Thierry Zarcone is Senior Researcher at the Centre National de la Recherche Scientifique in Paris, based at the Ecole Pratique des Hautes Etudes, Paris. He has held visiting professorships at Kyoto and Fribourg, Switzerland, and is an expert on Islamic Studies and the history of systems of thought in the Turko-Iranian region.

Angela Hobart is Honorary Reader at Goldsmiths College, University of London in Intercultural Therapy (Applied Medical Anthropology) and Honorary Research Fellow in Medical Anthropology, University College London. She also works as a psycho-dynamic therapist at the Helen Bamber Medical Foundation and teaches occasionally at the British Museum, London on the art and culture of Southeast Asia. She is Director of the Centro Incontri Umani (Cross Cultural Centre) in Ascona, Switzerland.

SHAMANISM AND ISLAM

Sufism, Healing Rituals and Spirits in the Muslim World

Edited by

THIERRY ZARCONE
AND
ANGELA HOBART

PUBLISHED IN ASSOCIATION WITH CENTRO INCONTRI
UMANI, ASCONA, SWITZERLAND

New paperback edition published in 2017 by I.B.Tauris & Co. Ltd
London • New York
www.ibtauris.com

First published in hardback in 2013 by I.B.Tauris & Co. Ltd

Copyright Editorial Selection and Introduction © 2013
Thierry Zarcone & Angela Hobart

Copyright Individual Chapters © 2013 Aurélie Biard, Bernard Dupaigne,
Patrick Garrone, Roberte Hamayon, Angela Hobart, Pedram Khosronejad,
Liliane Kuczynski, Manijeh Maghsudi, François Ruegg, Faiza Seddiq Arkam,
David Somfai Kara, Anne-Marie Vuillemenot & Thierry Zarcone

The right of Thierry Zarcone and Angela Hobart to be identified for their respective parts
has been asserted in accordance with the Copyright, Designs and Patents Act 1988.

All rights reserved. Except for brief quotations in a review, this book, or any part thereof,
may not be reproduced, stored in or introduced into a retrieval system, or transmitted, in
any form or by any means, electronic, mechanical, photocopying, recording or otherwise,
without the prior written permission of the publisher.

Every attempt has been made to gain permission for the use of the images in this book.
Any omissions will be rectified in future editions.

ISBN: 978 1 78453 745 6
eISBN: 978 1 78672 128 0
ePDF: 978 1 78673 128 9

A full CIP record for this book is available from the British Library
A full CIP record is available from the Library of Congress

Library of Congress Catalog Card Number: available

CONTENTS

List of Figures — vii

List of Plates — xi

Acknowledgements — xiii

Contributors — xv

Introduction — xxi
Thierry Zarcone

Vladimir Nikolaevich Basilov (1937–1998) A Pioneer of the Study of 'Islamised Shamanism' — xxxiii
Roberte Hamayon

Part I: Islamised Shamanism in Central Asia

Chapter One	Contextual Variations of Shamanic 'Healing' in South Siberia: From 'Obtaining Luck' to Relieving Misfortune *Roberte Hamayon*	3
Chapter Two	Healing in Central Asia: Syncretism and Acculturation *Patrick Garrone*	17
Chapter Three	Religious Traditions among the Kazakhs and the Kirghizs *David Somfai Kara*	47
Chapter Four	Muslim Shamans in Kazakhstan *Anne-Marie Vuillemenot*	59

Chapter Five	Interrelation to the Invisible in Kirghizistan *Aurélie Biard*	79
Chapter Six	Two Indigenous Healing Methods among Iranian Turkmen *Manijeh Maghsudi*	95
Chapter Seven	Shamans in Afghanistan? *Bernard Dupaigne*	115

Part II: From Central Asia to the Rest of the Muslim World

Chapter Eight	The People of the Air: Healing and Spirit Possession in South Iran *Pedram Khosronejad*	131
Chapter Nine	Shamanism in Turkey: Bards, Masters of the *Jinns*, and Healers *Thierry Zarcone*	169
Chapter Ten	The Bektashi-Alevi 'Dance of the Crane' in Turkey: A Shamanic Heritage? *Thierry Zarcone*	203
Chapter Eleven	Dreaming in the practice of African Marabouts in Paris *Liliane Kuczynski*	217
Chapter Twelve	Healing among Traditional Practitioners of the Algerian Sahara *Faiza Seddiq Arkam*	231

Part III: Islamised Shamanism and other Religions

Chapter Thirteen	Shamanism among the Gypsies of Southeastern Europe *François Ruegg*	259
Chapter Fourteen	Spirit Healing in a Hindu/Muslim Area: Shadow Theatre in Java and Bali *Angela Hobart*	281
Notes		303
Index		331

LIST OF FIGURES

Portrait of Vladimir Nikolaevich Basilov (1937–1998), a pioneer of the study of 'Islamised shamanism'   xxxiii

2.1. *A Kazakh shaman of Semipalatinsk playing the fiddle in 1927 (Photograph: F.A. Fiel'strup).*   29

2.2. *A female shaman playing the drum, beginning of twentieth century (Photographic Archives of Uzbekistan, Tashkent).*   30

2.3. *A female Tajik shaman playing the drum, Uratyube, 1995 (Photograph: P. Garrone and Th. Zarcone).*   30

2.4. *A Tajik shaman playing the drum during a healing ritual with a sick patient who is blindfolded, Uratyube, 1995 (Photograph: P. Garrone and Th. Zarcone).*   31

2.5. *A band of Qalandar dervishes singing, playing musical instruments and begging, beginning of twentieth century, Tashkent, Central Asia (old postcard, collection of Th. Zarcone).*   41

3.1. *Batïrkan a Kazakh* baksï *with his magic axe during trance, Bayan-Ölgii Province, Mongolia, 1994 (Photograph: László Kunkovács).*   53

3.2. *Kirghiz* bakshï *and* bübü *specialists during a midnight* jar *ritual, Talas Province, Kirghizistan, 1995 (Photograph: László Kunkovács).*   54

3.3. *Abdïkadïr Kirghiz* bakshï *during the ritual* (oyun) *performs a* talma biy *(shamanic dance) and climbs up the magic flag* (tuu, *Kizil-Su Kirghiz Autonomous Prefecture, Xinjiang, China (Photograph: Dávid Somfai Kara).*   55

4.1. The Kazakh shaman Kuat performing a shamanic ritual (zikir/dhikr) at Köktibie (Southeast Kazakhstan), 1994 (Photograph: A.-M. Vuillemenot). 64

4.2. The Kazakh shaman Kuat performing a shamanic ritual (zikir/dhikr) at Köktibie (Southeast Kazakhstan), 1994 (Photograph: A.-M. Vuillemenot). 65

6.1. Turkmen playing the dutar during a ritual (Photograph: Manijeh Maghsudi and Behrooz Ashtray). 102

6.2. Erejeb Porkhan during a healing ritual, village of Yel Sheshme, 1975 (Photograph: Manijeh Maghsudi and Behrooz Ashtray). 110

7.1. The healer standing in front of the sick patient and invoking the spirits, Northern Afghanistan, district of Jaozjân, 1974 (Photograph: B. Dupaigne). 122

7.2. The cotton wicks have been lit and the healer says incantations while beating his drum, Northern Afghanistan, district of Jaozjân, 1974 (Photograph: by B. Dupaigne). 123

8.1. Zar ritual near Abadan, Khuzestan, Iran, 2005 (Photograph: M. Rahmani). 154

8.2. Zar ritual near Abadan, Khuzestan, Iran, 2005 (Photograph: M. Rahmani). 155

8.3. Mama Zar, Zar ritual near Abadan, Khuzestan, Iran, 2005 (Photograph: M. Rahmani). 156

8.4. Zar ritual near Abadan, Khuzestan, Iran, 2005 (Photograph: M. Rahmani). 157

9.1. Drawing of demons playing the fiddle, end of fourteenth century ('Siyah Qalem', Manuscript 2153, Library of the Museum of Topkapı, Istanbul). 172

9.2. Drawing of a Qalandar dervishe (Ignatius Muradgea d'Ohsson, Tableau général de l'Empire othoman, divisé en deux parties, dont l'une comprend la législation mahométane, l'autre, l'histoire de l'Empire othoman. Paris, Imprimerie de Monsieur, 1791, vol 2, figure 137). 174

9.3. Turkish bard playing the saz, 1865 (private collection, Istanbul). 176

List of Figures

9.4. The Turkish bard and poet Neyzen Tevfik (1879–1953) playing the saz, beginning of twentieth century (private collection, Istanbul). — 177

9.5. A female Armenian healer healing a sick patient, mid-nineteenth century, Smyrna, Turkey (C. Constant, 'Le Magnétisme en Turquie. L'okoudmak, l'aghotèle', Le Magnétiseur, Genève, 11, year 4, 15 February 1863.) — 188

9.6. A miniature of Shehret ul-Nahr, the mother of the jinns with her 37 faces (from the 'Davetname', fifteenth century, manuscript of the Library of the University of Istanbul). — 194

10.1. Alevis performing the dance of the crane at Merdivenköy, Istanbul, 2008 (Photograph: Th. Zarcone). — 205

10.2. Ottoman calligraphy of a crane in the form of the Arabic prayer 'Bismillah', by the artist Mustafa Rakım, dated 1808–08 (in Aksel Malik, Türklerde Dini Resimler (Religious iconography among the Turks), Istanbul, Elif Y., 1967, p. 77). — 210

12.1. Drawing of a healing ritual, performed during a pilgrimage at the mausoleum of Moulay Abdallah at Tarhananet (Ahaggar, Algeria). The healer is in trance with a sword in her hands, a women, playing the lute/imzad (the drawing was made by Didi Slimane, a male nurse and Tuareg, whose mother was a Kel Ferwen from the Air district and his father a Kel Ghezzi from the Ahaggar). — 236

12.2. Drawing of a ritual called tindi in the Air district. The sick woman (in the centre of the picture) is in trance. She holds a headband decorated with horns. The men circle her with swords in their hands (drawing by Didi Slimane). — 237

12.3. Healing ritual of a baby possessed by the female and bird spirit called Oum e Sebian. The baby is wrapped up in a black cloth and a black cream is put on his body. Black is the colour of this bird spirit (Taberket, Tamanrasset, Algeria, 2002). — 244

13.1. Mausoleum of Sabri Husayn (Softa Baba), nineteenth century, at Tutrakan, Bulgaria, 2011 (Photograph: F. Ruegg). — 263

13.2. *Entrance of the mausoleum of Sabri Husayn (Photograph: F. Ruegg).* 264

13.3. *A detail of the mausoleum with the tomb of the saint Sabri Husayn in the background (Photograph: F. Ruegg)* 265

14.1. *Chatuhkaya with masks. Bali, Pejeng (W.F. Stutterheim, 1935.* Indian Influences in Old Balinese Art*).* 284

14.2. *Shadows on screen: noble Prince and ogre (Photograph: Jeune Scott-Kemball).* 285

14.3. *Kayon, Cosmic tree of life (Photograph: Angela Hobart).* 286

14.4. *Stage with puppeteer holding Prince Bima and musicians (Photograph: Per Horner).* 292

14.5. *Shadows on screen: Prince Bima receiving Holy Water from the Supreme God (Photograph: Giacomo De Caterini).* 293

14.6. *Spirit medium (Photograph: Angela Hobart).* 296

LIST OF PLATES

1. *The Kazakh shaman Kuat performing a shamanic ritual (dhikr) at Köktibie (Southeast Kazakhstan), 1994 (Photograph: A.-M. Vuillemenot).*

2. *Spirits with bull heads praying, from 'Ajaib al-Makhlukat', fifteenth century (Archives Metin And, Istanbul).*

3. *Oil painting of the dance of the cranes by the painter Oya Karakiz, Kahramanmarash, Turkey, 2008.*

4. *Zamanbek, a Kazakh shaman playing the fiddle (kobïz), Sayram, Kazakhstan, 1994 (Photograph: Jozsef Torma during fieldwork in common with D. Somfai Kara).*

ACKNOWLEDGEMENTS

The conference on *Shamanism and Islam. Sufism, Healing Rituals and Spirits in the Muslim World* was hosted at the Centro Incontri Umani (Socio-Cultural Centre) Ascona located on Lake Maggiore, on the border between Switzerland and Italy. The Centre seeks to encourage understanding, respect and peace internationally. The papers given at the conference form the basis of this work. We want to express our gratitude to all participants for their stimulating and reflective contributions and I.B. Tauris for their competent assistance in the publication of the book.

The shamanic journey reveals the unity underlying the separate and divided forms – 'it is one, it is unity, it is ourselves'. It is the way of compassion and poise that celebrates, heals, and transforms:

Jir jüzindaki avliya,	O saints who dwell underground,
Kün kuzindaki avliya,	O saints who dwell in the sky,
Marufdaki va Mashruqdaki avliya,	O saints from the East and from the West,
Turkistanda tumin bab,	O ten thousands of masters at Turkistan,
Sizdirdin midat tilayman.	I beg thy help.

(Translated from Kazakh Turkish: A. A. Diva'ev, 'Baksy, kak lekar' i koldun' (The *bakshi* as healer and spirit doctor), In *Iz oblasti kirgizskikh verovanii*, Kazan', 1899, pp. 3–4)

Thierry Zarcone and Angela Hobart

CONTRIBUTORS

Aurélie BIARD (CERI, Paris)

Aurélie Biard is a researcher at the Centre for International Studies and Research (CERI) in Paris and an associated researcher at the Centre for Turkish, Ottoman, Balkan, and Central Asian Studies (CETOBaC, CNRS). From September 2008 to August 2010, she was a doctoral fellow at the IFEAC (French Institute for Central Asian Studies), based in Tashkent, Uzbekistan. She holds a PhD in Political Science from Sciences-Po Paris. Her research focuses on Islamic clientelist networks and power struggles between Islamic actors as well as on ethical norms, business and Islam in Central Asia (Kyrgyzstan, Kazakhstan) and in the Russian Federation (Tatarstan). Her main publications include "The Religious Factor in the Reifications of 'Neo-ethnic' Identities in Kyrgyzstan," (in *Nationalities Papers*) and "Power, 'Original Islam', and the Reactivation of a Religious Utopia in Kara-Suu, Kyrgyzstan," (in *Central Asian Affairs*).

Bernard DUPAIGNE (Musée de l'Homme, Paris)

Bernard Dupaigne is a former director of the Anthropological department of the Musée de l'Homme, Paris. He is a specialist mainly of Afghanistan, Cambodia and Vietnam and has published five books on Afghanistan, as well as many papers about traditional society. His last book on the subject deals with art and history: *Afghanistan. Monuments millénaires* (Paris, Imprimerie nationale, 2007). The next book to be published describes iron metallurgy in ancient Cambodia.

Patrick GARRONE (independent scholar, Avignon)

Patrick Garrone, currently assistant editor of the *Journal of the History of Sufism* (Paris: Jean Maisonneuve) was a former civil servant of the French Ministry of Education and a cultural attaché in Africa. He is an independent scholar based in the South of France. His publications include *Chamanisme et Islam en Asie Centrale. La baksylyk hier et aujourd'hui* (Paris: Jean Maisonneuve, 2000). Another book on the bestiary of the beliefs of Central Asia is forthcoming.

Roberte HAMAYON (Ecole Pratique des Hautes Etudes, Paris)

Roberte Hamayon is Professor Emerita at the Ecole Pratique des Hautes Etudes, Paris. She is an anthropologist and has done fieldwork in Mongolia and Siberia since 1967. She founded the Centre and the Journal *Etudes mongoles et sibériennes*. Her main publications on shamanism are *La Chasse à l'âme. Esquisse d'une théorie du chamanisme sibérien* (Nanterre [Paris]: Société d'ethnologie 1990); *Taïga, terre de chamans* (Paris: Imprimerie Nationale 1997); and *Le chamanisme. Fondements et pratiques d'une forme religieuse d'hier et d'aujourd'hui* (Paris: Eyrolles, 2015). An English translation of her book Jouer. *Étude anthropologique à partir d'exemples sibériens* (Paris: La Découverte, 2012) was published under the title *Why you play. An anthropological study* by HAU/The University of Chicago press (2016).

Angela HOBART (Centro Incontri Umani and University College London)

Angela Hobart is the founding Director of the Centro Incontri Umani Ascona, Switzerland. She is Honorary Research Fellow of University College London (Medical Anthropology Department). She lectures at the British Museum on the Art and Culture of South East Asia. She also works as a psycho-dynamic therapist at the Helen Bamber Medical Foundation. She has published *Dancing Shadow of Bali, Theatre and Myth* (London, Kegan Paul International, 1987), *Healing Performances of Bali: Between Darkness and Light*, (Oxford, Bergbahn Books, 2003) and coedited *The People of Bali* (Oxford, Blackwell, 2001), *Aesthetics in Performance. Formations of Symbolic Construction and Experience* (Oxford, Bergbahn Books, 2005) and *Contesting the State: Dynamics of Order and Resistance* (Oxford, Sean Kingston Publishers, 2012).

Pedram KHOSRONEJAD (Oklahoma State University)

Pedram Khoronejad is Farzaneh Family Chair and Associate Director for Iranian and Persian Gulf Studies Program (IPGS) at the Oklahoma State University and also associated member of Groupe Sociétés, Religions, Laicités, CNRS-Paris, France. He obtained his PhD at the École des Hautes Études en Sciences Sociales (EHESS) in Paris. His research interests include cultural and social anthropology, the anthropology of death and dying, visual anthropology, visual piety, devotional artefacts, and religious material culture, with a particular interest in Iran, Persianate societies and the Islamic world. He is author of *Les Lions en Pierre Sculptée chez les Bakhtiari: Description et significations de sculptures zoomorphes dans une société tribale du sud-ouest de l'Iran, The Anthropology of Persianate Societies, Volume 2* (Sean Kingston). He is also the editor of several publications: *The Art and Material Culture of Iranian Shi'ism: Iconography and Religious Devotion in Shi'i Islam* (I.B.Tauris); *Saints and their Pilgrims in Iran and Neighboring Countries* (Sean Kingston); *Iranian Sacred Defence Cinema: Religion, Martyrdom and National Identity* (Sean Kingston); *Unburied Memories: The Politics of Bodies, and the Material Culture of Sacred Defense Martyrs in Iran* (Routledge). He is also chief editor of the *Anthropology of the Contemporary Middle East and Central Eurasia* (ACME). Pedram.khosronejad@okstate.edu

Liliane KUCZYNSKI

Liliane Kuczynski is a researcher at the National Centre for Scientific Research (CNRS, Paris). A specialist in the study of Muslim practices in urban contexts, Liliane Kuczynski completed a research program on African Muslim healers (marabouts) in Paris. In 2006 she was in charge of a lecture program on flexibility of religions practices in urban contexts. She has recently published a study of the celebration of the main Muslim feast Ayd al-kabîr in different towns of Senegal (*La Tabaski au Sénégal. Une fête musulmane en milieu urbain* (Anne-Marie Brisebarre and Liliane Kuczynski eds., Paris: Karthala, 2009)). She is also studying the development of Islam in a cross-cultural context: the French Caribbean. Her book *Les Marabouts africains à Paris* was awarded the Carlier Prize of the Academy for Ethical and Political Sciences (Paris) in 2003. She recently organised an international symposium on Religion on the Web (in collaboration, 2013) and edited a collective book resulting from this research: *Le Religieux sur Internet* (Liliane Kuczynski & al. eds., Paris: L'Harmattan, 2015).

Manijeh MAGHSUDI (Tehran University – ISRS Tehran University)

Manijeh Maghsudi is Assistant Professor at the Anthropology Department of Tehran University and a researcher at the Institute of Social Research Studies (ISRS Tehran University). She is the head of two Departments of Ethnology and Tribal Studies (ISRS Tehran University). She is an anthropologist and has done fieldwork in Turkman region of Iran. Her areas of expertise include: indigenous knowledge, traditional medicine and research method. She has carried out a great deal of research on Turkmen society, especially on women healers. Author of numerous articles on Turkmen society, her main publications include: *Indigenous Healing Methods of the*

Turkmen (Tehran, UNESCO, 2003), *Different Healing Methods among Turkmen* (Tehran, Afkar, 2003), *Cultural Variety, Ethnical Multiplicity and Social Solidarity* (Tehran, UNESCO and Azad University 2006), 'Women Healers in Turkmen Sahra in Iran and Caucasia', *Armenia: Arya Periodic* (Arya University) 2006, *Anthropology of Family and Kinship* (Tehran, Shirazeh, 2009).

François RUEGG (University of Fribourg)

François Ruegg is Associate Professor at the Institute of Social Anthropology of the University of Fribourg (Switzerland). Visiting Professor in Moscow, Timisoara, Cluj and Associate Professor in Bucharest, he also directed research projects funded by the Swiss National Science Foundation on Roma/Gypsies issues in Central and Eastern Europe (2003–2009). His published works include *Interculturalism and Discrimination in Romania: Policies, Practises and Representations* (ed. with C. Rus and R. Poledna, Berlin, LIT Verlag, 2006), *Nouvelles identités rom en Europe centrale & orientale*, Transitions (with A. Boscoboinik) (Vol. XLVIII-2, 2009, Geneva and Brussels), and many articles on Roma/Gypsies and intercultural topics.

Faiza SEDDIK-ARKAM (University of Franche-Comté)

Faiza Seddik-Arkam is a Ph.D. student working in a research team of socio-anthropology at the University of Franche-Comté (France). Her dissertation focuses on 'The magic, religious and therapeutic system of Tuaregs Kel Ahaggar (Algerian Sahara) from life narration of local tradipractitioners'. She has written articles on traditional music, magical therapy and possession among the Touaregs in several academic journals.

David SOMFAI KARA (Hungarian Academy of Sciences, Budapest)

David Somfai Kara graduated from ELTE University Budapest in 2000. He obtained MA degrees in Turkic and Mongolic Philology. During his university studies he started to conduct fieldwork among various Turkic and Mongolic peoples in Central and Inner Asia (Kazakh, Kirghiz, Uyghur, Karakalpak), Siberia (Tuva, Khakas, Altay, Yakut, Buryat) and Ural-Volga Region (Bashkir, Nogay, Kalmyk). He collected folklore, folk music and religious folklore (folk religion) among these ethnic groups. In 2007 he obtained his Ph.D. degree in anthropological linguistics (title of his thesis: 'Terminology of Religious Folklore among the Turkic and Mongolic Peoples of Inner and Central Asia'). He has been publishing his fieldwork materials in the Journal *Shaman*, Hungary, since 2004. He has also conducted fieldwork among minorities in China (Daur, Yugur, Salyr) since 2007. He worked at Indiana University as a visiting scholar and studied Western Sioux (Lakhota) folklore and religion in 2010, and conducted fieldwork in S. Dakota. Currently he works for the Institute of Ethnology (Hungarian Academy of Sciences) as a researcher.

Anne-Marie VUILLEMENOT

Anne-Marie Vuillemenot is a professor and member of the Laboratoire d'Anthropologie Prospective at the Catholic University of Louvain. His research focuses on the practices and uses of the body in space, first in Central Asia with Kazakh shepherds, then, in a comparative perspective between ritual practices in Kazakhstan, Uzbekistan and Ladakh, finally, to a contemporary dance company in Cape Verde. Among his recent publications are: *Intimité et réflexivité du chercheur*, in Investigations d'Anthropologie Prospective, codirigé par Defreyne E., Hagdad Mofrad G., Vuillemenot A.M, Academia-L'Harmattan (Louvain-la-Neuve: 2015); "Médiatiser l'invisible, Bitva ekstrasensov", in T. Boellstorff, B. Maurer, J. Mazzocchetti and O. Servais, eds., *Humanités réticulaires. Nouvelles technologies, altérités et pratiques ethnographiques en contextes globalisés* (Editions Academia, n. 12).

Thierry ZARCONE (National Centre for Scientific Research – CNRS – GSRL / EPHE Paris)

Thierry Zarcone is Senior Researcher (Directeur de Recherches) at the Centre National de la Recherche Scientifique in Paris (Groupe Société Religion Laïcité). His areas of expertise include Islamic Studies and the history of systems of thought in the Turko-Iranian region. Author of numerous articles on related scholarly topics, including the history of Sufism in the Ottoman Empire, Turkey, Central Asia, and Chinese Turkestan, he has also published on modern and contemporary Turkish and Central Asian history. His book *Mystiques, philosophes et francs-maçons en Islam* (Paris, Maisonneuve, 1993) was awarded the Prix Saintour of the Académie des Sciences Morales et Politiques. Zarconé most recent books are *Sufi Pilgrims from Central Asia and India in Jerusalem* (Kyoto, Kyoto University, 2009), *Le Soufisme, voie mystique de l'islam* (Paris, Gallimard, 2009), *Shamanism in Siberia and Central Asia* (with Charles Stépanoff, Paris, Gallimard, 2011), and *Le Croissant et le Compas. La Franc-maçonnerie dans le monde musulman entre fascination et détestation* (Paris, Dervy, 2015). Zarcone is also the editor of the *Journal of the History of Sufism* (Paris, Jean Maisonneuve).

INTRODUCTION

Thierry Zarcone

In this book we examine how shamanism, Islam, and especially Sufism, have interrelated over the centuries, and are still interrelating today. The area covered includes not just Central Asia, but extends to the Middle East, Africa and Indonesia.

Shamanism is often considered an 'archaic religion', in contrast to the monotheistic religions of Central Asia. Traditionally shamanism involved a 'shaman'; he or she was an expert of the spirit realm and sought to heal or relieve suffering through dance, trance or dreams. Yet the term shamanism commonly refers to a wide range of practices in various Muslim and non-Muslim parts of the world. However, they cannot be classified together. As the French anthropologist Philippe Descola (2005: 42–43), who specialised in Amerindian religion, persuasively argued it is meaningless to seek to unite all shamanic forms. This can be compared to classifying Brahmanism, ancient Greek religion and Christianity together on the grounds that a priest is important in all of them: he is a liturgical mediator between humans and the divine, as well as carrying out real or symbolic sacrifices. Essentially shamanism is a catch-all category for many different cults and belief systems. A unity can, however, be perceived between the shamanic practices of North Asia and Muslim Central Asia. Both share elements such as drum playing, the cosmic tree and certain rituals. This emerges, for instance, in contemporary times in the 'dance of the crane' (Figure 10.1 and plate 3), performed by the Bektashi-Alevis in present day Turkey, which is accompanied by music from a lute and sung mystical poetry. The dancers mimic the graceful movements of a crane – they bow, turn around, arch their necks elegantly and kick up their legs. The choreography of the dance retains a link to shamanism. Cranes and wading birds played an important role in Siberian shamanism; yet the dance has become a Mystic/Sufi ceremony.

This book is unique in the wide region of the world that it spans. This takes account of the rich oral and textual traditions that overlap, intertwine with or supersede one another. Concomitantly, varied ritual and performative genres have emerged that combine music, dialogue, song, poetry, participants and practitioners in countless different ways.

The introduction of Islam in Central Asia

The introduction of Islam to the oasis of Central Asia by the Arabs in the eighth century changed the religious face of the region. In the following centuries, the Samanid Persians, who succeeded the Arabs, and therefore the Muslim Turkic sovereigns (Qarakhanid etc.) who converted to Islam, brought this religion, by force of arms, into almost all of Central Asia, westwards to the Volga, eastwards to Southern Siberia and even to Northwest China. Consequently, some of the religions established for centuries in this area, namely Manicheism, Nestorian Christianity, Zoroastrism, Buddhism and shamanism, started to decline if they were not eliminated almost immediately. However, in remote Northern Asia, shamanism was still the main religion. The word 'shaman', adopted by Russian scientists in the mid-nineteenth century, comes from *saman* in Evenk language which is spoken by a Turkic population linked to the Tungus group living in Siberia. Similarly, *kamalanye*, the word used today by Russians and scholars for the shamanic rituals, originates from *kamlat* in the Tungus language, *kam* being also a synonym for shaman in other Siberian languages.

To return to Central Asia, although the sedentary Turko-Persian populations established in the major oases (Khiva, Bukhara, Samarkand, Kashgar, Qoqand) quickly converted to Islam, the nomads of the Kazakh steppe and of the mountain areas (Pamirs and Tian-Shan), today Kazakhstan and Kirghizistan, resisted the new religion. The latter population remained firmly respectful of their animist and shamanic past and had a veneer of Muslim culture only. Hence, Islam emerged with different faces in these two areas of Central Asia.

Islamised shamanism is better known since the beginning of the twenty-first century thanks to two seminal books by the Russian Vladimir Basilov (1992) and the Frenchman Patrick Garrone (2000) which combine historical and anthropological approaches. Both studies are based on a synthesis of all the research done in the nineteenth and twentieth centuries by Western, Russian and Soviet travellers and scholars, and on several fieldwork studies carried out before and after the collapse of USRR (1991). Basilov was the first to coin and problematise the concept of 'Islamised shamanism'. In addition, these two authors have brought a comparative analysis of Islamised shamanism and North Asian shamanism, and express above all their interest in the themes which are the subject of this volume, that is the mingling of shamanism with Sufism, the specific healing rituals which have developed in a Muslim context and the relation of the shamans with the spirits.

What associates shamanism with Sufism?

With the coming of Islam to Central Asia, shamanism, considered a pagan religion, was, contrary to the other monotheistic religions of Central Asia, condemned to disappear very quickly, at least in its original form. Actually, shamanism was reinterpreted through Islam or more precisely through Sufism or Muslim mysticism. The reasons for the close association, or more precisely for the 'syncretism' of shamanism and Sufism, are twofold. The first reason is historical, for Sufism was pivotal during the campaigns of Islamisation of Central Asia and has been, in the eyes of the populations of this area, entirely identified with the religion of the Prophet Muhammad. Actually, the Sufi shaykhs were the main propagators of Islam in the region, combining their mystical ideal with the holy war (*ghazza*). Many of them, according to historical chronicles and hagiographies, converted Turkish and Mongol sovereigns to Islam (Amitai-Preiss 1999). That was the case, for example, for Sayyid Ata, a member of the Yasawi Sufi order who converted Özbek Khan, the ruler of the Golden Horde, in the fourteenth century. There were also confrontations and even magical competitions between Sufi missionaries and shamans, to the detriment of the latter. According to some legends, the south of Siberia near the Irtysh River was Islamised in the thirteenth century by Sufis coming from Bukhara, though we do know, from documentary evidence, that it was actually in the seventeenth century that Islam reached the Irtysh and that a mausoleum was built for Hakim Ata, a Sufi saint originally from the Kharazm, in the district of Tyumen (Seleznev *et al.* 2009: 54–57; Bustanov, 2011).

The second reason for the association of shamanism and Sufism is based on the specificities of Sufism which, far from being a homogeneous movement, has both orthodox (sharia-oriented) and heterodox (more or less antinomian) trends. Shamanism was forced to Islamise its external appearance and its religious discourse (invocations to the spirits for instance), and to abandon some of its functions and ideas in order to be, if not totally accepted, at least more or less tolerated by the clerics of the new religion. Not surprisingly, it was the heterodox Sufi trends which pleased shamanism because of their flexibility and, in some cases even, their disrespect toward the implementations of the religious law (sharia). In this view, though many ideas and practices were borrowed from the whole of Sufism by the shamans, it was a particular group of Sufis, the Qalandar – an order composed of unmarried and wandering people performing 'ecstatic' dance – which closely combined with shamanism, insofar as in several cases the frontier between the Sufi and the shaman has remained vague and hazy. Moreover, an ambiguous figure, half-Qalandar and half-shaman, working as a healer, a bard and a foreteller has appeared over time in the epic literature. Generally called *ashiq* or *ozan* (bard) in Azerbaijan and in Anatolia, this figure is known under the name of *divana* (the 'enthusiastic') in Central Asia and Eastern Turkestan. Many foreign travellers met such *divana* in Asia up to the beginning of twentieth century.

To return to the question of syncretism, it must be said that the amalgam of shamanism and Sufism is based on a search for analogies and reinterpretation. First, the analogies are alleged resemblances between some shamanic and Sufi practices or concepts which have favoured their association. This is the case, for example, in Sufi repetitive litany (*dhikr*) which is equated in the eyes of the shamans with the shamanic invocative song. Also, the shamanic rituals are frequently named after the Sufi ceremonies: *zikir* in Kazakhstan, *jahr* (oral litany) in Turkmenistan and in Tajikistan. Also worth mentioning here is the Sufi dance which was considered similar to the gesticulations of the shaman, both being circular choreographies; and the Sufi saints integrated into the army of helper spirits of the shaman. Second, reinterpretation, as a rereading of the Sufi tradition, operates in favour of shamanism and its healing function to the detriment of the aim of Sufism. It means, for example, that the Sufi repetitive litany (*dhikr*) is reinterpreted as a magical incantation used to call the spirits and has lost its function of a personal mystical exercise (Zarcone 2000 and 2007). One wonders then, as Patrick Garrone in the present volume does, whether Islamised shamanism constitutes a definitively established corpus of syncretic beliefs or, conversely, if the ongoing confrontation between the two religious traditions of shamanism and Islam is an active process of mutual assimilation.

The Muslim shaman as healer

The syncretism of shamanism and Sufism continued over time and gave birth to manifold hybridisations of both traditions. The differences between these hybridisations depended on whether the influence of Islam was strong or soft, and where the hybridisation happened, that is among the sedentary populations dominated by sharia or among the nomads. Syncretism also means here that following the elimination of shamanism as an autonomous religion, a role played henceforth by Islam, two activities of the North Asiatic shamanism, healing and divination, were mingled with Muslim devotion and rituals. One reason for this is that healing and divination were, for the Muslim theologians, the less noxious elements composing shamanism. It is well known that healing and divination were two practices that actually already existed in Islam, though in a different form. It must be mentioned here, however, that, as demonstrated by R. Hamayon in this volume, 'contrary to many definitions of the late nineteenth century, healing is far from being the basic principle on which shamanism rests in Siberia; it is neither a primary function nor even the only activity of shamans'. Besides, we are told by history that although the Islamised shaman was known by various names, he was called *kam* in eleventh century in Eastern Turkestan, that is the name from which comes the term 'shaman', as seen above. This indication comes from a well known Turkish–Arabic dictionary written by a Turkish literati, which is a mine of information on the beliefs of the Turks. The author, Mahmut Kashgari, adds that the Arabic equivalent for *kam* is *kahana*, the pre-Islamic soothsayer, and that one function of the *kam* was to read incantations in order to heal the sick possessed by spirits (Boyle 1972: 178–9, 183–4; Dankoff 1975: 76–7). So the healing capacity of the Islamised shaman appears as its main function with divination alike.

The term *kam* was, probably very quickly, replaced by the term *bakhshi/baksy*, of Chinese origin (*boshi*), which designated, in the Chinese Empire, either Buddhist priests, or scribes, or even wizards. This term may have entered Central Asia with the Ilkhanide Mongols who conquered Iran, Anatolia and Irak in thirteenth century. Among the Ilkhanides, the terms *bakhshi* and *kam* referred first to the genuine shaman, and then, over time, to the Islamised shaman. Though the term *bakhshi* has been and is still nowadays more commonly used to qualify the Islamised shaman in a vast area which stretches from Azerbaijan to Chinese Turkestan, there are several other terms to distinguish the shaman (Garonne 2000: 12–21; Reichl 2001). The discrepancies between these terms hint at the specific activities accomplished by the shaman, all being nevertheless more or less linked to diverse ways of healing and foretelling practices. Thus, the terms *emchi* (healer in Mongolian) and *tabup* (doctor in Arabic) highlight the healing capacity of the shaman; the words *parikhan/porkhan, falbin, köz achiq* and *rammalji* refer to his activity as a soothsayer; *boqimchi* to the reading of incantations, and finally the terms *bakhshibazi* and *pirä oynitish* hint at the shamanic ritual, called here 'a play', as among some Siberian shamans this is a ritual to please the spirits, literally to make them play.

The shaman's family of spirits

The healing process operated by the Islamised shaman is based essentially on a negotiation or fight with the spirits. Thus, the spirits, and especially the auxiliaries or helper spirits of the shaman, fill a central position throughout the life of the latter, leaving him only after his death. The helper spirits, in a sense, are members of the shaman's family, particularly since we know that there are male and female shamans that say that they have experienced sexual symbolic encounters with spirits. This relationship is sometimes interpreted by the shamans as a kind of marriage. We should note also that it is through the spirits that Islamised shamanism has established a clear link with the ancient religions of Central Asia and with Islam, favouring a syncretism based on the belief that the spirits constitute a wide category of invisible beings everywhere and for all the epochs and all the religions. Hence, the army of spirits that are either helpers or enemies of the shaman is composed of spirits of various religious extractions: Turkic, Zoroastrian, Jewish, Christian and Muslim, plus the spirits of the ancestors.

In addition, through the spirits, shamanism is once again closely linked with Sufism because many of the luminaries of Central Asian Sufism, as deceased saints, are regarded as particularly powerful spirits and the first auxiliaries of the shaman. Their names are usually invoked at the very beginning of the rituals of healing. Hence, their tombs and mausoleums (*mazar*) became the sacred locus par excellence of Islamised shamanism. For example, the would-be shaman stays and sleeps in such places in order to be elected by the spirits through his dreams. Therefore, shamans frequently visit these places and sometimes gather there. The focus of popular fervour, tomb veneration is a dominant trend in Islam in general and in Central Asia in particular. Then, the presence of the shaman in such places is legitimised by his function as an intermediary between the men and the spirits. It is worth noting that nowadays the links between Shamanism and mausoleums are indisputably more frequent in Xinjiang than in Western Turkestan, since the prohibition on saint veneration hasn't been as systematic and merciless in China as it was in the USSR. We do know, for example, that a dynasty of Uyghur *bakhshi*, half-shaman half-tomb-caretakers, has been attached since at least the nineteenth century to the mausoleum of Ordam, one of the major shrines in Southern Xinjiang (Abbas 1993; Zarcone 2002), and that, at many other tombs, especially in Kizilsu Kirghiz Autonomous Prefecture (Xinjiang), the caretakers are also shamans or people performing shamanic healing rituals (Ghojesh, in press).

Finally, a word must be said about the opposition Islamised shamanism is facing in contemporary Central Asian society. On the one hand, although shamanism is considered in Kazakhstan as an important element in the Kazakh cultural heritage and an alternative medicine (Penkala-Gawęcka 2009), it is also regarded with caution and the shamans are depicted as charlatans and impostors. On the other hand, the shamans are fiercely fought by orthodox Islam and especially by its radical wing, Wahhabism, wherever its

Introduction   XXVII

representatives are established, usually in Uzbekistan and in Tajikistan. For example, in 1997 Thierry Zarcone found in Tashkent a Wahhabi booklet in modern Uyghur language, published in Saudi Arabia, with a chapter castigating the shamans (Abdil Ähät Hapiz 1989: 99). Shamans are also fought by the official mullahs of Kirghizistan, as shown by Biard in this volume. But the thread comes also from the State administration, as was the case in Tajikistan, in 2008, when the Tajik officials banned healers and foretellers on the grounds that healing activity was a 'parasitical industry that had grown to unacceptable proportions' (*Herald Tribune*, 4 July 2008).

Summaries of the chapters

The chapters of this volume, all based on original research, shed light on the situation of shamanism in the whole of Central Asia, including Turkey and the Balkans. Only one chapter, by R. Hamayon, doesn't concern Central Asia but Siberia. This chapter must be regarded however as an indispensable introduction to the whole of the volume insofar as it discusses the question of healing in northern shamanism and permits the measurement of discrepancies in the art of healing with Islamised shamanism. Patrick Garrone's contribution does not deal with a specific area of Central Asia but with the question of healing and disease among the Muslim shamans of this region with a comparative regard to the situation in Northern Asia. The focus is on the heterogeneous character of Islamised shamanism which is more linked to its Siberian counterpart when practised by Kazakhs and Kirghizs (called the 'nomadic' variant) than in the southern part of the region (the 'sedentary' variant) where the Uzbeks and the Tajiks live. In view of this, Garrone demonstrates that if the term 'Islamised shamanism' is a suitable definition for the first variant, the expression 'shamanised Islam' is more appropriate to define the second one.

Four chapters shine a new light on the present situation of shamanism in three republics of Central Asia. David Somfai Kara proposes a synthesis of his 15 years of fieldwork among the Kazakh and Kirghiz after the collapse of USRR in 1991. On the basis of his observations in the field, he comments on the 'Muslim' identity of the shamans, on 'popular Islam', on the legacy of Sufism upon shamanism and on the various rituals, while revisiting the definition of Islamised 'shamanism'. Anne-Marie Vuillemenot's contribution scrutinises the itineraries of two Kazakh shamans (*bakhshi*), male and female, and focuses on their increasing social and cultural role as healers in a changing society. She coins the expression 'neo-*bakhshi*' to reflect the changes in their healing activities. Moreover Vuillemenot questions the anthropologic dimension of the shamanic ritual called *zikir*, wondering especially to what extent Sufism and shamanism have mingled. The situation of the shaman in a changing world is also the subject of Aurélie Biard. The area concerned however is Kirghizistan. Biard considers the whole array of practices and representations of the healer as a 'symbolic world' and the remedy of the disease as a 'symbolic action'. In view of this, she reports on the rituals performed by three female shamans called *köz achïk* ('open eye'). Worth mentioning is the fact that the *köz achïk*, although healing the individuals, as is the rule in general in Islamised shamanism, heals also, to a certain extent, some 'collective ills related to the economic and political crisis'. Furthermore, writes Biard, the former president of Kirghizistan, Askar Akayev, used to consult a *köz achïk* who was a talented soothsayer. Manijeh Maghsudi's chapter is a comparative study of two classes of healers operating among the Turkmens of Iran (Turkmen Sahra district): the *porkhan*, a shaman who heals through a mediation with the spirits, living in remote and rural areas, and the *ishan*, a religious, more or less close to orthodox Sufism, living in town, who heals according to the rules of Islam while avoiding any contact with spirits. Both healers, however, recognise that disease comes from the spirits (*jinns*) and fight them with their own methods. Their rituals, although clearly different, nevertheless have some similarities that lead frequently to confusion about these two healers, that is regarding the *ishan* as a shaman. One particular feature of the healing ritual of the *porkhan* – that only exists among the Kirghizs and Uyghurs of Xinjiang – is the use of a sacred rope, equivalent to the cosmic tree of Siberian shamanism. Bernard Dupaigne's chapter on Islamised shamanism in Afghanistan is based on fieldwork carried out in 1973. Dupaigne's observations and analysis of this phenomenon are rare and unique as are those of Micheline Centlivres (1971) somewhat earlier. Since this period, Afghanistan has undergone drastic changes due to several wars, in particular that of the Taleban regime which persecuted many traditional trends of Islam, with special reference to Sufism and shamanism. Hence, Dupaigne's observations of shamanic rituals are precious testimony since these rituals will never be the same again. Dupaigne focuses on initiatory and healing rituals, both performed through intimate negotiation with spirits, and he questions the origin of the healing ritual. In so doing he recognises that some practices and ideas originate from ancient Iranian cults, as well as popular Islamic traditions and shamanic ceremonies.[1]

The situation of 'shamanism', or more precisely of shamanic ideas in Turkey, can be seen in the two chapters by Thierry Zarcone. In the first dedicated to the healers of Turkey, Zarcone highlights the historical process through which an Azeri/Anatolian religious figure, half-shaman and half-dervish, has became a bard over the course of time, and the role played by bardic music and musical instruments (the lute in particular) in the healing

Introduction   XXIX

process. Zarcone also discusses the case of some contemporary Turkish healers who show many similarities to the shamans of Central Asia. Zarcone's chapter therefore draws attention to the case of a guild of Anatolian healers that has its roots in shamanism but is structured after the Sufi brotherhood (*tarikat*) framework. Zarcone's second chapter deals with the 'dance of the crane' performed in the syncretic Alevi religion and by the antinomian Sufi order of the Bektashis. It aims to demonstrate that although cranes and wading birds play a role in Siberian shamanism and may have inspired this dance, this bird is also a mystical symbol that is widespread in Anatolia. Conversely Zarcone argues that the most interesting 'shamanic' background for this dance comes from its name, *oyun*, that is the name of the shaman and of the shamanic ritual in Xinjiang and in some areas of Siberia. François Ruegg's chapter shows that the Muslim gypsies of Rumania have preserved, due to their conservative feeling and attachment to tradition, several Ottoman and Turkic religious practices among which are shamanic ideas and divinatory healing rituals: control of the weather, the divination rite of the inspection of the bone of the left shoulder of an animal, ecstatic round dance, offering of food to the spirits and so on. Ruegg then draws attention to the conversion of these gypsies to Pentecostalism and makes a comparative analysis with the shamanists of Siberia who, like the gypsies, have enthusiastically joined this new religion.

Concerning the non-Turkic Muslim world, although there are many similarities between the healing movements existing in this area (Zar, Gnawiyya, etc.) and Central Asian Islamised shamanism, these movements have no links at all with shamanism. And if they have been depicted as 'shamanic' this is because ethnographers and anthropologists have coined a so-called 'descriptive category' to include any possession phenomena. Actually, 'Muslim exorcist cult', 'Muslim possession cult' or 'Muslim spirit cult' would be a better definition for these non-Turkic but Muslim possession practices which have their roots in the religious traditions of Africa, of ancient Arabia or of the Indonesian archipelago. It is of interest, nevertheless, to question the healing practices of these spirit cults, insofar as they share several elements with Asian shamanism and, first and foremost, because they have grown in a Muslim milieu and mingled Muslim symbols and rituals with archaic spirit or possession cults.

Five chapters in this volume investigate this phenomenon from Northern Africa to Indonesia and present the different ways adopted by African, Arab and Indonesian spirit cults of integration into Islam and how they have been re-interpreted by this religion. The chapters by Faiza Seddik-Arkam and of Pedram Khosronejad, which deal respectively with the healers and spirit cults of the Algerian Sahara and of Southern Iran, point to the interpenetration of Islam and African animism. Seddik-Arkam reports on the place occupied by Muslim saint cults, and pilgrimages to their tombs, and by the Sufi lodges (*zawiyya*), all being more or less in relation to the healers and their rituals. Khosronejad's chapter focuses on the *zar* ritual in Iran, an African spirit cult mixed with Arab animism that is widespread particularly in Sudan and Ethiopia. He shows that this cult has been amalgamated with Persian culture, a fact which is exemplified in its demonic pantheon where the *zar* spirits and other demons linked to pre-Islamic Africa sit side by side with *jinn*, *pari* (fairy) and *div* (demons) of Muslim Arabia and Persia. These three last demons are precisely invoked by the Islamised shamans of Central Asia. Liliane Kuczynski's chapter covers the diverse healing rituals of West African and Muslim male marabout living in Paris. One of these rituals is performed while the healer is dreaming through an invocation of spirits/angels to whom he is sometimes intimately related (a spirit is even considered the marabout's wife). As shown by Kuczynski, Islam and African shamanism are so inextricably linked in the practices of these healers that it is quite impossible to distinguish what belongs to each of them. More interestingly for the researcher, she writes, is the 'flexibility' and 'personal accommodations' manifested by the healers in particular through their interpretation of their own dreams and of the dreams of their clients. In the last chapter, Angela Hobart explores comparatively the significance of shadow theatre in Java and Bali in Indonesia, the most populous nominally Muslim country in the world. This genre is esteemed on both islands and illustrates how different traditions have been blended over the years. The puppet master is a healer and storyteller during the performance and conjures up for beholders the mythic world of ancestral spirits and epic heroes. Particularly in Java, the 'shamanic tree of life' at the beginning of a performance has Sufi and Hindu Vedanta resonances. Sultans of the nineteenth century watched plays for the mystical Sufi insights they provided. Then Hobart discusses the role of Balinese spirit mediums who counsel distressed clients during séances, and examines their affinities with shadow plays.

Bibliography

Abbas, Ablät (1993). 'Ordam tarikhidin omumi bayan' (A general presentation of the history of Ordam). *Yengishähär Tarikhi Materyalliri*, 1, 123–75.
Abdil Ähät Hapiz ['Abd al-Ahad Hâfiz] (1989). *Islam tadrisi - al-tarbiya al-islamiyya*, Jeddah, Dar al-Asfahani.
Amitai-Preiss, Reuven (1999). 'Sufis and shamans: some remarks on the Islamization of the Mongols in the Ilkhanate'. *Journal of the Economic and Social History of the Orient*. 421:1, 27–46.

Basilov, V. (1992). *Shamantsvo u narodov Srednei Azii i Kazakhstana* (Shamanism among the people of Central Asia and Kazakhstan). Moscow, Nauka.

Boyle, John Andrew (1972). 'Turkish and Mongol shamanism in the Middle Ages'. *Folklore*, 83: 3 (Autumn), 177–93.

Bustanov, Alfrid (2011). 'Sufiiskie legendy ob islamizatsii Sibiri' (Sufi Legends about the Islamization of Siberia). In: S. G. Kljaštornyj, T. I. Sultanov, and V. V. Trepavlov (eds). *Tjurkskie narody Evrazii v drevnosti i srednevekov'e*. Moskva, Izdat. Firma 'Vostočnaja Literatura' RAN, 33–78.

Centlivres, Pierre, Centlivres-Demont, Micheline, and Slobin, Mark (1971). 'A muslim shaman of Afghan Turkestan'. Pittsburg, *Ethnology*, 10: 2, 160–173.

Dankoff, Robert (1975). 'Kâšgarî on the beliefs and superstitions of the Turks'. *Journal of the American Oriental Society*, 95: 1, 68–80.

Descola, Philippe (2005). *Par-delà nature et culture*. Paris, Gallimard.

Dupaigne, Bernard (1996). 'Een exorcist in Afghanistan. Sjamanisme of niet ?'. In: Alexandra Rosenbohm (ed.). *Wat Bezielt de Sjamaan ? Genezing, Extase, Kunst*. Amsterdam, Koninklijk Instituut voor de Tropen, 1997, pp. 116–27.

Garrone, Patrick (2000). *Chamanisme et Islam en Asie Centrale*. Paris, Librairie d'Amérique et d'Orient Jean Maisonneuve.

Ghojesh, Gulbahar (in press). 'The Kirgiz bahshi and the mazar'. In Jun Sugawara, (ed.). *Studies on the Mazar Culture of the Silk Road*. Proceedings of the international workshop at Xinjiang University, Urumqi, August 2009., Tokyo, Toho Bunko.

Penkala-Gawęcka, Danuta (2009). 'Kazakh medical traditions in present-day Kazakhstan: locally rooted, regionally and globally flavoured'. In J. Pstrusińska, and T. Gacek, *Proceedings of the Ninth Conference of the European Society for Central Asia*, Cambridge Scholars Publishing, Newcastle upon Tyne, pp. 272–83.

Reichl, Karl (2001). *L'Epopée orale turque d'Asie centrale*. Paris, Centre d'études mongoles et sibériennes.

Seleznev, Aleksandr G., Selezneva, I. A., and Belich, I. V. (2009). *Kult' svyatykh v sibirskom islame* (The cult of saints in Sibirian Islam). Moscow, Izdatel'skii Dom Mardzhani.

Stern, David L. (2008). 'Fortunetellers see a bleak future. Tajik officials aim to ban whitchcraft'. *Herald Tribune*, 4 July 2008.

Zarcone, Thierry (2000). 'Interpénétration du soufisme et du chamanisme dans l'aire turque: chamanisme soufisé et soufisme chamanisé'. In Denise Aigle; Bénédicte Brac de la Perrière; Jean-Paul Chaumeil (eds). *La Politique des esprits. Chamanismes et Religions universalistes*. Nanterre [Paris], Société d'ethnologie, pp. 383–93.

_____(2002). 'Le Culte des saints au Xinjiang de 1949 à nos jours'. *Journal of the History of Sufism*, 3, 133–72.

_____(2007). 'The invocation of Saints and/or spirits by the sufis and the shamans: about the *munâjât* literature genre in Central Asia'. *Kyoto Bulletin of Islamic Area Studies*, 1, 52–61.

VLADIMIR NIKOLAEVICH BASILOV (1937–1998) A PIONEER OF THE STUDY OF 'ISLAMISED SHAMANISM'

Roberte Hamayon

Portrait of Vladimir Nikolaevich Basilov (1937–1998), a pioneer of the study of 'Islamised shamanism').

It is an honour for me to evoke here the memory of Vladimir Basilov, whom I was so fortunate as to know not only as a great scholar, but also as a very good colleague and friend. Vladimir Basilov can indeed be considered the person who injected new views in Russian approaches to shamanism in the late twentieth century and who, in particular, pioneered the study of 'Islamised shamanism' in Central Asia.

It is to this pioneering research work that the present book on healing in Central Asia is intended to pay homage. The concept of 'Islamised shamanism' has been successfully taken up and developed by Thierry Zarcone, Patrick Garrone and others, whose contributions to this book highlight the significance of our regretted colleague's approach to Central Asian realities.

What I personally – not being a specialist of this domain? – would like to stress here is the prominent part Vladimir Basilov played in the evolution of Soviet ethnography in the 1970 and 1980s, and in particular in the reassessment of shamanism as a religious phenomenon. This makes it necessary to briefly sketch the backdrop of his career at the Institute of Ethnography of the Academy of Sciences of USSR (presently called Institute of Ethnology and Anthropology). He joined this Institute as early as 1959, during which time he was greatly appreciated for his intellectual as well as human qualities. He came to be entrusted with the high position of scientific secretary for many years, and finally that of Director of Central Asian studies in the 1980s.

He was the one that local as well as foreign colleagues visiting the Institute could ask about everything: scholarly questions, help for elaborating materials ... He had a very acute analytical mind; open-minded and quick-witted, he was also an extremely kind and agreeable person. He was considered one of the most talented figures of the Institute and the best scholar in Central Asian studies. He had spent a huge amount of time doing fieldwork in Central Asia, and spoke Uzbek, which made him famous among local researchers and informants. Thanks to his perfect mastery of English language, he had a good knowledge of Western anthropological literature, which he generously passed on to young scholars. Finally, he also had a great aptitude for theoretical reflection, which was widely acknowledged by his colleagues. All this made him one of the most authoritative scholars in the Ethnographical Institute and beyond, in the Humanities department of the Academy of Sciences.

To better understand the great role Vladimir Basilov played in 'ethnography' as a discipline and more precisely in the study of shamanism in his country, it is necessary to briefly outline the ideological backdrop of the 1970s and 1980s. According to principles established from the beginning for his discipline, Soviet-educated ethnographers should have their research serve the building of a new society modelled on the ideal of *Homo sovieticus*.

Being an intellectual who was fundamentally both humanist and patriot, Vladimir Basilov was well aware that this model had become obsolete and that it was part of his duty to help it evolve, by better taking into account cultural diversity on the one hand, and psychological and spiritual concerns latent in every human community on the other hand.

Vladimir Basilov made a significant contribution to the evolution of the official theory, in particular with respect to shamanism and also, in a broader perspective, with respect to religion, spirituality and psychology. This evolution started with the publication of a book of collected papers: *Priroda i chelovek v religioznykh predstavleniyakh narodov Sibiri i Severa* (Nature and Man in Religious Representations of Peoples of Siberia and the North), 1970, which was followed by that of *Problemy istorii obshchestvennogo soznaniya aborigenov Sibiri* (Problems of the History of Social Consciousness of Siberian Aborigines), 1981. Both were published in Leningrad, by Nauka, the publishing house of the Academy of Sciences. Almost a decade before, Vilmos Diószegi, a Hungarian scholar who devoted his career to studying Siberian shamanism, had edited a volume consisting of papers devoted to the beliefs and folklore traditions in Siberia written by mainly Soviet and Hungarian scholars.[1] Vladimir Basilov joined this trend and wrote an innovative paper on transvestism in Central Asia on the basis of personally collected data in Uzbekistan intended as a contribution to the next volume edited by Vilmos Diószegi. Due to the latter's premature death, it was Mihály Hoppál who edited this volume at the publishing house of the Hungarian Academy of Sciences, with the title *Shamanism in Siberia* (1978). From then on, shamanism was more and more clearly assigned to the religious sphere, and considered as a set of beliefs and practices, which more or less explicitly challenged the official theory in use up to then, which was based on the assessment that shamanism was a relic of an early form of religion – hence primitive and wild – resulting from the neuropathic character of some individuals, the shamans.[2]

Vladimir Basilov gradually became the official representative of the Academy of Sciences of the USSR in the field of shamanic studies, owing to his position as authoritative scientist, his excellent command of English and his total reliability. Together with Mihály Hoppál, they planned to organise an international conference on shamanism in Hungary. This conference took place in the castle of Sárospatak, Hungary, in 1982. Its organisation was the result of their intense cooperation and involvement, which were decisive for carrying out this project. 'For the first time after decades of repression, could soviet scholars openly discuss about allegedly vanished for ever Siberian shamanism', Mihály Hoppál writes in the book dedicated to the memory of Vladimir Basilov (Kharitonova 1999: 18–9, my translation). The conference was intended as a sign that the attitude of Soviet authorities toward shamanism had changed and was to become from then on one of greater open-mindedness to psychology and toleration of cultural diversity. It was explicitly focused on shamanism as a religious phenomenon worth considering as a fully-fledged research topic. Vladimir Basilov was the head of the Soviet delegation – whose members he had himself selected, M. Hoppál adds *(ibid.)* The Proceedings were published in two volumes titled *Shamanism in Eurasia* (Hoppál 1984).

In the same perspective, Vladimir Basilov also prepared a book intended for the wider public. This short book, titled *Izbranniki dukhov* 'The Elect of the Spirits', was published in 1984 by the Publishing House of Political Literature *(Izdatel'stvo politicheskoi literatury)* in Moscow, a clear sign that the re-evaluation of shamanism put forth was officially approved. Two chapters of this book were translated in English, with the title 'Chosen by the Spirits' (Basilov 1990: 3–48), and a full German translation came out more recently (Basilov 2004). Indeed, we may say that this book had a decisive impact on the acknowledgement of shamanism as a form of religion characteristic of many autochthonous peoples who were part of the Soviet Union.

In this book, while sharing the idea that shamanism has vanished or is vanishing (the last chapter is titled *zakat shamanstva*, 'decline of shamanism'), Basilov stresses its basically religious character and, although still focusing on shamans as individuals (chapters *Professiya: shaman* 'Profession: shaman', *Teatr odnogo aktera*, 'Theatre of a single actor', *Zdorov li shaman?* 'Is the shaman sane?'), he denies all kinds of pathological interpretations and assumes the possibility of a 'mystical distortion'. He argues that the shamans' specificity comes from their being 'elected by spirits' (which motivates the title of the book), thus taking up the formulation adopted 60 years previously by Lev Ja. Shternberg. The latter called his presentation at the XXI International Congress of Americanists held in Göteborg in 1924 'Divine election in primitive religion' (Shternberg 1925), which was thereafter referred to as basic data by Eliade (Eliade 1951: 70–8). Since he had been banned by the Soviet regime, Shternberg had never been so extensively quoted as he was by Basilov. Throughout, his book which is also a broad overview of literature in Russian on shamanism, Basilov likewise cites a number of authors who, for political reasons, could not publish the results of their fieldwork in the 1930s (for instance, Prokof'ev). In the chapter 'Is the shaman sane?' (1984: 138–69), he particularly strives to clear the ground of some previous prejudices about shamans. Toward the end of the book, he takes into account what makes the shaman a representative and an agent of a religious system: he emphasises the importance of the clan and more generally of social organisation in the shaman's position and that of collective representations in his practices. (He will, in later works, more frankly disapprove of the Soviet tendency to give central importance to the person of the shaman, Mastromattei 1999: 4.)

Vladimir Nikolaevich Basilov (1937–1998) XXXVII

What he writes in the last chapter – 'shamanism is most deeply entrenched among the peoples of Central Asia and Kazakhstan. (...) Shamanism here had long been become part of Islam, and this is one of the reasons for its longevity' (1984: 204; 1990: 44) – introduces the topic of Basilov's masterful doctoral dissertation. He successfully defended it in 1991 before an Academician of the Tajik SSR, Professor B. A. Litvinskii, a corresponding member of the Turkmen Academy of Sciences, Professor S. G. Agadzhanov and E. P. Sokolova. All three were doctors in history, *doctor istoricheskikh nauk*, and he received the same degree. Then, he sent me the *Avtoreferat* (i.e. abstract and main argument) of his dissertation titled *Islamizirovannoe shamantsvo narodov Srednei Azii i Kazakhstana* (1991). It was still stamped by the Academy of Sciences of the USSR. I could then publish a shortened French version of this text in a special issue of the Journal *Diogène* (Unesco and Gallimard) (Basilov 1992a), which quickly also came out in the English version of *Diogenes*. Vladimir Basilov was happy that the full text of his dissertation could be published in Moscow, but the publishing house, Nauka, was henceforth that of the Russian Academy of Sciences. The title was slightly different: *Shamantsvo u narodov Srednei Azii i Kazakhstana* (1992b). It was soon translated into German: *Das Schamanentum bei den Völkern Mittelasiens und Kasachstans* (Mittelasiatische Studien 1), 1995, Berlin, Schletzer.

All this paints a backdrop that helps us understand how distressed our friend was when the USSR was dismantled. He had a great love for his country and was extremely proud of its achievements, even alongside an awareness of its defects and failures. Personally, he felt deeply concerned by the upheaval of everyday life and by the chaos caused by the brutal change of regime and by the disintegration of the Union, which made carrying out fieldwork in Central Asia scarcely imaginable. Things were better when he came to Paris in September 1997 to attend the fourth international conference of the International Society for Shamanic Research, which took place in Chantilly near to Paris. It was the last time that he met with many of us colleagues in shamanic studies – some of whom had become close friends, such Romano Mastromattei, from the University Tor Vergata in Rome, and Ioan Lewis, from the London School of Economics. His presentation became an article published in one of the two volumes of Proceedings (Basilov 2000: 361–9).

It was just one year later, in early autumn, that he passed away, in Portugal, swimming in the sea. His colleagues of the Institute of Ethnology and Anthropology in Moscow swiftly published a volume of collected papers dedicated to his memory in a collection of the Institute (Kharitonova 1999). The same year, Romano Mastromattei organised a celebration of a shamanic sacrificial ritual *tailgan* to commemorate Vladimir Basilov in the Ol'khon island of Lake Baikal in Buryatia, where he had been two years before with him thanks to his help. He also dedicated a book to his memory, which was published in 1999 as the first volume of the Venetian Academy of Indian Studies Series (Mastromattei 1999). Homage was paid to his memory at the Congress on shamanism held in Ulan-Bator in 2000. We may also consider as a homage the many references new shamans make today to his works. His book, *The Elect of Spirits* in particular, has become very popular among new shamans in Siberia. As a matter of fact, many of them belong to local urban or rural intelligentsias and are well-read in shamanic studies. They use Basilov's assessments on shamans as arguments to prove their legitimacy or justify some aspects of their practice.

Bibliography

Basilov, V. (1984). *Izbranniki dukhov* (The Elect of Spirits). Moscow, izdatel'stvo politicheskoi literatury, 1984, 208 p. (2nd edn. 1995).

―――(1990). 'Chosen by the spirits'. In Marjorie Mandelstam Balzer (ed.). *Shamanism: Soviet studies of Traditional Religion in Siberia and Central Asia*. Armonk, M.E. Sharpe, pp. 3–48. Re-edited in M. M. Balzer (ed.). *Shamanic Worlds, Rituals and Lore of Siberia and Central Asia*. Armonk, New York, London, England, North Castle Books, 1997, pp. 3–48.

―――(1991). *Islamizirovannoe shamanstvo narodov Srednej Azii i Kazakhstana. Istoriko-ètnograficheskoe issledovanie* (Islamized Shamanism of the Peoples of Central Asia and Kazakhstan, Historico-Ethnographic Research). Avtoreferat dissertacii na soiskanie uchenoj stepeni doktora istoricheskikh nauk, Moskva, Nauka.

―――(1992a) 'Le Chamanisme islamisé des peuples d'Asie centrale'. *Diogène*, 158 7–19. Reedited in Roberte Hamayon (ed.). *Chamanismes. Revue Diogène*. Paris, PUF Quadridge, 2003, pp. 127–145.

―――(1992b). *Shamantsvo u narodov Srednei Azii i Kazakhstana* (Shamanism among the People of Central Asia and Kazakhstan). Moscow, Nauka.

―――(1995). *Das Schamanentum bei den Völkern Mittelasiens und Kasachstans*. Berlin, Mittelasiatische Studien Band I, Reinhold Scheltzer Verlag, (translation in German of Basilov's *Shamantsvo u narodov Srednei Azii i Kazakhstana*, 1992).

―――(2000). 'Malika-Apa. Peripheral forms of shamanism? An example from Middle Asia'. In Denise Aigle; Bénédicte Brac de la Perrière; and Jean-Pierre Chaumeil (eds). *La Politique des esprits, chamanismes et religions universalistes*. Nanterre [Paris], Société d'ethnologie, pp. 361–9.

―――(2004). *Sibirische Schamanen. Auserwählte der Geister*. Berlin, Studia Eurasia Band IX, Reinhold Schletzer Verlag.

Bol'shaya Sovetskaya Entsiklopedia (The Great Soviet Encyclopedia) 1978. Moscow.

Eliade, Mircea ([1951]–68). *Le chamanisme et les techniques archaïques de l'extase*. Paris, Payot.

Hoppál, Mihály. (ed.) (1984). *Shamanism in Eurasia*. Göttingen, Herodot, 2 vols.

Kharitonova, Valentina I. (1999). *'Izbranniki dukhov' – 'Izbravshie dukhov'. Tradicionne shamanstvo i neoshamanism. Pamyati V. N. Basilova (1937–1998)* (The Elect of Spirits – Those who elect Spirits. Traditional Shamanism and Neoshamanism. In Memory of V.N. Basilov 1937–1998). Moscow, Rossiiskaya Akademiya Nauk, Institut etnologii i antropologii. Etnologicheskie issledovaniya po shamanstvu i inym tradicionnym verovaniyam i praktikam, t. 4.

Mastromattei, Romano (ed.) (1999). *Shamanic Cosmos. From India to the North Pole Star*. Venice, Venetian Academy of Indian Studies Series.

Shternberg, Leo [Lev Ja. in Russian] (1925). 'Divine election in primitive religion'. *International Congress of Americanists. Proceedings of the XXI Session held in Götegorg in 1924*. Göteborg, Göteborg Museum, pp. 472–512.

Tokarev, S. A. (1964). *Rannye formy religii i ikh razvitie* (Early Forms of Religion and their Development). Moscow, Nauka.

Vdovin, I. S.(ed.) (1970) *Priroda i chelovek v religioznykh predstavleniyakh narodov Sibiri i Severa* (Nature and Man in Religious Representations of Peoples of Siberia and the North) (1970). Leningrad, Nauka.

Vdovin, I. S.(ed.) (1981) *Problemy istorii obshchestvennogo soznaniya aborigenov Sibiri* (Problems of the History of Social Consciousness of Siberian Aborigines) (1981). Leningrad, Nauka.

Books and articles by Vladimir Nikolaevich Basilov: A Selected Bibliography

(1964). 'Teni svyatykh' (The shades of the saints). *Nauka u religiya*, 9, 54–7.

(1968). 'Nekotorye perezhitki kul'ta predkov y Turkmen' (Some vestiges of the cult of the ancestors among the Turkmen). *Sovetskaya Ètnografiya*, 5, 53–64.

(1970). *Kul't svyatykh v islame* (Cult of the Saints in Islam). Moscow, Izdatel'stvo 'Mysl'.

(1975). 'Traditsii zhenskogo shamanstva u kazakhov' (Traditions of female shamanism among the Kazakhs). *Polevye Issledovaniya Instituta Ètnografii 1974*. Moscow, Nauka, pp. 115–23.

(1975) with Niyazklychev, K. 'Perezhitki shamanstva y Turkmen-Chovdurov' (Vestiges of shamanism among the Turkmen-Chovdurov'). In G. P. Snesarev and V. N. Basilov (eds). *Domusul'manskie verovaniya i obryady v srednei Azii*, Moscow, Nauka, pp. 123–37.

(1975). 'O proiskhozhdenii Turkmen-ata: prostonarodnye formy sredneaziatskogo sufizma (On the origin of the Turkmen-Ata: popular forms of Central Asian sufism). In G. P. Snesarev and V. N. Basilov (eds). *Domusul'manskie verovaniya i obryady v srednei Azii*. Moscow, Nauka, pp. 138–68.

(1977). 'Novye materialy o shamanskom bubne uzbekov' (New materials about the shaman's drum of the Uzbeks). *Polevye Issledovaniya Instituta Ètnografii 1975*, 117–28.

(1978). 'Nekotorye materialy po kazahskomu shamanstvu' (Some data about Kazakh shamanism). *Polevye Issledovanija Instituta Ètnografii 1976*, 158–66.

(1978). 'Vestiges of transvestism in Central-Asian shamanism'. In Vilmos Diószegi and Mihály Hoppal (eds). *Shamanism in Siberia*. Budapest, Akadémiai Kiadó, pp. 281–9.

(1978). 'The Spirit world of an Uzbek shaman'. In *General Problems of Ethnography. papers by Soviet researchers*. Moscow, 10th International Congress of Anthropological and Ethnological Sciences – Delhi, 20–21 December 1978, Part 2.

(1980). 'The study of religions in Soviet ethnography'. In Ernest Gellner (ed.). *Soviet and Western Anthropology*. London, Duckworth, pp. 231–42.

(1982). 'Tashmat-Bola'. In *Glazami ètnografov*. Moscow.

(1984a). *Izbranniki dukhov* (The Elect of Spirits). Moscow, izdatel'stvo politicheskoi literatury, 1984 (2nd edn. 1995).

(1984b). 'Honour groups in traditional Turkmenian society'. In Akbar S. Ahmed and David M. Hart (eds). *Islam in Tribal Society. From the Atlas to the Indus*. London, Routledge and Kegan Paul, pp. 220–43.

(1984c). 'The Chiltan spirits'. In Mihály Hoppál. (ed.). *Shamanism in Eurasia*. Göttingen, Herodot, vol. 2, pp. 253–267.

(1986). 'Perezhitki shamanstva u Turkmen-gëklenov' (Vestiges of shamanism among the Turkmen-Gökleng). In V. N. Basilov (ed.). *Drevnie obryady verovaniya i kul'ty narodov srednei Azii*. Moscow, Nauka, pp. 94–110.

(1986). 'The shaman drum among the peoples of Siberia. Evolution of symbolism'. In I. Lehtinen (ed.). *Traces of the Central Asian Culture in the North. Suomalais-ugrilaisen seuran toimituksia*. Helsinki, Suomalais-Ugrilainen, pp. 35–51.

(1986). 'New data on Uzbek shamanism'. In *Beşinci Milletler arasi Türkoloji Kongresi*. Istanbul, TTK, vol. 1.

(1987). 'Popular Islam in Central Asia and Kazakhstan'. *Journal Institute of Muslim Minority Affairs*, 8:1, pp. 7–17.

(1990). 'Dva varianta sredneaziatskogo shamanstva' (Two variants of Central Asian shamanism). *Sovetskaya Ètnografiya* 4, 64–76.

(1990). 'Chosen by the spirits'. In Marjorie Mandelstam Balzer (ed.). *Shamanism: Soviet studies of Traditional Religion in Siberia and Central Asia*. Armonk, M.E. Sharpe, pp. 3–48. Reedited in M. M. Balzer (ed.). *Shamanic Worlds, Rituals and Lore of Siberia and Central Asia*. Armonk, New York, London,

England, North Castle Books, 1997, pp. 3–48 (English translation of two chapters of Basilov's *Izbranniki dukhov*, 1984).

(1991). 'Skifskaya arfa: drevneishii smychkovyi instrument?' (The Scythian harp: the most ancient bow-instrument?). *Sovetskaya Ètnografiya* 4, 140–54.

(1991). *Islamizirovannoe shamanstvo narodov Srednej Azii i Kazakhstana. Istoriko-ètnograficheskoe issledovanie* (Islamized Shamanism of the Peoples of Central Asia and Kazakhstan, Historical-ethnographical research). Avtoreferat dissertacii na soiskanie uchenoj stepeni doktora istoricheskikh nauk, Moskva, Nauka.

(1992) 'Le Chamanisme islamisé des peuples d'Asie centrale'. *Diogène*, 158 7–19. Reedited in *Chamanismes. Revue Diogène.* Paris, PUF Quadridge, 2003, pp. 127–145 (abridged version in French of Basilov's *Islamizirovannoe shamanstvo narodov Srednej Azii i Kazakhstana. Istoriko-ètnograficheskoe issledovanie*, 1991).

(1992). *Shamantsvo u narodov Srednei Azii i Kazakhstana* (Shamanism among the People of Central Asia and Kazakhstan). Moscow, Nauka.

(1993). 'Shamanstvo'. In *Svod ètnograficheskikh ponyatii i terminov.* Vol. 5 *Religioznye verovaniya.* Moscow, Nauka.

(1994). 'Texts of shamanic invocations from Central Asia and Kazahstan'. In Gary Seaman and Jane S. Day (eds). *Ancient Traditions. Shamanism in Central Asia and the Americas.* Nivot, Colorado, University Press of Colorado and Denver Museum of Natural History.

(1995). 'Blessing in a dream'. *Turcica*, 27, 237–46.

(1995). *Das Schamanentum bei den Völkern Mittelasiens und Kasachstans.* Berlin, Mittelasiatische Studien Band I, Reinhold Scheltzer Verlag (translation in German of Basilov's *Shamantsvo u narodov Srednei Azii i Kazakhstana*, 1992).

(1996). 'The 'shamanic disease'. In Uzbek folk belief'. *Shaman*, 3:1, 3–13.

(1997). 'Cho takoe shamanstvo?' (What is shamanism). *Etnograficheskoe obozrenie*, 6, 3–16.

(2000). 'Malika-Apa. Peripheral forms of shamanism? An example from Middle Asia'. In Denise Aigle; Bénédicte Brac de la Perrière; and Jean-Pierre Chaumeil (eds). *La Politique des esprits, chamanismes et religions universalistes.* Nanterre [Paris], Société d'ethnologie, pp. 361–9.

(2004). *Sibirische Schamanen. Auserwählte der Geister.* Berlin, Studia Eurasia Band IX, Reinhold Schletzer Verlag (full German translation of Basilov's *Izbranniki dukhov*, 1984).

Part I

ISLAMISED SHAMANISM IN CENTRAL ASIA

Chapter One

CONTEXTUAL VARIATIONS OF SHAMANIC 'HEALING' IN SOUTH SIBERIA: FROM 'OBTAINING LUCK' TO RELIEVING MISFORTUNE[1]

Roberte Hamayon

The view of healing as a shaman's main function became progressively predominant in Western ethnographic literature with the advance of colonisation throughout the nineteenth century.[2] The Tungus word 'shaman' eventually expanded to describe similar types of ritual specialist encountered in many societies all over the world. It came to totally replace the other terms used until then, such as priests of the devil, sorcerers, jugglers, soothsayers, magicians, etc., which designated characters found in medieval Europe. 'Shaman' was vague enough to encompass the various activities referred to by these terms. Its exotic character clearly discriminated colonised from colonising societies,[3] among whom no shaman could be identified. Finally, stressing healing as the main aim of shamanic rituals was tactful in a colonial context. On the one hand, helplessness in front of colonial pressure incited colonised peoples to multiply rituals that confirmed their 'traditional' view of the world,[4] and on the other hand, colonial modernising powers everywhere better tolerated rituals aimed at healing.[5] This created on both sides a trend to 'medicalise' shamanic rituals that were not basically meant for healing, and furthermore to 'medicalise' shamanism itself, given that the so-called 'initiatory illness' and some aspects of the shaman's ritual behaviour came to be likened to hysteria and interpreted as tokens of their suffering mental or nervous troubles.[6]

Thus, 'healer' became the most widespread feature used to characterise shamans, all the more since scholars failed to define shamanism as a religion, for lack of typical institutional features. The vocabulary of healing permeates the study of shamanism up to the present day (see for instance Atkinson 1992). Medicine-man is still widely used to refer to North-American shamans, and *curandero* (healer) is nowadays the vernacular term for shamans in South America. Likewise, a shamanic ritual is still currently called 'seance', a term borrowed from the vocabulary of spiritualism and also used in the field of psychoanalysis that emerged on the public scene at the time when the interpretation of shamanism as a healing procedure was blooming.

As this short historical reminder shows, the notion of shamanic healing is not self-evident. In this chapter, which is intended to question shamanic healing in South Siberia, I shall start from the following statement.

> If healing is understood as bounded within an experiential domain of suffering, then shamans are capable of healing their clients, providing relief from the chaos caused by illness, repairing personhood and offering new models of defining identity. Shamans do not cure disease; they seek to construct a life world in which disease has lost its meaning (Maskarinec 2004: 137).[7]

However, this definition will not apply in its entirety to all of the material produced below. This material is not, for a large part, personally collected field data, inasmuch as my fieldwork in Buryatia took place during the Soviet period (from the late 1960s to the late 1980s), a period marked by a strong repression of religious practices and, on the other hand, by noticeable development of biomedical health care. I could therefore observe no shamanic healing rituals. All my information comes from the rich ethnographic literature and the memories of my informants regarding the pre-Soviet and the beginning of the Soviet period, and from recent works regarding the present, post-Soviet period.

I shall argue that, contrary to many definitions of the late nineteenth century, healing is far from being the basic principle on which shamanism rests in Siberia; it is neither a primary function nor even the only activity of shamans. Indeed, the actuality of shamanic healing depends on a global set of representations, institutions and practices, which vary according to the type of context. Healing can be accounted for as an expanding branch of the basic structure of shamanism in particular contexts, where it coexists with the opposite activity: harming. Among the hunting groups of the Siberian forest in pre-Soviet times, healing was barely mentioned as a shaman's practice. However the shaman, on behalf of his community, conducted periodical rituals aimed at a general 'revival' or 'renewal of life' – one of the possible translations of their name among some Evenk groups, *ikenipke*.[8] His performance was held to 'revive' his fellows (which can be seen as a sort of healing if healing is defined as aimed to 'construct a life world in which disease has lost its meaning'), and these rituals also implied 'divining so that some people eventually die', as we shall see below.

By contrast, 'healing clients' was stressed as a shaman's main activity in the type of shamanism found among pastoral nomadic groups living in the steppe areas on the border of the forest; this context fostered healing (along with harming) for private purposes. It is significant of the above definition of healing as 'healing clients' that this was the only activity a shaman was paid for (always after it took place, sometimes only if it was seen as efficacious). Thus, a shaman could both heal and cause illness, depending on their client's request.

As to the forms of shamanism that are being revitalised today, they are of various types. On the one hand, some kind of shamanic healing can be identified among the services offered (for prior payment) by new shamans in consulting rooms to urban and foreign clients (who have to pay for them). On the other hand, shamanism is perceived as an abstract system of thought and claimed by local intelligentsias as the foundation of their ethnic tradition and identity; they call it 'shamanism without shamans', and perceive it as a philosophy of 'harmony with nature'; it is not associated with a particular mode of healing.

I shall briefly outline the type of 'ideological system' (understood here as a global set of representations, institutions and practices) at work in each of the two types of pre-Soviet South Siberian societies examined here: that found in the small chief less societies living by hunting in the forest, and that of the semi-pastoral Buryats living on the west side of Lake Baikal. Reference to the ideological background makes it possible to account for the place and form of healing in their framework. The development of healing from one to the other context is related to changes in their way of life, view of the world and system of values (Hamayon 2004).

Shamanic healing in hunting societies: 'exchanging vital force' with wild animal spirits[9]

Shamanism is the only ideological system in small chief less societies who live by hunting in the Siberian forest, such as the Evenk and Selkup of the Ienissei Basin (Anisimov 1958, Vasilevich 1957 and 1969, Prokof'eva 1976 and 1981). It is 'central' to society and encompasses all aspects of human life: it is essentially meant to make living by hunting possible. Hunting peoples conceive of themselves as one among other species, a party to the food chain that ensures life in the forest.[10] The inclusion of humans into the food chain is a crucial empirical element at the root of the conceptual construction that underlies their shamanism. This construction is based on a very simple idea: to catch the animals they wish to eat, humans should manage things so that the animals accept engagement through an exchange of food with them. It implies that animals are imagined as somehow similar to humans, endowed with intentionality and agency, hence having souls that 'animate' their bodies. Our analysis has led us to set 'animal spirits' apart from individual animal souls and to state that what is currently called 'animal spirit' is a sort of 'generic soul' that animates a whole species without being attached to any individual body. 'Vital force', carried by meat, is held to be necessary to feed spirits and souls just as meat feeds bodies. Thus, human souls and animal spirits have equivalent nature and function, which allows for social relationships between them. Conceived of on the model of relations between humans, relations to spirits are expected to give access to animal bodies.

Hunting peoples spell out clearly that life rests on an 'exchange' relationship between the human community and the spirits of the wild animal species they eat: just as humans live on game, consuming the meat and vital force of animals so, they argue, animal spirits feed on humans, devouring their flesh and sucking the vital force in their blood.[11] They define the exchange as being reciprocal and symmetric, in the shape of an everlasting mutual consumption that brings life and death to both humans and game animals. Thus, the hunting way of life implies the very notion of animal spirits animating game species, as if animal spirits were, so to speak, imagined in order to make hunting ideologically possible by turning it into an exchange where they serve as partners.

Souls are thought to be located in the bones, and destined to be reused from one generation to the other within the same human line or the same animal species after being somehow 'recycled' in the beyond. Everyone must have offspring; otherwise the exchange cannot be perpetuated. As a rule, hunters claim that they do not kill game animals and only take meat from them. Funeral rites performed on humans as well as those performed on hunted animals consist of preserving the bones and treating them so that the soul they convey can reappear in a new body for a new life.

Now, by its very principle, this exchange makes the progressive loss of vitality linked to ageing, as well as death, part of the natural order of things.[12] Sickness and death are seen not only as a kind of gift to the spirits in exchange for the game that people have eaten up to that day, but also as the prerequisite for the provision of food for future generations. This pattern of exchange seems to give no place to the notion of healing, which however somehow applies at individual and collective levels.

At the level of individuals: delaying the 'giving back' to animal spirits

On the one hand, nobody ever forgets the duty of exchange: being old and having grandsons, the hunter should go and 'give' himself back as 'food' to the animal spirits in the forest; yet this so-called 'voluntary death' is an ideal rather than an actual practice.[13] On the other hand, insofar as one should eat before dying – live as hunter before becoming quarry – people adopt various tricks to disconnect taking from and giving back to animal spirits so as to delay the deadly fate. The most current practice is feeding young wild animals they keep captive at home or smearing the small figurines they make to represent such young wild animals with fat, both currently called *ongon* in ethnographic literature since Zelenin ([1936]-52) popularised this Mongol word as a vernacular concept valid for all autochthonous peoples of Siberia.[14] It is believed that if the *ongon* (young wild animals, whether real or artefacts) are not fed, the animal spirits will be even more eager to devour humans or will refuse them any piece of game. The *ongon* are supposed to be able to both make men fall sick and hold game back. Feeding them is held to make them momentarily stop harming. Hence the crucial importance of 'feeding the *ongon*', *ongo edjeelüülhe* as Buryats say.[15] 'Do not get angry, eat', or 'take and give', are the ways in which a hunter addresses a figurine made of wood when putting bits of cooked meat in its mouth (Zelenin [1936]-52: 40; Lot-Falck 1953: 89).

In short, the part of the *ongon* is that of mediator in the exchange process. Their duty is to make humans die in the end on behalf of the spirits of wild animal species. Their two interconnected negative tasks – bringing sickness to humans and making their hunting unsuccessful – cannot be suppressed; it can only be postponed. Hence, feeding the *ongon* may be seen as a sort of 'healing', in so far as it connects the hunter's feeling of anxiety and ill-being to the current view of the world and leads them to acquire a sense of control over their fate. If hunting remains unsuccessful and weariness persists, a hunter may beat, insult or throw the figurine he fed until that point and start feeding another one.

At the group level: obtaining 'luck' for the human community

Hunting peoples say that they need a shaman to conduct their collective ritual aimed at obtaining 'luck' from the spirits for the hunting season to come. This ritual consists of setting up the institutional frame of the exchange. The frame is that of marriage alliance, which is the most constraining possible since it determines an endless string of such alliances. It is concretely expressed during the ritual by the shaman's 'marriage' with a wild animal spirit, imagined in the shape of a female elk or reindeer, the main game – which accounts for the shaman's costume, headgear (a crown adorned with antlers) and gestures. Only in his capacity as husband of a wild animal wife – only male shamans may perform this type of ritual – is he entitled to rightfully obtain 'luck', which she is supposed to let him take from her out of love for him.

The notion of 'luck' helps us understand this and other shamanic rituals. 'Luck' is required insofar as game cannot be produced and is therefore held to be accessible only through 'non-ordinary', somewhat 'magical' means. The shaman is to obtain luck in order that the hunters obtain game. Luck is understood as promises-of-game in the shape of animal vital force. The amount of 'luck' the shaman is able to take allegedly foreshadows the amount of game the hunters will be able to take. This conceptual background of shamanism is tied to hunting as an ideology rather than as an actual way of life. It survives when hunting decreases or disappears as an activity. By reasserting the exchange relationships with the surrounding world, such periodic collective rituals are expected to bring 'luck' not only in hunting, but also in other realms, which is tantamount to restoring belief in life. This explains why the notion of playing inspires the vocabulary and the whole atmosphere of the ritual, which may last for more than ten days. Dances and games meant to encourage matching and reproduction amongst animals as well as humans take place throughout the ritual. And this contributes to explain the renewal of shamanism in today's context; shamans are requested to call for 'luck' or 'fortune' in order to obtain various goods whose common point is that they cannot be manufactured: good health, good weather, fertility, love, money, business and all kinds of success...

Since it cannot be manufactured, what 'luck' is required for is necessarily limited in quantity: no one can be lucky at all times, and not all people can be lucky at the same time. It is marked by inequality and uncertainty. This is why shamans are always, necessarily, rivals of each other. The notion of 'luck' explains why the outcome of shamanic rituals is perforce undetermined and highly variable. If after the ritual the hunting season is good, the group will solicit the same shaman to conduct the next ritual. If the season is not good and too many people starve and die, another shaman will replace him.

At the end of this type of ritual, the shaman lies for some time completely motionless on his back, on a rug depicting a forest with wild animals, to let the spirits devour him. This ritual self-offering is intended to serve as a token of the group's future 'gift' to the spirits. The ritual ends with a divinatory sequence where the shaman proceeds to determine the supposed life expectancy of the participants. Some of them may then be marked out for dying soon. Thus, from inside the hut, the Evenk shaman shoots a small arrow through the smoke-hole for each participant; if the arrow falls close to the hut, it means that the participant concerned will die soon. The participants' eventual death will be interpreted as a forced gift to the spirits, like the old hunters' 'voluntary death': it is necessary that some members die for the group to survive.

Now, the idea of reciprocity with animal spirits is factually denied while remaining explicitly proclaimed. The shaman tries to 'take' as much 'luck' as possible and have the spirits take back as little human vital force as possible at the last possible moment. He is expected to use the disconnection between taking and giving back to act upon both the timing and the amount of human vital force the spirits take in their turn. This is perfectly true to the logic of exchange: loyalty rests on the nature of what is exchanged – meat and the vital force that goes with it. But like their animal models that lure one another, the humans resort to tricks. This is fully consistent with the explicit 'play' framework of the ritual. Tricking is part of the rules of the game, and the shaman must take advantage of it if he is to be fair with regard to the eventual loss in human vital force, which he can only reduce and postpone. This is why taking comes first in the exchange process and is embraced as the right attitude from an ideological standpoint. The shaman playacts his 'luck taking' in a very spectacular manner, but he keeps silent and motionless when giving his own vital force to the spirits.

Finally, the participants should give their formal approval to the shaman for his performance, for the ritual is under collective responsibility. Among the Evenk for instance, the shaman, blindfolded, throws a dissymmetric object (spoon, bowl, drum-beater...) on the ground. It is up to the participants to decide whether or not it has fallen on the lucky side (that is, cup side up), which they do with conventional exclamations. The shaman throws the spoon or the bowl again and again, either a limited number of times or as long as they proclaim the result as positive. Thereby, the participants commit themselves to having the ritual proved 'efficacious', that is they engage to try their best to successfully hunt or fish.

All this contributes to the deliberately playful, optimistic and willing turn that the ritual is expected to trigger in the hunters' minds: in the end, they have no option but to go hunting and face up to all kinds of risks and hardships.

Thus, while shamanism preserves people lives insofar as it ensures the group's defence and perpetuation, there is no shamanic ritual specifically intended for healing in this framework. Fertility rituals do exist, but they are not perceived as a type of healing; being sterile is not considered an illness, but a question of 'bad luck'. However, an aspect of the whole system of exchange with animal spirits, the human partners' reproduction, gives rise to what can be seen as a type of healing; it deals with the souls of those who die with no progeny and therefore cannot reappear again and 'animate' a new human body in their line: this is seen as a loss for the line and a possible source of trouble for its living members. The concern for the human life cycle develops as the role of hunting diminishes and it eventually becomes a major concern in the pastoral context. Anyway, it is obviously rooted in the duty of managing the exchange and expands as a branch from it, which justifies its coming under the shaman's responsibility and, on the other hand, its becoming more and more autonomous.

This is illustrated by the second case to be examined here, to which I now turn.

Shamanic healing among the semi-pastoral West-Buryats: bargaining with unfortunate dead souls

Among the Buryats, who live a mixed way of life (hunting and cattle raising) on the west side of Lake Baikal, shamanism coexists with another ideological system based on strong kinship principles of patrilineal descent and seniority;[16] it is also marked by the influence of Orthodox Christianity. As individuals, shamans are submitted to their clans; therefore they are thought to be always prone to rebellion and transgression. As representatives of their respective institutions, elders and shamans continually interfere and conflict with each other.

The shaman has but a small part in the periodic rituals, which the elders conduct in this context. The elders address ancestors from whom herds, pasturelands and nomadic routes have been inherited with prayers and sacrifices; they solicit from them rain, good grass, protection against wolves and so on, i.e. all that is necessary to breed stock; all this is encompassed in terms such as 'grace' or 'blessing'. The shaman's part consists of 'introducing the ancestors' blessing' into the sacrificial meat, which is seen as crucial to avoid misfortunes until the next ritual. According to my analysis, the herder's 'blessing' or 'grace' is to be interpreted in the line of the hunter's 'luck'.

While collective rituals are outside the shamans' domain, occasional private rituals have developed considerably and make their activity an important one for which they are paid, either in furs, domestic animals, meat or other food, cloth or cash. These private rituals are mainly aimed at divining and healing, any healing including divination. Of course, as in all shamanic systems, not all types of illnesses are subject to shamanic treatment and, conversely, shamanic healing concerns social and psychological rather than physiological disorders. Typical in this respect are all troubles perceived as threatening the patrilineal clan order, which accounts, on the one hand, for the current assimilation between illnesses and conflicts and, on the other hand, for the terminology of the shaman's coat – which is called 'armour' (*khuyag* in Mongol, *zebseg* in Buryat).[17] Such troubles may differ in kind and significance. Minor ones may require a mere 'repair' (*zahal*) ritual, which entails that any shaman should always be ready and able to 'find a means' (*arga*) adapted to the situation.

Skin diseases are held to reflect the punishment of some transgression; a shaman may then be called on to perform a ransoming ritual that consists mainly of addressing the ancestors with prayers and offerings. Shamanic healing is however more specifically required by those troubles that may affect the regular succession of generations within one's clan – and hence its perpetuation – the cause of which can be attributed to some unfortunate dead soul's revenge: a quite classical pattern.

More precisely, any trouble that impedes someone from living a 'normal' life (which implies having descendants) is subject to shamanic treatment. Troubles include marital strife, sexual incompatibility, loss of appetite and joy of life, etc.[18] All these troubles can eventually hinder the whole cycle of life, death and afterlife, and are considered to be caused by similar disorders in a dead person's life. The reason put forward is that the soul of anyone who dies without progeny loses the ability to be 're-used' for a new life on earth and is doomed to continual restlessness and wandering.[19] Moreover, out of frustration, such a soul is supposed to seek revenge among the living, either by abducting someone's soul or by taking its place in a living body, which makes the person suffer from nervous or mental illness. As a rule, any discontent with one's situation or any loss of taste for life is interpreted as being the departure of one's soul and its capture by a dead person's soul. Thus, the sufferings of both the living and the dead are interrelated and the shaman (either male or female) treats both of them jointly in rituals aimed at 'repairing' the life cycle of both living and dead human beings. In other words, the shaman should 'take care of the dead to heal the living'.[20] The shaman's first task is to establish which dead soul 'torments' the patient. To do this, he both openly carries out some kind of divinatory rite and secretly collects information from relatives and friends about persons that have died recently and their possible tribulations in life.

Then, during one ritual that may last for several nights, the shaman both addresses and impersonates the dead soul individually, treating it so as to reintegrate it into the 'normal' cycle of human life, death and afterlife, and make it eventually join the anonymous community of ancestors. On the whole, he consoles it with some compensatory worship: he offers food and clothes to its figurine and utters flattering words as to its intention. What matters in the reintegration process is the way a socially acceptable interpretation of the dead person's life and death is progressively constructed so that the hardship suffered receives an appropriate explanation. The reintegration is based on an interpretive construction of the dead person's unfortunate life story, which is made gradually in collective informal discourse and confirmed formally through shamanic divination. Subsequently, it takes the form of long songs sung by the shaman. Such songs start with addressing the dead soul in more or less compassionate or praising words and recounting how dreadfully hard its destiny was on earth, so as to assess its individual identity. Songs continue with expressions of the dead soul's supposed complaints and desires, the shaman then being considered as 'embodying' or 'impersonating' the dead soul. Thus, the shaman speaks alternately on the community's and on the dead soul's behalf. He plays the two parts, spells out questions and answers on both sides in a process of negotiation aimed at fixing the compensation (various offerings, and above all animal sacrifices) required by the dead soul to stop harming the living.[21]

Khangalov also mentions a practice called *hün dolyoo* 'human ransom' that consists of giving the spirit of the dead the soul of another human in exchange for the ill person's; it is supposed that the one designated to become 'ransom' will die sooner or later (Khangalov 1958, I: 209). This is one of the many reasons why everybody in a camp or village strives to attend such a ritual and refrains from sleeping throughout its unfolding for fear of being designated as 'ransom' to the spirits. It is believed to be easier to 'steal' a soul from someone who does not pay attention to what is going on.

Significantly, a ritual including an animal sacrifice is mostly called *khereg*, an 'affair', a 'bargain' among pre-Soviet West-Buryats.[22] The emphasis on such notions as bargain and ransom reflects the general idea that healing implies 'giving' the dead soul another being (be it a real animal or just the soul of a living human being) in exchange for the ill person. A recovery costs a death – a good reason to be permanently cautious not to offend dead souls, to offer their figurines comfort and food, and to take great care 'not to let a soul get and keep out of its owner's living body' (which may include forcing someone who is unusually silent and lacking appetite to talk and eat again).

It can also happen that the initially unfortunate dead soul becomes a famous individual spirit instead of being merely reintegrated into the ancestor's community. This is what incites Khangalov (a Buryat ethnographer of the late nineteenth century) to claim that the shaman's function is 'to make the evil dead become good'. It is possible that the conception of saints in Orthodox Christianity has influenced the construction of such spirits as individualised figures.

Much less attention is given to the living sick person than the dead person in such a healing ritual. As a rule, the shaman beseeches the sick person to recover, eventually under the threat of dying without progeny, now that he has freed his or her body from the dead soul's influence. He manages to attract the sick person's soul back into his body, which he always does by holding out a piece of food loaded with vital force, and calling for grace and blessings. This is called in Buryat *hünehe hariuulha* 'calling back the soul'.

In some cases, divining and healing cannot be separated from one another. An old woman I met in Buryatia in the late 1970s told me about a shamanic ritual carried out for her in her youth. She was not feeling herself (*she felt as if she was not the same person*) at that time; she was languid, silent and refused to eat. Her parents called a shaman. The shaman threw his beater on the ground several times. We might see this as his way of testing hypotheses on the possible cause of this girl's illness. He finally assigned the source of the trouble to a big piece of iron that was lying on the ground in the backyard and told the parents to throw it away. He mentioned no spirit and performed no other ritual. The girl recovered. When, as an old woman, she related this story several decades later, she still attributed her recovery to the shaman's intervention. From an analytical point of view, several factors can account for its positive effect. The shaman's designation of the 'culprit' was fully consistent with the family's worldview. His way of involving the family in the repair process provided an emotional support to the girl that helped her be reintegrated into the family and regain comfort and mastery over herself.

We observe that the major healing rituals that stage a bargain with a dead soul, as well as the minor ones of the type of 'repair' *zahal* or 'means' *arga*, are based on optimistic voluntarism similar to that observed at the end of the collective rituals of hunting societies. However, just as the logic of hunting life requires that some people die in order that the human community survives, and confines ritual actions to postponing illness and deadly fate, the economy of human relations in a pastoral lifestyle implies a permanent balance between the living and the dead, which entails that illnesses cannot be eliminated, but only transferred or delayed.

In the guise of a conclusion

Thus, as we saw in the first section of this chapter, one cannot properly speak of healing in relation to the pattern of shamanism associated with hunting life. Here, the playful rituals that are fostered are intended to have a positive impact on both the human community and the natural environment: both should be perpetuated in order that the exchange of vital force between them continues. A type of healing practice develops from the concern that, for the human community to continue, each member should go through the life cycle in its entirety, that is have descendants in whom his or her soul can be reborn for a new life on earth after being recycled in the afterlife. This type of healing practice becomes increasingly autonomous in the Buryat semi-pastoral society.

We can observe a whole series of changes in the latter pattern of shamanic practice compared to that typical of hunting life. The ideological emphasis passes from relations with the natural world, aimed at 'obtaining luck', to relations within the human society – specifically between the living and the dead – that are aimed to 'repel or relieve misfortune'. Concomitantly, as an institution, shamanism moves from a central position, marked by periodic rituals that give rhythm to a community's life, to a lower one, limited to 'repairing' private disorders, perceived as relatively marginal and subversive; in other words, from being a freely performed prestigious social duty it becomes a remunerative service to other people and, to some extent, from an exclusively male speciality it becomes one that is indiscriminately either male or female. Finally, the impact on health expected from the shaman's practice also evolves: an essentially physical orientation to health shifts to a more psychic understanding of the notion of vital force.

Significantly, in today's Mongolia and Siberia, new urban shamans currently use the word 'energy' to designate the healing effects on their clients whose expectations mainly concern the solving of such social or economic questions as unemployment, lack of money or divorce. The main or only physical problem is alcoholism, as vividly illustrated by Merli (2010). Energy appears to be often used as a complement to or in the place of the more conventional notions of fortune, grace or blessing in the discourse of new shamans. They perform mainly short rituals, which are intended to 'call for grace, fortune or energy', and are therefore perceived as divinatory and propitiatory. Again, shamanic action is thought of as bringing something positive rather than removing something negative.

Bibliography

Anisimov, A. F. (1958). *Religiya evenkov v istoriko-geneticheskom izuchenii i problemy prohiskhozhdeniya pervobytnykh verovanii* (The Religion of the Events in a Historico-Genetic Perspective and the Problems of the Origin of Primitive Beliefs). Moscow/Leningrad, Akademiya Nauk SSSR.

Atkinson, Jane Monnig (1992). 'Shamanisms today'. *Annual Review of Anthropology* 21, pp. 307–30.

Badamkhatan, S. (1962). *Khövsgöliin Caatan ardyn až bajdlyn toim* (A survey of the way of life of the Tsaatan living in the Hövsgöl province (Mongolia)). *Studia Etnographica* (Ulan-Bator) 2, 67.

―――(1965). *Khövsgöliin Darkhad yastan* (The Darhad of the Hövsgöl province). *Studia Ethnographica* (Ulan-Bator) 3, 1.

Baldaev, Sergei P. (1975). 'Objets descendus' et 'pierres écrites' dans le culte populaire bouriate'. *Études mongoles et sibériennes* (Nanterre) 6, 161–81.

Basilov, Vladimir. (1992). *Shamanstvo u narodov Sredney Azii i Kazakhstana* (Shamanism among the Peoples of Central Asia and Kazakhstan). Moscow, Nauka.

Bogoras, W. (1904–1910). *The Chukchee*. The Jesup North Pacific Expedition VII. Leiden/New York, parts 1–3 (Memoirs of the American Museum of Natural History, XI).

Cincius, Vera I. (1975–77). *Sravnitel'nyi slovar' tunguso-man'chzhurskih yazykov* (Comparative Dictionary of Tunguso-Manchu Languages). Leningrad, Nauka, 2 vol.

Donner, Kai ([1942]–46). *La Sibérie*. Translated from the Finnish, Paris, Gallimard.

Gemuev, I. N. and Sagalaev, A. M. (1986). *Religiya naroda mansi* (Religion of the Mansi People). Novosibirsk, Nauka.

Gracheva, G. N. (1976). 'Chelovek, smert' i zemlya mertvykh u nganasan' (Man, death and the land of the dead among the Nganasan). In *Priroda i chelovek v religioznykh predstavleniyakh narodov Sibiri i Severa (vtoraya polovina 19-nachalo 20 vv.)*. Leningrad, Nauka, pp. 44–66.

Hamayon, Roberte. (1978a). 'Soigner le mort pour guérir le vif'. *L'Idée de guérison. Nouvelle Revue de Psychanalyse*, 17, 55–72.

―――(1978b). 'Marchandages d'âmes entre vivants et morts'. In *Le Sacrifice II. Systèmes de pensée en Afrique Noire*, 151–79.

―――(1990). *La Chasse à l'âme*. Nanterre [Paris], Société d'ethnologie.

―――(2004). 'History of the study of shamanism'. In: M. N. Walter, and E. J. Fridman (eds). *Shamanism. An Encyclopedia of World Beliefs, Practices and Culture*. Santa Barbara, Denver, Oxford, ABC Clio, pp. 142–47.

Jochelson, V. I. (1905–1908). *The Koryak. The Jesup North Pacific Expedition VI*. Leiden/New York, parts 1–2 (Memoirs of the American Museum of Natural History).

Kehoe, Alice Beck (2000). *Shamans and Religion. An Anthropological Exploration in Critical Thinking*. Prospect Heights, Waveland Press.

Khangalov, Matvei N. (1958–1960). *Sobranie sochinenii*. Ulan-Ude, Buryatskii Institut Obshchestvennyh Nauk Buryatskogo Filiala Akademii Nauk SSSR, 3 vol.

Khomich, L. V. (1976). 'Predstavleniya nencev o prirode i cheloveke' (Representations of the Nenets about nature and man). In *Priroda i chelovek v religioznykh predstavleniyakh narodov Sibiri i Severa (vtoraya polovina 19-nachalo 20 vv.)*. Leningrad, Nauka, pp. 16–30.

Levin, M. G. and L. P. Potapov (eds) (1956). *Narody Sibiri* (The Peoples of Siberia). Moscow, Leningrad, Institut etnografii Akademii Nauk SSSR.

Lot-Falck, Éveline (1953). *Les Rites de chasse chez les peuples sibériens*. Paris, Gallimard.

Manzhigeev, I. A. (1960). *Yangutskii buryatskii rod* (The Buryat Clan Yangut).

Ulan-Ude, Buryatskii Filial Akademii Nauk SSSR.

Maskarinec, Gregory G. (2004). 'Healing and shamanism'. In M. N. Walter and E. J. Fridman (eds). *Shamanism. An Encyclopedia of World Beliefs, Practices and Culture*. Santa Barbara, Denver, Oxford, ABC Clio, pp. 137–42.

Merli, Laetitia (2010). *De l'ombre à la lumière, de l'individu à la nation. Ethnographie du renouveau chamanique en Mongolie postcommuniste*. Paris, Centre d'études mongoles et sibériennes/EPHE (Nord-Asie 1).

Olivier de Sardan, Jean-Pierre (1994). 'Possession, affliction et folie: les ruses de la thérapisation'. *L'Homme*, XXXIV: 131, 7–27.

Podgorbunskii. S. I. (1891). 'Idei buryat-shamanistov o dushe, smerti, zagrobnom mire i zagrobnoi zhizni' (Ideas of Buryat shamanists about soul, death, after life world and life). *Izvestiya Vostochno-sibirskogo otdela Russkogo Geograficheskogo Obshchestva* 21:1, 18–33.

Popov, A. A. (1976). 'Dusha i smert' po vozzreniyam nganasanov' (Soul and death in the representations of the Nganasan). In *Priroda i chelovek v religioznykh predstavleniyakh narodov Sibiri i Severa (vtoraya polovina 19-nachalo 20 vv.)*. Leningrad, Nauka, pp. 31–43.

Prokof'eva, E. D. (1976). 'Starye predstavleniya sel'kupov o mire' (Ancient representations of the Selkup about the world). In *Priroda i chelovek v religioznykh predstavleniyakh narodov Sibiri i Severa (vtoraya polovina 19-nachalo 20 vv.)*. Leningrad, Nauka, pp. 106–28.

_____(1981). 'Materialy po shamanstva sel'kupov' (Data on Selkup shamanism). In *Problemy istorii obshchestvennogo soznaniya aborigenov Sibiri*. Leningrad, Nauka, pp. 42–68.

Sandschejew, Garma D. (1927–28). 'Weltanschauung und Schamanismus der Alaren-Burjaten'. *Anthropos* 27, 576–613 and 933–55; 28, 538–60 and 967–86.

Shirokogoroff, Sergei M. (1935). *Psychomental Complex of the Tungus*. London, Kegan Paul, Trench, Trubner & C°.

Smolev, Ya. S. (1903). *Buryatskie legendy i skazki* (Buryat Legends and Tales). Saint-Petersburg, Trudy troitskosavsko-Kiakhtynskogo otdeleniya priamurskogo otdela Imperatorskogo Russkogo Geograficheskogo Obshchestva.

Vasilevich, Glafira M. (1957). 'Drevnie ohotnich'i i olenevodcheskie obryady u evenkov' (Ancient rituals of hunters and reindeer herders among the Evenks). *Sbornik Muzeyya Antropologii i Etnografii* 17, 151–85.

_____(1969). *Evenki. Istoriko-etnograficheskie ocherki (18-načalo 20 v.)* (The Evenk. Historico-Ethnographic Studies). Leningrad, Nauka.

Zelenin, D. ([1936]–52). *Le Culte des idoles en Sibérie*. Translated from the Russian, Paris, Payot.

Chapter Two

HEALING IN CENTRAL ASIA: SYNCRETISM AND ACCULTURATION

Patrick Garrone

Genesis of Islamised shamanism in Central Asia

Central Asia comprises a vast quadrilateral of approximately five million square kilometres. It includes the republics of Uzbekistan, Tajikistan, Kirghizistan and Turkmenistan, the steppe zone of Kazakhstan, the north of Afghanistan and Northeast Iran. The Chinese province of Xinjiang, formerly called Eastern Turkestan, is also part of the area. Throughout ancient history Central Asia exerted a considerable attraction on Turkish and Mongolian peoples originating from Upper Asia. Between 706 and 712 A.D. Islam conquered the main cities of the provinces of Sogdiana and Khwarazm. The contact between Turko-Mongolians and Arabo-Persians has determined the character of Central Asia to this day. It produced an Islamised form of syncretic shamanism, generally called *Baksylyk*, after the name of its eponymous officiant, the *bakshi*.[1] This shamanism, tinged with Islam, still manifests itself today all over the Central Asian area. Although it also occasionally penetrates the upper levels of society, it especially benefits from a strong anchoring in the popular classes. Its deep influence on people's minds in the area has enabled it to survive the turmoils of history and, in particular, to pass through the Soviet decades undamaged.

The syncretic character of this Central Asian shamanism, in which original shamanism and Islam are mingled, raises the following questions:

- Does this constitute a definitively established corpus of syncretic beliefs?
- Or, on the contrary, is the confrontation, still in progress, of two religious traditions, shamanism and Islam, an active process of assimilation?

Taking into account the economic, social and religious context in which the power struggles between shamanism and Islam take place in Central Asia, we might think that if the ethnographic data does not suggest the existence of a definitively established syncretism, but rather indicates an active process of assimilation, then it is clear that this process can only be carried out in favour of the Muslim faith. In the fight for the supremacy over souls, Islam gains advantages over shamanism from its more institutional nature, its financial power, its capacity to penetrate the highest levels of society and the international support it often enjoys.

Healing rites as indicators of acculturation

In order to try to understand the nature of the syncretism between Islam and shamanism, the shamanic cure is an obvious field for study: today the cure remains the last important prerogative of the Central Asian shaman. In Central Asia, the shamanic cure practically represents Islamised shamanism as a whole. Indeed, the Central Asian shaman no longer practises intercession for the benefit of the entire community like his alter ego of Upper Asia. He no longer appears as a master of the elements, an administrator of fortune or a regulator of the vital exchanges between the spirit of the Forest and a society of hunters. Admittedly, following the example of his Siberian equivalent, he still practises divination but, although this is taken for granted in rites, its importance remains marginal in Islamised shamanism. Besides, the symbolic and ritual dimensions of divination, even if practised for its own sake, are much poorer than those of the cure.

Although other classes of thaumaturges practising healing rituals also exist in Central Asia, the rituals used by Central Asian shamans are undoubtedly the richest, if only by virtue of the scale of their occurrence, the diversity of the situations in which they are performed and the abilities they require. The practice of shamanic healing enjoys widespread recognition among the indigenous people, and even manages to penetrate social circles supposedly inaccessible to it. This means that the cure, because it is extensively practised and socially widespread, and also because it occupies a central position in Central Asian shamanism, stands out as a particularly significant phenomenon. It meets three essential conditions for a better understanding of the syncretism observed in the Central Asian shamanism:

- the practices it entails are valid because they are considered extremely important by the natives;
- it clearly associates or juxtaposes a mixture of Muslim and shamanic elements;

- the ethnographic data concerning healing rites in Siberian shamanism allows us to appreciate the evolutions, changes and dynamics induced by the Muslim influence.

As regards the first condition, I have already underlined the importance of shamanic healing practices in Central Asia, both for the lower classes and for a significant proportion of the upper classes of society. As regards the second condition, the presence of mixed or juxtaposed elements related to original shamanism or belonging specifically to Muslim culture is obvious in Central Asian healing rites. Undoubtedly, shamanic themes are sometimes barely hidden by a superficial layer of Islamisation. Such themes are much more perceptible in practices carried out in places remote from urban centres and close to the areas of ancestral nomadism. Thus, they are predominantly found in northern areas, though still within Central Asia, i.e. in zones more particularly devolved to cattle breeding. This is hardly surprising, for, in Central Asia, the most immediately perceptible echoes and reminiscences of original shamanism seem to be directly connected to the later variant of Siberian shamanism, the variant attached to cattle-breeding communities, and not to the earlier form attached to societies of hunters. This parallelism could account for the influence of the cults of the dead and of ancestors in Central Asian shamanic cures. The dead and ancestors were indeed already closely involved in the healing ceremonies of Siberian shamanism of the cattle-breeding type (Hamayon 1990: 768). Lastly, purely Muslim elements – historical characters or saints, anecdotes and terminology, the invocations and references to the Old Testament – are particularly noticeable in a cure of Islamised shamanism because, unlike shamanic elements, they can be clearly revealed on account of their orthodox character.

The third condition justifying the choice of healing rites as a field for observation was the possibility of reference points uncontaminated by any external influence, to allow the appreciation of evolutions and changes. Such reference points are provided by the ethnographic data concerning Siberian shamanism from which the Central Asian form derived. Thus, I intend to make a structural comparison between the cure as it appears in Islamised shamanism of Central Asia and its Siberian source. Undoubtedly, there are several kinds of shamanic cures. This study is focused on those involving the most important ceremonies, either in terms of size or of the abilities requested from the officiant, that is to say those which are reserved for the most serious diseases and which are based on established and codified relationships with the powers of the unseen.

In conclusion, although healing does not constitute the basis of shamanism and although it is absent or unimportant in its most archaic forms (Hamayon

1990: 35), it nonetheless remains the only significant practice offering the possibility of comparative study in our research field. In Central Asia, no other phenomenon offers such possibilities for highlighting the presence of a definitively established syncretism between shamanism and Islam or, on the contrary, a still active process of acculturation between these two religions.[2]

Siberian shamanism and Islamised shamanism in Central Asia

At this stage of our study, it seems necessary to point out the main features which distinguish Central Asian Islamised shamanism from the original Siberian model. The present study is based on a conception of shamanism that differs from the long-prevailing version that presented shamanism as an institutionalised 'technique of ecstasy' (Eliade 1968). Siberian shamanism is much more than this, as shown by the work of Roberte Hamayon (1990). Originally, shamanism was connected to hunting. The 'intercourse' taking place in the Other World between the shaman and the daughter of the spirit of the Forest is the symbolic sign of an alliance between Nature and Supranature.

Several terms can be used to refer to the supernatural area beyond human perception, where the principles of all things dwell: 'Supranature', 'Other World', 'Hereafter', 'Heavens'. The choice of the term 'Supranature' is not meant to suggest any hierarchy between the various levels of perception, natural or supernatural: 'Supranature is "above" or "preceding" Nature only insofar as it animates and determines its "life"' (Hamayon 1990: 332). No words, because words are 'finite', can give an idea of infinity. The only way to recount these religious experiences accurately is, therefore, to adopt a negative definition: the zone which is the original abode of the spirits and to which Siberian shamans have access is, in fact, what Nature 'is not'. This means that the present study will focus rather on the relationship between 'Supranature' or 'non-nature' and Nature rather than on the concept of Supranature itself.

Through the bond he establishes between Nature and Supranature, the Siberian shaman contributes to regulating the constant circulation and nourishing exchanges between spirits and human beings, the former receiving human vital energy and the latter game. Later on, with the emergence of cattle breeding and agriculture, original shamanism evolved by establishing relationships with the dead and by incorporating the cult of ancestors. The Siberian shaman intercedes on behalf of the community and of private individuals. His intercessions may concern hunting, good fortune, weather or health.

In Central Asia, according to V. N. Basilov, Islamised shamanism is divided into two types, one defined as 'Turkish' or 'pastoral', the other as 'Tajik' or 'agricultural' (Basilov 1990, 1992 and 1997). The boundary between these two forms of Islamised shamanism can be placed north of the Syr Darya River, on the outskirts of the steppe area. In the present study, for clarity's sake, I will refer to the 'Turkish' or pastoral variant as 'nomadic' and to the 'Tajik' or 'agricultural' one as 'sedentary', even if today the opposition between the nomadic and the sedentary way of life no longer accounts for the social and economic reality of Central Asia as it did in the past. Indeed, although relatively recently urbanisation and settlement have gained ground and modified the way of life of the populations located north of the Syr Darya River, their original nomadism still determines people's frame of mind and also marks cultural, ideological and religious events.

Of those V. N. Basilov referred to as 'Tajik' or 'agricultural', it seems that only the term 'sedentary' can constitute a common denominator. Indeed, today, populations of the southern oases can no longer be considered mainly agricultural, because of the increasing role played by manufacturing and services in the area. In addition, referring to the southern variant of Islamised shamanism simply as 'Tajik' does not take into account the fact that these practices are also widespread among Turkish groups like Uzbeks.

Lastly, choosing terms like 'nomadic' and 'sedentary' refers to a geographical positioning that gives a better understanding of the adjustments of Islamised shamanism in Central Asia and of the degree of acculturation they have brought. Thus, unsurprisingly the most impaired and less expressive forms of shamanism are found in the sedentary areas where Islam has, for a long time, held sway over a structured, organised, not very mobile society necessarily submitting to its influence. Conversely, a form of shamanism, admittedly Islamised but less impaired and retaining traces of Siberian reminiscences, appears in the 'nomadic' area. In this area, Islam indeed exerts a weaker influence, insofar as it only plays upon smaller social units because the urbanisation process is still incomplete and settlement relatively recent.

In the 'nomadic' variant, north of the Syr Darya River, ceremonies are more paroxysmic. During these ceremonies, the shaman often accomplishes feats that recall original shamanism: treading on red-hot irons, swallowing swords or knives, etc. Healing ceremonies, in the south, in the 'sedentary' area, are less violent.

However, the present study will only try to highlight differences and similarities existing between these two types of Islamised shamanism when they seem relevant to illustrating the evolution of relationships between shamanism and Islam in Central Asia. These two types of shamanic practices will nonetheless be regarded as the local variants of the same syncretism mixing shamanism and Islam.

If the elements connected to original shamanism are generally more or less visible, depending on whether the event observed belongs to the 'nomadic' or to the 'sedentary' type, the Muslim character, conversely, is always clearly expressed in both cases. The specifically Muslim features of Central Asian shamanism, strengthened by the support of the now overruling power of Islam in the area, give the institution an outward appearance of respectability. For instance, ceremonies are often performed with the officiant turned towards Mecca, and ritual formulae are often in Arabic even if the speakers' knowledge of the language is decidedly approximate. Figures belonging to the Old Testament are also frequently invoked. The important differences between original Siberian shamanism and its syncretic Islamised counterpart from Central Asia have had an impact on healing practices. Consequently, before developing our analysis of these healing practices, it seems necessary to reassess the various conceptions of disease in each context.

Disease in original shamanism

In original Siberian shamanism, the main cause of disease is the 'desertion of the soul'. This 'desertion' can result from the soul migrating too far during its occasional wanderings, in particular during sleep. It can also be ascribed to abduction carried out by evil spirits. The soul then goes through a succession of events specific to prisoners: enforced stay, release etc. Other explanations are also offered: taboos have been broken, powerful entities have been offended, or the subject has been bewitched.

Roberte Hamayon has pointed out that the circumstances of this desertion of the soul, connected with disease, can range from sleep, in which case the desertion is harmless and reversible, to death, which makes it serious and irretrievable. She insists that disease is basically incurable, as it is part of the cycle of gifts and counter-gifts that ensure the permanence of life (Hamayon 1990: 566). Consequently, in Siberian shamanism, in the event of serious disease involving the 'desertion of the soul', the shaman will have to go and fetch it in Supranature in order to reinstate it in Nature, that is to say into the patient's body.

Disease in the Islamised shamanism of Central Asia

In the Islamised shamanism of Central Asia the shaman no longer enters Supranature, because nothing has been carried away there. Indeed, in most cases in this kind of shamanism, disease is no longer ascribable to a 'desertion of the soul' but to the fact that a place located in the real world, i.e. the patient's body, has been taken over or occupied by an evil spirit. Simply being close to an evil spirit is sufficient to produce a disorder. Thus, the redeeming intervention of the shaman has no need to call upon any celestial or infernal geography, as the harm is contained within Nature. The Central Asian shaman must free the patient's body of these unwanted evil spirits, banning them, and transferring them to some 'other place', a process sufficient to restore harmony without any need to call upon Supranature.

The aforementioned concept of 'banning' evil applies both to 'banning cures' strictly speaking and to those called 'transfer cures' as already defined in a previous study (Garrone 2000: 51–65). This does not imply that the preceding distinction between the two types of Central Asian cure is no longer relevant. In the 'banning cure' evil is forced to leave the patient's body immediately, whereas in the 'transfer cure' the disorders pass through a medium (i.e. a substance, a material) that is part of a process of coercion, lure or transaction. However, the 'transfer cure' is simply a specific variant of the 'banning cure', as the recovery and the translation of the disorders through a medium necessarily occurs after they have been dragged out of the patient's body. This is the reason why, in the present study, I use the expression 'banning' to refer to both kinds of shamanic cure in Central Asia. Moreover, the importance of the process of healing by banning evil suggests that, in the Central Asian Area, the concept of disease is not so far apart from the one prevailing in the oldest form of Siberian shamanism, in which possession was also considered as a possible explanation for the deterioration of the patient's health. It seems the Islamised variant of shamanism in Central Asia adopted those among the old beliefs that were acceptable to Islam.

The pressure exerted by Islam explains why the body is now at stake instead of the soul as it used to be in original shamanism. Consequently, the Central Asian shaman has no need to venture beyond natural limits.[3] To explain disease without involving a superhuman feat not admitted by Islam, such as the shamanic journey in Supranature, disorder is now located in a natural zone accessible to the shaman's performance, which thus remains acceptable: this zone is the patient's body or its immediate proximity. In Muslim Central Asia, crossing the boundaries between Nature and Supranature is a prerogative granted only to helping or evil spirits. This conception is then more admissible from an orthodox point of view, as Islam has already accepted a belief in *jinns* and their appearances.

A preliminary to the analysis of shamanic healing

The present study does not propose to classify and identify the different types of cure that have been described. I will take a particular interest in the geography, natural and supernatural, that constitutes the environment in which healing techniques operate, and in relation to which the actors engaged in the process, be they natural or supernatural, also interact.

However, I do not propose to make a detailed description of supernatural geography as it appears in native beliefs. These details are found abundantly in ethnographic literature. What interests us here is that there does exist a supernatural field with a geography of its own, where actions take place, just as they would in the real world: in original shamanism this world is a field of action for the shaman, whereas in the Islamised Central Asian variant, only spiritual entities live there or move in and out of this supernatural world.

Declensions of shamanic healing in Central Asia

As mentioned above, this study will focus on the most important type of shamanic healing used by Central Asian shamans. I will examine the type of cure, involving a complex ritual, that is used in the event of disorders requiring the greatest competence from the shaman and which demand the most institutionalised connections with Supranature. This kind of cure is generally referred to in Central Asian ethnographic research as *kamlenie*.

This study of shamanic healing should allow us to confirm either the existence of a still active process of acculturation and assimilation of shamanism by Islam or, conversely, the presence of a durably, perhaps definitively, established syncretism. Rather than detailing the various types of shamanic cures (*qaytarma, koch, ojun* etc.), which would blur the overall view, I will describe shamanic healing *per se*, that is to say the concept which has evolved, according to diachronic and synchronic circumstances, as it migrated from Upper Asia. For this purpose, the archetypal cure observed in Siberian shamanism, involving the quest for the soul in Supranature, will remain my reference.

Spiritual geography

The concepts of natural and supernatural geography have already been evoked. It is precisely the geographical aspect that will be used to highlight the significant changes expressed by the shamanic cure since its Siberian origin. For this purpose, I will henceforth prefer to write of 'spiritual geography', because this concept refers both to the natural and to the supernatural level.

If it seems fairly obvious that the concept and image of Supranature is related to the notion of 'spiritual geography', the inclusion of Nature itself remains to be justified. However, in the context of shamanic healing, Nature is not limited to its concrete, real elements. Actually Nature is also the place where powers, forces and entities connected to Supranature intervene. Most of the time they cannot be perceived by human senses, but the existence, activities and interventions of these powers are effective. To take them into account the shaman must adopt a less materialist and more spiritual approach. This is why Nature viewed from this angle, that is to say as the field of possible manifestations of Supranature, can be seen as referring to spiritual geography.

Healing practices take different forms according to local beliefs: either open intercommunication between Nature and Supranature is considered to exist, as in Siberian shamanism; or these two entities are believed to represent more or less separate worlds, as in the Central Asian Islamised variant. Thus, in Central Asia, Muslim influence has altered spiritual geography so significantly that original healing practices have been deeply modified. Incidentally, a similar evolution also takes place in regions where the type of spiritual geography prevailing in original shamanism has been transformed by enforced contact with another major established religion. For instance, in the Lake Baikal area the penetration of Lamaism has induced a change in the shamanic concept of Supranature by which the shamanic heavens accommodate recently introduced Buddhist deities (Hamayon 1990: 705).

In Central Asia there is no clear-cut division between these two polar conceptions of spiritual geography: the original shamanic variant in which an elect being – i.e. the shaman – is allowed to cross boundaries between Nature and Supranature; and the orthodox Islamic version in which the two worlds are absolutely separate and no mortal is allowed to cross. What actually takes place, according to geographical area, is a range of hybrid representations allowing various forms of relationship between the two worlds. As will be seen below, according to the dominant position of Islam and the type of spiritual geography it creates, the relationship between Nature and Supranature is either concealed or more or less openly asserted. The analysis of this relationship will prove particularly fruitful.

Spiritual geography and disease

As mentioned above, in original shamanism disease is the product of a desertion of the soul, which can eventually depart for the realm of Supranature. In the Islamised version of Central Asian shamanism, disease is neither produced by a desertion of the soul nor, obviously enough, by its departure for the realm of Supranature. Indeed, the soul is not generally referred to in the explanation of bodily disorders. The cause of disorder is strictly circumscribed to the natural world, for the spiritual geography induced by Islam erects a barrier between Nature and Supranature that is impassable by any human being. However, this barrier is impassable to human beings only. The separation between Nature and Supranature does not concern entities emanating from Supranature. Thus, in the Islamic religion, it is perfectly acceptable that creatures from Supranature should visit the natural world, as illustrated by the belief in *jinns*. Central Asian shamanism has taken advantage of this possibility. Consequently, disease finds its justification in the natural world, in particular when it is established that the patient is possessed. Indeed, although possession is due to supernatural entities, cases involving possession occur in the material world, they affect the patient's body and cannot be ascribed to a departure of the soul to some other territory belonging to spiritual geography.

The influence Islam exerted on the concept of disease through an imposed pattern of proscriptions and permissions in Central Asia provoked an evolution in the practices of shamanic cures in order to make them compatible with its requirements. Thus the mutations and the variations observed in the practices of shamanic healing testify to the degree of Muslim influence in the area. The limitation of the causes of disease to a strictly natural background, mentioned above, is one of the first mutations generated by the influence of Islam.

Healing in original shamanism and in its Islamised variants

There exists an obvious gap between healing practices in Siberian shamanism and the variants observed in Islamised shamanism in Central Asia.[4] This gap derives from their different conceptions of disease, whether they occur in Siberia, an environment considered by some academics as animist, or in the Muslim zone.

Thus, in traditional shamanic belief, the migration of the soul into Supranature compels the shaman to visit this zone. During the *journey* to Supranature the shaman generally assumes the paroxysmic behaviour of a wild animal, whereas his *stay* there is only expressed by a catatonic state which signifies his access to a metaphysical level from which ordinary mortals are excluded. It's during this stay in Supranature that the soul is recovered before it reintegrates into the patient's body. This reintegration of the soul into the patient's body restores the harmony that preceded the disease.

This journey to Supranature, which is considered indispensable for recovering the soul for its subsequent reintegration, has practically disappeared in the Islamised shamanism of Central Asia.[5] First of all because disease is not seen as a 'desertion of the soul' but, on the contrary, as a form of possession or harmful contact with evil spirits; and, moreover, because, in the eye of Muslim orthodoxy, man cannot free himself from his condition and have access to a place which is prohibited to him. Consequently, the shaman operates within strictly natural surroundings without any need to migrate to Supranature. Admittedly, he is led to perceive entities belonging to Supranature, to deal and interact with them, which involves abilities far removed from ordinary people's, but these events do not take place in some 'other place' that he would have to visit. When he cures the patient, the Islamised shaman of Central Asia has no need to travel geographically, because elements of Supranature are themselves moving within the natural world. This is shown by the eruption of evil spirits in or near the patient's body. These produce harmful effects, followed by the action of helping spirits needed for the healing process.

In Siberian shamanism, there exists a kind of geographical continuity between Nature and Supranature, and the shaman has to move along this continuum to intervene appropriately. Indeed, he even makes an explicit account of this trip, detailing the stops and adventures that punctuate it, conveying the idea that he has covered a physical, almost 'measurable', distance during his journey. Conversely, in Central Asian shamanism the prevailing spiritual geography shows an interpenetration between Nature and Supranature whereby the conditions of healing are present in the immediate surroundings of the shaman. In Islamised shamanism, especially in its 'sedentary' variant, the idea of a distance covered by the shaman does not generally appear. The competence which distinguishes the Central Asian shaman from the layman then consists in appropriating this spiritual geography in which Nature and Supranature overlap, and in interacting, to the best of his abilities, with the elements appearing in it, whether they are evil or helping spirits, patients or even audience.[6]

While in the Siberian shamanic cure the return to harmony means acting upon the positive element, i.e. the soul, in order to bring it back from Supranature to Nature, in Islamised shamanism it's just the opposite and one must act upon the negative element, i.e. the evil spirits, to eject them from Nature to Supranature. In Siberian shamanism the shaman intervenes over what is at stake in the disease, that is to say the soul, whereas in Central Asia he operates on the agents of the disease: the evil spirits. In both cases it is a question of subtracting and adding, but the fields of application are inverted: in the original shamanic environment the shaman 'subtracts' the soul from Supranature and 'adds' it back to Nature, where it belonged before its flight; in Muslim environments he 'subtracts' evil from Nature and 'adds' it back to Supranature whence it came. This inverted symmetry gives birth to two antagonistic versions of the founding acts of the healing process: in areas marked by original shamanism the recovery of the soul requires the shaman's presence in Supranature, whereas in the realm of Muslim obedience the expulsion of the evil spirits keeps him within Nature.

In Central Asian healing the problem no longer consists in searching some 'other place' for something absent in the natural world, i.e. the patient's soul, but in expelling the cause of the disorder. This expulsion of evil constitutes the founding of the cure in all local variants of Islamised shamanism, whether they belong to the 'nomadic' or the 'sedentary' type.

Expulsion of evil in the Islamised shamanism of Central Asia

Concerning the 'nomadic' type of Central Asian shamanism, A. Divaev describes a cure among Kazakhs during which the shaman, after achieving a few feats (insensitivity to fire etc.), flogs the patient or sometimes even a member of the audience. This process aims to expel evil from the patient or from any form of life to which it might become attached (Figure 2.1). The officiant's helping spirits also contribute to the process. Divaev adds that after calling his helping spirits the shaman leads them to battle. When the battle is over, a song of dismissal is sung in which the shaman asks them to take away the evil spirits. In this version Kara, the leader of helping spirits is unequivocally referred to as 'the expeller' (Divaev 1899: 28).

Still concerning this northern variant of Central Asian shamanism, J. Castagné mentions a cure among the Kazakh of the Kazalinsk district. Here again the report is very clear as regards expulsion. Indeed in this report the shaman is described as blowing into the patient's face; he also pretends that he is attacking an imaginary opponent with a sword and addresses the spirits in the following terms: '*bass* [choke], *tart* [draw out], *kess* [sabre], *ajda* [out]'. The shaman then throws himself upon the patient, biting and striking her while shouting '*chik* [leave]' (Castagné 1930: 103).

In the *kamlenie* related to Islamised shamanism ('nomadic' type, north of the Syr Darya River), the expulsion stage of the cure takes on a paroxysmic and demonstrative form. This can probably be explained by the fact that Islam's centre of influence is remote, situated further to the south. The spectacular character of the expulsion of evil in this area had already been mentioned in the early nineteenth century, at which time A. Levshin described a shaman who, in order to expel the evil spirits tormenting a patient, whipped him, spat at his face, bit him till he bled and pretended to cut his throat (Levshin 1832: 63).

Figure 2.1. A Kazakh shaman of Semipalatinsk playing the fiddle in 1927 (Photograph: F.A. Fiel'strup).

In the 'sedentary' variant, generally taking place south of the Syr Darya River, expulsion still constitutes the key element of healing, but no longer possesses this paroxysmic and demonstrative character. The patient is still struck to expel the evil spirit responsible for the disorder, but the blows are dealt without violence. In the case of a *kamlenie* taking place among Uzbeks in 1995, the blows were not only symbolic and scarce but moreover the shaman's outfit did not include such aggressive instruments as whips or knives. During this meeting, at the end of the fourth cycle or *halqa*, the shaman simply touched the patient's back several times with his drum, without violence, in order to expel the evil spirits (Garrone 2000: 78–82) (Figures 2.2, 2.3, 2.4).

Other accounts of this type of non-violent cure by symbolic expulsion, carried out in sedentary areas and consequently submitted to stronger Islamic influence, are reported by Taizhanov and Ismailov. They concern the practices of Toti Tabup, a Karamurt Uzbek shaman. This shaman would make seven strips of felt whose ends she plunged into a fire and, as soon as

Figure 2.2. A female shaman playing the drum, beginning of twentieth century (Photographic Archives of Uzbekistan, Tashkent).

they began to burn, withdrew them to beat the patient three times, before getting rid of them. Then she applied the same process using a switch made of seven different types of wood (Taizhanov and Ismailov 1986: 126).

So, we may conclude that both types of Islamised shamanism in Central Asia practise healing by expulsion, even if there are some idiosyncratic adjustments in each variant: the 'nomadic' one, because it is close to the area of

Figure 2.3. A female Tajik shaman playing the drum, Uratyube, 1995 (Photograph: P. Garrone and Th. Zarcone).

Figure 2.4. A Tajik shaman playing the drum during a healing ritual with a sick patient who is blindfolded, Uratyube, 1995 (Photograph: P. Garrone and Th. Zarcone).

original shamanism and further away from the centres of Muslim influence, is more inclined to spectacular paroxysm, while the 'sedentary' one is less violent because, for geographical reasons, it has submitted to Islamic influence and is more likely to comply with religious rules.

Displacement and 'fixation' of evil in Central Asian shamanism

By exclusively carrying out healing by expulsion, the 'nomadic' and 'sedentary' variants have now been clearly differentiated from the archetypal cure of Siberian shamanism. In fact, the expulsion of evil only constitutes the first phase of the cure. Admittedly, after expulsion, the patient is freed from evil, but complete recovery still demands that evil should be sent away and definitively fixed in some 'other place'.[7] This second phase, consisting of the removal and eventual 'fixation' of evil in a more or less remote 'other place' will sometimes involve discrepancies from the concept of spiritual geography imposed by Islam's domination in Central Asia. Thus, this 'other place', which ought to be, according to Islam, imperatively situated in natural surroundings, is sometimes located in Supranature. This is the case in some cures of the 'nomadic' type in which the memory of original Siberian shamanism has not completely disappeared, and where Nature and Supranature are again juxtaposed, thus creating an inviting 'spiritual area' that can be used. Nevertheless, in such cases this 'extent' will, *a priori*, be prohibited to the shaman and in fact only accessible to the evil spirits themselves.

'Fixation' of evil within Nature in the 'sedentary' variant

Muslim influence in the 'sedentary' area is powerful. The spiritual geography resulting from this influence imposes a rigorous separation between the natural and supernatural levels: elements of Supranature can break into Nature, but not the reverse. Consequently, after the expulsion phase, the Islamised shamanic ritual which takes place in such a context will try to remove evil and to fix it within Nature. The terms employed in the litanies chanted by shamans during the cures express the idea of a removal and a 'fixation' in Nature of the evil entity that has been dragged out of the patient.

Thus, another Uzbek shaman of the Karamurt group, Iris Tabup, after ordering the patient to squat, would slap his back, press on his temples, pull his ears, finally massaging him from shoulders to toes while repeating words aimed at evil spirits: 'Go away to the mountains, go away into the stones, go away across the steppe, leave this heart, get out of this nail' (Taizhanov and Ismailov 1986: 128). This confirms that evil is literally expelled from the patient's body (the heart, the nails) and then relegated and fixed in natural areas (mountains, stones, steppe), without any reference to Supranature. Moreover, the same passage confirms the non-violent nature of expulsion in this kind of Islamised shamanism, as the gestures made by the shaman are in no way comparable to the paroxysmic displays of expulsion seen in the 'nomadic' variant.

The expulsion of disorders and their 'fixation' within Nature is still attested in a *kamlenie* carried out in the Ura Tepe area in Tajikistan. Thus, in the following passage the shaman calls upon his helping spirits to take away the evil ones. Here again, obviously, 'fixation' takes place within Nature:

> This evil fate, take it away along the roads
> Take them away into the desert
> Take them away on the untravelled paths
> Take away this fate on the road...
> In the waters of the brooks
> Throw away this evil fate along the roads...
> (During and Khudoberdiev 2007: 94)

Here, again, the list of places where evil is to be taken away and 'fixed' is strictly circumscribed to the natural order.

The ethnographic material contains numerous examples of 'fixation' of disorders within Nature. Among Uzbeks in the north of Afghanistan, evil is thus transferred into coins then offered to a beggar, placed in a piece of bread which one gives to the dogs, or even put in bran thrown into running water (Cirtautas 1970: 46). Clearly, even after expulsion, the disorders are still regarded as remaining within a natural environment. Indeed, at least two of the previous cases imply that evil entities are considered sufficiently present to be offered substitutive victims by way of a new 'fixation'. Sukhareva gives a similar example amongst cures practiced among Tajiks of the Samarkand area. She mentions that at the time of the *kamlenie* the disease is supposed to migrate from the patient's body to a jug of water used for the occasion. According to local beliefs, whoever shall step onto this water, which has been spilt in a remote place, is likely to fall ill (Sukhareva 1975: 74). If the removal and 'fixation' of evil within a natural environment is characteristic of Islamised shamanism in the 'sedentary' area, there are also similar practices in the 'nomadic' zone.

'Fixation' of evil within Nature in the 'nomadic' variant

Although Muslim influence is weaker in the 'nomadic' area, it can nonetheless be felt. Indeed, even if healing takes on a more dramatic character than in the 'sedentary' area, the removal and the 'fixation' of evil usually still takes place in a natural environment. This is confirmed by V. N. Basilov, who mentions the practices of a Kazakh shaman of the Dzhambul district, Zhumakyz Baksy. When carrying out a cure, she would seize the lungs of a sacrificed sheep, sear them briefly in a fire, and use them to beat the patient's exposed body. Disease was supposed to be transferred into the lungs. The meat of the animal was then consumed during a feast. The bones and lungs were then gathered up and the shaman buried the whole thing in a remote place, deep enough that it could not be unearthed by the dogs (Basilov 1975: 120). Just as for the lungs, and without further explanation, the disease was also supposed to pass into the bones. Thus, the physical media (i.e. in this case the lungs) into which the disease has been transferred are buried in a natural environment, a practice that is similar to what usually occurs in southern areas. Indeed, no symbolic system is created here to evoke a possible removal of evil to Supranature.

Still referring to cures taking place in the 'nomadic' area, Castagné reports other examples of the 'fixation' of evil in Nature. In such cases the disease is transferred into animals' skulls, often dog skulls. At the end of the rites that aim to transfer the disease to a skull, it is left in a remote place. According to local beliefs, from this moment the disease is bound to the physical medium and the patient is freed from evil. The deposition place becomes dangerous for all those who would venture there, because of the evil spirits attached to it (Castagné 1930: 104–7).

However, in Islamised shamanism of the 'nomadic' type, the removal and the 'fixation' of evil are not always similar to the practices taking place south of the Syr Darya River. In the 'nomadic' variant Nature and Supranature are sometimes not rigorously separated in the spiritual geography, and this has a certain impact on healing practices.

'Fixation' of evil in Supranature in the 'nomadic' variant

The fact that the influence of original shamanism is more present in the 'nomadic' variant has an impact on the conception of spiritual geography expressed in the ritual. In these places, since this spiritual geography is less influenced by Islam, Nature and Supranature are sometimes perceived as not really mixed but rather juxtaposed. The original conception of Supranature as 'above' or 'preceding' Nature and somehow giving it life reappears here with additional strength. This different conception of spiritual geography has an impact on the course of some cures. Admittedly, in such infrequent cases, because of Muslim influence, the shaman no longer penetrates Supranature in the same manner as his Siberian alter ego, but he is nonetheless related to this zone in a mediating or symbolic way.

Castagné describes a *kamlenie* among Kazakhs in which the shaman, although respecting the Muslim prohibition of not entering Supranature, entertains a constant relationship with it:

> having cut the throat of [a sheep], the *baqça* takes out its lungs, then slits them twice with a knife; then he tosses them above the patient and shouts: *tart, tart* [pull, pull]. He then turns around the patient until he drops with exhaustion, after which he throws the lungs through the *changarak* and starts shouting: *chyk, chyk* [go out, go out]. The lungs having thus been thrown are immediately collected by a partner, carried away from the tent and buried' (Castagné 1930: 69; the words between brackets are taken directly from Castagné's original text).

The *changarak* is the 'smoke hole' situated at the top of the yurt. In addition, the axis of the *changarak* symbolises the axis mundi, the channel of communication between the world of Nature and Supranature. The lungs of the sacrificed animal, which have become the receptacle of the evil spirits, thus enter this channel and unequivocally migrate with them to Supranature. In this kind of Islamised shamanism, still close to the original kind, the dealings of a few elect with Supranature have not yet completely disappeared, and this is what the shaman more or less openly recalls when he sends the physical support of evil, that is the lungs, on a course which Islam forbids him to follow. In addition, the presence outside the house of a partner whose task consists of spiriting the lungs away, suggests that this more or less mysterious disappearance must be understood as a sign that they have now disappeared from Nature. This theatrical performance, together with the transit through the *changarak*, clearly signifies that the lungs and the evil spirits they held have been transferred into a zone forbidden to mere mortals, that is into Supranature.

The ethnographic material relating to the 'nomadic' variant provides other examples of removal and 'fixation' of evil in Supranature due to the survival of an old concept of spiritual geography. Thus, in the cure carried out among the Kazakh around Chimkent, mentioned above, the song of dismissal of the helping spirits in charge of the removal of the evil ones goes:

Oh you, Kara the expeller, send them back home, send them back,
all of them, bound hand and foot!
Make sure that all is well;
Seize them and send them all back home...
Follow your way up to the house without going back anywhere with the *jinns*.
There are unhappy widows whose *tunduk* remains open,
Well, follow your way up to the house and never turn your eyes towards this place.

(Divaev 1899: 28)

It is obvious that the role of the shaman's helping spirits is to send back and 'fix' the evil spirits, the *jinns*, in Supranature. This is shown in several passages of this song of dismissal. Indeed, there are several mentions of sending the *jinns* 'back home' and their appointed place of origin can only be Supranature. Mention is also made of a *tunduk* which 'remains open'. This is the name of the piece of felt which obstructs the 'smoke hole' of a yurt. Blocking it up during the night is expressly recommended, because the axis mundi goes through this 'smoke hole', thus enabling exchange between the worlds and making it possible for evil spirits to enter. This again confirms that the evil spirits which have been expelled are already, at this moment, within Supranature. Actually, it is recommended to 'Kara the expeller' that he not turn his eyes towards 'this place', that is towards the *tunduk*, which could offer the evil spirits an opportunity to burst into Nature again.

Even where nomadic populations have evolved toward a sedentary way of life, the 'nomadic' variant of the cure may yet preserve faint traces of the 'fixation' of evil within Supranature. Thus, in October 1914 in Lob Nor an Islamised shaman practising a healing ritual in a house, and no longer in a yurt, nonetheless persisted in making the physical support of evil go through the flue of the fireplace, a modern equivalent of the 'smoke hole'! After wrapping two wooden dolls in coloured rags and saying a few prayers over them, she set fire to them, passed them over the patient's face and threw them into the fireplace, where they burned (Malov 1918: 9). Here evil is sent into the 'Other World' just as the lungs were expelled via the *changarak*. Malov's description of the *kamlenie* also tells us that a *tugh* – a plaited rope whose ends are tied to a stake driven into both ground and ceiling and from which coloured rags are hung – was placed in the centre of the room. This is another symbolisation of the axis mundi, and it is normally via this axis that the evil spirits are evicted. The fact that they were evicted through the chimney, which is on one side of the room, is a good illustration of the acculturation phenomenon. Admittedly, some vague memory of expulsion through the 'smoke hole' has been preserved, but its close association with the axis mundi has been lost. This is a significant indication that acculturation is generated by changes in lifestyle, and that the gradual eradication of shamanic elements is brought about through the passage to a sedentary way of life, in particular.

These examples of cures in which evil spirits are moved to Supranature reveal that original shamanism keeps on exerting its influence. Actually, unlike other cures of the 'nomadic' variant and all those of the 'sedentary' type, the concept of spiritual geography in this case refers directly to Siberian shamanism and creates a specific kind of relationship with Supranature. Of course this only concerns the transit of the evil spirits, the Muslim prohibition that ascribes to the shaman the limits inherent to ordinary mortals being impossible to contravene. However, as long as it is possible in terms of spiritual geography, as in the cases above, the temptation exists for the shaman to have an immediate relationship with Supranature. Thus he will often go to the boundary separating the two worlds, illustrating that he feels the necessity for the shamanic journey, though he will never take the decisive step.

Other relations with Supranature in the 'nomadic' variant

The previous examples show that in some cases of the 'nomadic' variant, when spiritual geography fully reintroduces the idea of Supranature, the shamanic cure is modified. At the limits of its zone of influence, Islam can actually still put up with the passage of the disorders into the supernatural world. Thus, within the 'nomadic' variant it sometimes occurs that the conception of spiritual geography reintroduces the idea of a shamanic journey to Supranature. Nevertheless, because of Muslim imperatives, the shaman will not completely succumb to temptation. In some cures, one can see him simply suggesting the journey to the Other World in a truncated or symbolic form.

Chary Porhan, a Turkoman shaman of the Geklen group of the first half of the twentieth century, provides a good illustration. He carried out a 'nomadic' type of *kamlenie*. During such cures he used to tread on red-hot irons and tie himself to a rope hanging from the opening at the top of the yurt in order to call his helping spirits. He also tied his feet at the rim of the dome of the yurt and clapped his hands while hanging upside down (Basilov 1986: 101). Even if the shamanic journey to Supranature is neither really accomplished nor claimed, the symbolism of this part of the healing ritual is nonetheless significant: the shaman no longer ventures into the Other World, but stands on the border, at the opening of the path that leads there, that is on the axis mundi passing through the 'smoke hole'. In addition, part of himself, his voice, really penetrates Supranature, sufficiently at least to be heard by his helping spirits.

The passages of the healing ritual that concern the use of the *tugh* constitute an illustration of a symbolic or suggested shamanic journey. During the cure the shaman of the 'nomadic' type clings with one hand to the rope of the *tugh*, turning very fast around it. This creates a state of tiredness, even exhaustion, liable to make his head spin and, perhaps, also to modify his state of consciousness. In so doing, he places himself on the axis authorising communication between the two worlds, and his spinning movement, combined with the effect it produces in him, is highly significant, even if the journey to Supranature is not claimed as such. Branches, pieces of cloth and multicoloured ribbons are also tied to the *tugh* (Malov 1918: 6), decoration that refers to the 'sky pillar' allowing communication between worlds, symbolised by the central stake of the tent or the yurt among shamanic peoples of Upper Asia. The upper end of this stake is also sometimes decorated with coloured pieces of cloth (Eliade 1968: 213). All these elements connect the use of the *tugh* in this particular kind of cure to the 'nomadic' variant, and constitute a proof, albeit an implicit one, of an attempted shamanic journey.

A rather curious factor can also contribute to establishing that the use of the *tugh* by the shaman really constitutes an unexpressed attempt at a shamanic journey. Malov mentions that in the cure practised in the area of Aksu, in Xinjiang, a chicken is first buried for a short time at the foot of the *tugh*. Then the shaman dances on the place it was buried, after which it is exhumed, still alive and unscathed (Malov 1918: 15). This exploit seems to combine shamanic characteristics with the muffled and impoverished echoes of an older quest for the soul. One must not forget that, among shamanic peoples, the soul takes the appearance of a bird (Eliade 1968: 171). The burial of the fowl at the foot of the *tugh*, the axis of communication between the two worlds, probably symbolises the flight of the soul to Supranature. The shaman's dance above the place where the animal is buried, therefore near the *tugh*, appears to correspond to the shamanic journey, while the exhumation shows the happy conclusion of the search as well as the return of the soul to the natural environment, thus ensuring the patient's recovery.

In addition, an article by Gulibahaer Hujiexi, a Chinese Kirghiz scholar, allows us believe that even today the journey to Supranature is almost fully expressed by Islamised shamans in areas well away from strong Muslim influence. In a recent article, this scholar presents two pictures of a Kirghiz *Bakshi* (shaman) of Xinjiang (Kizilsu district) performing what appears indeed to be a journey to Supranature (Hujiexi 2009: 389, 395). In the first picture, the shaman is hanging at the top of the yurt and, in the second, half of his body is disappearing through the 'smoke hole'. In a private correspondence dated March 2010, Gulibahaer Hujiexi also confirms that the shaman is slipping through the 'smoke hole' to get in touch with his helping spirits. Therefore we have here a piece of evidence of a modest but real survival of a journey to Supranature in Islamised shamanism.

Finally, whether it concerns the 'fixation' of evil or the journey to Supranature, these openly shamanic ways of healing that belong to the 'nomadic' variant could indeed constitute the initial connection between original shamanism and the Islamised variant.

Synthesis of the analyses of healing in Central Asian shamanism

The cure, which is a minor phenomenon in Siberian hunter societies from which shamanism originates, is the main, if not the only, element of the variant of shamanism practised in Central Asia. In the Central Asian area, cure is almost synonymous with Islamised shamanism. The type of spiritual geography prevailing in the kind of shamanism which is the object of the present study is essential, because in fact it constitutes the matrix of the cure: actually, according to the conditions imposed by this concept, it potentially determines the healing practices to be implemented.

In Siberian shamanism spiritual geography takes the form of a continuum between Nature and Supranature. This continuum is the 'spiritual area' that must be travelled, and the Siberian shaman does so systematically, entering Supranature in order to recover the patient's wandering soul. In Central Asia, spiritual geography takes into account the prohibitions of Islam, and the disease manifests as an eruption of evil, originating from Supranature, into Nature. Actually, Islam usually forbids mankind access to the Other World, to Supranature, which is beyond human powers. Moreover, if we disregard the claims of Sufism and keep to the point of view of Muslim orthodoxy, this privilege was granted only once, to Prophet Muhammad himself. This power was bestowed upon him so that he might reach the divine level and contemplate God at the end of his celestial journey, the *mi'raj* (Böwering 1996: 206–7). Thus the Central Asian shaman will not have to travel to Supranature, elements of which can be seen and handled in a kind of quasi immediate relation.

Admittedly, the spirits responsible for disorders are not strictly part of the natural environment, as only the shaman can see and interact with them. However, they dwell in some undetermined 'other place', pretty close to Nature and overlapping with it, so that the shaman's actions can be described without any reference to an explicit geographical pattern. The cure is no longer a quest for the soul, but an expulsion of evil.

In the great healing rituals of Central Asian shamanism the expulsion of the evil spirits is followed by their 'fixation' in a place where they are supposed to be deprived of their harmful powers: in theory this place is within Nature because of the concept of spiritual geography prevailing in Central Asia. Actually, the strict separation between Nature and Supranature in this area makes it impossible, on man's initiative, for elements from the former to penetrate the latter: this affects not only the shaman, but also, *a priori*, the evil spirits he has expelled during the cure.

However, in the 'nomadic' variant it sometimes occurs that when the grip of Islam is loosened, the shamanic influence reappears with renewed vigour, at which point some discrepancies are revealed in spiritual geography. The concept of a continuum between Nature and Supranature re-emerges and practices of a more openly shamanic nature can again be detected in the cures, although they are never asserted as such: reinterpretation of the 'smoke hole' as an access point to Supranature into which disorders are sent, more or less avowed simulations of journeys to the other world and so on.

It can be seen that healing practices appear in a variety of forms across the whole Central Asian area. The shamanic elements which still appear in the cures of the 'nomadic' variant, even in a subdued manner, disappear almost completely in sedentary areas where Islam exerts absolute power. Thus the cure constitutes a remarkable example of syncretism between shamanism and

Islam. This syncretism associates the two elements in variable proportions: the emphasis on shamanism being reduced in increasingly urbanised areas. The question follows as to whether the process is over, or will continue until shamanic heritage eventually disappears.

Syncretism, acculturation and comparative elements

In order to identify the nature of the process we are confronted with in the case of Islamised Central Asian shamanism, I have searched Central Asian ethnographic material for other major field studies in which shamanism and Islam have mixed. Two such studies have been selected: one concerns Sufism, because some heterodox brotherhoods have retained shamanic elements; the other concerns collective imagination, in particular the legends of Korkut Ata, for the same reasons. The objective was to determine whether these studies revealed a durable and established balance between the two religions, or whether they instead indicated a long term process of eradication of the shamanic elements. The findings clearly reveal the phenomenon of the eradication of shamanism in favour of a triumphing Islam. Syncretism has only been a transitory stage, as shown in the following examples.

Disappearance of the most heterodox Sufi brotherhoods

In Central Asia, some Sufi brotherhoods that had maintained close relationships with shamanism were quickly submitted to a process of marginalisation, assimilation and, finally, extinction. I am referring here to the Yasawiyya and Qalandariyya brotherhoods. Various shamanic elements were detected in the dances practised within the Yasawiyya brotherhood, which appeared in the twelfth century (Köprülüzade 1929). The Yasawiyya fled from the Mongols in the thirteenth century, then, in Anatolia, merged with the Haydariyya, itself resulting from the very shamanic Qalandariyya. From the sixteenth to seventeenth centuries onwards, the presence of Yasawiyya decreased, and finally the brotherhood disappeared.

Central Asia and the surrounding area also sheltered the main trends of the Qalandariyya, founded in the thirteenth century and also containing elements linked to shamanism. This connection with shamanism materialises in the fact that the wandering dervishes of this brotherhood wear the *janda*, a kind of dress made of multicoloured pieces of cloth characteristic of the order and also worn by Burh, another name for Korkut Ata, an emblematic Central Asian figure of shamanism, as seen below (Figure 2.5).

Figure 2.5. A band of Qalandar dervishes singing, playing musical instruments and begging, beginning of twentieth century, Tashkent, Central Asia (old postcard, collection of Th. Zarcone).

The shamans invited their protecting and helping spirits to ritual feasts, and staged a bloody sacrifice named *degdzhush*. Qalandars prepared meals in a pot which they called *degdzhushi mavlon*, 'His Highness the burning cauldron' (Sukhareva 1975: 82–3). This symbolic cauldron is also present in the Yasawiyya, although a possible connection with shamanism is not borne out in this brotherhood.[8] The Qalandars no longer exist today in Central Asia, and in the first third of the twentieth century the only figures evoking them were some wandering characters existing outside any established institutional environment. They were called *duana* or *dîwâna*, and scholars of the time classified them as shamans (Chekaninskij 1929: 79) or mere healers (Castagné 1930: 127–34).

It thus appears that the Sufi brotherhoods which had some obvious elements in common with shamanism, like the Yasawiyya and the Qalandariyya, were gradually absorbed by other brotherhoods and finally vanished from the Central Asian scene. Islam refused any possibility of syncretism with shamanism. Although Muslim orthodoxy is naturally rather critical regarding Sufism in general, the pressure exerted on the Yasawiyya and the Qalandariyya must have been stronger than that on other brotherhoods which managed to survive in this area.[9]

Islam's refusal to admit any form of syncretism manifests itself not only in the cultural practices of ordinary people, but also in collective imagination, as shown by the legendary character of Korkut Ata.

Korkut Ata in the collective imagination of Central Asia

The character of Korkut Ata is a notable influence in the Islamised shamanism of Central Asia and the underlying corpus of beliefs related to it. He is also known in the area by other names, like Burkut or Burh.[10] This legendary figure is a good illustration of the slow process by which, in this area, Islam refuses any syncretism and assimilates any shamanic element until eventual eradication.

In the deepest layers of Central Asian collective imagination, Korkut possesses all the features of the shaman and expresses his supreme power totally and unreservedly. Thus, he is seen undertaking 'celestial' journeys during which he meets the Angel of Death, from whom he steals captive souls in order to bring them back into the world of the living (this feat is a characteristic element of a shamanic healing ritual). In the oldest corpus of stories relating to him, he also holds sway over natural elements, in particular over rain (Basilov 1970: 26, 33, 49).

With the arrival of Islam, Korkut appears as a domineering power, bullying and submitting the newcomer, that is to say Allah, to his will. He thus damages Allah's celestial throne because he refuses to intercede in favour of a childless couple. However, the power of Islam increased with time, and in episodes of his later legends Korkut appears as a ridiculous figure (Basilov 1970: 27, 31). One of the most significant episodes of his absorption into Muslim collective imagination is the mention, in a Kazakh legend, of the character wearing the *janda* of the Qalandars dervishes (Basilov 1970: 30). This is a good illustration of the process to which the figure of Korkut has been subjected throughout centuries of immersion in Islam. As a figure of pre-Islamic beliefs, Korkut could certainly not be integrated into Muslim orthodoxy without a period of 'acclimatisation', and for this reason his character must go through peripheral Islam, that is to say Sufism. One may also notice that the Central Asian collective imagination makes Korkut go through the Qalandariyya, one of the most heterodox brotherhoods, and one that shares some characteristics with shamanism.

Korkut's assimilation will not cease until his perfect integration into the Muslim sphere is achieved. Posterity will then represent him as a favourite servant of Allah, or as a counsellor of Muslim monarchs (Basilov 1970: 31–46), and finally as a saint who, although legendary, will be endowed with several mausoleums (Castagné 1910; Barthold 1963).

The disappearance of the most heterodox Sufi brotherhoods and the evolution of Korkut's character are examples, albeit in specific fields, of a complete process of assimilation of shamanism by Islam.[11]

Shamanised Islam and Islamised shamanism

In the 'nomadic' variant, the 'fixation' of evil in Supranature characterised an Islamised shamanism which definitely retained some conceptions of its 'original'. With some cures containing elements suggestive of the shamanic journey, even of the quest for the soul, one can say that we find ourselves at the outward limits of Islamised shamanism. Should the shaman take an additional step, both literally and figuratively, and thus penetrate Supranature, he would all but return to original shamanism. If such phrases as 'Sufised shamanism' and 'shamanised Sufism' have been used elsewhere (Zarcone 2000: 383–93), here a chiasmus is also appropriate: if the 'nomadic' variant in its most extreme forms can justifiably be described as 'Islamised shamanism' in consideration of the strong reminiscences of original shamanism it retains, conversely, the 'sedentary' variant could legitimately be described as 'shamanised Islam'.

Conclusion

As we come to the end of this study, it would appear that syncretism between shamanism and Islam is not definitively established, at least in a large part of Central Asia. What may be mistaken for established syncretism is only a particular moment in a still active process of acculturation and assimilation. It seems that this process will come to an end with the disappearance of the shamanic elements as they are driven out by Islam. The examples provided in the fields of Sufism and the collective imagination lead to this kind of conclusion.

Behind its monolithic appearance, healing in Central Asian shamanism is revealed to possess significant variations, and I have attempted to highlight the two main lines along which these differences are distributed. To this end I have introduced the notions of 'Islamised shamanism' and 'shamanised Islam'. It may well be that this distinction based on observed practices expresses a difference in their medium or long-term destiny.

'Islamised shamanism' might thus survive in the areas of minor Muslim influence, that is to say in northern Central Asia or in the Chinese province of Xinjiang. Indeed, in the latter region the Muslim religion is strictly controlled by authorities and is unable to give free rein to its proselytism and influence.

Conversely, south of the Syr Darya River, Muslim influence on mentalities is facilitated by increasing urbanisation. This makes the control of populations easier and allows organised religions, Islam in particular, to percolate and control the social environment. In addition, urbanisation also means that one can be in touch with large groups of people, whether through the media or modern transport: thus the religious influence of the neighbouring Muslim countries reaches the heart of Central Asian society. Lastly, urbanisation is also synonymous with education, giving an advantage to Islam, a religion based on written texts.

In southern Central Asia, for the same reasons, the share represented by clearly shamanic elements in cures tends to decrease, and popular practices already reveal the presence of a 'shamanised Islam'. It cannot be discounted that in urbanised backgrounds, Islam may, in the long term, find enough resources to totally eradicate the shamanic elements that appear in cures. These would then become practices referring to a peripheral Islam, but would already fall within a more-or-less orthodox sphere of influence. It seems that the first stages of this process can already be seen: in 1996 I observed an Uzbek shaman devoting himself to a talisman made by copying out Muslim prayers, while an informer assured me that the mullah was called when the recourse to the shaman had no effect.

In Central Asia, the cure thus seems to be a major indicator of the degree of assimilation of Islam by shamanism. The extent of Islamised shamanism in Central Asia has already been reduced to shamanic healing practices, as the community rites originally practiced in Siberia have disappeared. If this process of eradication of shamanic elements were to continue in the area of cures, in particular of the 'sedentary' variant, as has already happened in Sufism and in Korkut Ata's epics, shamanism would become increasingly absent in settled areas. The stage of 'shamanised Islam' that characterises the practices of the 'sedentary' variant today is perhaps one of the last spasms of a syncretism which only manages to survive north of the Syr Darya River in the form of an 'Islamised shamanism', or, in some areas in closer contact with modernity, as a shamanic revival of a 'New Age' type. This 'Islamised shamanism' would then constitute for a time (but for how long?) the last traces of a fleeting syncretism between shamanism and Islam in Central Asia.

Bibliography

Barthold, V. V. (1963). 'Mesto prikaspijskikh oblastei v istorii musul'manskogo mira' (The position of the Caspian Area in the history of the Muslim world) Raboty po istorii Kavkaza i Vostochnoi Evropy, Lekciya IX', *Sochineniya*, t. 2, razdel 2, Moscow, Nauka.

Basilov, V. N. (1970). *Kul't svyatykh v islame (Cult of the Saints in Islam)*. Moscow, Izdatel'stvo 'Mysl'.

———(1975). 'Traditsii zhenskogo shamanstva u kazakhov' (*Traditions of Female Shamanism among the Kazakhs*). *Polevye Issledovaniya Instituta Etnografii 1974*. Moscow, Nauka, pp. 115–23.

———(1986). 'Perezhitki shamanstva u Turkmen-gëklenov' (Vestiges of shamanism among the Turkmen-Gökleng). In V. N. Basilov (ed.). *Drevnie obryady verovaniya i kul'ty narodov srednei Azii*. Moscow, Nauka, pp. 94–110.

———(1990). 'Dva varianta sredneaziatskogo shamanstva' (Two variants of Central Asian shamanism). *Sovetskaya Etnografiya* 4 (July–August 1990), 64–76.

———(1992). 'Le chamanisme islamisé des peuples d'Asie centrale'. *Diogène* 158, avril–juin 1992, 7–19.

———(1997). 'Chosen by the spirits'. In M. M. Balzer (ed.). *Shamanic Worlds, Rituals and Lore of Siberia and Central Asia*. Armonk, New York, London, North Castle Books, pp. 3–48.

Birge, J. K. (1965). *The Bektashi Order of Dervishes*. London, Luzac and Co.

Böwering, Gerhard (1996). 'From The word of God to the vision of God: Muhammad's heavenly journey in classical Sufi Qur'an commentary'. In Mohammad Ali Amir-Moezzi (ed.). *Le Voyage initiatique en terre d'Islam. Ascensions célestes et itinéraires spirituels*. Louvain-Paris, Peeters, pp. 205–21.

Castagné, J. (1910). 'Mogila svjatogo Horhut-Ata' (The tomb of the holy Korkut Ata). *Trudy Orenburgskoi Uchenoi Arkivnoi Komissii, Drevnosti kirgizskoi stepi i Orenburgskago kraya*, v. 22, Orenburg, pp. 216–8.

———(1930). 'Magie et exorcisme chez les Kazak-Kirghizes et autres peuples turks orientaux'. *Revue des Etudes islamiques*, 4: 1, 52–156.

Chekaninskij, I. A. (1929). "'Baksylyk' sledy drevnikh verovanii Kazakov' (Baksylyk, vestiges of ancient beliefs among the Kazakh). In *Otdel'nnyi ottisk 1-go toma Zapisok Otdela Obshchestva*. Semipalatinsk, Semipalatinskii Otdel Obshchesva Izucheniya Kazakstana, pp. 75–87.

Cirtautas, I. (1970). 'On pre-Islamic rites among Uzbeks'. In *Traditions religieuses et parareligieuses des peuples altaïques*. Paris, PUF, pp. 41–7.

Divaev, A. A. (1899). 'Baksy v zhizni kirgiza' (The *bakshi* in the life of the Kirghiz). *Izv. o-va Arh., Ist. i Etn. pri Imp. Kazanskom Univ.*, 15: 3, 187–90.

———(1899). 'Baksy, kak lekar' i koldun' (The *bakshi* as a healer and a witch doctor). *Iz oblasti kirgizskikh verovanii*, Kazan, pp. 1–38.

During, Jean and Khudoberdiev, Sultonali, (2007). *La Voix du chamane. Etude sur les baxshi tadjiks et ouzbeks*. Paris, L'Harmattan - IFEAC.

Eliade, M. (1968). *Le Chamanisme et les techniques archaïques de l'extase*. Paris, Payot.

Garrone, Patrick (2000). *Chamanisme et Islam en Asie centrale. La Baksylyk hier et aujourd'hui*. Paris, Jean Maisonneuve.

Hamayon, R. (1990). *La Chasse à l'âme: esquisse d'une théorie du chamanisme sibérien*. Nanterre [Paris], Société d'ethnologie.

Hujiexi, Gulibahaer [Ghojesh, Gulbahar] (2009). 'Keerkeze zu samande zhouyu he shenge' (Songs and incantations of the Kirghiz shamans). In Jinxiang Seyin (ed.). *Saman xinyang yu minzi wenhua* (Shamanic Beliefs and Nationalities Cultures), Beijing, Zhungguo shehui kexue chubanshe, pp. 383–413.

Köprülüzade, M. F. (1929). 'Influence du chamanisme turco-mongol sur les ordres mystiques musulmans'. *Mémoires de l'Institut de Turcologie de l'Université de Stamboul*. Istanbul, Nouvelle série, 1.

Levshin, A. (1832). 'Opisanie Kirgiz-Kazach'ikh', ili kirgiz-kajsakskikh ord i stepei' (Description of the Kirghiz-Kazakhs or of the Kirghiz-Kazakh Horde and Steppe). *Etnograficheskiya izvesttiya*. X, 52–68.

Malov, S. E. (1918). 'Shamanstvo u Sartov Vostochnogo Turkestana' (Shamanism among the Sarts of Eastern Turkistan). *Ko dnju 80-tiletiya akademika Vasiliya Vasil'evicha Radlova (1837-1917 gg.)* 5, vyp. 1, 1–16.

Sukhareva, O. A. (1975). 'Perezhitki demonologii i shamanstva u ravninnykh tadzhikov' (The survivals of demonology and shamanism among the Tajiks of the plain). *Domusul'manskie verovaniya i obryady v srednei Azii*. Moscow, Nauka, pp. 5–93.

Taizhanov, K., Ismailov, H. (1986). 'Osobennosti doislamskikh verovannii u Uzbekov-Karamurtov' (The special features of pre-Islamic beliefs among the Uzbeks of the Karamurt group). *Drevnie obryady verovaniya i kul'ty narodov srednei Azii*. Moscow, Nauka, pp. 110–38.

Zarcone, Thierry (2000). 'Interpénétration du soufisme et du chamanisme dans l'aire turque: chamanisme soufisé et soufisme chamanisé'. In Denise Aigle, Bénédicte Brac de la Perrière, Jean-Paul Chaumeil (eds). *La Politique des esprits. Chamanismes et Religions universalistes*. Nanterre [Paris], Société d'ethnologie, pp. 383–93.

Chapter Three

RELIGIOUS TRADITIONS AMONG THE KAZAKHS AND THE KIRGHIZS

David Somfai Kara

I have been collecting data on religious traditions among the Kazakh and Kirghiz in Central Asia (Kazakhstan, Kirghizistan), China and Mongolia since 1994. Some of these traditions survived Communist rule, while others were revived after the Communist ideology disappeared from the region. I consider these traditions to be religious folklore – an integral part of folklore as a whole – that changes constantly. Elements within these religious traditions may disappear or evolve into something new, while new elements from different cultures and religions may be absorbed and incorporated. All the concepts and ideas in this chapter are based on my 15 years of fieldwork[1] among the Kazakh and Kirghiz. It is my intention that the data I have collected reflect a living tradition. I would like to avoid any kind of synthesis based on ethnographic data collected by others in the past.

The people in Central Asia have experienced a long process of Islamisation since the tenth century. Some pre-Islamic traditions have survived Islamisation (e.g. the respect for the Umay-ene fertility spirit among Kirghiz), but they have been absorbed by local Muslim traditions that have elements from Iranian, Arabic and other cultures. The vocabulary of these religious traditions also reflects strong Islamic and Central Asian influence, with 80 per cent of these terms having Arabic or Persian origin.

Muslim saints

The most important tradition is the veneration of saints (*awliya*)[2] and their spirits (*arwah*).[3] According to common beliefs, all human souls can turn into *arwah*, but usually only the spirits of special human beings (religious leaders, martyrs, legendary forefathers and heroes) can be seen by the chosen ones. There are other types of saints too. The *ghaib* is a magical figure[4] who can disappear or turn into an animal (e.g. Kirghiz Bugu-ene).[5] The strong spirit of Khidhr comes from Muslim mythology[6] and can appear as an old man to people with special abilities, sometimes initiating them or bringing them messages from the spirit world. The *chiltan* are 40 spirits who usually appear together and help people.[7]

Souls and spirits

In Islam every human being has one soul, which in Central Asia takes the Persian word *jan*. The Arabic word *ruh* is also used in certain cases, usually in the abstract sense. The word *arwah* is the Arabic plural of *ruh* and usually refers to respected, venerated spirits of special people. In this sense, the souls of certain deceased people turn into spirits to mediate between humans and God. This is completely different to the concepts of the Siberian Turks, who think that soul and breath are identical (*tïn*). Soul is a source of life and it ceases to exist after death. There is another special 'soul' (spiritual substance/force) inside humans, animals and sometimes non-living things (Turkic *kut* or Mongolian *sür/sünesün*)[8] that can leave them, travel and return. It does not cease to exist after death.[9]

Are there shamans among Muslims?

The religious specialists who mediate between the people and the spirits are usually called *bakshï* in Kirghiz and *baksï* in Kazakh.[10] One of the main problems in describing these religious traditions has to do with terminology. Soviet ethnologists commonly called these religious specialists 'shaman' and their activity 'shamanhood' or 'shamanism'.[11] However, the local people conducting or participating in rituals consider this to be a pure Muslim tradition (*musulmanchïlïk*). Soviet ethnologists argued that these traditions were the remnants of a pre-Islamic religion, which they defined as 'shamanism' or sometimes 'tengrism'[12] that was Islamised after the conversion of Turks in Central and Inner Asia. They speculated that Central Asian Turks, especially the nomads, were not 'real' Muslims and had only nominally accepted Islam, continuing to practise their old faith disguised by some Muslim traditions. After many years of research I have realised that this is not the right approach. It is not the ethnologists' task to judge whether people of an ethnic group are 'real' Muslims if they proclaim themselves Muslims. The term 'popular Islam' is also dubious, as it is very difficult to define what is official and non-official, or popular, in a religion.

Definition of shaman

But do some of these religious specialists qualify as shamans? It depends on the definition of the term 'shaman', which is also debated among ethnologists. Some Western scholars began to use the term 'healer' to avoid it, but that too is misleading.[13] Shamans can perform healing rituals, but their activities in society exceed the limits of healing, and some healers would not qualify as shamans at all. In my opinion, a shaman is a religious specialist who mediates between spirits and the community. Shamans receive their special ability through the help of the spirits who initiate them through dreams, visions (*ayan*) and sometimes illnesses (e.g. *talma* 'epilepsy').[14]

To limit the definition of shaman to a religious specialist who experiences 'spiritual journeys' during a state of trance is not a good approach either.[15] Shamans in Siberia can experience a spiritual journey or a possession trance, but the two types of trance can intermingle. Some religious specialists can communicate with spirits through trance, while others do not need to be in such a state to communicate with spirits. So in this sense, trance and religious experience in trance are irrelevant in defining shamans, although clearly they are important elements of some religious traditions. Shamans can go through all kinds of experiences depending on the beliefs and demands of the local community. Through these experiences they legitimise their position in the religious life of the society and are accepted as mediators between the community and the spirits. In my opinion, shamans and shamanic traditions can exist inside any given religion or religious tradition, regardless of whether its context is within what might theoretically be defined as a religion (e.g. Islam, Buddhism) or a folk belief (e.g. traditions of Siberian folk belief). Shamanic traditions are an integral part of the religious folklore of many ethnic groups in Central and Inner Asia and are based on the local religious ideas and folk beliefs.

Besides *bakshï* specialists, we find other demon-chasers (*dewana, kuugunchu/kuuchu*),[16] healers (*tabib, emchi-domchu*) and fortune-tellers (Persian, *falgir*; Kazakh, *balger*)[17] in Central Asia. These different religious specialists have their own functions, but they all proclaim divine qualities, usually received through spirits. Female *bakshï* specialists are called *bübü* in Kirghiz (from Persian *bibi*),[18] while Kazakh female healers prefer the term *balger*. There is also great rivalry between the different specialists, with claims that others are evil (*kara*, 'black') and deal with black magic and witchcraft. Most of the specialists talk about their religious activity as the 'white way' (*aktïk*).[19] That is why some of them wear white clothes during rituals. Some of these specialists do qualify as shamans, and specifically as Muslim shamans. The shamans I met did experience trance or ecstasy, but this was neither possession trance nor shamanic journey. They usually felt the presence of the invoked spirits and sometimes could see them.

Ethnic or indigenous traditions

Religious traditions and folk beliefs have no ethnic boundaries, just as with other types of folklore. We cannot actually talk about Kazakh or Kirghiz shamanic traditions, because they are a real cultural phenomena. Nor is there a nomadic and sedentary division. Traditionally nomadic ethnic groups (Kazakh and Kirghiz) share most of their rituals and beliefs with sedentary groups (Uzbek, Uyghur and Persian-speaking Tajik). Some of the rituals labelled pre-Islamic can be found among sedentary people, but nomadic groups do not practise them. Soviet ethnologists believed that nomadic groups accepted Islam much later than sedentary people, and that their Islamisation was not complete. However, these assumptions cannot be justified by data.[20]

Sufism and its legacy

One of the traditions we must mention is Sufism. The *bakshï* specialists usually call their spirit-invoking rituals *zikr* and *jar* (Arabic, *dhikr* and *jahr*),[21] and these are well-known in Sufi tradition. They sometimes invoke the spirits of famous Sufi saints[22] (Arslan-bab, Ahmad Yasawi, etc.)[23] during rituals. Among their helping spirits (*arwah*) we also find martyrs (*shahid*), some Islamisers (e.g. Baba Tükles)[24] and even local epic heroes and legendary forefathers (e.g. Manas),[25] and political and religious leaders (e.g. *pir*, *es-han*).[26] Their real or supposed tombs (*mazar*) are also venerated and are the scenes of rituals and pilgrimage (*ziyarat*).[27] If no tombs are available, local people choose natural features (e.g. springs, lakes, trees or rocks) to be used as *mazar*. Their mentioning of the Sir-Darya River[28] in shamanic songs and *zikr* rituals probably stems from the fact that most of the sacred sites and tombs of saints venerated by the nomads are situated by it. Religious specialists use different means to legitimise their abilities and practices. It includes their connection with the spirits of Sufi and other Muslim saints, their tombs and other sacred sites, as well as legends about them.[29]

Special ability granted by God

The ideology behind local religious traditions is that Allah grants special ability (*khasiyat*) to places and people.[30] This special ability can be mediated by the spirits of Muslim saints. These spirits can be seen only by chosen people ('the open-eyed ones'; Kirghiz, *közü achïk*).[31] The ability to see and to communicate with the spirits is received through a dream or vision (*ayan*). During the dream, the future *bakshï* usually meets the spirits who give him food or drink, and by which he symbolically receives the special knowledge.[32] The initiated person's eyes open up to the spiritual world. Some of the spirits can appear in the form of animals (*bugra*, 'male camel'; *kochkar*, 'ram'; *yïlan*, 'snake').[33] Spirits can mediate good health and fortune (*salamat, baraka*) to people (also expressed by the old Turkic term *kut*), and healing power (*shifa*) from God. On the other hand, people believe that misfortune is caused by evil power (*shaytan*), which can appear in different forms (*jinn, dew-pari, albastï, yel-mawïz*).[34] Misfortune can be provoked by other people through witchcraft (*ters du'a*, 'converse prayer'), cursing (*kargïsh*) and the evil eye (*yaman köz* or *nazar*, 'bad eye or look').[35]

Shamanic rituals

During shamanic rituals (*jar, zikr* or *oyun*)[36] shamans usually sing a spirit-invoking song. They invoke their helping spirits, who can be Muslim saints (*awliya*) or different obedient demons (*dew-pari*)[37] that appear in the form of different animals (e.g. camel, ram, snake etc.). There were *baksï* specialists among the Kazakhs who also used the fiddler-like *kobuz* to achieve the trance state.[38] Nowadays, most shamans only sing or dance. The *dewana* specialists use a special kind of magic stick ('*asa*; Kirghiz, *asa-tayak* or *asa-musa*)[39] with little rattles on it. Other shamans grab a horse-riding whip (*kamchï*), which they use to symbolically chase away evil spirits. The whip can be replaced by other tools (e.g. axe or knife)[40] (Figures 3.1, 3.2). Sometimes spirits are invoked by the burning of special candles (*sham*).[41] Many elements of Muslim shamanic rituals can be found among Sufi practice too. Chanting prayers and texts from the Qur'an is also an important part of the rituals. Among the

Kirghiz and Uyghur, a rope with a white cloth tied between the ceiling and the floor called *tug/tuu* ('flag') is used during rituals[42] (Figure 3.3). Another common idea is that demons causing illnesses can be transferred to different objects (*köchür-*)[43] or can be chased away by blowing air (*dam sal-*), spitting water (*uchukta-*) and by smudging (*alasta-*). Performing animal sacrifice to God and the spirits (*qurban*) is also part of most of their rituals.

Remnants of pre-Islamic beliefs

Although we know little about the pre-Islamic beliefs of the nomadic Turks, the Kipchaks in Central Asia, there are some elements of modern folk belief that can be traced in Old Turkic and among the Turks of Siberia. One of them is the veneration of Umay-ene, a fertility spirit among the Kirghiz.[44] Umay-ene helps women to become pregnant and to deliver a healthy child. But shamans also invoke her during rituals for assistance. Another remnant is the notion of *kut*, which people do not identify as 'soul' anymore, though it is still something that can leave the human body causing illness or misfortune.[45] Sometimes *kut* is replaced by the word *ürey/üröy* which is related to the Arabic word *ruh*, 'soul'. There are various explanations when the *kut* leaves the body, and special rituals are performed to return it to a person or a house.[46]

Connections between religious specialists and epic storytellers

While the term *bakshï* is used in the eastern and northern parts of Turkestan (Kazakh, Kirghiz, Uyghur and Eastern Uzbek) for a religious specialist (shaman), the same word is used in the western and southern parts of Turkestan for an epic storyteller or bard (Turkmen, Karakalpak, Western Uzbek). In that region shamans are called *porkhan*.[47]

After interviews with many Kirghiz epic storytellers (*manaschi*), I have realised that their initiation into the spiritual world and their practice of performing epic stories are very similar to those of the *bakshï* specialists. These peculiarities are also based on the same religious ideas and beliefs. Epic storytellers experience trance (*talma*) during initiation and performing, they have initiation dreams ('*ayan*) and connections with different helping spirits.[48] So, in that sense epic storytellers are also a sort of shaman as spirit mediators. They usually do not heal, but have special abilities and can sometimes foresee the future.

Religious Traditions among the Kazakhs and the Kïrghïzs

Figure 3.1. Batïrkan a Kazakh *baksï* with his magic axe during trance, Bayan-Ölgii Province, Mongolia, 1994 (Photograph: László Kunkovács).

Fundamentalist attack against local traditions

In recent years fundamentalist Muslims have begun to put forward the idea that all these traditions should be excluded from religious practices, because they are not part of 'real' Islam. They cite work from Soviet scholars that argues for the pre-Islamic origin of these traditions. In reality most of the religious traditions now labelled pre-Islamic or shamanic can be traced in Muslim sources, throughout the centuries, as Muslim traditions. People who practise or participate in these religious traditions are usually devoted

Figure 3.2. Kirghiz *bakshï* and *bübü* specialists during a midnight *jar* ritual, Talas Province, Kirghizistan, 1995 (Photograph: László Kunkovács).

Muslims. Most of them are religious people who pray five times a day (*beshwaqt namaz*) and some of them go on the Mecca pilgrimage (*hajj*). They regard saints merely as mediators between Allah and human beings. They do not worship them or their sacred sites. They worship Allah, who transfers his power (*qudrat*) through those spirits and sacred sites. The acceptance of these rituals also varies between different age groups, between male and female members of the society, and between urban and rural areas. Women tend to be more accepting of these traditions and they attend rituals more often. Sometimes couples do not agree on the effectiveness or legitimacy of the rituals, but that does not cause conflict in their families or personal relationships. Male members of the society prefer official Islamic religious practices, and most of the Muslim clerics (*molla* and *imam*) reject rituals performed by *bakshï* and other religious specialists outside the so-called 'official' Islam.

Post-Soviet changes in religious traditions

After the collapse of the Soviet regime, and even during the era of 'Perestroika', many of the forbidden traditions were revived. People who used to practise them secretly started to hold public rituals. But significant changes also occurred. Most of the people from younger generations turned away

Figure 3.3. Abdïkadïr Kirghiz *bakshï* during the ritual (*oyun*) performs a *talma biy* (shamanic dance) and climbs up the magic flag (*tuu*) Kizil-Su Kirghiz Autonomous Prefecture, Xinjiang, China (Photograph: Dávid Somfai Kara).

from religious traditions during Soviet times. Nowadays, partly due to the lack of a good healthcare system, many of them turn back to esoteric healers (Russian, *ekstrasens*) who usually live in cities and claim to be 'traditional', but who have little in common with pre-Soviet religious traditions and healing methods. They use a lot of elements from other medical traditions, but try to legitimise their activity through the legacy of Central Asian religious practices. They also claim that they were chosen by the spirits, and that Allah granted them special abilities to see the future or to heal people. We should make a clear distinction between the post-Soviet and the pre-Soviet traditional practices.[49]

Bibliography

Aytpaeva, Gülnara (ed.) (2007). *Mazar Worship in Kyrgyzstan: Rituals and Practitioners in Talas.* Bishkek, Aigine Cultural Research Center.

Basilov, Vladimir (1992). *Shamanstvo u narodov Srednei Azii i Kazakhstana* (Shamanism among the people of Central Asia and Kazakhstan). Moskva, Nauka.

Bayalieva, Toktobübü (1972). *Doislamskiie verovaniia i ikh perezhitki u kirgizov* (Pre-Islamic Beliefs and its Remnants among the Kirghizs). Bishkek (Frunze), Ilim.

Bellér-Hann, Ildikó (2004). 'Uyghur Healers (China)'. In Marico N. Walter and Eva Jane Neumann Fridman (eds). *Shamanism: An Encyclopedia of World Beliefs, Practices, and Culture.* Santa Barbara, California, ABC Clio, pp. 642–6.

DeWeese, Devin (1994). *Islamization and Native Religion in the Golden Horde (Baba Tükles and the Conversion to Islam in Historical and Epic Tradition).* Pennsylvania State University Press, University Park.

De Heusch, Luc (1971), 'Possession et chamanisme'. In De Heusch, Luc. *Pourquoi l'épouser?* Paris, Gallimard, pp. 226–44.

Divaev, Abubakr (1899). 'Baksï kak lekar' i koldun' (The *baksi* as a healer and a witch doctor). In *Izvestiia Obshchestva arkheologii, istorii i etnografii pri imperatorskom Kazanskom universitete,* XV/3, 307–41.

Grzywacz, Zuzanna (2010). *Traditional Kazakh Medicine in Change.* Poznań (Poland), Wydawnictwo Naukowe Uniwersytetu im. Adama Mickiewicza.

Hamayon, Roberte (1993). 'Are 'Trance' and 'Ecstasy' and Similar Concepts Appropriate in the Study of Shamanism'. *Shaman,* 1, 3–25.

Johansen, Ulla (2003). 'Shamanistic Philosophy: Soul – A Changing concept in Tuva'. *Shaman* 11/1–2, 29–49.

Kehl-Bodrogi, Krisztina (2006). 'The Reassertion of Religious Healing in Post-Soviet Uzbekistan'. *Asian Anthropology,* Hong Kong, Chinese University Press, vol. 5, pp. 111–29.

Kenin-Lopsan, Mongush (1997). *Shamanic Songs and Myths of Tuva,* ISTOR book 7. Budapest, Akadémia Kiadó.

Malov, Sergei (1918). 'Shamanstvo u Sartov Vostochnogo Turkestana' (Shamanism among the Sarts of Oriental Turkestan). *Sbornik Muzeia Antropologii i Etnografii,* V/1. St. Peterburg, pp. 1–16.

Mélikoff, Irène (1987). 'Ahmad Yesevi and Turkic popular Islam'. In *Utrecht Papers on Central Asia.* Utrecht, Utrecht Turkological Series No. 2, pp. 83–94.

Potapov, Leonid (1991). *Altaiskii shamanizm.* S. Peterburg (Leningard), Nauka.

Somfai Kara, Dávid (2003). 'Living Epic Traditions among Inner Asian Nomads'. In Mihály Hoppál and Gábor Kósa (eds). *Rediscovery of Shamanic Heritage*. Budapest: Akadémiai Kiadó, 179–94.

———(2004a). 'On a Rare Kyrgyz Ritual' (Field Report, photo László Kunkovács). *Shaman*, 12, 161–66.

———(2004b). 'Kirghiz Shamanism'. In Mariko Namba Walter, Eva Jane Neumann Fridman (eds). *Shamanism, an Encyclopedia of World Beliefs, Practices and Culture*. Santa Barbara, California, ABC Clio, Vol. II, pp. 579–82.

———(2005). 'The Last Kazakh *Baksï* to Play the *Kobïz*' (Field Report, photo József Torma). *Shaman*, 13, 181–87.

———(2006). 'Batïrkan, a Kazakh Shaman from the Altay Mountains (Mongolia)' (Field Report, photo László Kunkovács, musical analysis János Sipos). *Shaman*, 14, 117–38.

———(2007). 'The Sacred Valley of Jay Ata and a Kirghiz Shaman from Xinjiang, China' (contributor Mihály Hoppál, musical analysis by János Sipos). *Shaman*, 15, 47–68.

———(2008a). 'An Uighur *Baxshi* from the Ile Valley, Kazakhstan' (Field Report, photo: László Kunkovács). *Shaman*, 16, 143–54.

———(2008b). 'Rediscovered Buriat Shamanic Texts in Vilmos Diószegi's Manuscript Legacy'. *Shaman*, 16, 89–106.

———(2008c). 'Mazars and Shamans: an Animist Concept of Worshipping Nature in the Popular Islam among the Kyrgyz'. In Mihály Hoppál and Zsuzsa Simonkay (eds). *Shamans Unbound*. Budapest, Akadémiai Kiadó, pp. 185–92.

———(2009). '*Ominaan*, a Revitalized Daur Shamanic Ritual from Hailar' (contributor Mihály Hoppál, musical analysis by János Sipos). *Shaman*, 17, 141–69.

———(2010a). 'Some Fieldwork Notes on Bashkir Folk Medicine' (Field Report, photo: László Kunkovács). *Shaman*, 18, 187–96.

———(2010b). 'Baba Tükli and the Swan Girl: Legitimising Elements in the Turkic Epic Edige'. *Acta Orientalia ASH* 63, 117–32 and in *Shaman*, 15, 47–68.

Chapter Four

MUSLIM SHAMANS IN KAZAKHSTAN

Anne-Marie Vuillemenot

This chapter analyses some examples of *bakhsi* (shaman-Sufi) practices that are linked to new forms of popular Islam in contemporary Kazakhstan. After the independence of Kazakhstan, *bakhsis* reappeared spontaneously, along with their typical practices linked to Sufism and shamanism. Although shamanism in Kazakhstan is often reduced to narrowly-defined 'cures', a careful analysis shows that it encompasses all sorts of evils, misfortunes and illnesses. In practice, people tend to consult *bakhsis* with regard to all their everyday-life problems. Since the 1990s, the term *bakhsi* has been used to refer to all different kinds of healers, soothsayers or Zoroastrian faith healers. It also includes some mullahs who demonstrate the power of healing and whose practices are tinged with local and global influences. It refers to old traditional forms of shamanism and Sufism as well as to new social constructions commonly called 'neo-shamanism' and 'neo-Sufism' which borrow from alternative Western cure methods. Thus defined, *bakhsis* seem to be more and more numerous in Kazakhstan, yet vary widely in terms of power and strength.

Here I offer two examples of post-Soviet Kazakh *bakhsis* (Kuat and Khaiat). This chapter describes their personal practices and shows how the position of *bakhsi* or of neo-*bakhsi* is changing and expanding in contemporary Kazakh society. Kuat (Power) was born in Taldykorgan; today he works in a traditional medical home in Pavlodar, but as the oldest *bakhsi*, he goes from one place to another to heal people who ask for him. At Karnak, near the town of Turkistan, lives Khaiat; this young *bakhsi* girl presents a very interesting combination of components of pre-Islamic religions, Central Asian Sufism and contemporary Kazakh Islam.

The new figure of the *bakhsi* takes part in the revival of identities and the intermingling of tradition and modernity. Hence, the *bakhsis* play a role in the socio-cultural transformations of contemporary Kazakh society.

Bakhsis *and neo*-bakhsis

The Kazakh *bakhsi* is traditionally seen as a Sufi shaman. Since Kazakhstan became independent in the 1990s, the term has been extended to cover different categories of persons: shaman, Sufi shaman, diviner, healer, seer, *kobiz* player (this two-stringed viola-like instrument is traditionally associated with Kazakh shamans), Zoroastrian healer. The term is also applied to mullahs who are thought to have the power to heal sickness, and whose otherwise Islamic religious practices have been influenced by local customs. Neo-shamanism and neo-Sufism are becoming important parts of daily life through a sort of post-Soviet 'new wave' of *bakhsi* activity. The specific practices associated with this changing environment are present in rural and urban areas. They are in fact flourishing throughout the country, and more and more people from all strata of society consult *bakhsis* in order to find solutions for the many personal crises caused by the political and economic upheavals the country has experienced.

New systems of representation and belief have sprung up everywhere in the former Soviet Union, from charismatic movements such as Pentecostalism to alternative movements making mystical and therapeutic claims, descendants of neo-Sufism, the post-Soviet 'new age' and even the 'new age' movement in the West that rose during the 1970s...and there are still others. Our question in this case is the following: If the therapeutic orientation has become more and more important in the practice of the *bakhsis*, how has this affected their traditional social position and other practices?

What is happening in contemporary Kazakhstan appears to me to have to do with a very wide range of strategies and practices, many intended to alleviate the difficulties involved in the country's passage from a command economy to 'cowboy capitalism'. In a search for solutions, the Kazakhstani population[1] is turning towards belief systems that look back to the heroic figures of ancient empires of Central Asia. The economy poses a problem, but nationalism is also in play. Within this framework, the figure of the *bakhsi* begins to appear as a dependable point of reference, in the context of a future fraught with uncertainty. The practice of going to see a *bakhsi* is engaged in by people of all ethnicities, from every social class, seeking help of an unspecified kind. As a result, the number of *bakhsis* is growing.

The entire range of contemporary practices of this nature is determined in two main ways: on the one hand by traditions, and on the other, by Islam.

Muslim Shamans in Kazakhstan 61

What traditions and what kind of Islam are we dealing with? The roots of the main traditions reach back to Siberian shamanism, to the old Zoroastrian religion, and to the influence of Buddhism and Nestorian Christianity. The Muslim population for the most part is influenced by Sufism. There is currently a popular interest in 'holy places' to which one may make a pilgrimage. There also seem to be a large number of individuals claiming to have worked medical miracles, and people claiming to have witnessed them. All my informants affirmed that even during Soviet times they visited *bakhsis*, or someone else in their family did. Of course, not all the *bakhsis* are considered equally powerful in healing.

The question of the influence of Sufism on Central Asian shamanism can be addressed more or less in these terms: how can two fundamentally different systems coexist in a single ritual time and space? I will attempt to cast light on this subject by examining and analysing in terms of space a rite of *zikir* (*dhikr*) I participated in, in 1995 in Kazakhstan.

Certain researchers appear to consider this kind of ritual as something that belongs to ethno-history, that is, the original ritual has disappeared, or else it has undergone such transformations as would make it representative of a sort of deviation from both shamanism and Sufism. On this subject, Bruce C. Privatsky has said:

> Late nineteenth century reports showed that the Kazakh *baqsi* (shaman) was a visible, but more and more marginal figure in Kazakh communities, his rhetoric Islamised, and his role as a healer eclipsed by *täwip*s (*tabib*, doctor) practicing Muslim healing arts. Then came the advent of the Soviet medical system, accompanied by the attack on the old healing arts as superstitious and unscientific. Although the Kazakh shamans have left behind no accounts of their suffering, it is clear that they were thoroughly suppressed during the Soviet period[2] (Privatsky 2001: 2).

The purpose I shall pursue over the course of these few pages is in defence of a concept of permanence through transformation, and a view of practices that reach across the centuries to leave their imprint on the present, a view that gives them great ethnographic value. As Bertrand Hell has emphasised, both shamanism and possession can be characterised by a 'principle of adaptability' (Hell 1999: 9), when the therapeutic and the religious are woven together: 'It is striking to observe that what some researcher considers as a religious ritual ends up being studied by someone else as a medical practice, and vice versa' (Laplantine 1992: 346). The following examples reinforce these observations.[3]

I would like to dwell at some length upon the personalities of two Kazakh *bakhsis* in order to examine not only the current state of individual practice, but even more importantly, to show that the position of the *bakhsi* or neo-*bakhsi* changes and expands; the *bakhsi* of today can essentially be viewed as being in the 'business' of renewing identities.

Kuat[4]

I met Kuat *bakhsi* in 1994 (his name means Power). He invited me to follow him through an initiatory process: seclusion, abstinence, fasting, purification, symbolic death of the participants, followed by a new way of life in which each of the initiated would be other than he or she had been and act in a different way. Name-giving, like many other things, is accomplished according to rules in Kazakhstan. Kuat's grandfather was a powerful *bakhsi* recognised as such by those around him and actually mentioned in certain Kazakh writings of the early twentieth century. His given name, Power, is linked to this family history and to an arrangement by means of which the role of *bakhsi* is transmitted to a member of the family after having skipped one generation. No one can become a *bakhsi*; one is born a *bakhsi*. The ancestors will designate the person who is to become a *bakhsi*, and after this has been accomplished, the initiation of the new *bakhsi* by others *bakhsis* can begin.

The question of power and of the gift of healing, as this understood in Kazakhstan, remains of central importance when we consider a *bakhsi*. He is the one who assumes responsibility for confronting the different kind of spirits that are potentially dangerous for human beings, and he is required, at regular intervals, to demonstrate his capacities to the entire community. Moreover he must respond to challenges from other colleagues[5] that arise from time to time.

The observation that the power of the *bakhsi* is declining these days is true, as brought up in the writings of Bruce C. Privatsky, Maria M. Kosko and many other researchers. But within the communities that recognise Kuat, and in the view of my oldest informants (who were children during the 1930s), there is no doubt that the power of this *bakhsi* is considered to be as great as that of any other in living memory. It appears to me that what is happening here does not have as much to do with the importance of how to classify the powers and accomplishments of traditional *bakhsi*, as with their ranking in terms of legitimacy and recognition within the communities in which the *bakhsis* of today operate. As Vladimir Basilov has observed, this field of operation today has to do essentially with cures (Basilov 2003: 135);

within this framework, ineffectiveness is punished by an unsatisfied patient. This might happen to a bad doctor practicing modern medicine, who then gets labelled a quack.

However, especially in Kuat's case, his field of action and intervention is far more extensive than merely curative in relation to the range of services he is regularly asked to provide across the entire country – including a house being haunted, someone disappearing, malicious magic being practiced – i.e. everything that enters into the complex conception of evil, unhappiness or sickness. He may deal with all these ailments alone, or in a group, as when he requests that a community come together with him for a collective ritual.

The practices examined here are not improvised. The rites involved come directly from the Kazakh Sufi tradition. The help of a *bakhsi* is always sought in cases of disorders that penetrate the social, familial or individual order. These disorders are systematically interpreted within Kazakh society as related to *jinns*.[6]

The Sufi *dhikr* – *zikir* in the Kazakh language – comes to the fore here, the process being both therapeutic and religious. Kuat appears to consider making recourse to this kind of ritual as a 'major operation' associated with other techniques of care and transformations of the evil-unhappiness-sickness complex. The rite examined here is one of many constructed and based on the same model. It highlights certain recurrent themes, but leaves a significant amount of leeway for invention and improvisation in relation to the particular circumstances, in a manner appropriate to the place where the rite is to be performed, all being possibly further determined by the specific situation of the persons for whom the rite is being performed. For example, rites performed for children and for adults are based on a general structure, but are not performed the same way.

Kuat lives today in a city in the northeast of Kazakhstan called Pavlodar. For the first time in his life, he is set up in an official therapy center, but he continues to travel. Over the course of the years he has perfected his practices, techniques of health and care that are not necessarily linked to his initial designation as a *bakhsi*. However, this does not make him a 'neo-*bakhsi*'; he is a *bakhsi* of his own time, affected by a certain kind of globalising modernity in which traditional practices coexist with the widest imaginable range of techniques, some of which passed at one time from east to west, and some of which are being rediscovered in the former Soviet Union today, having gone around the world.

In August 1995, I met Kuat at his family home in Taldykorgan. A group of patients surrounded him as is standard, and had been doing so for several weeks (Vuillemenot 2000: 345–60). I was present at and participated in a *zikir* offered for two children: a young boy who stuttered and a (male) baby that had never spoken.

Figure 4.1. The Kazakh shaman Kuat performing a shamanic ritual (*zikir/dhikr*) at Köktibie (Southeast Kazakhstan), 1994 (Photograph: A.-M. Vuillemenot).

The rite took place in an open courtyard attached to an isolated house at the edge of the steppe. The participants formed a circle, and Kuat took up a position to the southwest. Behind him on a table, books lay open – the Qur'an and books that had been given to him by those who initiated him into shamanism and Sufism. There were also ritual objects that he had obtained over the course of his many experiences: cloths, weaving, a bag containing the 41 divinatory beans of the *kymalak*,[7] his musical instruments (a *dombra*, a Sufi combination of large and small drum), and finally the umbilical cord from a sheep that had just given birth.

The *bakhsi* began the ritual by beating with one hand on his large drum (Figures 4.1, 4.2). The participants had earlier arranged themselves in a circle, each occupying their own space. The circle encompassed children who were too young to dance or who had fallen asleep during the rite. The circular ritual space had to remain closed for the entire duration of the performance of the rite. Everyone at some point began to dance and repeat the sacred formula of the *zikir*: *lâ ilaha illa Allâh*, while remaining in the same place.

Kuat stepped into the centre of the circle and executed a series of movements that seemed to resemble more closely a series of gestures than a dance; at night certain animals were asked to help, not just invoked or evoked; these were the eagle and the camel.

Muslim Shamans in Kazakhstan 65

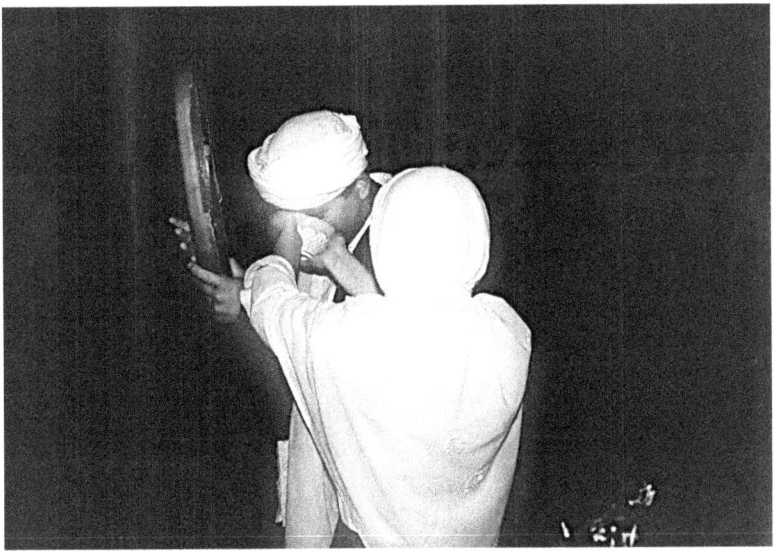

Figure 4.2. The Kazakh shaman Kuat performing a shamanic ritual (*zikir/dhikr*) at Köktibie (Southeast Kazakhstan), 1994 (Photograph: A.-M. Vuillemenot).

The *bakhsi* can also invoke his own *jinns*, that is, spirit figures that are always with him, sustaining him and giving him power. But this is not the case with the animal figures, which are supposed to present themselves to him according to the necessity of the moment. Kuat explains that they come to help him in the process of curing; they become active within him and are not subject to his will. It is they who dance, using his body as a vehicle. And where is he at that moment? His answer is complicated. He points out that he is both 'present' while at the same time travelling in the sphere of the beyond, attempting to find the guilty party. One possible way of understanding this simultaneous location might be linked to the belief held in Turco-Mongol culture that a dead person is in more than one place at the same time (Kaskabasov 1984: 71; Roux 1984: 255). There is no contradiction involved according to the life-principles[8] of the *bakhsi*, the privileged mediator between two worlds being found at one and the same time in different spaces.

There is another aspect of this that is even more disturbing: Kuat says that in situations like this he is taking a double voyage, one of a shamanic type and one of a Sufi type, the sort in which one seeks to rejoin the divine light in order to seek healing. These two voyages are superimposed one on top of the other, and it is precisely because they are thought of as belonging to a single space-time that they can coexist.

In the middle of the ritual circle, a fire had been lit, kindled in a circular pit; on the north side of the fire there was a black hen. Kuat grabbed the hen and stuck a long skewer through her throat. At first the hen seemed asleep. Before she died at the end of the *zikir* she revealed a number of predictions that Kuat announced at the end of the rite.

Kuat danced, first on one foot and then on the other, to the rhythm of spoken formulas pronounced by those in attendance, while turning in a taut circle from west to east, within the circle of the participants, keeping the hen held in his hands in front of him. Then he came closer to the stuttering child seated on the northwest side of the fire, within yet another circle lying between the circle traced by the feet of the *bakhsi* and the outer circle, a circle that was obviously reserved for the entrances and exits of the two patients for whom the rite was being conducted.

The baby was being held in his father's arms to the northeast of the fire, across from the young boy. Kuat puffed and spat, no longer singing. He turned three times from west to east, around the stuttering boy, holding out the hen. Finally he wrapped the child in a white sheet and completely covered him, including his head. This sheet would be divided between all participants at the end of the *zikir*. The child was in this way kept covered during the entire rite, the purpose being to keep him safe from attacks by other spirit-apparitions who might be in the area for nefarious purposes.

The case of the baby who had never spoken was more complicated. The *jinns* affecting the baby might be chased away, but it would be possible for them to attack the other child involved. Clearly there were precautions to be taken.

Putting the boy to the northwest symbolised that he too found himself between two worlds. The fact that he could not speak with fluency indicated that he still belonged partially to the worlds of the West and of the North. The West is the direction of the dead, the ancestors, and also of the life of the pre-human being. The North is the direction of the elders and the recently deceased.[9]

Kuat then walked over to the fire and plunged his hands into it, and then stomped on it, catching a few clinkers and putting them in his mouth. Then he began to turn the small patient around in order to stop his suffering and unhappiness, while chasing the *jinns* away from him with fire – fire that burnt in a circular hearth, similar to the one found inside yurts.[10]

Two practices are linked together here. One is related to an elaborate multifaceted pattern of significations: 'turning around', *ajnaly*, in a Kazakh context signifies the initial and most basic form of care and protection that *bakhsis* can administer, but which can be accomplished by any person who wishes to intervene in order to support or to help a person in difficulty.

This type of practice is common and is witnessed in cases when mothers and sick children interact. The other type is represented by spectacular demonstrations provided by some Sufis and dervishes who are obliged to give evidence of their 'supernatural' powers. In the example given here, a strong odour of burning flesh was perceptible during the rite, but Kuat had no visible burns at the end. I should mention that Kuat at no time during the ceremony swallowed any food or drink that might give credence to the hypothesis of psychotropic substances. I have not been able to determine the cause of these phenomena.

Then Kuat began to involve the participants in the ritual circle, according to a technique that he uses repeatedly and systematically during the *zikir* rite: he comes up in front of a person, takes hold of this person's head with both hands and bends it back with some force, a piercing cry sometimes accompanying this gesture. In the ritual discussed Kuat turned again to the fire, and put his hands and feet into it. Other participants continued to repeat the same formula mentioned earlier, in the manner of a psalm, while dancing in one spot, following the rhythm chanted. The stuttering child remained covered by the white sheet.

Upon a sign from Kuat, all fell silent and the participants sat down. As the shaman directed his attention to the baby, a young man passed him the fresh sheep's umbilical cord. Kuat placed the cord around most of the baby's neck, and held the suspended baby. He carried the baby towards the fire and laid it in the lap of its father. Then the baby was passed three times between the legs of Kuat, and from grandmother to father, always from west to east, in accordance to where they sat. The baby still had the umbilical cord around its neck. Kuat then took the cord and placed it around his own neck, and gave the baby to its father. Subsequently the cord would be boiled in the *kazan*,[11] cooked by the grandmother, and given to everyone in the family the following day.

This re-enacted birth experience had the purpose of enabling the mute child to enter the human world, freed of the handicap that marked it whilst at the intersection of two worlds, when it was an incomplete human. In Kazakhstan, when children are born, they are not considered 'new-born': they have passed through other lives beforehand. The previous life should come to an end in the direction of the west, the direction of ancestors and the ancient ones. Upon a person's earthly death vital principles (soul, breath, luck, destiny) return to the place from where they originally came, moving via the west, after having crossed by way of the north. Interestingly, the word for death in the Kazakh language is *katis boly*, *katy*, to go back, to return.

It seems that at the beginning of the ritual, the baby simply did not exist. The infant was held by his father, who occupied the position as master of a house within the innermost circle of a yurt while guests were present at the northwest place, i.e. the positions of the participants in the ritual were like those inside a yurt. Kuat's actions during the ritual process of symbolically 'bringing a child into this world', allow us to interpret why the baby was held in its father's arms all this time. The re-birthing is carried out by the father's mother, the paternal grandmother, who in Kazakh kinship terms can function as the mother because the baby is the first born of her eldest son, and lives with her as a younger son. He would learn to call his grandparents father and mother, and his father and mother brother and sister.

Since the paternal grandfather in this case was dead, the biological father was able to step into the role of father.

This entire sequence is remarkable for more than one reason. First it has great symbolic coherence; since the ritual concerns a birth, it is performed 'from west to east' following the path outlined by the life-giving principles, and indeed by the soul itself as it seeks reincarnation. On another hand, in the mythic universe the organisation of worlds are superimposed on each other (high, middle, and low). The inhabitants of each of these worlds wear their sashes or belts in different ways in order to show which level they belong to. The baby who is still in the liminal state between two worlds thus wears the umbilical cord of a sheep until it is reborn. In the Kazakh language the umbilical cord is designated by a single word, *kendek*, which also designates the centre of a yurt and the position of a fire pit in the centre. The same fire that burns in that circular area is symbolically present during the ritual in the centre of the circle of participants, bringing to mind the notion of a cord, and also representing the space inside the typical yurt. At the end of the rite Kuat scattered the coals of the fire. While spitting and blowing he counted the people lying down – an act intended to awaken them fully again. If a participant did not stir even after that, the *bakhsi* called his or her name while turning from west to east around them (Plate 1).

At the end of the ritual, he called out the name of Allah and everything came to a halt.

Kuat then reseated himself to the southwest, covered himself, and began to tremble. After a period of complete silence he began to speak, giving some advice to each patient, and revealing parts of the words supposedly conveyed by the chicken; these had indicated that the baby, then two years old, would begin to speak at the age of five, would be in perfect health at seven, and by fifteen would emerge as a powerful *bakhsi*.

As regards the actual baby, who was finally removed from the white cloth around him: the question was asked whether he had been frightened by an alcoholic. If so, such a situation must never happen again; it would be otherwise impossible to cure him. The predictions continued including a few general remarks about the future of the country, the economy, the Chinese menace, the danger of nuclear radiation, etc. The focus of the predictions were that hard times would come, but that Kazakhstan would stay out of war, unlike other countries in Central Asia.[12]

One more interesting observation is worth noting: speech was almost absent from a rite that was conducted on behalf of the two children, one who stammered and the other mute. Moreover there was no singing to Allah, no improvisation on recurrent themes, only the breathing of Kuat could be heard. The only words communicated were in effect those spoken by the chicken, who predicted the future of the mute child (to become a shaman); he would indeed speak, and speak fluently – this speech would enable a dialogue with spirit figures of the beyond and the divinities.

With regard to his helper spirits, Kuat did not mention them at all, but chose to finish this 'silent' *zikir* by invoking the name of Allah. Was this because children were involved? When the *zikir* is performed for adults, it usually ends with the previously mentioned formula, '...and now leave me alone with my *jinns*'.

Jean During (1988: 22) has examined the exclamatory use of the name, 'Allah!' as one of the effects that Sufi music seeks to produce, using the power of sound and sonorous vibrations to set off a change in the body. Such special names can also have an inspirational effect, as has been pointed out by Gilbert Rouget (1980: 38); a Sufi is hence in a state between communion and possession in his exchanges with Allah during the *dhikr* trance.

The account of the data presented here raises once again the question of the 'legitimacy' of a shaman in a Muslim territory, especially a Sufi territory. Despite an apparent equivocation, this formula exactly reflects the truth of the subject', as Vladimir Basilov wrote.[13]

Khaiat[14]

The rehabilitation of the city of Turkistan has had an effect on the surrounding area and also upon the entire region, where holy places have been multiplying. This is also true for Karnak, a small town located about 40 km from Turkistan. At Karnak, there lives a young female *bakhsi* who presents an interesting example of cross-cultural influence between pre-Islamic religions, Sufi Islam of Central Asia, and modern Islam.

Khaiat was contacted for the first time by spirit apparitions when she was in the first year of graduate school. A man with one Cyclopean eye appeared to her then, and every year since, a new spirit figure has come to teach her a sura of the Qur'an. She said that nowadays the figure comes accompanied by 11 other spirit figures dressed all in white. Besides these figures, there are also sometimes figures dressed in black; she considers these apparitions to be malicious, and she fights them. Her paternal grandfather, who was himself a healer, had in fact spoken to her of a Cyclops figure who had appeared to him. At the death of her grandfather, the Cyclops appeared to her.

At the age of 14, she fell seriously ill, and temporarily became deaf and mute; her organs began to fail one after the other. At that time her father drank alcohol and when an alcoholic came to her house she would get a continuous attack of hiccups.

Her sicknesses at this time disappeared thanks to the intervention of two *bakhsis* from another village, who were accompanied by powerful *jinns*. These *bakhsis* gave her four pieces of white sugar to swallow. On the first day, after swallowing the first piece of sugar, one of her ears opened up. On the second day, having swallowed the second piece of sugar, her other ear opened up, and then her voice came back and finally her various illnesses disappeared. In order to complete the treatment, the *bakhsis* attempted to beat her with a whip in order to make sure that the malevolent *jinns* that had possessed her were gone, but she grabbed the whip and beat the two *bakhsis* instead. Thus it was recognised that the spirits that were accompanying Khaiat were more powerful than those that had accompanied the two *bakhsis*, and the whip became her first instrument. She embarked upon her own work as a *bakhsi* after having received a *bata*, that is, blessing, from yet another *bakhsi* of the region.

Her 11 spirit helpers were all masculine, and although she was not married they let her walk free. She said that she prefers not to get married because whenever she has to battle against powerful evil *jinns*, she becomes sick afterwards and the sickness lasts several days. At any rate, in order for her to consider a man as a potential husband, he must be a non-smoker, a non-drinker and must say his five daily prayers.

She insisted that the social position of the *bakhsi* was not what she would have chosen for herself, but there was nothing she could do about it. She must take on this role, or else fall sick. The first phase of her initiation was completed several years later by a second initiation.

Our initial analysis allows us to observe that the succession of events that have marked the life of this young woman, as someone recognised and followed by spirit figures, is similar to other examples that have been reported from Central Asia, including among others those mentioned in many works of Vladimir Basilov concerning a region somewhat to the south in Uzbekistan (Basilov 1970; 2000; 2001); shared features being designation by apparitions, sickness, acceptance, healing, dual initiation by spirits and by more experienced *bakhsis* as well. Recognition and acceptance on the part of existing shamans completes and reinforces the first designation by spirits. As with Kuat, prohibitions on tobacco and alcohol are included in the shaman's practice and described as specifically Islamic prohibitions. The use of sugar instead of salt is interesting. White foods – salt or flour – are used to attract evil from outside the body so that malicious *jinns* can be captured. This is a widespread practice that is not limited to *bakhsis*. But these foods are usually placed in a container next to the sick person. Sugar is ingested, and works on the evil spirits from the inside, dissolving them.

Ak, white, is the colour of a certain kind of purification, and also the colour of nobility, in accordance with Kazakh society being divided into white bones (nobles) and black bones. 'The white bone is composed of khans and their offspring' (Hudson: 1938: 55). Religious leaders and Muhammedan wise men are also given noble rank. By using foods or other objects of the noble colour, humans deceive *jinns* and offer them targets other than those they have seized.

Of importance here also is the fact that Khaiat could not marry and thus could not become a daughter-in-law. In other writings I have shown that the roles of *bakhsi* and daughter-in-law are complementary and central to the equilibrium of Kazakh society (Vuillemenot 2009); the actors in both roles seem to perpetuate and preserve a dialogue with other worlds, inhabited by a variety of divinities and figures from both the spirit and the human worlds. A single person cannot be a *bakhsi* and a daughter-in-law at the same time. Only young and elderly women can enter the entire complex of rites performed by *bakhsis*.

The narrative of the second initiation of Khaiat takes a very interesting turn whereby Islam is revealed to be the justification of the entire symbolic construction.

Khaiat told this story: she did not go out for 41 days; this included 11 days spent reclining without making the slightest movement. She described her captivity among initiatory spirits, in the major phase of this initiation, after which she was released by the spirits. During this period she appeared to her family to be someone poised between life and death. Later she would say that she had travelled to Mecca, following the lead of the spirits. The proof that she had been there was this: the arches of her feet and her heels were covered with blisters and her legs were swollen. Furthermore, villagers who had actually been on a pilgrimage to the tomb of the Prophet said that they could recognise, in Khaiat's descriptions, things they had seen with their own eyes. After this test was concluded, two *bakhsis* who had accompanied her during her struggle gave her a knife that would become her second instrument, to be used to cleanse houses of malevolent *jinns* and to combat mental illnesses.

Whenever she had to fight one of these powerful *jinns*, she recited one of the suras she had memorised in order to put up a wall of resistance that kept evil from her. She used her whip, her knife and sugar in order to chase away the dangerous *jinns*. She wrote down in a notebook the things that her invisible helpers told her, but she was not supposed to let anyone else read it. Friday was her only day off, a day on which she was free and alone and unencumbered by the constant influence of the invisible helpers. On Friday she dressed as she liked and used makeup.

She only proffered her services to believers of whatever confession and she took steps to protect herself against unbelievers and the *jinns* that go with them. She did not provide every kind of cure that exists in *bakhsi*'s work and when she felt she could not help, her invisible helpers told her to send the suppliant to a doctor or hospital.

The spirit helpers asked her to undergo a third initiation, but she refused for as long as possible for fear of the ever more intense suffering involved. When speaking of these things she used the concept of energy and its transferal to describe in part how the spirit helpers connected with her.

Khaiat received her clients in a small one-room building just outside her family's home. The young woman presented herself and saw herself as the instrument of invisible helpers who diagnosed illnesses, prescribed, counselled and advised solutions.

Now let us explore again the elements of this narrative one by one: first, the number 41. The number 40 evokes a certain number of Qur'anic references and 41 is linked, in Kazakhstan, to the *kymalak*.[15]

The number of elements in each pile and their position are later interpreted by someone who practises divination. The diviner concentrates upon the great recurrent themes of daily life, but sometimes tries to answer a precise question. Khaiat said that she was prohibited by her invisible helpers from telling the future, but her experience was inextricably linked symbolically to the universe of prediction.

In Khaiat's speech, the number 11 does not appear to be linked to any particular reference, except in so far as each family in the Kazakh tradition has a lucky number and a lucky day of the week in terms of potential for happiness and quantity of vital principle, *kyt*.

The mention of suras that are transmitted and learned by the intermediary of invisible helpers underlines the fact that the term derives from Islam, while on the other hand the recitation in which they are embedded, in this case, does not correspond, strictly speaking, to any sura. Actually, a series of onomatopoeic phrases are involved that are repeated out loud by Khaiat – different phrases for different contexts. The literal meaning of these phrases appears to be almost irrelevant, since what counts is that they belong to the body of speech drawn on in order to address to the gods – to Allah in this case. Certainly, we are at this point in an area in which euphemisms are frequently employed, and in which speech conceals within itself the power to alter the entire social organisation, but Khaiat continues to insist that her practices belong to the Islam of the ancients.

It appears to me that there might be an interesting connection between the oral employment of euphemisms and Khaiat's secret writing in the notebook. In the writings of *bakhsis* that I have been able to study, they contain groups of signs that can only be deciphered by the invisible helpers or the *bakhsi*. These might be described as pictorial euphemisms.

Khaiat's use of the term energy is actually a borrowing from contemporary international speech in which the concept of energy is in the process of becoming the zero signifier that Claude Lévi-Strauss described. In this Central Asian context energy comprises situations as diverse as altered states of consciousness, trance, possession or the transfer of vital principles.

Khaiat feels that it is very difficult to describe what is happening inside her. The moments when her invisible helpers interact with her are tinged with fear and wariness. The physical power of speech cannot be discounted in this socio-cultural context. It is even possible that she is protecting herself from presences that inevitably must accompany a foreign woman who has travelled to Kazakhstan, and who employs a transcultural vocabulary with some facility.

Conclusion

From a historical perspective of examining the practices and beliefs in Central Asia, the contemporary ritual universe presents a thorough coherence. The principles according to which spirit helpers designate persons is the same everywhere, and the same is true for the process of initiation, as the necessity of resolving in a communal fashion those disorders introduced through the complex notion of evil/unhappiness/sickness. The persistence of a plurality of symbolic universes that harmoniously coexist must certainly allow some diversity in religious practice, and new tendencies may simply be assimilated.

The intermingling of Sufism and shamanism seems in some cases to go well, and in other cases less so. Yet this phenomenon remains true and is well attested 'and intrinsic' to the range of contemporary practices; further it is one of the most often encountered varieties within the sphere of Central Asian ritual. In the cases of *zikir* that have been described here, the articulation between the spheres of safety and *bakhsi* can be discerned through the use of a spatially oriented vision that emphasises a superimposition of two kinds of practice and belief that are linked together. Nonetheless, a question that arises in the course of this reflection, one which is infinitely more complex, remains still 'untouched': it hinges on a point raised by Jean During in relation to 'the musical East': 'something is happening!'.[16] The reflexive (in French) *se passer* captures the movement by which a certain kind of transmission occurs from one person to another. This operation is not dichotomous: tradition versus modernity. It participates in a complicated system, which is very ancient, where different primordial universes coexist, as well as different representations and ways of being in the world. This is not something that has been constructed recently, but has to do with the construction of a vast complex of transformations that over the centuries have allowed Islam to come to terms with ancient practices without covering them over completely.

Jean During characterises the musical universe of Central Asia in this way : 'the migrant leitmotif, the empty square that must always be "found", but which can never be pointed to, since it is always elsewhere, irremediably empty in its place' (During 1994: 424). This leitmotif is the keystone of an arch that allows one to faithfully reproduce, as well as to inexhaustibly reinvent a great Sufi master, and seems to me to illustrate in a remarkably appropriate manner what 'happens' in the Kazakh *zikir*.

There is indeed a systematic re-appropriation of the *zikir* through the person of the *bakhsi* who in each performance reconstructs a unique and singular rite, in accordance with a situation that is to be brought back into balance at a particular moment, and which is based on a certain number of pieces of evidence: the circular nature of the rite, the presence of participants who make it possible to perform the rite, the invocation of Allah, the summoning of spirit helpers, the ubiquity of the person of the *bakhsi*, the two voyages, the representation and the legitimacy, in effect, of 'something happening'! Something is happening that is not just a matter of transmission, reciprocal influence or 'bricolage', something that brings into play the entire range of relationships constructed between what lies beyond. The transmission and process of learning that are accomplished during the *zikir* in connection with persons who in most cases had never participated in such a rite, belong to the society's concern that a certain equilibrium with regard to the other worlds should be re-established or preserved through the exchange of speech with those worlds. And this means of re-establishment is in effect systematically privileged in Kazakh society, as in daily life in moments that are not 'ordinary',[17] and in times of ritual performance. We are not speaking, of course, of ordinary speech, but of artistic speech: poetry, epic, blessing, prayer, the words of a prayer that are apt to seduce the various entities of the other worlds. In the space-time of the rite, the *bakhsi* is precisely the person that is in charge of this art-speech.

Moreover, the ritual of the *zikir* reveals, in its delimitation of a space and its setting in motion of various functions and actors (whose roles can also be switched), a theatrical dimension. We are thus witnessing the establishment of 'ritual theatre' within which individual trajectories are bound together in a common space all tending towards a single goal: the alleviation of evil fortune.

This quest for ritualised unity has nothing to do with the dimension of fusion that links a creator to his creation; this is a constant in the Kazakh universe before Islamisation and after it. The question of a creator or creators does not arise, or at least it does not arise in terms of omnipotence and omniscience.

These worlds *are*, and it is necessary to preserve their equilibrium at any price. In such a framework, harmonious cohabitation between Sufism and shamanism appears to be indispensable. This alliance is precisely what allows equilibrium to be maintained between universes which, *a priori*, should never meet.

The model of the Kazakh *zikir*, as presented here, points to the singularity of the two voyages, of the shaman and the Sufi, juxtaposed within a single space-time, and juxtaposed as well within a thought system that no longer thinks of one of them without the other, and which constructs the greatest harmony from the greatest contradiction in an effort to please the gods.

As regards Khaiat, every part of her narrative juxtaposes pre-Islamic beliefs and practices (largely shamanic) with Islamic justifications. The progression of stages of her initiations, each more difficult to bear than the last, indeed show that Khaiat is the instrument of the spirit helpers, and that she is at their service, in exchange for which they allow her to heal, to cure, to alleviate suffering and to resolve various problems presented by those who come to consult her. The fact that she speaks about this arrangement in terms of captivity is related to her difficulty in fully accepting even now the enormous responsibility that weighs upon her. In effect, there are few who desire to become a *bakhsi*, a designation which cannot be refused and which proves very constraining. It is not a question of gaining more power, but only of accepting her duty and of accomplishing tasks that are required of her.

Like Kuat, Khaiat inherited her 'gift' from her grandfather. And thus she was brought into contact with the forces of the invisible, and the difficulties of the set evil/unhappiness/sickness. As a young woman, she has access to different techniques that are still available and it does not seem impossible that she will someday practise the *zikir*. And what would happen if she decided to marry? Traditional Kazakh society is articulated around two foundational axes: masculine/feminine, and elder/younger. Kuat already finds himself occupying the category elder/masculine – something that gives him great legitimacy. Khaiat remains within the sphere of those designated younger/feminine, a position that cannot be improved unless she becomes a daughter-in-law. The position of this young woman is thus far from enviable. In accepting the will of fate, that she become a *bakhsi*, she also accepts being cut off from the possibility of the social legitimacy of a married woman – but if she refuses to go along with the designation the spirit helpers have made, she would be putting her life in danger.

In these two examples, we do not see the emergence of instrumental reason, already present in Soviet medicine. There is only the simple observation that the *bakhsis* are participating in current socio-cultural transformations. The latter come in answer to a great diversity of demands and appear as guarantees of the social order. Whatever changes may come, they remain the pivots of a society that for a very long time has developed in terms of the reciprocal influence of beliefs, practices and cultures.

Bibliography

Barba, Eugiénio and Saverese, Nicolas (1985). *Anatomie de l'acteur. Un dictionnaire d'Anthropologie théâtrale.* Cazilhac, Bouffonneries Contrastes.

Basilov, Vladimir (1970). *Kylt sviatikh v Islame* (The Worship of Saints in Islam). Moscow, Akademiia Obchestevennikh nayk, Instityt naytchnove ateizma.

──(2000). 'Malika-Apa. Peripheral forms of shamanism? An example from Middle Asia'. In Denise Aigle, Bénédicte Brac de la Perrière, Jean-Paul Chaumeil (eds). *La Politique des Esprits.* Nanterre [Paris], Société d'ethnologie, pp. 361–9.

──(2001). *Spedneaziatskii etnografitcheskii sbornik vipysk IV* (Central Asian Ethnographic Collection, Vol IV). Moscow, Rossiiskaia akademiia nayk, Instityt etnologii i antropologii NN Miklykho-Maklaia.

──(2003). 'Le Chamanisme islamisé des peuples d'Asie centrale'. In Roberte Hamayon (ed.). *Chamanismes – Diogène.* Paris, Quadrige/PUF, 2003, pp. 127–45.

During, Jean (1988). *Musique et Extase. L'audition mystique dans la tradition soufie.* Paris, Albin Michel.

──(1994). *Quelque chose se passe.* Paris, Verdier.

Hamayon, Roberte (1979). 'Le Pouvoir des hommes passe par le langue des femmes: variations mongoles sur le duo de la légitimité et de l'aptitude'. *L'Homme* XIX: 3–4, 109–139.

Hell, Bertrand (1999). *Possession et Chamanisme, Les maîtres du désordre.* Paris, Flammarion.

Hudson, A.C. (1938). *Kazak Social Structure.* New Haven, Yale University.

Journal d'histoire du soufisme (2004). Special issue on 'La danse soufie', 4. Paris, Librairie d'Amérique et d'Orient – Jean Maisonneuve.

Kasabekov, A. (1994). *Jakin altaev kazak filosofiiasinin tarikina kerespe* (Forewarning of Kazakh Philosophy's History). Almaty, Er-Deylet.

Kaskabasov, Smet (1984). *Kazaktin khalik prozasi* (Kazakh National Prose). Almaty, Kazak SSR-inin Gilim.

Kazakhi, ictoriko-Etnografitcheckoe iccledovanie (The Kazakhs, Historic and Ethnographic Research) (1995). Taizhanova (ed.). Almaty, G.E.

Kosko, Maria M. (2002). 'Shamanism: an essential component of the Kazakh worldview'. In Andrzej Rozwadowski and Maria M. Kosko (eds). *Spirits and Stones, Shamanism and Rock Art in Central Asia and Siberia*. Poznan, Instytut Wschodni UAM, pp. 13–27.

Kultura kotchevnikov na rubezhak vekov (XIX-XX, XX-XXI): problem genezisa i tranformatsii (The Nomadic Culture during Centuries, XIX-XX, XX-XXI: Genesis Question and Transformations) (1995). Chakhanova (ed.). Almaty, N.J.

Laplantine, François (1992). *Anthropologie de la maladie, Etude ethnologique des systèmes de représentations étiologiques et thérapeutiques dans la société occidentale contemporaine*. Paris, Payot.

Privatsky, Bruce G. (2001). *Muslim Turkistan, Kazak Religion and Collective Memory*. Richmond, Curzon Press.

Rouget, Gilbert (1980) *La Musique et la Transe. Esquisse d'une théorie générale des relations de la musique et de la possession*. Paris, Gallimard.

Roux, Jean-Paul (1984). *La Religion des Turcs et des Mongols*. Paris, Payot.

Sembin, M. K. (1994) 'Sever i kazakhskoj toponimike' (North in Kazakh toponymy). *Khabarlari izvestija* 1, 63–8.

Vuillemenot, Anne-Marie (1998). 'Chamanisme au Kazakhstan: renouveau et tradition'. *Religiosiques*, Special issue on 'Les marges contemporaines de la religion' 18, pp. 79–97.

———(2000). 'Danses rituelles kazakhes : entre soufisme et chamanisme'. In Denise Aigle, Bénédicte Brac de la Perrière, Jean-Paul Chaumeil (eds). *La Politique des Esprits*. Nanterre [Paris], Société d'ethnologie, pp. 345–60.

———(2004). 'Quand un bakhsi kazakh évoque Allah'. *Journal of the History of Sufism* 4, 131–41.

———(2006). 'L'islam populaire kazakh et ouzbek: enracinements locaux et mondialisations'. In *Recherches Sociologiques et Anthropologiques*. Louvain-la-Neuve, Catholic University of Louvain, pp. 63–78.

———(2009). *La Yourte et la mesure du monde. Avec les nomades au Kazakhstan*. Louvain-la-Neuve, Académia-Bruylant, Collection anthropologie prospective.

Chapter Five

INTERRELATION TO THE INVISIBLE IN KIRGHIZISTAN

Aurélie Biard

In the context of brutal transformations – on a Kirghiz scene that is fragmented and scattered due to the decline in living standards, widening social inequalities and political instability – a category of Kirghiz therapeutic actors and specialists of communication with the supernatural, the *köz achïk* ('open eye'), try to thwart or solve what might at first sight seem unavoidable: misfortune, mishap, illness. They partake of the 'Kirghiz way' or *kïrgïzchïlïk*, that is the 'Kirghiz ways of doing' – which are supposed to be ancestral and perennial – like other specialists such as the sorcerers[1] and certain *moldo*[2] (Kirghiz: mullah). All these specialists assign the nefarious events suffered by one or several individuals either directly to impersonal forces or to the effect of the will of 'another' (sorcerer, spirit, etc.), and define and associate in their own style the officiant, the patient and the origin of the illness/ailment. The *köz achïk*, like the *moldo*, tries to bring solutions to the ills affecting the local population in its everyday life, in an unstable post-colonial sociopolitical and economic context. They mobilise a whole array of practices and representations, which, in my view, form a symbolic world.[3] Each of the specialists, who claim to take part in the Kirghiz way (*kïrgïzchïlïk*), partake of this symbolic world in their own way, this symbolic world being articulated to orthodox Islam in a complex manner. In fact, with the re-Islamisation of society and the spreading of neo-*Hanbalî* movements through Central Asia (in particular in the Uzbek Ferghana) from as early as the mid-1970s – that have benefited locally from the weakening of the *Hanafiyya*[4] and the decline of the mystical orders (Dudoignon 2001: 71) – there is a struggle over ritual practices and the re-interpretations of social practices such as the healing rituals practised by the healer-diviners, who are denounced as 'non-Muslim' by most of the representatives of Islam.

Throughout this survey, it has seemed necessary to study this symbolic world not just from a therapeutic perspective; as the role of the *köz achïk* is not solely to free their patients from an illness, but rather to 'open a path (*jol*[5])' to them, that is to 'see' to it that there should be no obstacle[6] on the 'path' (the fate of an individual), which underlies a spatial conception of human destiny in a pastoral society with a nomadic tradition. Thus the role of the *köz achïk* is also that of predicting the future of their patients, finding an object or an animal that has been lost or stolen,[7] even predicting electoral results, and above all answering to the 'why' of their misfortunes.

The main function of the *köz achïk* thus seems to be, to a certain extent, to heal certain collective ills related to the economic and political crisis by relying on widely shared representations within the Kirghiz society. The rituals of the *köz achïk* – by trying to conjure evil or more rarely to favour happiness – become a bet on the future, an attempt to change a random future, especially in an uncertain social and political context. Furthermore, Kirghizistan directly suffered from the economic collapse following the fall of the Soviet Union. Since its independence, Kirghizistan has implemented market-oriented measures following the precepts of the great Western organisations (i.e. the World Bank), thus marking a radical disengagement of the State. In this new economic context, the deterioration of the health system shows the limits of the management of public health for the major part of the population (a severe lack of means in the public hospital structures, the lack of accessibility of high quality medicines, and the problematic loss of credibility of the health system, among other things in the psychiatric field, etc.).

People sometimes turn towards the *kïrgïzchïlïk* because of the obstacles preventing access to health services in rural areas – though this is not the only explanation. However, the local population that shares this symbolic world, albeit with doubts and uncertainties, first go and see the *köz achïk* because they recognise their efficiency.[8] Indeed, the population looks for a different credibility in this form of medicine, which is considered traditional and more holistic.

This field survey focuses to a large extent on three healer-diviners through their respective biographic discourses: Gülayïm (village of Kïzïl-Oy, district of Jayïl), Joldoshbek (village of Chaek, country town of Jumgal) and Zarïlkan (village of Chaek). Although the life stories of these three *köz achïk* are not strictly speaking representative of all the healer-diviners of the region – and we must be cautious not to approach them in a totalising and reifying manner – however stereotyped they are structurally the content of the patterns of these narratives nonetheless differ from one healer-diviner to another. Moreover these narratives form an essential part in legitimising the individual in his function.[9]

My ethnological surveys have shown the importance of the 'disease-election', the spirits teaching through dreams, the relationships of 'inspiration' (section 1) and the *emic*[10] conceptions of ills (section 2). The last section will focus on the processes of legitimation and de-legitimation at work in this symbolic world: the legitimation of these practices by the healers, the acceptance of this legitimacy by the patients, and the processes of marginalisation of these representations and local practices considered non-Muslim by the representatives of an orthodox Islam (section 3).

Interrelation between the köz achïk and the spirits

The mode of election of the köz achïk

Before being invested in their function, the healer-diviners themselves go through the trial of suffering, of misfortune, which represents in their case a 'call from the spirits'. Elective diseases have no particular characteristics, except for the fact that they are persistent, and are generally so despite other attempts at recovery. During this 'initiation disease' or 'election disease' (de Sardan 1994), the spirit(s) (more often than not the *arbak*, i.e. 'ancestral spirits', or *peri* (fairy, angels)) inflict sufferings of calling to the future healer-diviners. These spirits will put an end to these sufferings as soon as an alliance is entered into with them. The election by one or several spirits is lived as a curse by the person who suffers it. He/she cannot refuse it for fear of death (or of seeing one of his relatives die). It manifests itself by a crisis whose symptoms are stereotyped (Hamayon 1990: 440–41) such as, for example, paralysis, a symptom which is often likened to a symbolic death or abdominal wind.

A dream (more rarely a vision) is often at the origin of the calling of many *köz ačïk*, who are supposed to have had a revelation given through a dream by certain spirits (in particular those of a 'distant relative', that is to say of an ancestor, or of a Muslim saint) a figure of sainthood exterior to the *köz achïk*'s family, which comes from a lineage of Sufi brotherhood and was the object of an hagiographical study; of Manas, the hero of the great Kirghiz epic,[11] and so on. These spirits urge them to start treating patients. In these dreams, the future healer-diviner makes contact with these spirits and through them he/she acquires a knowledge from which he/she will draw his/her ritual powers.

The crisis suffered by the future *köz achïk* doesn't necessarily translate into a physically afflicting disease; other forms of misfortune can affect him/her or his/her family, such as the fact of surviving from a disaster in which many others died or from the cruel death (the loss of a child, etc). This was precisely the case of a woman, Tinatin, close to Gülayim (a *köz achïk* from the village of Kïzïl-Oy, district of Jayïl), who started throwing stones (*tölgöchü*, 'the one who throws stones') (using 41 pebbles) in order to predict the future after the death by drowning of her 15-year-old daughter in the river near their home. Her desire to be initiated into some of the techniques used by the *köz achïk*, which she compares to 'taking one's vows', appeared to her, she told me, as a means 'not to become mad'.[12] Sometimes, there may only be expressions of conventional symptoms, the important thing being to reclaim the legacy of the tutelary spirits – as long as, in a lineage, others had had some *kasiet* (property [of healing]). The idea of 'misfortune' is there to impose the legacy absolutely. Taking over a legacy also means that it has to be formalised, insofar as a dead person is tormenting you so that you take care of him, and then stops doing so once you have recognised him. As a result, it would be better to say that misfortune has been lifted rather than healed.

What is interpreted *a posteriori* as an 'election-disease' can be illustrated by the example of Gulayïm.[13] Gülayïm is a 37-year-old *köz achïk* who lives in the village of Kïzïl-Oy, in the region of Chüy. She confesses that she has not found a husband yet because of her position as a healer-diviner. Gülayïm comes from a family of ten children and is the youngest daughter; one of her brothers is also a *köz achïk* near Bishkek. Gülayïm started to treat patients in 1989, after being initiated by a 99-year-old *köz achïk* whom she calls a 'master' (*ustat*) and who lived in Jumgal. Her life and studies were upset by long bouts of illness against which the doctors she consulted were powerless, according to her. As there was no hospital in the village where she was born and the journey to the hospital would have been too expensive, her family sent her to a *köz achïk*, despite the ideological reservations of her father, who was strongly Communist, but who nonetheless urged his children 'to respect and to fear the *arbak*'. Her father, who was worried about his daughter's health, agreed to his daughter being treated by a healer-diviner.[14] Gülayïm complained of heart pains and headaches: 'her heart was tight' (*jürök baylap saluu*), which was interpreted as a sign of election by the *köz achïk* they consulted.

> The man who cured me told me: 'You have the capacities to become a *köz achïk*. Do you want to? I can put you on the path. Can you do it?' I answered that I wasn't, because 'I am very young, I've just ended my studies, I have to make something of my life.' 'I'm going to stop your capacities, your *kasiet*,' he then answered. I returned home and the spirits of this man tortured me. I came back to him after a year.

Faced with Gülayïm's refusal to embrace the profession, this *köz achïk* would have then sent her his own *arbak*, the ones that protect him (*koldoochu arbak*) in order to compel her to accept the function of healer-diviner. During that period, Gülayïm's dreams were full of strange figures, of sunbeams, and so on. Gülayïm thus ascribes to these *arbak* an intention to blackmail her, in order to make her yield to their pressure and therefore to the desires she ascribes to them. She eventually accepted her condition, and 'went down on the path' (*jolgo tüshüp kaldï*) of the *köz achïk*, thus being freed from the sufferings that overwhelmed her. Now, it's her task to send her *arbak* in order to cure the pains her patients are suffering from. Gülayïm now considers that she has 'found her path', that of the *köz achïk*. Gülayïm leads a life that she does not consider easy, because the *arbak* are in control of her life and she has to obey them in every respect. She thinks that she inherited her *kasiet* – which she considers as a gift from God (*Kuday*) – from her mother, who would not have accepted it and who would have transmitted it to her when she died. Gülayïm also made clear that the *koldoochu arbak*, that is to say the 'guardian *arbak*', generally hands down the *kasiet* to the person they loved most when they were alive. And yet, this gift for healing is perceived as a burden, which is not chosen, but endured, and it manifests itself against the will of the person bearing it. The handing down of the *kasiet* thus generally happens along the lines of genealogical kinship (in the paternal line as well as in the maternal line).[15]

Even if some healer-diviners are destined to be considered 'social misfits' because of their relationship with the spirits, as in the case of Joldoshbek (village of Chaek, country town of Jumgal) who spent several months in a psychiatric clinic before embracing the profession of *köz achïk*, the crisis they experience is part of a necessary journey towards social recognition, so that their *kasiet* will be much sought after.

Relationships of 'inspiration'

The conception of the relations between the healer-diviner with his/her spirits, excludes any attempt to formalize it, remaining fluid. One of the characteristics of this symbolic world and of similar phenomena is that the officiant manifests physically that he is in 'direct contact' with the supernatural entities. It can even be said, following the argument made by Roberte Hamayon, that 'the direct aspect of a contact lies on its bodily expression, which it somewhat proves' (1994: 189). This contact is considered to be the means of action of the healer-diviner, thanks to which he can achieve multiple functions deemed indispensable to the life of the local community. The notion of contact entails a metaphoric relationship, for the partner with which one is in contact with is invisible (most of the time it is established with the 'protective *arbak*' (*koldoochu arbak*), the 'ancestral spirits, tutelary spirits' (Jacquesson

2007) which are the representation of the same and are necessary to the perpetuation of the group). The physical expression of this 'contact' – Zarïlkan, *köz achïk* and *ektraseans* from the village of Chaek, for instance, signals this 'direct contact' by yawns, sighs accompanied by the tensing of the jaw – is above all a social code intended for the audience. The arguments used in Kirghizistan to qualify this 'contact' are rarely in a language of incorporation but rather a language of alliance. The healer-diviners 'remain themselves' during a healing ritual, but their knowledge derives from the spirits or from 'elsewhere': the spirits talk to them, give them advice, tell them about certain events in their patients' lives. They reach an understanding of what causes the misfortune of their patients, an understanding that would rather pertain to 'inspiration'. This explains why there is an ambiguous zone in the relationship between the healer-diviners and the spirits, an ambiguity that appears to be a necessity of function.

We can then wonder about the use of the inspired 'words' which are implemented through the example of a session of divination given by Gülayïm. Gülayïm considers the *arbak* as the souls of the dead, which are talking to her through her ancestors. She explains that, during a healing ritual, she calls upon her ancestors 'with her consciousness', and then they call her *arbak*. I was able to see a ritual during which she was making a diagnosis on the health of her patient, while delivering a few general reflections on his life (the potential presence of obstacles on his way, etc.) before eventually telling him the future. In performing this ritual, she told her patient that she 'was going to see him' (*adam körüü*) and that she was going to talk to her ancestors (*ata-baba*). When the patient desired to obtain pieces of information on such or such event of his life, the patient sometimes asked her questions; she answered him by consulting her *arbak*, to which she addressed herself in a low voice, with her eyes half-closed, while she was saying her rosary (*tespe*). She asked them, in a familiar tone bordering on invective, what they thought of the person in front of her, if she could repeat to him what they said and if the patient would bear it. During this 'session', she just repeated the words of her spirits while asking them for their permission beforehand (as she claims it, the spirits' answers to her question come to her head and she just passes the information to the patient). The *köz achïk* thus speaks on behalf of the spirit or spirits which she replaces. She authenticates the speech as coming from the spirit or spirits. The mediation introduced by this imaginary presence takes away her sense of responsibility and vouches for the truthfulness of her speech. Who would dare, indeed, to question the word of the *arbak*?

As the ultimate source of knowledge, the spirits also know, according to Gülayïm, the political future of Kirghizistan. The first time I met Gülayïm was just after the so-called 'Tulip' Revolution of March 2005, and thus before the presidential elections that saw the victory of the actual Kirghiz president, Kurmanbek Bakiyev. Gülayïm explained to me that if her *arbak* were available at that moment, that is if they were anxious to tell their secrets, they could give her the name of the future president, but only a short time before the elections. According to Gülayïm, certain deputies would demand she supported their candidate, which would tend to prove the importance of the 'knowledge' that she claims she has from her spirits in the eyes of the local community, a 'knowledge' that would hardly be questioned. A *köz achïk* such as Bursulsun, settled in Narïn, had even been the unofficial *köz achïk* of the former Kirghiz president Askar Akayev; she enjoyed increased political prestige, and in particular her task was to predict his future and to warn him about the presence of possible 'obstacles on his way'.[16] Bursulsun thus declared:

> I had predicted the 11 September 2001 attacks in the United States. I also predicted the troubles in the region of Batken[17] six months in advance. I can predict the obstacles that someone might meet on his way. When people are sick, they come to see me. I treat them. In 1993, I had dreams concerning president Akayev and I wrote poems on his destiny, his greatness. He gave me this house. A politician who is now part of the opposition offered me an apartment in Bishkek. My neighbours have a very hostile behaviour towards me. Some believe I'm mad.

This statement tends to show the sway of this phenomenon in spheres that might be considered out of its reach. However, President A. Akayev consulted Bursulsun only unofficially and in a private capacity. Many of healers do not have a high status and are sometimes marginalised.

Emic conceptions of ills

How does this symbolic world present the different misfortunes affecting the body, the possessions and the social life of individuals, as a disorder in this life? What are the recurring etiological schemes of these nefarious events: witchcraft, the evil eye, willingness to harm attributed to certain spirits, breach against interdicts, bad energy, imbalance between principles and moods, and so on? According to *emic* representations, no misfortune is unwarranted, and therefore it is necessary to look for its cause, which is a feature of divination. From a heuristic point of view, 'the issue is less to discover a hidden cause than to attribute one, (it wouldn't almost matter which one) to be able to act on it' (Schlemmer 2004: 142). During the divination, the *köz achïk* 'chooses an agent, an origin and a solution (or a configuration) among the possible agents, origins and solutions (or the etiological configurations) of the disease' (Zempléni 1985: 38).

For many healer-diviners, it seems that no natural cause can be attributed to the disease (biological misfortune, that is to say ill fortune in the life of a body), which is supposed to be inflicted by the action of the spirits. As a result, there is no natural remedy to the disease, but it leads to a symbolic action. Within the framework of this interpretation, there are reminders that illness, and more generally misfortune, can result from a certain number of causes, for there are several possible reasons for the spirits' desire to harm. As we saw when we broached the issue of 'disease-election', some sufferings result in a somewhat improved status of the victim.

Other mishaps are only justified on negative grounds and call into question the responsibility of the individual as well as mistakes of ritual: funeral rites badly performed, forgetting the cult of the ancestors, and so on. Misfortune (physical or otherwise) would thus be the sanction of a previous social misbehaviour. It should be remembered that the *arbak* are supposed to punish breaches of the moral and social order, which they are responsible for, through the means of disease-sanction (in particular epilepsy and 'illnesses of the soul'). Thus, like Andras Zempléni, one wonders 'not how an individual uses the means offered by the society he belongs to, but how this society, or his culture, uses his "illnesses" to ensure its own reproduction or to cope with its own changes' (1985: 19).

Some conceptions, however, tend to repudiate the patient's responsibility: misfortune or disease happens arbitrarily, which corresponds to two types of etiologies: on the one hand, a social and 'intentional' causality (one is attributed to an 'other' – *kara köz achïk* or supernatural 'beings' – the desire to harm), and on the other hand, an antisocial etiology, of which the agents – principles or moods – are impersonal (bad energy, etc.). Let us consider more fully the first conception. The illness, whether physical or mental, occurs after a spirit has 'struck' an individual or when the latter has been scared by a spirit. This fear can emerge in different circumstances: by seeing an *arbak* in a cemetery, by passing above a place of sacrifice, and so on. It is said that chance encounters generally happen with wandering spirits that are considered to be harmful. These spirits are never *arbak*, which are put into the category of the self, but they are representatives of otherness, the *jin kapïr* (non-Muslim *jinn*), the *albarstï*,[18] and so on. Thus, the *jinns* in Kirghizistan were generally thought of as being agents of evil and not unpredictable spirits with no connection with Satan. The *jinns* are pathogenic agents that make the people they 'haunt' or harass sick. The treatment precludes any negotiation with these spirits, who are considered malevolent. Thus Gulayïm sometimes treat the diseases and misfortunes engendered by the *shaytan*, the *jin ooru* ('the diseases of the soul'). These diseases are induced either by the fear engendered by a 'bad spirit', which can take a zoomorphic shape (that of the animal which is the most likely to frighten its victim; for example the snake) or an anthropomorphic shape (that of an *arbak*...), or else the victim, a weak individual, will have let himself/herself be seduced by the *shaytan*, which from then on will run his/her life for him/her, which tends to put in perspective the taking away of responsibility from the individual.

Thus a *köz achïk* like Gülayïm sometimes treats a disease through exorcism[19] or thanks to 'biological energy', according to the terminology used by some *köz achïk*. All ills – including diseases – are enemies. Therefore, Joldoshbek, in each of the healings which I witnessed (which took place in his own bedroom, under huge posters representing Mecca, hung on the walls), used a whip (*kamchi*) and a knife to fight the so-called evil spirits. He whipped his patient in order to drive out the pathogenic agent; as for the knife, he used it to 'lift the heart' of those who are (or were) afraid of something ('when you have been afraid, you feel like your heart has fallen down, then it must be lifted back up'). Joldoshbek also makes knots with a reel of thread that has previously been unwound, above the spot where the patient feels pain; by doing so, he explains that the course of the disease 'is cut off'.

The practitioner really 'cures' the subject by extracting the culprit, or what is the effect, from the suffering body, whenever there is an attack by a 'mean spirit'. What is at stake is to expel an ill, that is to exorcize. The healer-diviner can also use his 'biological energy' by laying his hands, which are supposed to be sources of heat, over organs which may have 'caught a cold'. The *köz achïk* jointly use references to the spirits and to 'bio-energy', even in rural areas.

It is interesting to note that the *köz achïk* does not always succeed in eliminating what is a constituent of the illness, but he can transfer it, in a more general manner, through space (an animate or inanimate support) and through time (when the patient will have become mature enough to bear his *kasiet*). We thus saw Joldoshbek carry out a healing with a transfer onto an animate support. It was a ritual that consisted in 'stopping the *kasiet*' of a patient who had trouble bearing it, which was making him sick. He suffered from headaches, and often fainted. After reciting the Fatiha (the opening sura in the Qur'an), Joldoshbek did *dem-saluu* – blew – on his rosary (*tespe*) before passing it over a candle's flame. He then proceeded with the *tespe* making movements along the arms of his patient, from the shoulder to the hand, as if to extract something from him. After this, he felt his pulse and dealt him a few blows on the shoulders with the *tespe*. Then he brought in a black goat that was provided by the patient and placed it by one of his daughters next to the patient. He wound some thread around the young man's head and, with the other end, did the same around the goat's horns. Once the man and the animal were thus connected, he used the *tespe*, the whip, and the knife alternately, passing each one over the flame three times, in order to transfer the illness from the patient to the goat; he then does the same movement over the arms of his patient, then along the thread. He then unwound the thread, and threw it in a cup of water in which he quickly made the patient spit three times, then hastened to get rid of the cup's content outside the house. The medium was a black goat. A castrated male is preferred. The *köz achïk* transmits to it his patient's illness and consequently it must never be sacrificed. Once the ritual is over, the goat will remain for seven days at Joldoshbek's who will regularly pray during this period. If the goat does not die from the effects of the transfer of the illness during the week, it should go back to its flock, within which it will bear a distinctive mark and will from now on be considered sacred, unsuitable for any kind of consumption. When this animal dies, what is constitutive of this illness will be considered as being definitely destroyed.

Some *köz achïk* readily recognise their powerlessness to treat certain ills; then the tutelary spirits indicate this (is the illness a matter for the methods specific to the *kïrgïzchïlïk* or, conversely, for scientific medicine?). They may sometimes send their patients towards medicine practised in hospitals. Sometimes patients combine both approaches: you can thus go to the hospital to receive a symptomatic treatment and return to the healer-diviner for an etiological treatment. The local population looks for a different credibility in this form of medicine, which is considered more holistic. However, in the context of the increasing importance of reference to Islam in the Kirghiz society, the unity of this symbolic world is questioned by certain local social forces of an Islamic nature.

Marginalisation of these practices by the representatives of Islam

Exercising the function of *köz achïk* inside a patrilineal society with a Muslim majority and with a nomadic tradition like the Kirghiz society, rarely corresponds to a central, masculine and enhanced position of power, but more to the expression of a form of fragmented, feminised and sometimes marginalised, or even denigrated, counter-power. The functions of *köz achïk* (and/or *tabïp* (*tabib*), *bakshï*, etc., as these categories are not exclusive from each other) seem indeed to have been feminised since the last decades of the Soviet period. The so-called 'traditional' practices of healer-diviners may be, at least in some aspects, the result of a recent economic and social evolution. Some women *köz achïk*, as well as their main role of healer, represent a form of spiritual authority in their villages, which sometimes puts them in competition with the local imam or sheik (Dudoignon 2001: 75). This may be one of the reasons why the symbolic world specific to the *köz achïk* is violently denounced today as non-Muslim, even more than Sufism and the cult of saints, by the representatives of orthodox Islam. Such practices as the cults of ancestors and saints and visits to sacred sites (*mazar*)[20] are loudly decried by some new social and religious actors (new mullahs, local preachers (*davachi*), 'missionaries', tablighis, etc.), some of whom claim to adhere to a teaching strongly marked by a salafi inspiration, if not an ikhwani one. These new actors uphold a dogmatic and ritual purism and set up a project of radical reform of Islam through preaching (ar. *da'wa*; kir. *davat*), among other things against practices they consider blasphemous. All the *salafi* movements present in Central Asia systematically condemn the local *urf u 'ada* ('customs'), even when they don't challenge questions of dogma, on the grounds that they are innovative (*bid'a*) when compared to original Islam (which itself must be reconstructed).[21] Of course, they display the greatest hostility towards the healer-diviners, who synthesise practices and representations (and pretend to ensure the perpetuation of Kirghiz society in reference to its ancestors), widely shared within Kirghiz society. The symbolic world specific to the diviner-healers, which is intimately connected to the cult of the ancestors and within which Islam puts up with some practices similar to shamanism, is thus condemned as a whole by all the salafi movements.[22] These social and religious actors have been trying to dissuade the local population from following these local practices, which they perceive as relics from pre-Islamic cults. To rely solely on *emic* representations, these practices could be described as what are widely held to be the ancestors' 'ways of saying' and 'ways of doing', so the efforts of the new actors to have these practices banned has provoked much unrest among the local population.

However, the different neo-Hanbali movements are not the only ones to condemn strongly the practices of healer-diviners, who also come up against the hostility displayed by many 'institutionalised' mullahs (i.e the mullahs who are part of the 'nationalised' framework of Hanafi Islam authorised in the region). The actors of Islam condemning the practices of the diviner-healers, whether these actors are institutional religious figures (traditionalists who tend to display an apolitical conservatism in search of the sole re-traditionalisation of society, reformists, radical Hanafi, etc.) or not, press their criticisms with very strict theological stands. In their arguments, the *köz achïk* as well as those who consult them are considered to be irreligious and 'associators' (ar. *mushrikun*), because of their invoking of spirits and the help requested of the saints or the spirits of ancestors. They are generally accused of living on popular gullibility, of being impostors.[23] Thus, Anashkan Tashkïdjaev, an official Kirghizistanese Uzbek imam from the central mosque of Osh (in the Kirghiz Ferghana, therefore in a strongly Islamised environment) – who told us that he spoke Arabic, had been to Saudi Arabia eight times, had done the *hajj* (the pilgrimage to Mecca), and had been trained at the well-known *madrasa* Mir-i Arab in Bukhara – explained:

> The *köz achïk* say that God gave them *kasiet* but God alone can do that. It is forbidden by the Qur'an to ask something to the dead, to pray for the dead, for dead people. You have to read the Qur'an and that is all. The *shaytan* is their God. [...] The Prophet says that you must not believe in the *köz achïk*. What the *köz achïk* say are the words of the *jinn*, words that do not exist in the Qur'an. [...] The *köz achïk* invent words by saying these are *sura* from the Qur'an.

In order to legitimise his judgement, this imam was basing it on the sura al-Falaq (The Dawn, 113: *Qul 'auzu bi rabb al-falaq*), the sura al-Nâs (sura 114: *Qul 'auzu bi rabbi n'nas*).

However, the modalities of interaction between the *köz achïk* and the other power holders such as the mullahs (in particular the 'institutionalised' mullahs, most of them being traditionalists) turn out to be much more complex. In the context of the setting up of new economic, social and political relationships in the Kirghiz rural space, the *köz achïk* and the *moldo* are admittedly competitors who share the same territory and, consequently, fight over influence in the local community, but they are also constantly negotiating due to the richness of rural sociabilities, which greatly facilitate social and religious communication. As a result, the confrontation between the mullahs and the *köz achïk* takes different shapes: compromise, negotiation, resistance or even cooperation. The *moldo*, especially if they have received a solid religious education,[24] naturally hold the highest rank in the local hierarchy, like the *imam-i juma* in particular. A higher authority is quite often recognised to the *moldo* by the *köz achïk* themselves. Thus, Gülayïm, *köz achïk* from the village of Kïzïl-Oy, who claims to be submissive to God's will, considers that the *köz achïk* are 'experts' for life here below, while the *moldo* prepare individuals for the beyond. Gülayïm thinks, moreover, that it is the duty of the *moldo* to 'raise the moral standards in the Muslim community'.

> In the Soviet era, the *moldo* were against the *köz achïk*. Now, there are good relationships between us. I don't do the prayer, the *namaz*. Each of us has a role. The *moldo* prepare people for life after death; the *köz achïk* are specialists for this life. I'm in favour of the *moldo*. If it is necessary, I can be a subordinate to the *moldo*. The duty of the *moldo* is to raise people's moral standards, raise the Muslims' moral standards.

My fieldwork has shown, however, that the moral register is not exclusive to the *moldo*; indeed, the *köz achïk* appropriate a moral discourse on the practices that are considered deviant (too much vodka consumption, careless cult of the ancestors, etc.) and, as a result, are trying to embody the social standard in effect.

Quite often, the *köz achïk* send the person who has come to consult them to the mullah, and the reverse also happens. Therefore there is an ambivalence about some mullahs, who can sometimes give their blessing (*bata*) in order to allow an applicant to take on the function of diviner-healer, in turn call upon a *köz achïk*[25] to heal them, or again proceed themselves to healing sessions following 'the Muslim way of healing' (Privratsky 2001: 193), that is with the recitation of the appropriate Qur'anic verses. Thus certain mullahs (*Hanafi* but often tinged with the Naqshbandiyya Sufi brotherhood, in particular in the south of Kirghizistan) have been partly initiated with persons they generally consider as living saints, and they too practice exorcism after the universal ways of Islam. The ills, the diseases due – according to what these 'healer-mullahs' said – to the *jinn* are treated by them with divine science (*ilm-i ilahi*), with the reading and recitation of prayers, blessings, recitation of the sura Ya Sin (36) in particular, and so on. However, some 'healer-mullahs' do not just recite the appropriate verses in order to drive out the trouble-maker *jinn* from the patient's body, but also use a knife like the *köz achïk* (most of the time in order to 'block' the path of an evil spirit), or even a stick with which the patient is beaten, as the spirit alone is supposed to feel the pain caused by the blows.

As for the *köz achïk*, they inscribe their activities in a Muslim perspective, even in the less Islamised areas. Moreover, the superior degree of religiosity attributed to some healers plays an important role in their legitimation, in their being socially recognised, in the foundation of their credibility and the acceptance of their authority. Some *köz achïk* insist on the fact that they have received the necessary blessings directly from the saints and/or from mullahs or from Sufi cleric/*ishân* (Basilov 1992: 18). The prayers they address to these saints as well as the pilgrimages that some of them (especially women) make to the tombs of Muslim saints allow them to establish their credibility. Some healer-diviners try to legitimise their practices and the techniques to which they resort by claiming that Prophet Muhammad did the same: for Tursun, a *köz achïk* from Narïn, 'Muhammad used the whip and threw stones too like the doctor (*tabïp*)'.

My path, [claims Gulzat], is to try to follow the Qur'an. I throw the stones. Sometimes I use cards to predict the future, but I know it is against Islam. If the patient asks for cards, I use them. Some people are pure and others are thieves. But everybody can come to my place. I also heal. I recite suras from the Qur'an.

Moreover, the healing sessions sporadically use Arabic, the liturgical language of Islam, and Qur'anic reminiscences (sura learnt by heart) are far from rare. However, almost no healer speaks Arabic and very few have read the Qur'an, even if Kirghiz translations exist. But the *köz achïk* say they practice religion in their dreams and have learnt to recite the Qur'an in dreams. Some verses of the Qur'an seem, according to them, impenetrable, but as Zarilkan, a 40-year-old healer who specialises in the loss or the theft of the cattle[26] in Isïk-Köl district (*oblast*), testifies:

> When I make the *shaytan* go out by *dem-saluu*, it can come back to my place and ask me: 'Why did you make me go out?' I then read the Qur'an or recite a sura (kir. *kelme*: typical sentences from the Qur'an) like 'Bismillah...'. What matters is to deeply believe in this sentence, to know how much I believe in it. If I don't understand this sentence, it even increases its reach.

Another healer-diviner, Tursun states:

> I pray God. I heal only thanks to God. I ask God: 'Help me'....) I was very ill for a year. When I was eighteen, I cured myself almost by myself. An old doctor (*tabïp*) helped me, he advised me to read the Qur'an. I don't understand Arabic but with all the force of my heart, one has to believe in these sacred sentences.

There were also many healer-diviners who strongly encouraged me to embrace the Muslim religion and thus displayed a certain proselytism: 'I know – Zarilkan told me – that you will come back to live here [in Kirghizistan] for the rest of your life and that you will convert to Islam.'

Conclusion

In an instable post-colonial political and economic context, the *köz achïk* appear, in *emic* representations, as the guardians of the 'tradition', of the 'Kirghiz ways of doing' (*kïrgïzchïlïk*), even as they show their capacity for innovation and their resourcefulness (percolation of a new vocabulary such as that of 'biological energy', modern spiritualities, etc.), which facilitates adaptation to change and modernity. This symbolic world can thus adapt itself to changes as well as to the challenges it encounters. The free will of the *köz achïk*, who all claim they submit to God and are 'good Muslims' – in spite of their being condemned for their practices and representations by different representatives of Islam – would not be incompatible with the 'traditions'. The flexibility of this system, which has to do with its oral nature – in spite of the *köz achïk* being attached to the Muslim healing tradition, the references to the Qur'an, the propitiatory expressions – allows infinite adaptation and re-creation.

Bibliography

Abramzon, Saul M. (1949). 'Rozhdenie i detstvo kirgizskogo rebenka' (The Kirghiz and their ethnogenetic, historical and cultural links). *Sbornik muzeya antropologii i etnografii*, XII, 78–138.

_____(1971). *Kirgizy i ikh etnogeneticheskie i istoriko-kul'turnye svyazi* (The Kirghizs and their ethnogenetic, historical and cultural relations). Leningrad, Nauka.

Basilov, Vladimir N. (1987). 'Popular Islam in Central Asia and Kazakhstan'. *Journal of Muslim Minority Affairs* 8: 1, 7–17.

_____(1992). 'Le Chamanisme islamisé des peuples d'Asie centrale'. In *Diogène* 158, 7–19.

Castagnè, Jean (1930). 'Magie et exorcisme chez les Kazaks-Kirghizes et autres peuples turks orientaux'. *Revue des eètudes islamiques* 1, 53–156.

_____(1951). 'Le Culte des lieux saints de l'Islam au Turkestan'. *Ethnographie* 46, 46–124.

Delaby, Laurence (1976). 'Chamanes toungouses, monographie'. *Études mongoles et sibériennes*, 7.

Dor, Rémy (2004). *Parlons kirghiz, Manuel de langue, orature et littérature kirghizes*. Paris, L'Harmattan.

Dudoignon, Stéphane, A. (2001). 'Islam d'Europe ? Islam d'Asie ? En Eurasie centrale (Russie, Caucase, Asie centrale)'. In Andrée Feillard (eds). *L'Islam en Asie du Caucase à la Chine*. Paris, La documentation Française, pp. 21–80.

During, Jean and Khudoberdiev, Sultonali (2007). *La Voix du chamane, Étude sur les baxshi tadjiks et ouzbeks*. Paris, IFEAC-L'Harmattan, Collection Centre-Asie.

Even, Marie-Dominique (1988–9). 'Chants de chamanes mongols'. *Études mongoles et sibériennes*, 18, 19–20.

Garrone, Patrick (2000). *Chamanisme et Islam en Asie centrale, La Baksylyk hier et aujourd'hui*. Paris, Librairie d'Amérique et d'Orient Jean Maisonneuve.

Hamayon, Roberte (1982). 'Des chamanes au chamanisme'. *L'Ethnographie*, 87–88, 13–48.

―――(1990). *La Chasse à l'âme, Esquisse d'une théorie du chamanisme sibérien.* Nanterre [Paris], Société d'ethnologie.

―――(1994). 'En guise de postface: qu'en disent les esprits?'. *Paroles de chamanes, paroles d'esprits, Cahiers de Littérature Orale*, 35, 189–215.

Jacquesson, Svetlana (2007). 'Le Cheval dans le rituel funéraire kïrgïz. Variations sur le thème du sacrifice'. *Journal Asiatique*, 295: 2, 383–414.

Olivier de Sardan, Jean-Pierre (1994). 'Possession, affliction et folie : les ruses de la thérapisation'. *L'Homme*, 131, XXXIV: 3, 7–27.

Pike, Kenneth, L. (1947). *Phonemics, a Technique for Reducing Languages to Writing.* Ann Arbor, University Michigan Press.

Privratsky, Bruce (2001). *Muslim Turkistan. Kazak Religion and Collective Memory.* Richmond, Surrey, Curzon.

Rasanayagam, Johan (2006). 'Healing with spirits and the formation of Muslim selfhood in post-Soviet Uzbekistan'. *Journal of the Royal Anthropological Institute*, 12, 377–93.

Schlemmer, Grégoire (2004). 'Vues d'esprits, La conception des esprits et ses implications chez les Kulung Rai du Népal'. Ph.D. Diss, Nanterre, Université Paris X – Nanterre.

Seleznev, Aleksandr G. (2000). 'Le Syncrétisme islam-paganisme chez les peuples türks de Sibérie occidentale'. *Cahiers du Monde russe*, 41: 2–3, 341–56.

Vuillemenot, Anne-Marie (2000). 'Danses rituelles kazakhes: entre soufisme et chamanisme' in Denise Aigle; Bénédicte Brac de la Perrière; Jean-Pierre Chaumeil (eds). *La Politique des esprits, chamanismes et religions universalistes.* Nanterre [Paris], Société d'ethnologie, pp. 345–60.

―――(2004). 'Quand un bakhsi kazakh évoque Allah', *Journal of the History of Sufism*, 4, 131–141.

Zarcone, Thierry (2000). 'Interpénétration du soufisme et du chamanisme dans l'aire turque, "soufisme chamanisé" et "chamanisme soufisé"'. In Denise Aigle; Bénédicte Brac de la Perrière; Jean-Pierre Chaumeil (eds). *La Politique des esprits, chamanismes et religions universalistes.* Nanterre [Paris], Société d'ethnologie, pp. 383–96.

―――(2003). 'Le Chamanisme islamisé après la disparition de l'URSS'. In Roberte Hamayon (eds). *Chamanismes,* Diogène, Paris, Quadrige/PUF, pp. 147–58.

Zempléni, Andras (1985). 'La "Maladie" et ses "causes": introduction'. *Ethnographie*, LXXXI: 96–97, 13–44.

Zeranska-Kominek, Slawomira and Lebeuf, Arnold (1997). *The tale of Crazy Harman. The Musician and the Concept of Music in the Türkmen Epic Tale Harman Däli.* Warsaw, Academici Publications Dialog.

Chapter Six

TWO INDIGENOUS HEALING METHODS AMONG IRANIAN TURKMEN

Manijeh Maghsudi

As with anywhere else in the world, indigenous healing methods in Iran have arisen either from core cultural and social realities in the context of the prevailing ecology (particularly plant life) in a specific residential place, or they have adapted themselves to these conditions by adoption of more or less acceptable forms. These healing methods are not found in urban areas, and townspeople regard them as mere folk superstition, folklore even. However, they have sustained their value and credibility to locals; and have even became an inseparable constituent of the life and culture of rural people, to the extent that they consider their effects undeniable facts.[1]

Despite different historical roots and cultural attachments, certain indigenous healing methods have been mistakenly identified with one another, due to some similarities in their appearance. Among these, one could point out *guvati*, practiced in Sistan and Baluchistan Province (southeast of Iran); *zar* in Bandar Abbas (south of Iran); and *porkhani*[2] (shamanic) ritual in the Turkmen Sahra region.[3] Because of the application of music and certain symbolic acts that bestow dramatic character to them, and also the belief in the existence of intruder evil spirits that penetrate the soul of the patient, the boundaries separating these three healing methods are not clear-cut. The healer in each attempts to exorcise such spirits from the patient's body.

In Bandar Abbas and Qashm Island (one of the 14 Islands of Iran), *Ahl-i Hava* is an expression applied to persons who are considered haunted by the wind, which perhaps symbolises the intruder evil spirit? The healer, who if male is called *babazar* and if female *mamazar*, takes advantage of music in the form of an orchestra and also of symbolic acts such as the clapping of hands by those accompanying the patient, in order to lead the patient into a state of ecstasy and drive the wind (evil spirit) out of his body (Saidi 1968: 45). *Guvati* has almost the same procedure. In this rite, the healer, who is usually a man called *khalifa*, orchestrates the music and symbolic acts in order to exorcise the intruder spirit from the patient's body (During 1988: 2). It is very rare to have a female healer perform this rite. *Porkhani* is different from the other two rituals mentioned. In this rite, good metaphysical forces operate in favour of curing the patient. Therefore, the healer (*porkhan*) serves as a link between those forces and the patient for the purpose of driving out the bad or intruder spirits from the body.

The point I intend to make and clarify in this chapter is that the healing procedure in *porkhani* enjoys certain characteristics which render it difficult to reduce this kind of healing practice to what is observed in *guvati* and *zar* rituals, or to any other form of treatment by music or dramatic acts. The musical and dramatic aspects are indeed significant in *porkhani* rites. The effects of music or drama might account for the tendency of patients to recover to a normal state. In my view, from the standpoint of anthropology, the best way to define the phenomenon of *porkhani* can be found in the relation between *porkhan* and metaphysical forces with the goal of curing the patient's sickness (Maghsudi 2006b: 25).

Any other definition for this phenomenon – other than the one based on the tenets of the indigenous society – risks interrupting the link between the researcher and the cultural reality of the subject of study. This could present the danger of all sorts of deliberate and intractable definitions emerging. Despite enjoying the music and watching the dramatic acts (they sometimes clap their hands to encourage *porkhan* to continue them), people who go to the *porkhan* (patients and their relatives) do not consider them the actual factors that cure sickness. They believe that only the good metaphysical forces are able to accomplish this task. In my opinion, we cannot neglect this cultural reality, one which accounts for the *porkhan*'s equivalence to a shaman, a point which I stress throughout this chapter.

The most dramatic acts pertain to male *porkhan*. I have not, in person, seen any female *porkhan* conduct displays. Nevertheless, people do believe in the healing potential of women *porkhan* – invested in their power which finds its origin through their relations with the metaphysical dimension. Dramatic acts are not regarded as determining criteria for a definition of the *porkhani*. If this were the case, we would have to exclude female *porkhan* from *porkhani*'s definition, and our investigation would likewise lead to a deadlock.

While taking the above point into consideration, we have employed the same approach to distinguish and classify different indigenous healing methods in the Turkmen Sahra region. The counterpart for *porkhan* in this new study is the *ishan* (plural = *ishanan*[4]). *Ishanans* put greater emphasis on the religious aspect of healing (such as writing special prayers for the patient) than *porkhan*. In their healing method, the relationship with the metaphysical forces is only feasible and permissible through dreaming and mystical conduct, that is, through spiritual knowledge. I should warn readers that the term '*ishani*' is not sufficiently exact and clear, and it sometimes includes shamans too. However, here in this chapter, we use this term in the first sense explained above.

Methodology

I am an anthropologist who conducts field research. I take the utmost pleasure in probing into the hidden cultural layers of the society concerned. Through this investigation, I discover my own self too, and gain knowledge of my inner states. I emphasise that I am a field researcher anthropologist. The points I make in this study not only serve as a reminder of certain historical facts, but are based on the foundation of direct observation and my personal field research. Though I am to some extent familiar with Turkmen language, I always have interpreters and guides accompanying me during my visits. In most cases, I record the conversations and interviews on a CD or a tape, and then write the translation of the recorded content down to study later in more detail. In certain cases, where some sensitivity is involved or the situation is such that it is not appropriate to record the live incident, I resort to observation, progressing the dialogue and taking notes about the event in question.

My research projects were initially and primarily focused on and limited to the issues of marriage, divorce and family relations among members of Turkmen society. Some seven years ago, I became acquainted with certain female healers, and this meeting paved the way for the transfer of my attention to the healing methods that existed within this community. I previously had some information about *porkhans*. However, I did not know that female *porkhans* existed, occupying an important and specific position in the indigenous healing system. This finding astonished me, and I was even more surprised by my unawareness of this fact. Since that time, that is, over the last seven years, I have become acquainted with many female healers known by various titles, such as *porkhan, ishan,* Prayer Writer, Bonesetter, *daamaar tutan*,[5] *qarakh Yaasin*[6] and *zikr-i khanjar*,[7] and have continued collecting information about their lifestyle, profession and conventions. I have likewise had meetings with male *porkhans*, and I should say that a comparative study of these two groups could be fascinating. However, my own investigations are mainly concentrated on female healers. These women have extraordinary humanistic and emotional characteristics; but the dramatic aspect of their work is indeed insignificant. This is why they have not attracted the attention of non-indigenous observers.

The final outcome of this research will appear in a book. In this chapter, I highlight the preliminary results of my observations with my comments so far. The issues are raised here briefly, and tend to be rendered in the form of conclusions drawn from statements made on the basis of my observations, rather than a detailed analysis of case studies being presented.

The ethnic roots

As one of the tribes of Oghuz – one of the great ethnicities in Central Asia – the Turkmen are known as 'Seljuk Oghuz', from the name of their leader, Seljuk. During the era of Samani rule in the tenth century, they received permission to settle in the northeast of the Iranian plateau (Muin 1993: vol. 6, 387). A short while after the overthrow of the Samanid Dynasty and the establishment of the Ghaznavid's, some Turkmen tribes received permission from Sultan Mahmud to settle down in the present lands of the Iranian Turkmens, now called the Turkmen Sahra region (ibid.).

Following several wars, the Iranian plateau decreased in scale, some parts of it becoming the present-day countries of Afghanistan and Turkmenistan (Guli 1987: 70–71). The larger Turkmen society was likewise divided into two smaller communities, the Turkmens of Iran and the Turkmens of Turkmenistan. Of course, as a consequence of the invasions and triumphs of the Seljuks (a dynasty established in Iran by the Turkmens), a large number of Turkmens scattered, forming small ethnic groups in the neighbouring countries (Ashtiyani, Abbas 1973: 43).

Iranian Turkmens belong to three large tribes: Yamut, Guuklan and Tekke. Each in turn is divided into smaller tribes. In Iran the Guklan reside in the Gulidagh and Kalalaha lands at the foot of the Gulidagh Mountains situated on the eastern side of Turkmen Sahra. Guuklan was the first tribe among the Turkmens inclined to settle in one place, and they began practising agriculture, gardening and honey bee breeding, along with animal husbandry (Lugashva 1979: 23–4). The Yamut tribe resides in the western part of the Turkmen Sahra region. Unlike the Guuklan, they did not abandon nomadic life easily. It was only under pressure from the state then in power – around a century ago – that they were obliged to settle in one place, finally giving up their resistance and adapting themselves to the new lifestyle. The Tekke tribe is a smaller community than the Guuklans or the Yamuts, and its residential area is Jargalan, and also to the north of the city of Bujnuurd (Azami and Gunbad 2003: 15).

According to the statistics provided in 1997, the total population of Turkmens in Iran had reached two million. They therefore make up one-third of the total number of Turkmens worldwide, and 2.5 per cent of the Iranian population. While preserving their ethnic identity, the Turkmens are dispersed in rural areas as well as in four towns in the Turkmen Sahra region, including Gunbad Kavus, Gumishan, Kalalah and Bandar Turkmen. This region currently belongs to the Gulistan province, where you can likewise find a certain number of ethnic Fars, Baluch, Ozbek and Kazakh (Maghsudi 2006a: 55).

The ideological roots

The Turkmens came to the Iranian plateau from Central Asia where Buddhist, animist, totemist, shamanist, Mazdak and Zoroastrian tenets and beliefs were common (Azami and Gunbad 2003: 15). It is therefore natural that the Turkmens received influences from these ideologies, or at least become familiar with them. However, their belief in the existence of the sky god (Tangeri) and earth goddess (Atagen); their faith in several gods and goddesses for natural phenomena such as day, night, wind, rain, moon, sun, etc.; and also their belief in the sacredness of the water, fire and ancestral spirit and in a specific site for contact with the spirits, are among the most ancient and consistent convictions of Turkmens (ibid). They could be regarded as the Turkmens' ideological system, at least in so far as it has been recorded by historians. In this study, I focus attention on the last point, the possibility of making contact with other spirits, which undoubtedly has a shamanic structure. But it is first necessary to conduct a short review of some points relating to the time, place and method of the Turkmens' conversion to the religion of Islam.

As mentioned earlier, in the tenth century the Seljuk's Oghuz gained permission from the Samanids to settle down in the north of the Iranian plateau. Since the Samanids were Muslims, it is probable that with the Oghuz's residence in Iran came the obligation or encouragement to convert to Islam. Or it may simply be that the Turkmens gained interest in the new religion of Islam as a result of associating with Muslim people. The name Turkmen seems to have been applied to them from that time, that is from when

Seljuk's Oghuz were considered Muslim Oghuz (Muin 1993: vol. 6, 387). This process certainly could not have happened instantaneously, but probably evolved over a period of one or two centuries. In other words, during this time span, the Turkmens seem to have preserved their own beliefs and rituals while accepting those of the new religion of Islam. In documents remaining from this era, we see some hints about both the Turkmens' totemism and irreligiousness (Ibn-i Fazlan 1985: 48). What is certain and undeniable, is that their adoption of Islam serves as a turning point in the history of this new religion. With their warlike character, the Turkmens greatly contributed to the expansion of Islam over other lands, particularly in the Middle East.

The Iranian Turkmens are mainly Sunnites and belong to the Hanafi school. Otherwise, the Naqshbandiyya Sufi order is influential among the Guuklans and there are individual Turkmens who call themselves 'Awlad' and attribute their family tree to the Rashidin Caliphs. They are in turn divided into four groups: Shaykh, Makhdum, Ata and Khvaja (Maghsudi 1989: 74).

The shamanic elements

The basis of shamanic belief is the relationship of the shaman with metaphysical forces. From the standpoint of the indigenous people, either the healer or the patient, there is no division between the natural and the metaphysical. The latter is an inseparable and real component of the former. The metaphysical is even considered as the natural; or vice versa, that it, nature, is a part of the metaphysical. The same is true for the soul. It is regarded as a real phenomenon. It is true that in day-to-day life the soul does not appear to everybody; however, the healer (shaman) is capable of establishing contact with souls, spirits and metaphysical forces. It can even be to the extent that the shaman is able to exert control over the souls, spirits and metaphysical forces, and most importantly to resort to them for curing a disease. It is the latter ability that makes a person a shaman, and allows them to enjoy a specific standing, distinguishing them from the other people who can contact spirits and souls. The relation of the shaman with the metaphysical world is a positive one, pursuing the goal of healing a patient. The special aptitude of a shaman for curing sickness rests on this specific form of relationship. Should they be deprived of this ability, they will no longer be able to cure the disease. Even if they were able to heal a patient without this particular relationship, they would no longer be regarded as shamans.

This is the very reason for depicting Erejeb Porkhan as a shaman (Khurmali 1999: 48). He is one of the most famous indigenous healers among the Iranian Turkmens, as well as a classic example of a Muslim shaman. It is believed that 'he is in contact with an army of *jinns* (metaphysical creatures) and benefits from them to cure the patient' (Khurmali 1999: 48). Just imagine, Erejeb Porkhan standing there, giving commands to a populous army of *jinns*, and everyone obeying him. Erejeb Porkhan is nevertheless very humble and does not boast about his power or this ability. He says that it is in fact the *jinns* who give instructions and ask him to cure the patients, and that they likewise show him how to treat the disease, and help him for this purpose. However, what is important from the viewpoint of semantics is the exceptional ability of Erejeb, which provides him with the possibility of establishing links with the metaphysical forces and seeking help from them to treat the patient. This is why Erejeb is considered a shaman.

In the *porkhani* method, this significant shamanic element sits comfortably and tangibly beside the other Islamic cultural elements, such as prayer and spell. The image rendered by Porkhan from metaphysical creatures and the descriptions of his distinct experiences with them, reveal a combination formed from these two cultures. Moreover, the practice of Islamic teachings in Porkhan's personal life and the constant presence of them in the special ceremonial treatment, along with specific applications of music, song, objects and body gestures, that is, the very symbolic shamanic elements, all point to the interaction of the two cultures.

There are four different aspects to the healing method of Erejeb Porkhan that serve as essential structural constituents of this specific healing method. To put it another way, *porkhani* is defined with and through these four aspects. Each aspect has caused various and sometimes even opposing interpretations from the viewpoint of semantics, as well as the particular importance attributed to the *porkhani* when a definition is given. The four aspects are as follows:

1) *Metaphysical.* The relation with metaphysics (here, the *jinns*) is for the purpose of seeking help to cure the disease. Erejeb Porkhan has a sack, from within which the army of *jinns* contacts him and leads the music towards the state of ecstasy; and hence the link is made.
2) *Musical.* The *dutar* is the Turkmens' traditional musical instrument, played by a musician called a *bakhshi*. The music is conducted in the Navaiya system which is one of the most famous musical branches among Turkmen. On certain occasions, the *porkhan* himself takes his *dutar* and plays it for a while, outside the ceremony. At present, music is broadcast on a tape recorder. He believes that the *jinns* are gathered through playing the music. He himself reaches a state of ecstasy by

Figure 6.1. Turkmen playing the *dutar* during a ritual (Photograph: Manijeh Maghsudi and Behrooz Ashtray).

    listening to the music and it prepares him for getting contact with them, spiritually (Figure 6.1).

3) *Dramatic.* The performance includes certain objects such as a sword, wooden pieces and a rope made of camel's fleece and hung from the ceiling, a spatula, a lash and a series of dramatic acts such as climbing up the rope when in a state of ecstasy and swirling around its axis, tapping the sole of the patient's foot with the spatula, putting a hand into the patient's mouth and taking out the agent of the disease with the help of two wooden pieces placed at the back of the patient's neck in order to be hit by the sword.

4) *Islamic.* This is contained in the very act of prayer writing. The ideological content of these prayers is naturally based on Islamic beliefs. When the ceremony is finished, the *porkhan* writes and gives a special prayer to every patient.

    The first three aspects are related to shamanic culture, and the fourth to Islamic culture. We therefore find a combination of both shamanic and Islamic elements in the *porkhani* ceremonial. I contend that the second and third aspects in this ceremony – though very attractive because of their dramatic manifestations – are less valid as evidence for the existence of a shamanic element in the healing method of *porkhani*. Despite this, in certain studies, a special and determining significance is bestowed upon the second aspect; whereas in certain others, it is the third aspect which enjoys this position. As we shall see, the *porkhani* ceremony is sometimes reduced to a musical treatment and on other occasions to a dramatic treatment. The literature likewise attempts to interpret and justify the various musical and dramatic elements within the *porkhani* ceremony using psychological approaches, and thereby also grants legitimacy to this practice.

This approach is neither reliable nor unhindered in its coming to an understanding of the concept of shamanism. The analytical study of the first aspect, that is, the relation of the *porkhan* with the metaphysical, does however supply us with such a possibility. Through consideration of this relation we are able to reveal the shamanic element in the healing method of the *purkhan*. The musical and dramatic elements in the healing method of Turkmen healers, however, have many similarities to those practised in other regions of Iran, for instance, among the Zabuli, Baluchi and indigenous people of Bandar Abbas, and which have cultural and geographical origins different to those of shamanic ritual.

There is neither exact nor sufficient information about the decoration of the scenes of these performances, in order to be able to compare and contrast them with those prevalent in shamanic eras, before the conversion of Turkmens to Islam. The past cultural elements have either been destroyed or changed drastically and become mixed with other nations' cultural elements, to the extent that we cannot consider purely Turkmen or purely shamanic characteristics. The similarity of the *porkhan*'s spatula to that of a certain shaman in another part of the world, or the gesture of climbing up the rope practised by both a *porkhan* and a shaman elsewhere, do not serve as firm evidence to consider a *porkhan* as a shaman, unless the existence of the dramatic and musical aspects – regardless of their content – are seen along with the first aspect (contact with the metaphysical) that is held as a necessity for a *porkhan*'s activity. They only create a suitable atmosphere for the realisation of healing practice. The primary factor involved in the treatment is the *jinn*. Erejeb Porkhan says himself that 'the sound of the *dutar* forces the *jinns* to come and gather here'. Elsewhere, he adds that 'the *jinns* tell me what to do and how to treat the disease'.

The main difference between *porkhan* and *ishan* (another group of Turkmen indigenous healers who have an Islamic method of healing) lies here. While *porkhan* have a positive and useful relation with the *jinns* and seek help from them to cure the patient, *ishan* take great care to avoid the *jinns* and consider them the very cause of the disease. The viewpoints of these two groups hence have very different foundations.

Islamic elements

This study has undoubtedly adopted an anthropological approach to the object of investigation. Generally, there are three distinct Islamic perspectives on any issue. One is the formal view. The second view is specific to the jurists as well as to the independent thinkers. And the third one is that of the public. According to formal Islam, these healing methods, particularly *porkhani*, are rejected and prohibited (Rajabiyan Tamak 2004: 37–8). In this view, interference with metaphysical phenomena and affairs, in particular penetrating and mastering them, are beyond human capability. People are only able and allowed to seek help from God and the saints, through prayers and accomplishment of good deeds. Or, we may remain inactive and mere observers of unnatural phenomena (such as miracles). Human beings are incapable of manipulating these phenomena or exerting their will over them. As a result, the majority of Islamic jurists and independent thinkers look at the healing procedure with scepticism and do not give it much credence. Of course, certain indigenous religious men support the *ishan* and cooperate with them. Hence, it is only in indigenous popular culture – and mostly among the lower classes of rural society – that the healing ritual enjoys a high status and value. As a consequence, the domain of this study pertains to the Islam reflected in the beliefs and customs of rural people.

As mentioned earlier, the Turkmens' healing methods combine shamanic and Islamic components. These healing methods could form a spectrum, with various degrees of mixing between the elements. At one pole, we could place *porkhan* and at the other, *ishans*. The *porkhani* method of healing is the most shamanic; the *ishani* method serves as the most Islamic indigenous healing method in the region of Turkmen Sahra (Maghsudi 2006b: 111). The *porkhani* way of healing relies on a positive relation with the *jinn* as its main feature. However, *ishani* is regarded as a healing method based upon practising religious duties; they avoid the *jinn* and are of the opinion that the main agent of disease is the *jinn*'s penetration into the body. *Porkhans*, however, possess the capability to recognise *jinns* and have them driven out from the body and living environment of the patient (Maghsudi 2003a: 65).

There are two groups of *ishans* among the Turkmens: one of normal *ishans* and the other of *ishans* with exceptional aptitudes. The first group consists of those who have attended theological school in a classical way and received religious teachings. Afterwards, through their own choice of a devotional and ascetic life, they have obtained a spiritual ranking and embarked on the profession of prayer writing for patients. They are thus called 'prayer writers' or 'prayer writer clergymen'. This group is excluded from the scope of this investigation, which concentrates on the second group, the *ishans* (Ishhaans in Turkmen language) who enjoy exceptional capabilities. From this point when we write of *ishans* reference to the second group is to be understood.

The *ishans* are themselves divided into two sub-groups. The first consists of *ishans* who, like the 'normal' *ishan*, have passed lengthy courses of religious studies, as well as performing prayers and *zikrs* (Sufi litanies), practising fasting and leading an ascetic life, and who have undergone a sudden drastic change and spiritual revolution from within. The second sub-group belongs to those who – like *porkhan* – have not received religious teachings or are illiterate, and nevertheless experience an internal unexpected transformation, without willing or attempting this inner reformation. These two sub-groups both gain knowledge of their own new aura and spirituality through psychological upheaval and bodily confusions (such as being struck by sickness). Daydreaming and illusions may either follow or precede this situation. This change of mood is interpreted by their relatives as a spiritual designation to render services to people, and, to reach this end, they have been endowed with special and exceptional abilities. The two groups, despite taking different routes towards their inner revolt, now set foot on a common path to the goal of becoming a healer. First, they should be accepted by a spiritual master or guide who is an experienced veteran *ishan*. This master examines the conditions of the potential candidate's soul, or listens to their claims, in order to confirm if he or she really enjoys the exceptional aptitudes required to be chosen for the task of healing patients, or, on the contrary, to decide that they are a liar or merely a sick person. If they are diagnosed as a chosen one, they are sent to a clergyman who will likewise subject the candidate to certain tests. If they pass, they will be sent to reside in a sacred place to undergo a course of spiritual refinement (usually a shrine that is consecrated for this purpose). The length of this course can be either short or long, depending on the spiritual and corporal states of the candidate, after which they ready themselves to practise healing. However, permission for an independent life is not granted yet. They must stay in their master's house for a while in order to receive the necessary training. When the trainee says that they are prepared to begin work, and this is approved by the master, they can finally become independent and practise healing alone.

The *ishans* – particularly those who have not received religious teachings – have significant similarities with the *porkhan* with respect to their being chosen, gaining exceptional capabilities and undergoing formalities to reach the stage of healing (*ishani*). The main difference rests on their contrasting attitudes towards *jinn*. The *ishans* avoid any kind of contacts with *jinn* and consider them harmful creatures. They therefore have a negative view of *porkhans*, rejecting them totally and believing that they are irreligious because Islam has banned any contact with *jinn*.

Avoiding dance, music and physical touching of the opposite sex, and even separating female gatherings from male ones, are further features that distinguish the two healing methods. Female *ishan* avoid touching a man, observe physical distance from them, and do not accept male patients. Under the influence of the new political and cultural conditions after the Islamic Revolution, they even put aside their Turkmen kind of scarf and, instead, put on a white one, wearing it in such a way that not a single strand of their hair can be seen. Female *porkhan*, by contrast, are still faithful to their Turkmen scarf. Moreover, they do not wear it seriously, or see much importance in covering their hair. They do not even care if their hands touch the hand or the body of a male patient. This is of course a general description. We could find, for example, a female *ishan* who behaves in a free manner and does not abide by such religious restrictions. The influence of social and geographical milieu can be detected in the distinction between *porkhans* and *ishans* and in the apparent differences between *ishans* themselves. The *porkhans* usually live in mountainous areas, in villages far from city life. They are therefore far from the control exerted by the state regarding Islamic rules for women's appearance. Conversely, *ishans* live in villages near a town or in its suburbs, or even in a town. Consequently, the closer they are to city life, the more their observation of the Islamic codes for appearance after the Revolution (for instance, the special way of fixing their white scarf on the head) can be sensed. Whether their adoption of the new specific mode of Islamic appearance is out of compulsion (fearing the risk of losing their position) or due to ideology (their beliefs which distinguish them from *porkhans*) is a subject that needs further investigation.

The *ishans* are committed to the observation of Islamic laws with respect to their appearance and religious duties such as reading the Qur'an, saying *zikrs*, fasting, praying for long periods, giving alms and writing prayers. Illiterate *ishans* try to be in touch with the previous group. Sometimes they draw certain incomprehensible signs and lines on to the patient, as if they have accomplished their religious duty. However, the *ishan* is not a normal prayer reader or writer. He or she is an exceptional entity chosen for the task of healing in a special way.

The *ishan* can diagnose if *jinn* have penetrated the patient's body, and know how to treat this. It is true that they do this through the reading of the Qur'an and praying; however, there are certain formalities and rituals that should be observed, which cannot be done by just anyone. The *ishan* know the *jinn*, separate them from one another and employ a particular mechanism for driving them away from the patient. Moreover, they are in contact with the saints through their dreams and visions gaining insights and inspiration from them, or being told directly what method should be used for curing a disease.

Here, we can detect a similarity to shamanism, a common, yet hidden, aspect that should not be overlooked. Although *ishans* do not establish a natural and real contact with metaphysical forces, this relation is realised indirectly through dreaming. This contact is sometimes accomplished between the state of consciousness and sleeping, so they are not able to exactly describe it. They do not know if these incidents take place when they are asleep or awake. As a result, there are ambiguities which cannot be overcome and, according to some researchers, the boundary between *porkhani* and *ishani* methods of healing is hence not clear cut. This is the reason why some authors consider the *ishans* to be shamans, the same way *porkhans* are.

The manner of writing or reading the prayer, the choice of a suitable time for this purpose, the method of putting the patient on the floor and the position of healer with respect to the patient (beside, over the head or below the feet), as well as the way of organising the objects in the patient's room, opening and closing the door and windows, and discovering any evil eye or harm from neighbours are all carefully observed and coded by the healer, in accordance with the special character of the patient and the *jinn*, as these have a determining effect on the treatment of the disease. Here, we can notice the dramatic and mysterious aspect of certain *ishans*, in which their characters and healing methods become close to those of shamans, insofar as the apparent manifestations – not their rules and principles – are concerned.

Case studies: two healers, porkhan *and* ishan

I now present the biographies of two healers: one a male *porkhan*; the other a female *ishan*. What follows is a narration of interview discussions with them, recorded on cassette tape. The first narrative is based on the dialogue between one of my Turkmen MA students (who was conducting research on *porkhani* ritual, and authored an MA dissertation under my supervision) and Erejeb Porkhan (Khurmali 1999: 78–9). The second is based on the dialogue I had with a female healer called Zubayda Ishan. My aforementioned MA student assisted me during this meeting, serving as translator and guide.

Erejeb Porkhan

Talking about his first encounter with metaphysical forces, Erejeb Porkhan says: 'One day, from behind the window of a religious school, I noticed the presence of two metaphysical creatures. As soon as I saw them, they sat upon my shoulders and asked me to accompany them.' He added that since his father and grandfather became insane because of their disobedience towards the fairy creatures, he decided to avoid the same destiny by complying with their instructions. At the age of 14, in the company of the fairies, he went to the shrine of Takiya Baba.[8] He recounts the rest of story as follows:

> One night, after three days of ascetic fasting, I visited a tall elder. He came beside my bed and massaged my body. It was as if he transferred his power and energy into my being. He then whispered this advice in my ears: 'Do not abandon the five-times prayer under any circumstances. Be clean and always with ablution or ritual washing. Always be a medium. Do not put a fixed price on healing, but accept the money for this as alms.'

He then adds:

> This elder put an army of *jinns* under my control, the number of which reached 72 million, and their leader is a Muslim called Al. He then asked me to call myself a medium and disappeared. I returned to my homeland with this rank.

Erejeb continued by saying that from that date people knew him as a *porkhan*. But he himself did not know what this term meant. The zeal of his *porkhani* practice reached its climax at the age of 20: Erejeb Porkhan is seriously involved with the task of driving evil spirits out of his patient's bodies, and this responsibility becomes his whole life's objective. On the other hand, his problems with people who do not understand him increase day by day, to the extent that he is obliged to decide to leave his home place.

> My actions and gestures during the special ritual of driving away the spirits were something new and unprecedented amongst the people, and they regarded my fortune telling as opposed to the exoteric aspects of their religion. The problem arises because I could not objectify the world of *jinns* and make it accessible to them. Therefore, I had to leave my homeland.

Consequently, Erejeb Porkhan embarks on a wandering life, going from one village to the other with his old donkey and the symbolic paraphernalia of *porkhani* practice such as a sword, a rope, a cloth sack, a spatula, a whip, and wooden pieces which are placed in the *siliqua* sack. He describes his method of healing in this way:

> When I am supposed to go to a village, at the time of sunset and before conducting the ritual, the village alcove is cleared of people and objects, and they place the patient in a corner. I enter the alcove with a whip

in my hand. Throwing an angry look at the whip, dagger and heated spatula, I get near to the patient with this gesture. I lay beside him on the floor, and musicians come and play the music. Various spirits are then attracted by the music and incite me. I therefore cry loudly, and, in order to direct them into the cloth sack hung on the wall, I hang myself from the rope, and through swinging my body I separate the pure spirits from the bad ones, and can feel the internal world of the patient. I then stand with bare feet on the heated spatula, or I lick it or hit the sole of the patient's foot with it. Simultaneously, the village girls form a choir, singing aloud together, and seeking help from God for the exit of the evil spirit from the body of the patient. When struggling with a psychological patient, I can sense the assistance of *jinn* and the transfer of energy by them. I tame the patient, make him submissive, overcome him and give him orders as to what to do or not to do.

In his middle age, Erejeb quit the wandering life, and resided for a while near the village of Yel Cheshme, together with his wife and seven children. However, he got into quarrels with certain neighbours who interfered, and therefore left the place and went to the village of Niyazabad, where he still lives at the time of writing. Erejeb receives the patients in groups, and his hosting of them sometimes last for two or three days.

Erejeb Porkhan is an elderly, short-bearded man of average height. Like a tribe's respected elder, he wears a long white shirt, with a white and yellow turban on his head. The *porkhani* ritual is usually performed after the sunset prayer. During the ceremony, the sound of the *dutar* accompanied by the song of the *bakhshi* (the Turkmens' traditional singer) is broadcast from a cassette tape. Erejeb begins his programme by delicate, dramatic movements, such as swirling and rolling and looking astonished at his surroundings. While accomplishing these acts, he talks to the patient and jokes with them. Then, as a symbolic act, he hits the sword on the backs of the attendees' necks. A rope is hung from the ceiling, and Erejeb hangs himself from it when in a state of ecstasy, and twists around from it. Erejeb also holds a cloth sack which serves as one of his working tools. He says that by turning around the rope, he leads the *jinn* towards his sack. He then gets his head close to the opening of the sack and contacts the spirits. Before the end of the ritual, when Erejeb takes the spatula from the floor, all the attendees of this ceremony, both the patients and their relatives, stretch out their usually bare feet from the folded position. Erejeb then hits their heels hard with the hot spatula. They say that they receive a good feeling throughout their bodies with this stroke. At another stage of the ritual, Erejeb takes his sword and asks one of those present in the gathering to help him. He gives two wooden pieces to

Figure 6.2. Erejeb Porkhan during a healing ritual, village of Yel Sheshme, 1975 (Photograph: Manijeh Maghsudi and Behrooz Ashtray).

them. At this moment, all the women present bend their heads towards the front and in this way, their long woven hair comes forward, too. They then put aside their Turkmen scarf. Erejeb asks his assistant to place two wooden pieces at the back of each woman's neck, which he hits with his sword. This is repeated with everyone attending the ceremony, men and women, patients and their relatives alike (Figure 6.2).

Zubayda Ishan

Zubayda is a 45-year-old woman who was married at the age of 19, and now has 6 children. She began healing patients when she was 35, and she describes her story as follows:

> In a state of sleep or half-sleep, I saw a man with a turban on his head. I sometimes fainted, too. At one of the nights of the Qadr event,[9] when I was dreaming about such persons, they woke me up and whispered into my ears, saying: 'Zubayda! From now onwards, you should heal people.'

For a while Zubayda was astonished, and she discussed the matter with her husband and relatives. At first, her husband took a negative view of the event.

But, seeing Zubayda's spiritual states frequently leading to weakness, fainting and fits of ecstasy, he became frightened. Zubayda realised that she could not decline the responsibility that was being placed upon her shoulders, that is, to heal the sick. Her husband finally reached the same conclusion and understood that there was no other way forward but to grant his permission for this practice (Maghsudi 2003b: 283). However, Zubayda did not find the courage and capability within herself to take on this responsibility. She constantly told herself 'I am not literate, nor have I a master to train me. So, how can I heal?' She then continues:

> One night I slept, having these thoughts in my mind, and dreamed that a blind little girl asked me to cure her. I did not know how to do that. I heard a voice saying to me, 'Zubayda Ishan! Read out the verse *Alam tara kayfa* of the Qur'an.'[10] Without knowing how to read the Qur'an, I read out the verse and began the job of healing with these verses.

Concerning a girl haunted by *jinn* who was not accepted by the mental hospital, she says:

> I took her to the shrine of Takiya Baba and fastened her to the tomb frame with a band, and opened it the next day. I was inspired to let the patient go. The girl, who suffered from an arrhythmic heart, became sound and well. Her parents invited me to their home and celebrated this happy occasion.

The following statements clearly reveal that their *ishani* healing method is different from that of *porkhani*, insofar as the kind of relation with metaphysical forces is concerned. Zubayda says:

> I don't have a *jinn* in my possession or under my control. It is through reading Qur'anic verses that I exorcise the *jinn* from the patient's body. I am with god. Of course, the *jinn* want me to be with them, but I have never accepted their request and will not do that. I follow the saints and imams.

Conclusion

All the above terms and expressions indicate people who enjoy metaphysical or supernatural powers and are in contact with the metaphysical world. This is a world that cannot be seen with the merely physical eye. Only shamans can observe it, communicate with the forces there and take advantage of their power for their own purposes, such as healing patients (Maghsudi, Manijeh 2006c: 7). The *porkhans* take these metaphysical forces into their possession, and through following the instructions given by these forces, as well as commanding them to lead toward their goals, they reach their objectives. Turkmen Sahra's *porkhans* have these shamanic characteristics, and they are hence considered by Turkmens to be blasphemous, behaving in the opposite way to that of approved, exoteric Islam.

Shamanic beliefs and ideologies are deeply rooted in Turk tribes, and exist in a special way among Moguls. All Turk tribes believe that shamans regard themselves as mediums between human beings and metaphysical forces or creatures. They are in contact with the other world, and talk about it. With their immigration to the western part of Asia they eventually become Muslims, leading to the presence of Islamic tenets and conventions, as well as a series of Islamic cultural dispositions in the shamanic ritual, thus causing changes to it. What we observe today in *porkhani* ritual is in fact a combination of shamanism, Islamic beliefs and Turk tribal culture.

Shamans and *porkhans* are known as magicians, according to the beliefs of Turk tribes (Asghar 1976: 388). They are people who can cure patients, not just treat them. They recognise the spirits or *jinns* as the factor causing the sickness, and through exorcising them they drive the disease out of the patient's body. It is said that the magicians suck the blood of the patient to cure them. Similarly, in *porkhans*' ritual, something is taken out of the throat of the patient. In a rare *porkhani* ceremony, I witnessed a *porkhan* place a patient on the floor and begin sucking his mouth, as if he was taking the agent of the disease out of his throat, the same way that magicians suck the patient's blood to cure the disease. Erejeb Porkhan, by putting his hand down the throat of the patient, transforms the pain or the disease into a small ball of fleece or interlocked hair, and takes it out of the patient's body. These similarities are significant and need further research.

It should be pointed out that when treatment is referred to here, what is meant are the methods and procedures practised to overcome the disease. In other words, through experience and repetition, trial and error, practitioners have worked out methods and techniques for this purpose. However, in the case of cure, treatment is done without using the methods gained through experience, and without an intermediate stage, that is, the treatment occurs automatically. For this reason it can be said that the patient is cured rather than treated.

It is also necessary to mention a delicate point in connection with the difference between a physician and a healer such as a *porkhan*. A patient asks the doctor to cure him. He does not necessarily have a particular ideology or a certain faith, and considers the treatment one of the physician's duties and specialisations, and thus expects him to give him treatment. However, when a patient asks a healer (*porkhan* or *ishan*) to cure him they go to the healer with a strong faith and belief, seeking the cure, and the treatment happens automatically without an intermediate stage. The patient does not regard the treatment as one of the duties of *porkhan*, but asks to be cured. This process, that is, the patient's request to be cured by the *porkhan* and the intervention of ideology and belief, constitute the recovery process. In other words, the patient's belief and faith are inactive, playing no role in the physician's treatment; whereas the patient, through their faith and belief, has an active and determining presence in front of *porkhan* during the whole process of cure.

Bibliography

Asghar, Agha Beigui (1976). 'Turkmen Society'. *Journal of Sahand*, 4, 386–91.

Ashtiyani, Abbas (1973). *Mongol history*. Tehran, Amir Kabir.

Azami, Rad and Gunbad, Durdi (2003). *Nigahi ba hayat-i madi va manaviya Turkamanha* (A Glance at Turkmen's Material and Spiritual Lives). Mashad, Mashad University Press.

During, Jean (1988). 'Govat: ecstatic ritual in performance'. *Journal of Presentation* 43(2), 37–57.

Guli, Amin-Allah (1987). *Seyri dar tarikh-i siyasi-ijtima'iya Turkamanha* (A Review of the Historical and Social History of the Turkmen). Tehran, Nashr-i Ilm, pp. 1–256.

Ibn-i Fazlan (1985). *Safar-nama Ibn-i Fazlan* (Travelogue of Ibn-i Fazlan). Translated by Abulfazl Tabatabai. Tehran, Nashr-i Bunyad-i Farhang-i Iran.

Khurmali, Abdulhakim (1999). *Barrisiya Darmangariya Bumiya Ja'ma'iya Turkman: ayin-i Porkhani* (An Analysis of the Indigenous Healing Method in the Turkmen Community: the Porkhani Ritual). Tehran, Iran, Azad University of Iran.

Lugashva, Bibi Rabi'ia (1979). *Turkmanha-yi Iran* (Iranian Turkmen). Translated by Husayn Tahvili and Cyrus Izadi. Tehran, Shabahang.

Maghsudi, Manijeh (1989). 'Khanavada va Khishavandi dar miyan-i Turkamanha' (Family and kinship bonds among Turkmen). Ph.D. thesis, Sorbonne University.

———(2003a). 'Darman-e Bumiya Turkmanha' (Indigenous healing methods of the Turkmen). *Sub-Regional Training Workshop: Role of Women in Safeguarding and Transmission of the Intangible Culture Heritage*. Tehran, UNESCO.

———(2003b). *Teknikha-yi gunaguna darmāangari dar miyan-i Turkmanha: dar zan va farhang* (Different healing methods among the Turkmen: among women and in the culture). Tehran, Afkar.

———(2006a). *Tanavvu-yi farhangi, kisrat-i qumi va hambastagiya ijtimayi* (Cultural variety, ethnical multiplicity and social Solidarity). Tehran, UNESCO and Islamshahr Azad University.

———(2006b). 'Different techniques of indigenous healing among Turkmen'. *Mongolia Traditional Medicine Faculty*. Second International Conference on Traditional Medicine – Current Situation and Future Status. Mongolia, Ulaanbaatar, Mongolia Traditional Medicine Faculty, pp. 65–72.

———(2006c). 'Zanan-i darmangar-i bumi dar Turkman-Sahra dar Iran va Qafqaz' (Iranian Women Healers in Turkmen Sahra in Iran and Caucasia). *Armenia: Arya Periodic*, 1, 1–10.

Muin, Muhammad (1993). *Farhang-i farsi* (Dictionary of Persian). Tehran, Farhang-i Ilam, 6 vols.

Rajabiyan Tamak, Sadiq (2004). *Rad-i avham bar asas-i Qu'ran va Sunnat* (Rejection of illusions on the basis of the Qu'ran and of the Islamic tradition). Mashad, Astane Godse Razavi.

Saidi, Ghulam-Husayn (1968). *Ahl-i Hava* (People of the Breath). Tehran, Amir Kabir.

Chapter Seven

SHAMANS IN AFGHANISTAN?[1]

Bernard Dupaigne

September 1974. For two months, we have been living in a little village in northern Afghanistan near Sar-e Pol ('the Head of the Bridge'), in the province of Jaozjan. The region is populated with Uzbeks of the oriental Turkish language group who came to Afghanistan mostly between the eleventh and the sixteenth century. Some are still semi-nomadic and have maintained the old ethnic subdivisions. Most, however, have adopted a sedentary life and now live as agriculturists. The village where we are established[2] is a village of assimilated Arabs who have lost their original language and speak the Persian of Afghanistan, called *farsî*, in the local nomenclature, but *dârî* according to official terminology. Of the Arab groups who arrived in Afghanistan at the very beginning of the Arab conquest (eighth–eleventh centuries) and then, again, in 1401 CE from Baghdad with the army of Tamerlane, those who call themselves Qôreysh (from the name of a major tribe in what is now Saudi Arabia) and still speak Arabic, only presently inhabit four villages in Afghanistan.[3] The other Arabs, all of whom are non-Arabic-speaking, are prominent in the northern regions of the country from the province of Faryab in the west, to the province of Takhar in the east, and are predominantly found in the provinces of Kondoz, Balkh, Samangan and Jaozjan. In this remote area, the Arabs have assimilated Uzbek culture. It could be said that their poverty has allowed them to conserve the ancient traditions better than the Uzbeks themselves. It is these Arabs who live in the most beautiful yurts, and it is their daughters who weave for their dowry the most delicate bands of felt for the yurt and make the finest decorated felt.[4]

Most people are poor and do not work on irrigated fields. They cultivate spring wheat in dry-farmed hills and raise fat-tailed sheep, or Astrakhan lamb. Our Arabs from Sar-e Pol are agriculturists; cultivating wheat in irrigated lands, but mostly in non-irrigated fields. They spend the winter in the same flat-roofed, sundried earthen-brick houses as their Uzbek neighbours. From spring to fall they follow their cattle to pasture, living in yurts; the circular, portable, dwellings of the semi-nomadic Turks of Central Asia, built of willow wood and covered in felt. By the beginning of March, they make the one-hour walk west of the village to the nearby hills and stay there until mid-June. Afterwards, they migrate upwards to about 500 metres above sea-level looking for green pastures, a six-hour walk to the south, where they stay two and a half months on non-privatised land that is owned by the government (though each year they return to the same plots which are traditionally reserved to their families). While moving back toward their villages before the coming of the cold, they spend one or two more months in the yurt, east of the houses, with the door oriented towards the rising sun. Since the mid 1960s, they have spent winters in houses.

We were trying to meet an exorcist, or a shaman, a *bakhshî*, whom we were told lived in the area. The term *bakhshî*, well known in northern Afghanistan and in Turkic Central Asia, means 'priest', 'shaman' or 'scribe'.[5] The copyist of the 'Miraj-nâma', the impressive manuscript conserved in the National French Library in Paris is signed with the name *bakhshî*.[6] The *bakhshî* is, therefore, if not necessarily a scholar, at least a knowledgeable man, having studied under a master who, after initiating him, bestows upon him his powers and authorises him to practise the art of healing.

The healing ceremony, though not clandestine, is performed in private homes by the *bakhshî*. The local men of religion, that is the mullahs, or those in charge of the mosques, take a dim view of the rite as a 'practice of the ignorant'. The local Islam itself, however, is superficial and impregnated with old superstitions. Pilgrimages to the tombs of saints are still widely practised and at the time of festivals many people gather around the shrines and attend family picnics. After the prayers, the circumambulation around the tomb, and the prayers in front of candles or oil lamps burning in the crevice of the grave, both men and women share a meal, but in separate places.

In a region where the sanitary conditions are appalling, the mullahs are often called to pray at the bedside of the sick. They invoke the name of Allah and give the sick person a talisman, *tawiz*; a religious handwritten text, meticulously enclosed in a small leather case which is held by, or affixed to the clothing of, the sick. This talisman may contain, in addition to the written blessing, some earth taken from the foot of a nearby saint's tomb or a splinter of the tree that grows at the head of the tomb. To this tree are affixed *ex votos*, or fragments of coloured cloth each of which carries a prayer. Each saint has his own specialisation: curing the blind, treating infertility or mental illnesses.

So as to not provoke the anger of the mullahs, no healing ceremonies are carried out during the sacred month of fasting, Ramadan. Likewise, the villagers affirm that 'the *bakhshî* can cure only if God allows it. If he doesn't authorise such a practice, how can the patient be cured? The sick is cured only if God makes the situation better; if he doesn't want it to happen, nothing will be healed!'

We finally met our *bakhshî* in his village, thanks to the help of his nephew who is the chief of the village. His nephew was sceptical about the alleged powers of his uncle. He said that his uncle is not very strong and that he 'doesn't have any powers'. There are also other *bakhshî* in the province, both Arabs and Uzbeks. Two female *bakhshî* practise in the area, one of whom is Arab, and the other Uzbek. But a male *bakhshî* is also able to heal female patients.

We wanted to see one of the rituals performed by a *bakhshî*. It was therefore our responsibility to visit his home and ask for permission. His protective spirits are very powerful, he told us, and the rule is that those who need his help must come to him, personally. He was cautious about us and didn't want to linger too long in meeting us. He was frightened, he said, that his *jinns* would punish him by making him sick. The long negotiations come to a close during our third visit, when we payed the fees of the ceremony: a hen for the sacrifice, one kilogram of butter, and two *gaz* (about two metres) of white cotton cloth. We had then only to wait for a sick person to ask to be healed.

The initiation of the shaman

In order to perform healing ceremonies, the *bakhshî* must have been previously initiated. This ceremony gives him the legitimacy and the power to face the mysterious powers that he will meet along the long and symbolic journey he will undertake in the course of the healing ceremony. One doesn't choose to become a *bakhshî*, he or she is claimed by supernatural forces and must obey the message coming from the other worlds. Our *bakhshî* was called in his infancy. His mother, starting with his conception, prayed and fasted for nine months and nine days, because all her previous newborn babies had died at a very young age. When he was still a small child, the *jinns* attempted to throw him off the horse he was riding and he was very scared. In adolescence, he was ill for an entire year with a terrible headache, and he was unable to walk. His hands stayed twisted and he was unable to work. He was ill for seven years; seven years during which he was unable to eat salt (it means that he could not eat properly cooked rice and other foods). 'The *jinns* can weaken the people', he said. They sent him dreams to invite him to come join them. A master exorcist in the area realised that the young boy would not heal until he responded to the call of the spirits. Thus, this master initiated the boy when he was only 18 years old. Having completed the initiation with 'the belt tied, and the waist knotted', his health returned to him: 'the *jinns* had sent the sickness to me', he said. 'When I accepted and responded to their invitation, I was cured; my body once again became strong'. It is worth mentioning that before his initiation, the young boy already possessed, as he said, exceptional talents: 'if someone had stolen something in the region, I knew who did it. When a dispute broke out, I knew the reason'.

The initiation of a *bakhshî* is similar to the traditional rite of an artisan.[7] This ceremony of initiation, called *kamarbandî* (tying of the belt) consists of the fastening of a belt round the coat of the young apprentice; this action will make him a 'man', an initiate. The belt is an essential element of men's clothing and symbolises the man's strength. A man without a belt is simply not dressed. He is nothing more than an irresponsible child that hasn't been well tended to. The belt is the tie that connects the artisan to generations of masters who came before him. In the same way, it links the *bakhshî* to his or her predecessors. The initiation ceremony of the *bakhshî* is called *kamar basta kardan*, literally 'tying the waist'. The spiritual master, *ûstâd* or *khalîfa*, of our *bakhshî* is an old Arab from a neighbouring village (who was himself initiated by an Arab master from the nearby village of Baghali), who came with his assistant to tie our *bakhshî*'s waist and in doing so, linked him to the lineage of the masters. Our *bakhshî* was thus authorised to heal.

The initiation ceremony took place at night. A cow and a lamb having been sacrificed, the *bakhshî* tells me that:

> I submitted myself to two masters; I put myself under their feet and the masters tied my waist (with a belt). Then, they did the benedictions (*khayrât* – thanksgiving) and I distributed the food to my neighbours in the village. I also gave them the blood of the animals. My masters didn't tell me what I was supposed to do during the rituals, neither the words nor the prayers. After the initiation, at the start of the first ceremony that I officiated, the *jinns* came by themselves. That which needed to be done was written upon my own body.

The *bakhshî* finishes, perhaps exaggerating a bit, 'since then, I, myself, have initiated twenty other *bakhshî*'. If the powers of a spiritual master are strong enough, he or she may be able to perform the initiation him or herself.

'Of the two female *bakhshî* who practise in the district, I initiated one and the other was initiated in the city', he continues. I am told that the female *bakhshî*s dress in a white cotton robe and prepare a torch by covering one end of a stick in fat, which they then light and pass along the length of the body of the patient. This is called a ceremony of the lit torch, *âlâs*, 'flame', as described by Pierre Centlivres.[8] I, however, have not seen such a ritual performed by our male *bakhshî* during the healing ceremony.

The healing ritual

We will be taking part in a ceremony that is still practised in northern Afghanistan in the populations of Turkish origin.[9] The seance normally takes place in the evening, in the house of the sick person, with the participation of only family members of the patient. Because of the demands of photography, this seance will take place during the day and we have been authorised to record the entirety of the ceremony.[10]

The women of the family of the sick person are preparing thin, round wheat pancakes that are fried in oil and will be distributed to all the participants as a symbol of communion. The wife of the *bakhshî* is making 20 candles, *luqtcha*, by rolling cotton wicks around wood sticks. She has to stretch the cotton fibres collected from the cotton plants in the garden, and wrap them around a stick while rolling it along the edge of a glazed clay pot.

One woman brings butter, with which the *bakhshî* coats the wicks using a piece of cotton. He then arranges the 20 candles in a ceramic bowl filled with ashes from the household, laid on the ground on the two *gâz* clothes of white cotton. This will stay between the healer and his patient as a symbolic separation throughout the ceremony. The *bakhshî* then smears more butter on the upper section of the bundle of the wicks that have been gathered together and crosses three long cotton wicks at the top of the candles. He repeats to me several times that I will be frightened during the ritual, because the *jinn* spirits will appear.

The patient is a woman who suffers from headaches. The audience is composed uniquely of women from her family accompanied by their young children. The sick woman is squatting, dressed in a robe of red cotton with large floral print (the fabric is imported from nearby Uzbekistan). A red, cotton scarf printed in Pakistan covers her hair. Outside, the female neighbours of the family wait with their children.

The *bakhshi* draws several black points on the feet, hands and breasts of the sick woman who is still squatting. The ink is made of a mix of indigo dye and a few drops of blood taken from an incision on the still-living hen. The *bakhshî*, a man of 53 years, has a long salt-and-pepper beard. He is dressed all in white with bare feet, loose cotton pants and a long white cotton shirt that is open on the right shoulder in the Uzbek fashion and tied with a cotton belt.

After having said *bismillâh*, 'in the name of God', an Islamic prayer that precedes every new action, he takes his belt, which had been placed in the drum (*dâyra*), and ties it around his waist. The *dâyra* is a large tambour drum with a wooden frame that is covered by a sheepskin, this one without any ornamental designs. The *bakhshî* will play this drum during his trance. This musical instrument is normally reserved for women in northern Afghanistan.[11] There are iron rings affixed to the inside of the wooden frame that sound when the tambour is beaten. The *bakhshî* places a leather whip in the *dâyra* and wraps his head in white fabric that is fixed behind the head by a string, hiding the top of his head and his ears. The preparations have lasted one hour.

The sick woman opens her hands at eye-level in the sign of a prayer while the healer is on his feet, hands apart, intoning the ritual Islamic prayer. The question is if this prayer, and the other Islamic incantations that will reoccur regularly throughout the healing ceremony are a form imposed by the dominant religion, a concession to Islam meant to make the ancient, non-orthodox practices less scandalous, or if in fact the healing ceremony has inserted itself in popular Islamic practices. The *bakhshî* is beating the drum with his hand, singing and invoking Sheytân (Satan). Standing, he chants and uses a match to light the cotton wicks that have been coated with butter. This flame will separate, for the length of the ceremony, the patient and the healer.

The *bakhshî* chants incantatory formulas that are incomprehensible, but we are able to make out Islamic words and invocations to Allah and his prophets. His voice swells and he shakes his head, grumbling, murmuring and imitating indistinct cries of animals. The tension and the emotion mount. The *bakhshî* seizes the *dâyra*, which has been lying on the floor between him and the flame.[12] Later, he will reveal to me that his own master performed healing ceremonies with a *kobuz*, a two-stringed fiddle with an open sound box, but that he lost it when a flood carried it away. Nowadays, there are no longer craftsmen who are skilled enough to make a *kobuz*, and the *jinns* would beat them if they tried.

While uttering incantations, the *bakhshî* shakes and beats the *dâyra* with its back-side turned towards him. Squatting down, he puts the *dâyra* in front of the fire and flings himself backwards. He cries out, shakes his head and beats his skull with the frame of the drum. He shakes his head and, with his whip in one hand, he beats the drum, facing the sick woman. He coughs, beating harder and harder on the drum. He greets a spirit who has just appeared, and defends himself against demons and evils spirits. He appeals to his masters for aid by invoking their names; when they appear, he greets them. The *bakhshî* is engaged in a voyage in which he will fight, with the help of his allies, the spirits who have brought on the illness. He invokes the creatures from the 'salty sea' and saints (*hazrat*). While chanting, he beats the women and everyone else in the room (except us) with the edge of the *dâyra*. He invokes the Prophet Mohammed, the mountains he has climbed, and the valley of the river Helmand. He says 'hello' (*salam aleykhum*) to a *jinn* from 'Arabia' that he has just met. He invokes the spirits of protection and evil spirits, beating his head with the drum. While uttering a litany, he stands up straight and breaths upon the sick to draw out the evil spirit (Figure 7.1). The language that he uses is mostly incomprehensible. He crouches down again and resumes his litany while beating the drum. Standing up, he places himself to the left of the patient and orders the evil spirits to leave her body. Then he stops, looking up towards the sky, and cries out again. He makes noises with his nose, swallows, defends himself against some danger and bites down on his own wrists while beating his head. He imitates animal noises. He is most probably meeting animal spirits (perhaps a chicken, 'cot, cot, cot'). He beats the woman with his *dâyra* while appealing to the prophets of Islam, the saintly men (*Khoja*), the 'angel (or fairy) of the mountains' (*peri-kohistân*), and other fairies. He invokes the help of the 120,000 prophets: Isâ (Jesus), Mûsa (Moses), Dâoûd (David) and even the Prophet Ingel (!), 'the Gospel', and many other saints and *pîrs* (masters). At one moment, the *bakhshî* names us and his wife throws him a terrified glance. One hour later, he rubs the ears of the sick in the name of the prophets, breathes and taps her back, invoking the 72 animals (the 72 animal *jinns*). The ceremony finally ends with an '*Amin*' (Amen) which is then repeated in chorus by everyone present.

The *bakhshî* puts his belt and the whip in the frame drum. The cotton wicks have burned down completely (Figure 7.2). After some Islamic formulas, his voice returns to normal. The woman is still squatting, not moving. The other women keep silent, motionless. They didn't participate in the ceremony. The *bakhshî* is exhausted. He distributes the fried cakes to each one of the women present at the ceremony and to the neighbours outside. The hen hasn't been sacrificed; they have taken only a small amount of his blood to draw the signs on the body of the sick woman. Later, it will be killed and cooked, its meat distributed to the relatives and the neighbours of the sick as a benevolent act (*kheyrât*).

No price has been fixed for the ceremony, but I give the *bakhshî* 500 afghanis to thank him, the equivalent of 7 chickens or of 70 kilograms of wheat. Usually, when the *bakhshî* is brought to Sheberghan, the capital of the province, 60 kilometres in the north, he is paid twice this price. The woman doesn't yet know if the 'cure' has helped. She will only know its effects later. However, she is concerned about our presence during the ritual; she fears the revenge of the *jinns*: 'if the healer is not pure, the *jinns* will punish him'. Our *bakhshî* also seems scared. *Jinns* are dangerous; if they want to take revenge on him, they will cut him in two. In the end, he asks me not to play the

Figure 7.1. The healer standing in front of the sick patient and invoking the spirits, Northern Afghanistan, district of Jaozjân, 1974 (Photograph: B. Dupaigne).

recordings that I have taken while still in Afghanistan, 'otherwise the *jinns* will punish me'. I can, however, play them abroad.

The *bakhshî* has no memory of what he said and did during the ceremony, not even which languages he used: 'the spirits came and took me', he says. Nevertheless, he knows that they came in great numbers to meet him. He saw 7,000 of them speaking every language there is. 'Only God knows how many came to visit me'. He only knows that he was in the mountains, at a *ziârat*, the tomb of a saint; this is a 'dangerous place', he says, and 'any other man who went there would die'. His task achieved, the *jinn* that was tormenting the sick woman has been appeased and has returned to his home.

Figure 7.2. The cotton wicks have been lit and the healer says incantations while beating his drum, Northern Afghanistan, district of Jaozjân, 1974 (Photograph: by B. Dupaigne).

Spirits and protectorate spirits

There are, says the *bakhshî*, 72 different kinds of *jinns*: those on earth and those of the sky. Each of them can make men sick. If a man inadvertently touches a *jinn*, he will be sick in the part of the body that was in contact with the spirit; the *jinns* can make any part of the body sick. He can call a specific *jinn* by beating the *dâyra* with its favourite tune. He can then ask this spirit which *jinn* has made the patient sick.

His protectorate saints allow him to defend himself while surrounded by all of these spirits. He, himself, benefits from seven protective spirits, the Seven Masters *pâdeshâh* ('kings') that were transmitted to him by his spiritual master. Their names are, in the order given by the *bakhshî*:

- Sâqî: a name.
- Mâmâ: 'maternal uncle'.
- Zard Pari: 'the yellow angel'.
- Mollâh Bâbû (*Bâbû* being the informal term for 'mister' in India).
- Yûnis Ayjân: from *ajän*, 'spirit-master' in Mongolian (a term probably derived from '*jinn*'). Yunos is the Persian equivalent to Jonas: so Yûnis Ayjân should therefore mean the 'spirit of Jonas'.
- Almasti: Al, 'scarlet', is the pre-Islamic she-devil of the Turks. Albasti is the king of the *jinns* in Uzbek tradition. He is always a male, according to

Gunnar Jarring.[13] Besides, Albasti, on the other hand, is known among the Turks, the Kirghizs, the Kurds and the Iranians as the 'scarlet illness'. The scourge of death, or the puerperal fever which must be kept out of the house for the first 40 days after giving birth (*al*: scarlet; *basti*: crushed).[14]

- Sheyâtûn: probably derived from Sheytân, Satan. Sheyâtûn is his most powerful protector: 'he spends six months of the year under the sea, and the other six months in the clouds'. It is he who indicates to the *bakhshî* which spirit is responsible for the ailment of the sick person.

In one single healing ceremony, two *bakhshî* cannot officiate together unless one of them is the master who initiated the other. The powers of two *bakhshî* who were initiated separately are antagonists. 'They will fight each other' inevitably, because their spiritual masters are not the same. An exorcist can treat, if he is powerful, two patients in the same house. If his power is less strong, two *bakhshî* will be necessary. But if the sick are from two separate houses, two separate ceremonies should be organised. However, there is no *bakhshî* who is able to heal heart disease. In the end, upon my request, the *bakhshî* specified that he is not a wizard, *jâdû*, for he doesn't know how to prepare love potions or talisman against enemies.

Using iron in the ritual called here *bâqum* demands a special initiation from the master, an authorisation that is not given to all the *bakhshî*. The ritual of the shovel, i.e. 'to make the shovel glow red' (*bîl sukhte kardan*), is only performed for the most grave cases and can only take place at night. It is expensive and requires two seances on two consecutive nights. Iron is a precious and rare substance that is the product of a mysterious transformation that can only be the work of the gods and plays a prominent role in shamanistic ceremonies in Siberia, Mongolia and Central Asia. According to Evelyne Lot-Falck, 'iron is the protector *par excellence* against hostile forces, but it scares all different kinds of spirits indiscriminately'.[15]

Our *bakhshî* has received the authorisation to perform such a ritual from his master, and he tells us the details of the ceremony. He puts two or three *gaz* of white sheet over the head of the sick person. After having sacrificed an animal (a lamb or an ox), he heats two iron shovels until they are red hot. Then, he pours a cup of water on the shovels and guides the steam produced towards the sick and the participants in the seance. Only this ritual can expel the spirit of a 'worshipper of fire', *âtech parast* or *alau parast*: if it is a *jinn* 'worshipper of fire' (that is to say, one who follows the ancient religions of the Iranian plateau) who is making the person sick ('to tie a man', *adam basta kardan*), only the ceremony of fire and iron can deliver him.

This ritual is dangerous for the healer who performs it, for he can be killed by the *jinns* if 'he doesn't have a pure heart', meaning if he is not in a state of ritual purity. Our *bakhshî* has not authorised the women of the region whom he initiated to heat the shovel until it is red hot and direct the vapour over the sick person (we might ask if women generally have the right to perform such a ritual).

In conclusion, the significance of this ritual poses a problem of methodology. Is this a ceremony left over from Siberian or Mongolian shamanism, or simply a cure intended to expel the evil spirits from a sick? Is it the remnant of an ancient tradition that was forbidden by Islam or a local elaboration associated with heterodox Islam, impregnated with old popular practices? In Central Asia, similar healing rituals have been observed among Kazakhs, Kirghizs, Uzbeks, Turkmens and the Uyghurs in Xinjiang.[16] We find in the course of this ceremony a number of classic elements of Siberian and Mongolian shamanistic practices: the role of fire, of light, and of iron; sickness and dreams; the signs that the spirits have chosen someone to perform the ritual; the initiation as a link to the lineage of masters; protectorate spirits who help the healer when he or she meet evil spirits; travel in search of evil spirits in order to fight them; and the return to earth at the end of the cure. Nonetheless, this could be nothing but the expulsion of an evil spirit from the body that it torments. Nothing seems to hold the evil spirit after it is expelled from the body; there is nothing into which it is transferred after the expulsion. In the end, this ritual seems to be more aimed at expelling the spirit from the body that it is tormenting than a ritual journey to the hereafter in order to bring back the wandering soul of a sick person to his body.

Obviously, the *bakhshî* is not, like the Siberian shaman, searching in the sky for the scattered souls of the sick, a situation that produces instability and sickness. Finally, in the ritual of the *bakhshî*, the sick person remains passive and never participates in his recovery. This is not the case in the Siberian ritual where the sick person, along with the other people present at the ceremonial, are implicated in the search for the stolen soul. The *bakhshî* ceremony observed in Afghanistan could therefore be interpreted as the Islamisation of pre-Islamic rites with the invocations of the Prophets of Islam and the orthodox formula and rituals.

Pierre and Micheline Centlivres, two renowned ethnologists and specialists of Afghanistan, observed the same ritual of 'playing of the *bakhshî*' in May 1968, in the wide oasis of Tash-Qorghan, also in Northern Afghanistan. The urban and rural populations of this area are composed of Tajiks, Uzbeks and Arabs. Of the three *bakhshî* that they met, two are poor Arabs, of the same poor Arabs that we met who don't own very much agricultural land and who have preserved the ancient Uzbek traditions better than the other Central Asian ethnicities. The initiation ritual is similar to the ritual I have described in this chapter: white clothing, cotton wicks dipped in oil and wrapped around a willow stick, Qur'anic benedictions and invocations to God, stances and trances and animal cries, calling to the spirits, and the use of a musical instrument to beat the sick person. But here, in the oasis of Tash-Qorghan, the musical instrument used by the *bakhshî* is different. Instead of a drum, the healer plays the *kobuz*, the two-stringed horsehair fiddle with an open soundbox, decorated with pieces of iron, without any skin on the soundboard. This *kobuz* is present, both as a ritual and a profane instrument in many other areas of Central Asia, particularly among the Uzbeks.[17]

Bibliography

Barfield, Thomas J. (1981). *The Central Asian Arabs of Afghanistan. Pastoral Nomadism in Transition*. Austin, University of Texas Press.

Basilov, Vladimir N. (1992). 'Le Chamanisme islamisé des peuples d'Asie Centrale'. *Diogène*, Paris, 158, pp. 7–19. Reedited in Roberte Hamayon (ed.). *Chamanisme*. Paris, PUF Quadrige, 2003, pp. 127–145.

Çagatay, Babur, and Sjoberg, Andrée F. (1955). 'Notes on the Uzbek culture of Central Asia'. *The Texas Journal of Science*. 7:1, 72–112.

Castagné, Joseph (1923). 'Survivances d'anciens cultes et rites en Asie Centrale'. *Revue d'Ethnographie*, 15, 245–55.

_____(1930). 'Magie et exorcisme chez les Kazak-Kirghizes et autres peuples turks orientaux'. *Revue des Études islamiques*, 4, 53–151.

Centlivres, Pierre; Centlivres-Demont, Micheline, and Slobin, Mark (1971/1988) 'A Muslim Shaman of Afghan Turkestan', *Ethnology*. 10:2, 160–73. Reedited in Centlivres, Pierre, and Centlivres-Demont, Micheline. *Et si l'on parlait de l'Afghanistan?* Neuchâtel-Paris, Ed. de l'Institut d'ethnologie – Maison des sciences de l'homme, 149–67.

_____(1972). *Un bazar d'Asie Centrale, Forme et organisation du bazar de Tashqurghan*. Wiesbaden, Dr Ludwig Reichert Verlag.

Centlivres-Demont, Micheline (1997). 'Un corpus de *risâla* du Turkestan afghan'. In Grandin, Nicole and Gaborieau Marc, (eds). *Madrasa, La transmission du savoir dans le monde musulman*. Paris, Arguments, 84–91.

Chadwick, Nora K., and Zhirmunsky, Victor (1969). *Oral Epics of Central Asia*. Cambridge, Cambridge University Press.

Dupaigne, Bernard (1976 a). 'Yourtes de jeunes mariés dans le nord de l'Afghanistan'. *Etudes turques 1. Actes du XXIXe Congrès International des Orientalistes*. Paris, 49–54.

_____(1976 b). *Musiques classiques et populaires d'Afghanistan*. Disk 33, Paris, SFPP.

_____(1982). 'Les Arabes arabophones d'Afghanistan'. In Jean-Pierre Digard, (ed.). *Le Cuisinier et le Philosophe. Etudes d'ethnographie historique du Proche-Orient. Hommage à Maxime Rodinson.* Paris, Maisonneuve et Larose, 89–96.
Farhadi, Ravan (1967). 'Languages'. *The Kabul Times Annual.* Kabul, 83–5.
Findeisen, Hans (1951). 'Zur Kenntnis des Perichonswesens bei der sesshaften Bevölkerung Ost-Turkestans'. *Der Forschungsdienst,* 4, 1–15.
Hamayon, Roberte (1990). *La Chasse à l'âme, Esquisse d'une théorie du chamanisme sibérien.* Nanterre, Société d'Ethnologie.
Jarring, Gunnar (1939). *On the Distribution of Turk Tribes in Afghanistan.* Lund, Lunds Universitets Årsskrift, 35, 4.
Kieffer, Charles M. (1976–80). 'L'Arabe et les Arabophones de Bactriane (Afghanistan)'. In *XXe Congrès international des Sciences Humaines en Asie et en Afrique du Nord,* Mexico, 9 August 1976, 1–20. Published as 'L'Arabe et les Arabophones de Bactriane (Afghanistan): I. Situation ethnique et linguistique'. *Die Welt des Islams, International Journal for the Study of Modern Islam,* N. S., 20, 3–4, 1980, 178–96.
Krueger, J. (ed.) (1963). *The Turkic Peoples: Selected Russian Entries from the Great Soviet Encyclopedia.* Bloomington, University of Indiana Press.
Levchine, Alexis de (1840). *Description des hordes et des steppes des Kirghiz Kazaks ou Kirghiz-Kaïssaks.* Paris, Arthus-Bertrand.
Lot-Falck, Évelyne (1953). *Les Rites de chasse chez les peuples sibériens.* Paris, Gallimard.
Massé Henri (1938). *Croyances et coutumes persanes.* Paris, G.-P. Maisonneuve.
Menges, Karl (1968). *The Turkic Languages and People: an Introduction to Turkic Studies.* Wiesbaden, Harrassovitz. Revised edition, Wiesbaden, Harrassovitz, 1995.
Mir Haydar (1436). 'Mirâj-Nâme'. Herât. Copied by Mâlek Bakhchi. Manuscript Suppl. turc 190, Bibliothèque Nationale, Paris.
Nicolas, Michèle (1972). *Croyances et Pratiques populaires turques concernant les naissances.* Paris, Presses orientalistes de France.
Radlov, W. (1870). *Proben der Volklitteratur des türkischen Stämme Süd Sibirens.* St-Petersburg, Commissionäre der Kaiserlicken Akademie der Wissenshaften.
_____(1893). *Aus Sibirien: lose Blätter aus meinem Tagebuche,* Leipzig, T.O. Weigel.
Roux, Jean-Paul (1958). 'Le nom du chaman dans les textes turco-mongols'. *Anthropos,* 53, 1–2, 133–42.
Sana, Sanaoullah (1975). 'Les Arabes (arabophones) dans un milieu turcophone de la Bactriane (Afghanistan)'. In *Acculturation turque dans l'Orient et la Méditerranée, Emprunts et apports.* Paris, Colloque international du CNRS.
Schurmann, H. F. (1962). *The Mongols of Afghanistan, An Ethnography of the Moghols and Related Peoples of Afghanistan.* The Hague, Central Asiatic Studies 4.

Sidky, M. H. (1990). 'Malang, sufis, and mystics. An ethnographic and historical study of shamanism in Afghanistan'. *Asian Folklore Studies*, 49, 275–301.

Slobin, Mark (1976). *Music in the Culture of Northern Afghanistan.* Tucson, The University of Arizona Press.

Snesarev, G. P. (1969). *Relikty do musul'manskich verovanij abrjadov u uzbekov Khorezma.* Moscou, Izdatel'stvo Nauka. English translation (2003): *Remnants of pre-Islamic Beliefs and Rituals among the Khorezm Uzbeks.* Berlin, Schletzer.

Zorz, Annie, and Dupaigne, Bernard (1976). *La Fiancée.* Film 16 mm, 26 mn. col., Paris.

Part II

FROM CENTRAL ASIA TO THE REST OF THE MUSLIM WORLD

Chapter Eight

THE PEOPLE OF THE AIR: HEALING AND SPIRIT POSSESSION IN SOUTH IRAN[1]

Pedram Khosronejad

In the memory of Ghulam Husayn Sa'idi (1936–85)

Iran has a cultural attitude all its own. It is Persian, but not as a matter of ethnicity. And it is predominantly Moslem, but with an entirely different experience of Islam than its brethren in faith. For all its seeming marginality in the world today, this is a place painfully alert to the world; it is where new cultural schemes are born in the wake of unimaginable human calamities, where world religions are hatched, and where people have always found a way to make convivial and compelling lives (Babaie 2008: xi).

Iranian *zar* had not been one of my main research topics, although I had had direct observations of some of the *zar* spirit possession rituals during fieldwork in Bashagard of Hurmuzgan (1994–1996), an arid and exceptional area of the Persian Gulf which remains largely obscure to the eyes of researchers. My aim here is to translate integrally the specific chapter of Ghulam Husayn Sa'idi's book – *Ahl-i Hava* (*The People of the Air*, 1967) – where, for the first time in the history of Iranian studies, he introduces *zar* and its details (Sa'idi 1967: 44–64). Many researchers have previously quoted and even translated some parts of Sa'idi's book, but never before has an entire chapter been translated for use in the wider academic debate regarding *zar* in Iran. Therefore readers of this chapter should know that a great part of this chapter is based directly on Sa'idi's observations, which I have interpreted and explored with my own direct experiences in Bashagard, as well as with comparative data from other research done on this topic.

This chapter contains two major sections. In the first I present *zar* in the view of other anthropologists who have observed this procession spirit ritual in other societies, especially among Muslim communities. The second part is dedicated to *zar* in Iran. This section begins with a brief history of black slavery and slavery trade in Iran. I think, generally speaking, *zar* is an imported belief and procession ritual which came to Iran via black slavery. Basic knowledge about the existence of black slavery in Iran can help the reader understand why communities who practice *zar* in Iran are mostly black Iranians who today live in the south of Iran beside the Persian Gulf. This section will continue and finish with the presentation of *zar* in the south of Iran. Most of this section is based on my translations and interpretations of Sa'idi's text. His own original text (in Persian) is not edited very well and I therefore worked a great deal on his words and also where necessary added the ideas of other anthropologists including myself. I thus consider my chapter to be one of the first ethnographical treatments in English on *zar* in Iran, one in which I also attempt to trace some preliminary connections between *zar cult*, and the history of slaves and slavery in Iran.

Introduction

Anthropologists have long struggled with the problem of how best to conceptualise and account for the observable diversity of religious belief and practice in various Muslim societies and communities. This diversity has been a problem not only for students of Islam but for the Muslim community itself.

Ladislov Holy (1991: 4) proposes that in spite of the fact that Islam does not recognise any institutional religious authority or organisation entrusted with defining the 'official' religious view, 'the relationship between "official" and "popular" religion has not disappeared but has rather become more subtle and intricate'. This distinction has often been used to assess beliefs and ritual practices.[2] Azam Torab (2006: 18) argues that: 'the first, defined as an "official" or "orthodox" Islam, is associated with the learned scholars (*ulama*), who are conventionally men while the second implies a "local" Islam or "popular" practices and beliefs that are primarily linked with women, the illiterate and the rural.' The relationship between religious beliefs and political attitudes among Muslim communities has recently been at the forefront of academic and public debate. The question of whether high levels of piety or religious attendance are associated with certain types of political attitudes and behaviour has been a major area of interest for scholars.[3]

After the Islamic revolution of 1978–79, within Iran, 'which is the only regime in the Muslim world that is directly ruled by the clergy', the place of religion in public and also private arenas is restricted and guided by the Islamic state. Abdolmohammad Kazemipur and Ali Rezaei affirm that 'the state took over all formal institutional spaces of religious collective activity and has since drawn upon religion as the main cultural resource for political legitimisation purposes' (Kazemipur and Rezaei 2003: 357). Also, under the Islamic state, most non-Islamic practices have been considered serious threats to 'Shiite Islam' and, of course, seriously damaging to the 'existence of actual regime in power'.

Away from urban areas, especially among small-scale societies and pastoral nomads, the diversity of religious beliefs and practices in Iran are clearly different. It seems to me that members of such communities effortlessly 'juggle local and multiple identities – villager, tribesman, female – with the broader identity of believer and to legitimize them all' (Eickelman and Piscatori 1990: xiv). I agree with Holy (1991: 1) when he states that 'there are numerous ideological and practical accretions present in all Muslim societies which account for the actual diversity of Islam'.

In such a religious, cultural and political climate, a topic which has not, until now, attracted much serious attention in Iran is that of popular healing practices and spirit possession ceremonies, during which, by the help of healers and mediums, illness can be cured. The position of orthodox Islam and Muslim states, including Iran, regarding these kinds of healing ceremonies is not clear and more research needs to be done in this field. According to Iranian law, every kind of healing is considered an intervention in medical matters; for this reason, formal advertising of any kind of healing is forbidden (Javaheri 2006: 179).

Much of the anthropology of healing, spirit possession in general and also in Muslim communities, has sought to explain it in terms of strategies aimed at overcoming socio-economic disadvantage, or at securing material or social benefit. Some of them interpret spirit possession as the means by which marginal actors in society, often women, gain some measure of authority, agency and sense of community (Doumato 2000; Lewis 1998); in terms of charisma and strategies to gain legitimacy among other healers and clients (Bellér-Hann 2001; Lindquist 2001) or as the response of disillusioned, marginalised groups in post-colonial societies to the incomprehensible processes of globalisation, which leave them destitute while others around them prosper (Comaroff and Comaroff 1999).

Other anthropologists, however, have criticised such explanations as reductive (Boddy 1988; 1994; Kapferer 2003; MacPhee 2003; Nourse 1996).

The analyst, Johan Rasanayagam (2006: 380) believes: 'imposes his or her own system of rationality and so fails to grasp the full significance of sorcery and possession practices. Instead they suggest that possession and sorcery should be examined in their own terms.'

If such non-orthodox and popular activities are based on Islamic beliefs and thoughts and performed during sacred months and rituals attached to such periods, they may be accepted. In her stunning film 'Standard-bearers of Hussein: Women Commemorating Karbala', Ingvild Flaskerud (2003: 35) shows how a female healer in Shiraz, based on Sufi-Islamic thoughts, can open an official private practice for herself and become a popular healer among Shiite families in this city.[4]

But besides such Islamic (Shiite) healing ceremonies, performed mostly among urban societies, in Iran one can still find many healing and spirit rituals and ceremonies which have some connection with popular beliefs but which are not based on Islamic thought or religious texts. There are many reports by anthropologists and ethnographers who did their fieldwork around Iran during the last century where the presence of traditional healers or local doctors in the shape of one religious man or woman (mullah) is mentioned.[5] Many of these popular religious practices in the Islamic world and also in Iran (*cafbini*[6], *falbini*, *ayinabini*, *jinngiri*, *raml- va usturlab*...) are associated with magic.[7] Students of the history of religion have linked some of these magical practices in Islam with pre-Islamic Middle Eastern and East African customs.

One of the most notable of these customs is *zar* (Hentschel 1997; Savage-Smith 2004). Based on my observations in the field, I believe that *zar* belongs to one of the two kinds of popular spiritual healing practices among non-urban societies of Iran.[8] From Abadan to Chabahar, different ethnic groups practise and perform *zar* as a spirit possession ceremony and healing ritual for curing sufferings that are created mostly by supernatural entities, in the majority of cases, *jinns*. Some of these *jinns* can penetrate the body of a person and change the nature of their spirit, their soul and consequently their normal life. According to local beliefs, the only way to be at peace with such extra-human forces is to perform the *zar* ritual.

While we do not have much information or academic reports on *zar* before the Islamic revolution of 1978–79 in Iran,[9] after this period, surprisingly, we start hearing more about this spirit possession ceremony.[10] The Shiite state in Iran not only does not appreciate such non-orthodox and non-Islamic ceremonies, it also, as much as it can, bans them. Despite the fact that *zar* uses drumming, dancing and chanting as a means to cure an illness (thought to be caused by an external spirit which has penetrated the body of the patient), for the majority of its history it has been prohibited by Islam in some Islamic countries (including Iran), and branded as a pagan practice.

Today the only official way that *zar* healers and their groups can perform and show their activities with the permission of state and local governors is in the guise of folkloric music festivals, where they can come with their group onto a stage and perform their rituals as public performances. Of course, local communities continue to organise and perform their private *zar* ceremonies as a healing system based on spirit possession, but for the most part one can be sure that such activities are private and far from public view. Under such clear religious and political pressure, it is unsurprising that the lives of healers and their followers may be endangered if they become too exposed.

What is zar?

Zar, which refers to both the beliefs and practices associated with a certain kind of spirit, is still best known as a type of *healing cult*. As far as research shows, people in communities of different ethnical origins, religious faiths (Muslim, Christian, Falasha) and geographical areas are attracted to *zar*. Today there is a wide variety of beliefs and practices focusing on *zar*, not all of them entailing possession by the spirits. There are also varying indigenous uses of the term *zar*. For instance, it can denote the hierarchy of *zar* spirits, or an individual spirit belonging to this group; the ceremonies focusing on these spirits; a person who is possessed by a *zar* spirit, or the psycho-physical result of possession by a *zar* spirit: malady, trouble, dissociational states, or general feeling of being 'out of sorts'; in sum: 'altered states or capacities'.[11]

Much of the debate until recently has focused on the origins of *zar*, on whether it was derived from an African or Middle Eastern source.[12] There is little controversy among scholars today about the *zar* cult having been introduced into the Middle East during the last century by slaves from Ethiopia, where it is thought to have originated. However, this lack of controversy seems to be based on an unsubstantiated consensus rather than evidence. While there is still a general debate about the origins of *zar*, there is no doubt that it is an exported phenomenon that expanded in some coastal regions in Southern Iran.

S. I. Rahim (1991) sees *zar* as an expression of psychological disorder, whereas I. M. Lewis (1991) prefers to consider it a therapeutic outlet for marginal members of society, especially women. While Michael Lambek (1980; 1993) has focused on *zar* as a distinct system of communication and knowledge, Janice Boddy (1988; 1989) considers it to be a meta-language, a type of counter-hegemony within the larger patriarchal society. Fritz Kramer (1993) believes that the richness and complexity of *zar* rituals and beliefs reinforce the argument that this is indeed a very old ritual system, and one which, furthermore, tells us a great deal about 'the whole spectacle of life with all its contradictions and problems'.

Boddy (1988: 12) also believes that the *zar* rite is a kind of cultural therapy; its curative powers derive less from a virtual experience of trance than from the entire possession context that renders it, and countless other experiences, meaningful. Indeed, an individual's experience of trance is largely constructed by its context. In short, the relevant issue in the case of the *zar* is not trance *per se*, but trance firmly situated in a meaningful cultural context – possession – having medical, social, psychological and often profound aesthetic implications. Before considering these, the nature of the illness that signals possession remains to be addressed (1988: 12).

Generally speaking *zar*, in the sense of possession, is usually (though not exclusively) inherited. It is frequently passed on from parents to their children, or to a close relative, who in this sense 'adopts', or is adopted by, the spirit of their relative. This process may result in certain physical symptoms or disorders reappearing in successive generations. *Zar* is also contagious and may strike at any time (Kenyon 1995: 111).

The *zar* as a *cult* is a relatively recent scholarly device which has been left undefined by most, if not all, writers on the subject.[13] Natvig (1987: 670) argues that this lack of clear definition has reduced the value of many ethnographic reports and much research on what authors have termed *zar* or *zar cult* since the reader is uncertain as to what the author really means.

If the term *zar cult* is to make any sense at all, *cult* must be understood as a typology of religious organisation, and not as referring to cultic devotion (to *zar* spirits). According to Richard Natvig, cult, as a typology of religious groups, designates a group that is at one end of a continuum of religious organisations, ranging from *cult* via *sect* to church. In general terms, *cult* refers to a small, often local, more loosely organised and more individualistic group than the others mentioned (*ibid*). A cult's beliefs and rites tend to make a fundamental break with the main religious tradition of the society in which it exists, without, however, being consciously schismatic. In fact, cults are often little concerned with doctrine and belonging to a cult is independent of allegiance to a particular set of doctrines, and does not preclude membership of other kind of religious groups. Instead, cults tend to lay emphasis on religious rituals and practices, often of an instrumental kind aimed at the achievement of immediate, concrete results or benefits for the individual member, such as mental or physical healing, comfort, or personal ecstatic experiences, rather than long term salvational benefits (Natvig 1987: 670). With this in mind, *zar cult* may be prototypically defined as referring to a religious group of the cult type, where the basis of recruitment of members is *zar* spirit possession and where meaningful long-term relationships with spirits are cultivated by means of a ceremonially provoked spirit possession on a regular basis. An individual becomes a member of the cult by virtue of an initially uncontrolled and, therefore, harmful possession experience, which is brought under control and turned to their advantage, or at least neutralised, by the individual's active participation in a *zar cult* group's recurrent ritual activities. A *zar cult* group is headed by a person who is usually possessed as well, and who, after a period of assisting a senior *zar* group leader, or through the direct intervention of the *zar* spirits, has obtained the specialised skill and knowledge of how to deal with the *zar* spirits (Natvig 1987: 671).

There are ceremonial and cosmological differences and the socio-sexual catchment areas, as well as the consequences of participating in the *zar cult*, vary from place to place. The aim of the cult, however, is the same: the curing of illness or misfortune caused by possession by a species of spirit called *zar*.

Very briefly, the theory of the *zar cult* is that there exists a great number of *zar* spirits, euphemistically called lords, masters, angels or blessed ones. When disturbed they are liable to possess human beings, thereby causing some sort of illness or deviant behaviour patterns in the victim. It is possible, however, to come to terms with the spirits and this is the purpose of the *zar* ritual (Natvig 1987: 57). A person suspected of having been possessed by a *zar* spirit is taken to the local *zar* leader, usually a woman or man, who considers the circumstances of the affliction. To settle the case, the *zar* leader may then suggest a ritual diagnosis, during which contact with the *zar* spirit world is established. If the ritual diagnosis shows that the person is indeed possessed by a *zar* spirit, steps have to be taken to reconcile the spirit. One has to satisfy the spirit's terms for withdrawing the affliction. These terms, which are revealed during the ritual diagnosis, regularly consist of the victim celebrating a sacrificial ceremony for the spirit. Furthermore, in this ceremony the victim has to wear special clothes, ornaments and amulets, the types of which are decided by the particular spirit possessing her/him. In order to maintain the new relationship with the spirit, the possessed person has to renew the agreement with the spirit by repeating the sacrificial ceremony in accordance with this agreement, usually once a year (Natvig 1987: 57–8). Those possessed by *zar* spirits become members, by virtue of that possession, of *zar cult* groups that consist of a community of fellow sufferers, with a *zar* leader who is also possessed. The sacrificial ceremony can be regarded as a ritualisation of the introduction into a cult group of a person who has already been 'elected' by the *zar* spirits (Natvig 1987: 58).

Etymology of the term *zar*

The etymology of the term *zar* is obscure, and I think today it is impossible to say precisely where it comes from. It also seems to me that the word has many origins based on different regions, religious beliefs and rituals. I think its meanings and functions have changed repeatedly over time and during its long diverse journeys.

One can also add another difficulty: the negligence of pioneer observers (who registered *zar* ceremonies) towards the local languages and dialects to find out more about origins of the word *zar*. Many of them re-recount explanations which they heard from others who were mostly unfamiliar with local traditions and folklores. Therefore, we should not be surprised when we see that more acceptable interpretations and hypotheses regarding the etymology of *zar* came only at the beginning of the twentieth century.

Generally speaking, I think we can divide all of these hypotheses into two main categories. First, one considers the origin of the word *zar* to be from Africa, mostly Ethiopian sub-cultures, namely Abyssinian. The second category proposes that the origin of the word *zar* is somewhere among Arabic-speaking regions of the Persian Gulf. My observations would suggest that a combination of these two ideas is more accurate: that is, that the origins of the word *zar* remit to a mixture of African and Arab culture with a strong connection to North African Islamic beliefs.

As we said, to many scholars it seems that the word *zar* has Abyssinian origin.[14] Enno Littmann (1950) collected a great number of Abyssinia magic scrolls in which the word *zar* occurs in the shape of *zârt*, *zârit* and *jâr*. Also, Stefan Strelcyn (1972), in his precious work on 34 magico-medical divinatory manuscripts from Ethiopia (with Amharic influence), shows that the word *zar* appears to designate a spirit or the head of a group of spirits which cause illnesses. In this regard, many scholars, following Enrico Cerulli, suggest *zar* is an Amharic word,[15] probably derived from the Cushitic supreme god, *djar* in Agau, which in Christianised Abyssinia became a malevolent spirit. 'The name is of non-Semitic origin, probably derived from the name of the supreme divinity of the pagan Cushites, the God-Heaven called in Agau *gar*, and in Sidamo languages: *Kaffa yaro*, *Buoro daro*' (Cerulli 1934: 1217).

But it seems that Kahle rejects this theory. While he seems to have been undecided about the origin of the zar cult when he wrote 'Zar-Beschworungen in Egypten',[16] he was evidently intrigued by Frobenius's observation of the strong similarities between *bori* and *zar* ritual and beliefs. After Frobenius's book was published, Kahle wrote in a letter to Elisabet Franke that 'it seems to me that here we have the key to the Zar'.[17] Four years later, Max Meyerhof wrote: 'the Zar has formerly been traced back to Abyssinia; recently,

Mr. Prof. Kahle has informed me that he will soon be able to present important evidence for its origin in Inner Africa, especially Hausaland'.[18] Kahle, however, never published the results of his investigations (Natvig 1987: 674). Seligman also refuses Cerulli's idea:

> In Spiro's vocabulary of the colloquial Arabic of Egypt *zar* is translated by 'negro incantation' and no plural or derivation is given. It was suggested to me by an Egyptian that it meant 'visitation' and came from the Arabic verb *zâra*, 'the visited'. In the Sudan I only found the word *zâr* used to mean the ceremony, the spirits themselves being spoken of as *asaid*, 'masters' (Seligman1914: 300).

Other scholars who worked among Northern Sudanese spirit possessions report different etymologies regarding the term *zar*. Ahmed al-Shahi proposes the following:

> ... *zâr* (possibly from the Arabic *zâra*, to visit, though this derivation is disputed), which implies that when spirits desire certain things they visit an individual through whom these things are obtained for individual's benefit; and *zahar* (Arabic: *zahara* 'to appear'), imply that the spirits appear, commonly through dreams, and reveal their identity to the possessed and to the master of ceremony. In these regions *zar* also is referred to as *al-jâma'a* (Arabic: group) a term to indicate all the spirits and also known by term *asyâd* (Arabic: masters), indicating the power of the spirits over individuals (Al-Shahi 1984: 29–30).

There are some accounts from Somali that the word *saar* describes a state of possession by a spirit also called *saar*. This spirit itself (*saar*) in the Islamic setting, is described by Lewis (1956: 146) as a kind of *jinn* whose malignant powers cause certain types of sickness.[19] From Aden, Lidwien Kapteijns and Jay Spaulding (1996: 175) report that the term *zar* has been used as *zuhr*, which presents the custom of many Muslim women to hold harmless meetings that are simply a sort of social gathering whereby women meet to pass a few hours listening to small drums being played and sing songs.[20] Other historical evidence leads to interpretations of *zar* as an Islamic religious fetish which helps to hunt down the demons that attack humans (Artin Pacha 1885: 185, n).

As regards the Arabic origin of the term *zar*, the earliest report is the work by Christiaan Snouck Hurgronje (1970: 124–8). Snouck Hurgronje argues that *zar* is not an Arabic word *per se* but originally came from Eastern Arabia, somewhere in the province of Oman. He states that the word also has a plural form: *zeeran*. Strangely, he goes on to say that he has been told that the word is Arabic and denotes a sinister 'visitor' (*zara yezuru*) who makes his or her abode and so possesses the victim (id: 124). Later, Samuel Zwemer (1920: 228) follows the popular Arabic etymological explanation which connects the word *zar* and the Arabic verb *zâra*. John Walker (1934: 62) also states that the word *zar* could come from the Arabic word *ziyara*, meaning visitation, inasmuch as persons possessed by demons are said to have been 'visited' by spirits (*el-assayad*), or it could have been derived from the town of Zara in Northern Iran (i.e. unknown). It has also been suggested by Taghi Modarressi (1968: 150), and Farrokh Gaffary (1986: 92–7) that the word *zar* is Persian. Modarressi (1968: 150) states that the term *zar* was applied to the Iranian culture when it was introduced in Southern Iran by African sailors from the southeast coast of Africa in the sixteenth century.

In contemporary Persian literature, the term *zar* has two main interpretations. The first usage is in the form of a prefix and complex verb (*zâri*): *zârikardan* or *zâridan* (*zârzadan*), which means crying, lamenting or mourning. The second usage is in the shape of a suffix adjective which describes a 'bad situation or condition': *hal-i zar* (bad feeling), *kar-i zar* (act or work which ended badly).

Origin of zar

As Natvig (1987: 685) proposes, 'the ultimate origin of the *zar cult* is open to conjecture'. Historical evidences report that the *zar cult* as a topic of research came to the attention of Western scholars from several fields and with different viewpoints after the second half of the nineteenth century. Not only did most early scholars, such as Michael De Goeje (1890) and Theodor Nöldeke (1890), try to work on this issue, but later researchers up until today have also tried to find the origins of the *zar cult*,[21] which, it seems, is yet to be satisfactorily pinned down. It seems to me that the *zar cult* as a simple observation is mentioned perhaps for the first time in a letter by Luci Duff Gordon (1902: 380).[22] But Natvig (1987: 671), argues C. B. Klunzinger (1877: 395), who resided in Qusayr as a former quarantine doctor, was the first European writer who described the *zar cult* in Egypt.

> Among the women *zikrs* are not indulged in, but the tendency to ecstasies is even much greater among the more nervous sex, and to gratify this inclination they have adopted a practice which is said to have been introduced by Abyssinian female slaves, and which gradually spread to such an extent that the government felt itself called upon to forbid it. Nevertheless, it is still common among high and low, especially in Upper Egypt. The *sar*, a certain *ginn*, is the powerful

genie of sickness, who throws himself upon the women by preference (Klunzinger 1877: 671).

Later, in the second volume of his work, Snouck Hurgronje describes the *zar cult* as a female practice in Mecca (Snouck Hurgronje 1970: 124–8).[23] de Goeje (1890: 480) and Noldeke (1890: 701) both reached the conclusion, independently of Klunzinger, that 'the *zar* is introduced from Abyssinia, most likely by the slave women'. Based on the reports of others, especially Klunzinger, Natvig (1987: 672) argues that the *zar cult* is a foreign element in the Middle East and was brought to this area during the nineteenth and early twentieth century by slaves. Pamela Constantinides's (1972: 263) investigations of Sudanese oral traditions showed that many of the earliest remembered cult leaders were described as being Egyptian. However, 'Closer enquiry as often as not revealed that these were "dark complexioned" Egyptians, probably in fact the wives and descendants of Mohammed Ali's model army of slaves, recruited principally from the south and south-western Sudan.'

Along with the fact that we find no evidence of a notion of spirits called *zar*, or of the existence of *zar* cult-like practices, in any part of the Middle East, including Northern Sudan, earlier than around the middle of the nineteenth century, it is reasonable to conclude that the *zar cult* was indeed introduced into the area, probably in the first half of the twentieth century by slaves (Natvig 1987: 674).

Other theories have occasionally been put forward, none of them able to challenge the older Abyssinian theory. These theories propose either an African origin for the *zar cult*, or a Persian one, or a combination of both. Thus, Frobenius, struck by the similarities between *bori* rituals that he observed in Hausaland and the *zar* ritual which he saw in Omdurman, suggested that both had their origin in a system of beliefs ultimately derived from Persia, which had spread throughout the grassland belt, from Abyssinia in the east to Hausaland in the west, due to an early Persian influence in the area via Nubia (Frobenius 1913: 561–4).

A double origin of the cult was proposed by Brende Seligman (1914), who suggested that the name *zar* and the belief in *zar* spirits had been introduced from Abyssinia, while its ritual had been introduced by black slaves from South and Southwestern Sudanese tribes and derived from their cult of tribal and ancestral spirits. Another double origin theory combining an African with a Persian origin has been suggested by Modarressi (1968: 149). According to him, the name *zar* is Persian and was applied to the cult when it was introduced in Southern Iran by black sailors from the southeast coast of Africa in the sixteenth century. All of these theories are marred by speculations, uncritical use of sources, or self-contradictions and must be rejected.

The *Encyclopedia of Islam* (Cerulli 1934: 1217) supports Duncan MacDonald and C. B. Klumzinger's contention that the word *zar* is Ethiopian in origin. Similarly, Simon Messing (1958: 1123) states that the *zar cult* is highly developed in Northern Ethiopia, with its centre in the town of Gondar. Also, in Iran the origin of the word *zar* is obscure. Although many scholars have carried out research on the subject, their interpretations are different and unrelated. Sabaye Moghaddam (2009) in the *Encyclopædia Iranica* classifies this activity as ceremonial, calling it a trance or healing dance: in some parts of Persia, musical exorcisms are performed to relieve those thought to be afflicted with evil spirits.

Zar *and gender issues*

Generally speaking, most literature on spirit possession assumes that it affects women more than men, for women are less free, more disenfranchised and more in need of a proxy.[24] Many of these anthropological studies demonstrate that among non-urban societies, spirit attacks are most likely to occur when women are in transition from one phase of life to another. Also, many scholars explain *zar* as a kind of female strategy for taking on the privileges denied them in their un-possessed state, or for articulating subaltern positions on the established political order.[25]

Historically also, most of the observations on the *zar cult* are almost unanimous in noting that the cult and its leadership were dominated by women. In fact, *zar* beliefs are found among both men and women, but practices associated with the *zar* ritual as an organised *possession cult* lie firmly in the hands of women (Kenyon 1995: 109). Thus, it is evident that at least at the time when the *cult* had gained enough popularity to attract the attention of outside observers, it was under the control of women. Such literature on predominantly female possession rites is particularly rich in examples from the Muslim world, especially in the Middle East.

According to C. B. Klunzinger (1877: 397), the *zar* leader was usually a slave woman. In an article published in 1885, Yacoub Artin Pacha mentioned a shrine (*zawiya*) in Cairo called *Shaykh Bidak*, where freed 'negresses' used to assemble 'for delivering themselves to their fetish (*zar*) that consists to hunt the demon – which penetrated and attacked the body of the possessed person – by the help of music, and sacrifices of sheep'.[26] At the turn of the century, Eugénie le Brun also became acquainted with the *zar* ceremony when her Sudanese maid resigned because the spirit that possessed her disapproved of the sombre black dresses her mistress used to wear. Le Brun credited the 'negresses' with a predominant role in the cult and claimed that three-fourths of the women who considered themselves possessed by the devil ('le Diable') were black. She also referred to the *zar* leaders as black women and mentions one in particular; the aged leader of the most renowned cult group in Cairo. She was the freed slave concubine of a prince and spoke nothing but Turkish (Le Brun quoted by Salima 1902: 255–98).

In countries situated in the Persian Gulf, female slaves also evidently had a hand in the cult's leadership. Snouck Hurgronje (1970: 101) wrote about 'the *Sheikha* (female *zar* leader) and her slave girls, who must attend these functions with beat of drum and with a species of song...'. In this century, Fanny Lutton of the American Mission also described the *zar cult* in Muscat and referred to a 'Devil dancing' performed by black slave women (quoted in Zwemer 1920: 234). According to Dirk Dykstra, a member of the Arabian Mission in Bahrain, blacks and Arabs intermingled in *zar* ceremonies, while the Shiites of Bahrain did not mingle with others: 'the only outsiders they have with them are the negro musicians' (Dykstra 1918: 20). Lastly, Thomas Bertram (1931: 261) described the *zar cult* in the fishing villages of Oman and reported that the *zar* leader was often an old black woman. More recent observations from Bahrain (Holes 2000), Dubai (al-Zakari 1998) and Saudi Arabia (Doumato 2000: 170–84) also confirm the dominant role of women in *zar* ceremonies.

Most scholars who wrote after Sa'idi on the *zar cult* in South Iran have completely ignored the importance of gender issues in this procession ritual (Aghakhani n.d.;[27] Modarressi 1968; Mirzayi 2002; Marsden 1972; Sharifiyan 2002; Boloukbashi n.d.; Riyahi 1977; Masudiyah 1977 and 1985; Darvishi 1991, 1998 and 2001; Muhibi 1995; Safa 1988, Gharasu 2008). A documentary film made by Mehrdad Oskoui (2004), and also some parts of Mahmud Rahmani's documentary film (2007), are the only official visual representation where we can understand the importance of gender, especially the role of women in *zar cult* in South Iran. Oskuyi's film demonstrates why and how the majority of *zar* believers and participants in South Iran (Qashm Island) today are women who belong to the lowest classes of society. Here, we see clearly how women talk about their personal psychological and social problems in their society and with their family, especially their rapport with their husband. While most studies of *zar* show that most possessed patients are women, the masters of ceremonies and head of rituals can be both women and men. Also, in such ceremonies, in most cases, music performances are executed by a group of men and not women.

Iranian zar

As I mentioned before, in this part of my chapter I will first present a brief history of black slavery in Iran as I think that it was via this maritime human commerce that *zar* arrived into Iran for the first time. In the second part I will talk in detail about the *zar* ritual in Iran.

A brief history of black slavery in Iran

Slave trading to the Persian Gulf began well before the Islamic period. Medieval accounts refer sporadically to slaves as household servants, bodyguards, militia men and also seamen in Southern Iran and the Persian Gulf (Ricks 1988: 66). For historians of Iran and the Persian Gulf, the subject of slaves and slave traders is a relatively new field of research. There are virtually no published materials available in English or French about African communities in Iran, and Joseph Harris (2003: 325) states that he was also unable to find an Iranian who knew of any such study in Arabic or Persian. But Mohammad Bastani-Parizi (1961: 307–476) argues that the existence of towns and villages such as Zangiabad (a village built by Africans), Qala Zangiyan (Castle of Africans) in Baluchistan and Dah-i Zangiyan (village of Africans) in Kirman refer to an African background (slaves) in Southern Iran.

Trade in the Persian Gulf was an ancient activity for the people of Persia and the Arabian Peninsula. With the rise of the Sasanids (A.D. 226–640), seafaring in the Gulf became an integral part of Persia's commercial and maritime activity (Ricks 1970: 339).[28] Additionally, the predominance of Persians in the Gulf trade in pre-Islamic times is indicated by the many Persian words used by merchants and sailors of the Gulf during the medieval period.[29]

The shift from Sasanian to Islamic hegemony in the Gulf had little effect on the economic structure of the coastal ports. The Arab invasions (ca. A.D. 640) of Persia and the subsequent turmoil along the coastal ports of the Persian Gulf brought a new and lasting dimension to the commerce of those regions, particularly during the later medieval period (Ricks 1970: 343). Persian merchants and ships from the Gulf continued to trade antinomy, rugs and precious stones from Syria (al-Sham) and Egypt, along with woven fabrics, cotton, horses and pearls to India and the Far East (Toussaint 1966: 45; Lewis 1960: 87–8). Slaves, ivory, teakwood, ambergris, tortoise shell and gold continued to be brought from East Africa on Persian ships, while peppers, camphor and muslin, as well as other spices and piece goods, were brought to the ports of the Gulf from India and the Far East to be carried overland to the cities of Iran and the Fertile Crescent (Lewis 1979: 343).

From the ninth century onwards, Arab and other Muslim writers provide information on the movement of slaves from the black lands towards the North and the East – across the Red Sea and Indian Ocean to Arabia and

Iraq, down the Nile to Egypt, and across Sahara to the slave-markets of North and Northwest Africa.

Abu Zaid (ca. A.D. 877–915), himself a merchant from Siraf, noted that Sirafi merchants visited Jidda in the Red Sea and the Zanzibar coast (Ferrand 1922: 130; Nadvi 1966: 130). Finally, Isfahani (A.D. 893–970) relates the report of Hasan b. Amr al-Sirafi, a merchant from Siraf, who visited the land of Kanam in the Sudan (Marvazi 1942: 54; Brockelmann 1943–44: 117, 221; ibid. 1937–1942: 117, 221). During the tenth century, Sirafi captains and merchants were actively engaged in both the Red Sea and India-China trade. Arab and Persian sources reveal that the Persians were still dominating trade around the coasts of Arabia as far as Jidda and the other Red Sea ports (Hourani and Carswell 1995: 79; Wiet 1955: 82–83). Historians and geographers did not indicate the composition of the population of Siraf in this period or its political structure, but it is known that Persians, Arabs, Jews, Indians and other national groups, including Africans, formed its population.[30] Al-Masoudi (A.D. 896–956) describes the route taken by the Sirafis to the East African coast as being a direct course from the Persian Gulf to the Island of Qanbalu (Zanzibar), the principal port along the coast in the sea of Zangibar (bahr al-Zanj) (al-Masudi 1962: 94). In addition, trade to East Africa from Siraf during the tenth century usually consisted of spices, cotton cloth, perfumes and kitchenware, in exchange for ivory, gold and slaves.[31]

By the twelfth century, the Island of Kish had become the chief commercial centre in the Persian Gulf and one of the principal trading towns with East Africa regarding slavery. The Cairo Geniza documents in this period also indicate trade competition between Aden and Kish for the markets of East Africa, particularly for slaves, which resulted in several naval clashes between the two states (Goitein 1954: 247–8).

During the fourteenth century the Island of Hurmuz became the principal commercial centre for Indian Ocean trade into the Persian Gulf. The East African trade in gold, ivory and slaves continued to be an important part of the Gulf's commerce on this island. Historians frequently note the cosmopolitan population of the island and the great number of Indian, Arab and Persian merchants, as well as African slaves (Aubin 1953: 77–79). In this period, the towns of destination for the African slaves were rarely the port-towns themselves, but rather the distant hinterland towns, such as Kirman, Shiraz or Baghdad. In the nineteenth century, however, slaves were sent to a variety of locations, including relatively small towns along the Gulf littoral and into the villages of the Iranian hinterland.[32]

By the nineteenth century the trade (slavery) from the Caucasus had largely dried up, mainly because of Russian advances in that area and consequent reconfiguring of the economy. Thus, Iran and the Ottoman Empire became much more heavily dependent on Africa as a source for slaves and black slaves consequently grew in number (Martin 2005: 152). From many historical sources, it is clear that this century witnessed a dramatic rise in slave trading into the Persian Gulf region from East Africa, by way of the pilgrimage trade from the Red Sea and by way of Oman (Ricks 1988: 68). A reasonable idea of the volume of the mid-nineteenth-century slave trade can be drawn from the British reports (Ricks 1988: 66). In this period, the black slaves came under two types: *habashis*, coming from Abyssinia; and *zangis*, from Africa itself. *Habashis*, who were of a lighter complexion with features closer in type to those of Middle Eastern people, were twice the value of *zangis* (Martin 2005: 152).

By British calculations, in the early part of the century import numbers of slaves to the Persian Gulf as a whole were regularly estimated as between 10 and 20,000, the main centre of trade being Muscat (Kelly 1925: 414–6). With regard to Iran, in 1842 the British estimated the number to be 1,080 in Boushihr and other Iranian ports. None of the Iranian ports sent vessels directly to Zanzibar, except for Langah, from which 3 or 4 boats sailed annually, each returning with about 70 slaves. According to a questionnaire of 1842, some 3,000 slaves (two thirds male and one third female) arrived in Bushahr each year, but only about 170–80 remained there, the rest moving on to Ottoman territory (Martin 2005: 214). About one quarter were sold at Bandar Abbas and a small number at Langah and Kangirun (Issawi 1971: 125). In 1847 it was estimated that importation on the Iranian coast amounted to 1,150 'negroes' and 80 Abyssinians per year on average, although this did not include the comparatively small number who were brought back by pilgrims.[33] They were of all ages between 4 and 60 and many women and children were not bought but stolen.[34]

The first steps towards the suppression of the slave trade in Iran were taken between Sheil, the British Representative, and Haj Mirza Aqasi, the Grand Vizier, in 1846. However, the coming to power of Amir Kabir (1807–52) brought a major shift in policy. An agreement was reached between him and the British at the end of 1851 and made effective from 1 January 1852, granting the British the right of seizure and temporary detention of Iranian vessels engaged in the slave trade (Martin 2005: 214).

Winds (spirits) in South Iran[35]

In reply to the question of what exactly *zar*, *nuban* and *mashayikh* define, any local person in the south of Iran and the Persian Gulf who is even slightly familiar with the riparian culture and way of life will answer: all of these are winds (*bad*). Sa'idi argues:

Winds are forces which control the entire world, both within and beyond the earth, and everything is subject to their influence. All imaginary and fantastical creatures, such as fairies (*pari*), devils (*div*) and both good and evil spirits, are all winds, hallucinations or airs and all human beings are the targets of both good and bad winds.[36]

It is the above-mentioned people leading a riparian life on islands (Qashm, Kish) and in coastal areas (Bandar Abbas, Bandar Lengah, Bandar Boushihr, Bandar Jask) who are the potential victims of the winds. Among them, it is a common belief that most of these winds emanate from Africa and India, while a few come from Saudi Arabia and other countries of the Persian Gulf. In South Iran, it is said that blacks and poor people are in the first line of attack from the winds.[37] Fishermen, seamen (*jashu*) and women who work in palm-groves are the secondary targets. Generally speaking, poor women are in greater danger than poor men, as they are always hungry, sick and in trouble with other members of their society. Rich people who give offerings and arrange ceremonies never become the winds' target; poor people who do not have any money or goods to offer for such ceremonies are the most vulnerable. People who live in the mountains and deserts or on the sea shore are also good targets for the winds, although rich people living in comfortable houses and safe places are excluded from this risk. Most of the seamen who live on the coast permanently will immediately be attacked by the winds. A wind has no pity and will attack any member of society, from little babies to old people who are awaiting death. However, a wind loves young and strong targets as they possess a great amount of energy and can make a good mount (*markab*). The person who becomes the target of the winds is named *markab*, a mount, or *faras*, a horse, while the wind which is on a mount (patient/victim) is called *habub*, which is an Arabic word and which is also known as *pehpeh* in local riparian language.

Sa'idi reports that all winds, just like human beings, are either Muslim or infidel (*kafar*). Whichever the case may be, after selecting their target all winds will render their *markab* sick and futile (*havayi*). Infidel winds are very dangerous and in some cases even kill their mounts. However, such violation or destruction of their target is rare among Muslim winds. All of the winds are contagious and are capable of transferring from one body to another. For example, if a person is in love with or hates another person, they can pass on their wind to this person, or, conversely, catch their wind. This is also the same in the case of the *baba* and *mama*, who can offer their good winds to those whom they chose, or make someone sick by giving them bad winds (Sa'idi 1967: 48).

According to one manner, we can divide all winds into two categories, the first of which comprises winds which can see (*bina*), watch and walk with open eyes. These winds know everything about the entire world. If one can bring them in (*ziravardan*), they can talk and provide answers to all questions. This type of wind has definitely had offering ceremonies and votive meals (*sufra*), drunk blood, heard poetry and songs and had people performing on kettledrums for it. Most of the winds of the *baba* and *mama* fall into this category, which means that their winds are clear-sighted (*bina*). Among 'the people of the air' (*ahl-i hava*), these kinds of winds are named 'clear or pure winds' (*bad-i saf*) which never disturb their mounts (*markab*).

The other category is that of 'blind winds' (*bad-i kur*). 'Blind winds' will bother and perturb their *markab* and are never calm and clear (*saf*). These winds have never had offering ceremonies, drunk blood or heard poems or the sound of kettledrums. During the assemblies and rituals of 'the people of the air', these winds will be brought down and rendered pure, clear and clear-sighted. It is under these conditions that their targets become calm and tranquil.

According to Sa'idi, the most important winds in South Iran are as follows:

- *Zar*: all of these are infidel (*kafar*), although there are a few exceptions. Locally they are named *bad-i surkh*, or 'red winds'.[38]
- *Nuban*: these make their targets sad, handicapped and infirm.
- *Mashayikh*: all of these are Muslim. These winds are kind and pure (*pak*) and have settled on Muslim coasts.
- *Bad-i jinn*: these all belong to the earth or the subterranean world; they are all inter-connected, like a chain, and are very dangerous.
- *Bad-i pari* (fairy): there are two different kinds of winds in this group, namely infidel fairies and Muslim fairies.
- *Bad-i dib* or *div* (demon): these are very large and tall, with a height of more than 40 metres, and live in deserts and on islands. If they touch a human being, he or she will immediately die and become a statue.
- *Bad-i qul* (ogre): from afar these look like drunks (*shutur-i mast*) and may kill everybody.

Baba *and* mama

For a person who becomes the victim of winds, there are a number of avenues for seeking help at times of difficulties and illness. With the increasing belief in the power of medicine, people may consult a medical doctor first rather than seeking the help of a religious man, but the reverse is also true. In the south of Iran, for a long time during such situations, medical attention was the first port of call for help; when told by doctors that nothing could be done, the afflicted would generally seek a mullah or a religious person (*duanavis*) in an effort to find a solution.

If it was found that these experts could not help the patient, it would be evident that he or she had been made the target and 'mount' (*markab*) of a wind. This wind can be a *zar*, a *nuban* or one of the thousands of other winds. In a word, nobody is capable of assisting such patients except *babas*, or 'fathers', and *mamas*, or 'midwives'.[39] All *babas* and *mamas* were initially victims of one or several winds and *zars*. Little by little, after spending time, and after much exercise and training, they gained a power for controlling their winds and *zars* and for becoming their master. Besides their specialty regarding winds and *zars*, *babas* and *mamas* normally also work as local traditional medical doctors.

To escape from the pain and torture of a wind, targets should go directly to the *baba* or *mama* of that specific wind, as each wind has a particular *baba* and *mama*. *Baba* and *mama* inherit their profession and responsibility from their parents; most of them are either black or mixed race and are dark skinned. If they are not successful in healing their patient, they have no choice but to send them to a *gaptaran*, the biggest and most powerful *baba* or *mama* of another region. Each *baba* and *mama* has their own stand (*basat*) with different goods and objects, such as kettledrums with different names, special clay pots for incense (*gashtasuz*), and other musical instruments that they use during their ceremonies. The *baba* and *mama* will drink the blood of animals sacrificed during the rituals; indeed, in their community, they can gain increasing credibility and importance according to the amount of blood they consume.[40] A *baba* or *mama* should nominate their successor during their lifetime, for which purpose they hold special ceremonies. If this is not carried out, after their death 'the people of the air' will gather together and nominate one of the blacks among themselves to be their *baba* or *mama*.

Bad-i zar

In most regions of Iran where *zar* is found, the cult is basically a woman's religious activity, considered unorthodox and as such often criticised and ridiculed by men and the educated. In Iran, *zar*, which is shunned by the Muslim clergy and educated people in particular, exists within a field of orthodox Islamic spiritual beliefs stipulating that God is the only power. Regardless of the fact that *zar* is a trance religious ceremony that uses drumming and dancing to cure an illness thought to be caused by a demon, it is technically prohibited by Islam as a pagan practice.[41]

In Iran, *zar* concerns the belief in the existence, influence and power of spirits (winds). Women, and less commonly men, are possessed by a variety of *zars*, each of which makes its specific demands. Although men may be victims of spirit possession, like many other countries they refrain from joining in the *zar* ceremonies for fear of ridicule. In such societies, 'although men do not deny the existence of spirits, in the context of Islam' (Callan 2008: 400), they are likely to regard women who appease spirits as un-Islamic; 'proper Muslims appeal directly to Allah' (Masquelier 2001). The effects of possession (*zar*) on the possessed person (*markab*) are that he or she is likely to suffer from an illness with psychological and physical symptoms. Once these demands are satisfied, the possessed person feels better and the *zars* will be satisfied, placated and appeased. The possessed person will be the victim of *zars* for their whole life and there is no complete cure for such patients.

After Sa'idi the most important *zars* in the south of Iran are Maturi, Shaykh Shangar, Dingmaru, Umgarah, Bumaryam, Chinyasih, Pehpeh, Daykitu, Bujambah, Babur, Namrud, Taghruri and Ghisas. Sa'idi reports that in the south of Iran, *zar* is the most dangerous and most prevalent of all the winds. All *zars* are infidel (*kafar*) and originate in different parts of the world. The most dangerous come from the eastern coast of Africa, namely Zanzibar, Somalia and Ethiopia, which have enjoyed commercial relationships with the cities situated on the southern coast of Iran for centuries. The other *zars* come from India and Saudi Arabia, which Sa'idi claims have very strange mountains and wide seas (Sa'edi, 1967: 51). One can recognise the sea or country of origin of each *zar* from the language that they speak. Each *zar* will be brought down and will begin to talk after drinking blood; they will talk only to the *baba* or *mama* of the *zar* from the interior of each target, via his or her larynx. The manner and method of the outbreak of each *zar* is different, and they normally reside on the coasts.

It seems that every human being is considered potentially vulnerable to being possessed by a *zar* spirit or spirits. But humans differ considerably in their degree of vulnerability and certain situations are considered particularly inviting to the *zars*. Most of these situations are points of psychological or social stress (Messing 1958: 1121). Therefore, all human beings, regardless of their age, are potential victims of *zars*. A sort of psychic predestination is responsible in other cases. Victims are 'chosen' by the *zar* for their melancholy natures or weak personalities. In some cases the illness plays the role of a religious revelation, which 'calls' the chosen into the *zar cult*. In this connection it is interesting to note that it is not only weaknesses which create points of stress for attracting a *zar* (Messing 1958: 1121).

Children or adults both form good mounts (*markab*) for *zars*. When the *zar* captures its victim and enters into the body of its target, it will make them sick and no medical doctor will be able to resolve this sickness. Like the other winds, each *zar* is the cause of a specific illness. Messing states that symptoms of possession by *zar* spirits include proneness to accidents, sterility, convulsive seizures and extreme apathy (Messing 1958: 1120). As in the south of Iran, where more than 72 different *zars* are in existence, one can recognise around 72 different illnesses in such patients.

A *zar*, like most winds, will penetrate its victim's body in the form of a *jinn*.[42] The first reaction of the *baba* or *mama* of the *zar* should, therefore, be to bring out the *jinn* from the victim's body. The healer (*mama* or *baba*) is himself *zar*-possessed, but has 'come to terms' with the spirit. His first task is to diagnose the specific spirit, or syndrome of spirits, which ails the patient.

Preparation for the ceremony

As mentioned above, the *zar*'s intention is almost always signalled by sickness. The diagnosis is made by *baba* or *mama* of *zar* assisted by his or her *zar* devotees (*ahl-i hava*). One can become a member of *ahl-i hava*, 'the people of the air' if one succeeds in escaping the winds safely subsequent to having become their target. When someone becomes a 'member' of *ahl-i hava*, they should always wear clean white clothes, constantly take baths and use perfume.[43] 'The people of the air' should never use alcoholic drinks and should never perform any bad or illegal actions, as otherwise their wind will trouble them again.[44] There are many prohibitions for *ahl-i hava*, some of which include the following:

- They are not permitted to touch dead bodies, including human and animal corpses and remains.
- They should not touch any kind of uncleanness (*nijasat*) or make themselves impure.[45]
- If someone wants to light their cigarette with the fire of the shisha (*qalyan*) of 'the people of the air', they should ask for their permission first; if not, their wind will trouble them.
- They should never become drunk.
- They should never make love with strangers (*namahram*).

Baba or *mama* and the possessed person work towards two goals. First, they must regularise the relationship between the *zar* and its victim by learning who the *zar* is and what it demands in return for removing the sickness. Second, they must expel the purely physical aspects of the sickness which the *zar* has inflicted (Young 1975: 571–2).

When the victims are brought to the *baba* or *mama* and they recognise that the wind is a *zar*, they will keep the patient indoors and out of sight for a period of seven days.[46] They will wash and clean the body of the patient[47] and he or she should not see a woman, dog or hen during this period. The patient should also not be seen by any women (*mahram/namahram*) and, if the patient is a woman, she should be kept far away from men.

For this reason, a *baba* or *mama* will keep their patients far from the city in a hut constructed from bamboo (*kapar*) situated on the seashore. During all periods of disappearance from public view (*hijab*), the *baba* or *mama* will massage the body of the patient with a special unguent (*ma'jun*) at night. Locally, this unguent is named *girkou* and is made from 21 different ingredients, such as: basil, saffron, *bukhish* (a kind of local plant), cardamom, walnut, chicken's tongue and *gasht* (a kind of Indian wood from Mumbai). All of these ingredients should be soaked in rosewater and the victim's body should be covered with this mixture each night; they are also given some to drink. In the morning following the period of seclusion, the *baba* or *mama* should again wash the patient's body and cover it with *girkou* and another unguent. This new liquid is composed of the dust of seven paths (*khak-i haft rah*), mixed with seven leaves of seven thornless plants.

Before the *zar* ceremony officially begins, the *jinn* which has penetrated the victim's body should be brought out from it. In order to achieve this, the patient should be laid down, their toes tied by the hair of a goat, and some fish oil (*sifah*) rubbed on his/her body and some goat's hair burnt under their nose. At this moment, the *baba* or *mama* will verbally threaten the *jinn* by holding and moving a bamboo stick (*khiyzaran*) in their hand to force it to leave the victim's body. The *baba* or *mama* should then strike the victim's body with this bamboo stick until the *jinn*, with a piercing and sad scream, deserts its mount (*markab*) and escapes.[48]

After the *jinn* has fled, only the *zar* remains settled in the patient's head and body. In order to bring it down, the *baba* or *mama* should organise a ceremony in which they sing songs,[49] perform music, give votive meals (*sufra*),[50] and sacrifice an animal and drink its blood. On the day prior to such a ceremony, a woman (*khiyzarani*) who is a member of 'the people of the air', holding a bamboo stick, should go to the houses of the other devotees and call all of them, especially young women (*dukhtaran-i hava*). *Dukhtaran-i hava* 'daughters of air' are young women who are still virgins and have pleasant singing voices. These women are able to dance well and their presence beside the men in such ceremonies (*bazikardan*) is crucial. Besides 'the people of the air', there are other participants who are not patients and come solely to play musical instruments and sing songs, who are traditionally named *safi* or 'people of love' (*ahl-i ashq*).[51]

At the beginning of the *zar* ceremony some charcoal is placed in the incense-pot (*gashtahsuz*) to which some *kundruk* (a kind of local plant) is added. The *baba* or *mama* then fumigates all the musical instruments and puts them in their respective places. They spread a large cloth on the floor on which they arrange many things, such as various foods, fragrant wild herbs, lotus fruit (*kunar*), dates, and the meat and blood of the sacrificed animal. This blood belongs to the *zar*'s sacrifice, which is normally a goat (*kahar*) sacrificed on the day of the ceremony and whose blood is placed in a dish as part of this spread.[52] The *zar* will not begin to speak until it drinks this blood; thus, in order to better understand the *zar*'s requests, the patient should first drink this blood.[53] Drinking the blood also demonstrates the connection of the target to the 'people of the air'. Additionally, as previously mentioned, the credit and rank of the *baba* or *mama* is directly connected to the number of times blood has been drunk; for example, it is said that a particular *baba* has drunk blood three times, or that a *mama* has drunk blood five times.

During the *zar* ceremonies, in contrast to the rituals for Muslim winds, nobody is permitted to pronounce the name of God, the Prophet or the 14 holy persons (*chahardah ma'sum*); if someone should utter such names by mistake during the ceremony, the *zar* will never be brought down.

Upon arrival in the ceremonial venue, each participant should remove their shoes outside and sit beside 'the people of the air' and the other participants without greeting them. Furthermore, while sitting there they should not speak to anyone. If tea or coffee is brought, they should not place the cups on the floor after it is consumed, but should rather wait until someone comes and collects them by hand. The ceremony opens with the installation of the *baba* or *mama* at the head of the scene, with their special large kettledrum (*mudendu*) placed just in front of them. The *mudendu* is one of the biggest kettledrums of 'the people of the air' and the person designated to play it should sit on a stool behind it. On the floor in front of this kettledrum a silver tray is placed bearing dishes of *gashtahsuz* and *kundruk*, which are dried herbs used as incense[54] (Figure 8.1).

Generally speaking, the *zar* ceremony should be performed when everybody is seated on the floor; men and women sit beside each other and sing and dance simultaneously. It is possible for the ceremony (*bazi*) to take as long as two or three days, especially in cases where it is the first ceremony of the victim. It lasts for such a long period as the *baba* or *mama* requires time to bring down the wind from the head and body of the patient. During these periods, none of the participants has the right to leave the venue; if they are tired, they may sleep there (Figures 8.2, 8.3, and 8.4).

By a movement of their bamboo stick the *baba* or *mama* will indicate that the ceremony has officially begun and everyone will begin to play

Figure 8.1. *Zar* ritual near Abadan, Khuzestan, Iran, 2005 (Photograph: M. Rahmani).

(*bazikardan*). The *baba* or *mama* will perform on the *mudendu* and start to sing and all the participants will respond in chorus. At first, most of the songs are sung in Persian, but after a few minutes they change to an unknown (Swahili) language. While there are few local people who understand these kinds of poems or songs – even among the black *babas* or *mamas* – even if they do not know what they are singing, they may continue such a ceremony for many hours.

During the ceremony the patient sits beside the *baba* or *mama*. After the commencement of the ceremony and the singing and dancing, the patient gradually begins to move and tremble; this indicates the movement of the *zar* within their body. When the trembling of the patient increases it transfers from his head to all parts of his body. At this stage his head will lower and he will drink from the blood that is placed in front of him. The kettledrums will then be played more strongly and the singers will sing louder; it is then possible that the *zar* may penetrate the heads of the other participants and all of them move their heads and bodies in unison.

As previously mentioned, the *zar* will be brought down with one of the special songs and it is at this moment that the *baba* or *mama* can talk with the *zar*. They will ask the *zar* its name, from where it comes and why it has captured the body of its victim. They will say that this target is poor,

Figure 8.2. *Zar* ritual near Abadan, Khuzestan, Iran, 2005 (Photograph: M. Rahmani).

unfortunate, is a fisherman or seaman and that the *zar* should leave him. The *zar*, in its own language, will answer from where it comes, what its name is and for which reason it has chosen its victim; all of this communication takes place in the native language of the *zar*. Most of them can talk in Arabic, Indian or Swahili, without any relation to the native language of their victims, which may be completely different to these languages.[55]

After these introductions, the *baba* or *mama* will ask the *zar* to leave its victim's body as soon as possible. The *zar* will reply that this is not a simple matter and that it needs a votive meal (*sufra*) in order to come down. It also requests bamboo (*khiyzaran*), ankle-rings (*khalkhal*) and clean clothes. The requests of all the *zar*s are not similar or at the same level. Some of them,

Figure 8.3. *Mama Zar*, *Zar* ritual near Abadan, Khuzestan, Iran, 2005 (Photograph: M. Rahmani).

such as *Maturi*, ask for many things and want all of these goods in gold; others request little and are happy with small gifts.

On this issue, al-Shahi reports:

> Spirits of the *zar* are thought to be hidden powers, and their influence on human beings manifests itself when these spirits desire certain demands (*talabat*) such as items of clothing, golden and silver ornaments, drinks, cigarettes and other goods. Demands vary, and whatever the spirits ask for will be for the benefit of the possessed individuals and for the satisfaction of the spirits. Spirits are thought to be very sensitive in relation to their demands; they become anxious and afraid that what they have asked for may not be granted. This is reflected in the changed personality of the possessed: he or she becomes anxious

The People of the Air: Healing and Spirit Possession 157

Figure 8.4. *Zar* ritual near Abadan, Khuzestan, Iran, 2005 (Photograph: M. Rahmani).

that all demands must be satisfied. Once these demands are met, the spirit in question pardons the possessed person and enters into peace (*salam*) with him or her. Thus the reciprocity and mutual relationships between a person and a spirit: if peace of mind is to be maintained, then demands have to be met in order to pacify and appease the spirits. Another significant factor in the context of reciprocity is the belief in the infinite duration (*abadiyya*) of the possession because the spirit may need the person, at some later date, to execute a wish or a demand. Hence the belief that in the *zar* spirits are not exorcised but propitiated (al-Shahi 1984: 31).[56]

One of the most important things requested by most of the *zar* is a piece of bamboo. Some of them will ask for just one, while others will demand many; normally this type of bamboo is imported from Muscat. On the day of the ceremony (*bazi*), when the *zar* is brought down the *baba* or *mama* will ask him what kind of bamboo he wants. The *zar* will select its bamboo with regard to the bamboo's cords (*bul, band*). The bamboo stick should generally have two silver heads or be ornamented with silver rings. In order to prepare the bamboo, on the day before the ceremony they will cover its surface with henna (*hana*) and fish oil so that they may polish it; later they will ornament its surface with silver. Besides bamboo, 'the people of the air' and especially *zar*s need clean, white, perfumed cloths, as well as a special large veil (*lang, languta*). The *languta* is made from two pieces of a special textile, *shateh* (a type of local handmade textile), each piece of which should not be less than eight metres in length. These two pieces of *shateh* are sewn together with blue, yellow and green silk thread.

If the victim is a very poor person who cannot pay for all of the *zar's* requests, the *baba* or *mama*, instead of the victim, will instead give some credit as a promise (*rahn*) to the *zar*. For this purpose, they will attach a piece of textile or iron to the arm of the patient; in reality, this is a sign of the promise made to the *zar* so that it will wait and give its mount (*markab*) a chance to provide for all of its requests. Some of the *zar*s will accord their victims a short period of time; if, on its expiry, the promise remains unfulfilled, the *zar* will again resume its work.

When all of these requirements have been prepared, in another *zar* ceremony the *baba* or *mama* will bring it down and ask if it is happy with these offerings. If the *zar* accepts these gifts and offerings, the victim will be free to go; however, if the *zar* is unsatisfied, the patient should repeat this stage until the *zar* accepts their offerings.

When the victim is in a state of trance, they will be held from behind and laid down on the ground, although care should be taken that their head does not touch the ground. Another person will hold the patient's feet and move their body so that it faces the direction of Mecca (*qibla*). The *baba* or *mama* will ask the victim to strike their own chest hard with their fist; once the patient does this, the *zar* will suddenly leave its victim's body. At this instant, nobody should speak; if they do so, it would be possible for the *zar* to penetrate their body. Only the *baba* or *mama* can recognise and confirm the departure of the *zar*. When the *zar* leaves its victim, they should move the victim into a sitting position so that their toes touch the floor. After the ceremony, once it has been brought down and satisfied, the *zar* is no longer dangerous. Meanwhile, its victim will never return to their normal situation and, to some extent, the wind will remain in their head.

In some cases, despite all the efforts of the *baba* or *mama*, the *zar* has no desire to leave its victim's body and does not accept any *sufra*, music, offerings, songs or even blood. The ceremony will be repeated for durations of three, seven and finally twelve days; if at the end of these periods, and despite all such attempts, the *zar* remains resistant and decides not to be brought down, the *baba* or *mama* will cease to work on such a patient. Traditionally, such a victim is called *tahran* (no special meaning). *Tahran*s are unpopular within their societies, become notorious and hated and are obliged to leave their villages.

Conclusion

Organising and participating in spirit possession cults, 'sacralizing their own space at the shrine complex, sharing grievances and a sense of community' (Callan 2008: 401) are all signs of the strive for agency of Muslim women, who are 'marginalized at or excluded from the mosque' (Doumato 2000; Mazumdar and Mazumdar 2002; Mernissi 1975) and other male-dominated religious areas in Iran and other Muslim communities. Based on the recent documentary film of Mehrdad Oskoui we understand that in the south of Iran *zar* is a spirit possession ritual, a cult, and also a *'lieu de culte'* which expresses the psychological problems of the subordinate position of women in male-dominated communities. During the period of *zar* possession, women step outside the conventional social patterns of behaviour and are free to express their personal cresses, which, in normal situations, are neither tolerated nor respected (al-Shahi 1984: 39). We see also in this film that *zar* ceremonies also allow women to express their problems, enjoy a temporary freedom to behave without the constraints of social conventions and have their own space (Oskoui 2004). Also, confirming Dykstra (1918: 23, *zar* rituals in Iran certainly provide women with a great deal of fun and excitement and give them a distinction and authority which they would otherwise not have.

I feel that within such societies in Iran, if women are more restricted than men in other ways, they are less constrained with regard to religion: they are neither expected to become familiar with matters of liturgy and doctrine, nor to have sufficient moral strength on their own to uphold them. Phrased positively, as Boddy (1988: 10) argues, 'this means that women are relatively freer to embrace what men consider folk beliefs, those having so-called pagan elements and in whose company they place the *zar*'.

It seems to me the only way that *zar* could have been introduced into the Iran plateau was via black slavery commerce. While we know not all of the black slaves who arrived in Iran stayed in southern coastal regions, today *zar* can be found and is practised only among riparian and small scale societies of the Persian Gulf. It shows us that there may be connections between the professional job and commerce of people of these societies and the *sea*. Today we definitely need more ethnographical field works in the Persian Gulf in order to open new windows onto this forgotten spirit possession ritual in Iran.

Bibliography

Abu-Lughod, Maryam (1993). 'Islam and the gendered discourses of death'. *International Journal of Middle East Studies*, 25, 187–205.

Adamiyat, R. (nd). 'Uza'i Ijtima't'. In R. Shafaq (ed.). *Siminar*, II, 144–51.
Aghaie, Kamran (2005). *The Women of Karbala: Ritual Performance and Symbolic Discourses in Modern Shi'i Islam*. Austin, University of Texas Press.
_____(2004). *The Martyrs of Karbala: Shi'i Symbols and Rituals in Modern Iran*. Washington, University of Washington Press.
Aghakhani, Nader (1998). 'Le Bâbâ et l' 'autre', le 'jeu thérapeutique' et les 'gens de l'air'. MA, Haute Bretagne, Université Rennes 2.
_____(2005). 'Le Processus de symbolisation à travers le 'jeu' des 'gens de l'air'. Ph.D, Nord Villetaneuse, Université Paris 13.
Aghakhani, Nader and Doubille, Olivier (2002). 'Symbolisation du pulsionnel dans le rite 'thérapeutique' des 'gens de l'air' (Iran)'. In Clotte Sabatier and Olivier Doubille (eds). *Culture, Insertions et Santé*, Paris, L'Harmattan, pp. 49–78.
Amam, Muhammad Ali (1963). 'Manabi'-i iqtisadi-yi Khalij-i Fars' (Economic Resources of the Persian Gulf). In Rizazadih Shafaq; Mustawfi, Ahmad; and Muhammad Ali, Sayyid (eds). *Siminar-i Khalij-i Fars*. Tahran.
Al-Masudi (1962). *Les Prairies d'or*. Translated and edited by Barbier de Meynard and Pavet de Courteille. Paris, Société asiatique.
Al-Shahi, Ahmed (1984). 'Spirit possession and healing: The zar among the Shaygiyya of the Northern Sudan'. *Bulletin (British Society for Middle Eastern Studies)*, 11:1, 28–44.
Al-Zakari, Mohamad A. K. (1998). 'Folk Beliefs of Arab Women of Dubai Prior to Oil Discovery in 1966'. MA, University of Exeter.
Amanat, Abbass (ed.) (1983). *Cities and Trade: Consul Abbott on the Economy and Society of Iran, 1847-1866*. London, Ithaca Press.
Amedroz, H.F and D.S. Margoliouth (1921). *Continuation of the Experiences of the Nations*. Oxford, Blackwell.
Artin Pacha, Yacoub (1885). 'Zul-Kadr et Bab Zoueyleh'. *Bulletin de l'Institut égyptien*, 2e série, 6, 166–202.
Asadian, Muhammad (2004). *Gusha-i az danish va bavarha-yi 'amah dar shahr-i Qashm* (Notes on Popular Knowledge and Popular Believes in Qashm Island). Tahran, Rushanan.
Aubin, Jean (1953). 'Les Princes d'Ormuz du XIIe au XVe Siècle'. *Journal asiatique*, 241, 77–138.
Azadarmak, Taghi and Tezcur, M. Gunes (2008). 'Religiosity and Islamic rule in Iran'. *Journal for the Scientific Study of Religion*, 47:2, 211–24.
Babai, Sussan (2008). *Isfahan and Its Palaces: Statecraft, Shi'ism and the Architecture of Conviviality in Early Modern Iran*. Edinburgh, Edinburgh University Press.
Bastani-Parizi, Muhammad. E. (1961). *Tarikhi-i Kirman*. (History of Kirman). Tahran, Behnam.
Beck, Lois (1992). *Nomad: A Year in the Life of a Qashqa'i Tribesman in Iran*. California. University of California Press.

Bellér-Hann, Ildikó (2001). 'Rivalry and solidarity among Uyghur healers in Kazakhstan'. *Inner Asia*, 3, 73–98.
Belgrave, James. H. D. (1952). 'A brief survey of the history of the Bahrain Islands'. *Journal of the Royal Central Asian Society*, 39:1, 52–64.
Belo, Jane (1960). *Trance in Bali*. New York, Columbia University Press.
Bertram, Thomas (1931). *Alarms and Excursions in Arabia*. London, Allen & Unwin.
Boddy, Janice (1988). 'Spirits and selves in Northern Sudan: The cultural therapeutics of possession and trance'. *American Ethnologist*, Medical Anthropology, 15:1, 4–27.
_____(1994). 'Spirit possession revisited: Beyond instrumentality'. *Annual Review of Anthropology*, 23, 407–34.
_____(1989). *Wombs and Alien Spirits: Women, Men, and the Zar Cult in Northern Sudan*. Madison, University of Wisconsin Press.
Boloukbashi, Ali (n.d.) *Ahl-i Hava* (People of Air). Online resources: http://www.cgie.org.ir/shavad.asp?id=130&avaid=4156.
Bourguignon, Erika (1973). *Religion, Altered States of Consciousness and Social Change*, Columbus, Ohio State University Press.
Broch, Harald Beyer (1985). 'Crazy women are performing in Sombali: A possession-trance ritual on Boneraté, Indonesia'. *Ethos: Journal of the Society of Psychological Anthropology*, 13, 262–82.
Brockelmann, Carl (1943–44). *Geschichte der Arabischen Litteratur*, Leiden, Brill (Supplementbände 1–3, Leiden, Brill, 1937–1942).
Callan, Alyson (2008). 'Female saints and the practice of Islam in Sylhet, Bangladesh', *American Ethnologist*, 35:3, 396–412.
Comaroff, J, and J.L. Comaroff (1999). 'Occult economies and the violence of abstraction: notes from the South African postcoloniality'. *American Anthropologist*, 26, 279–303.
Cerulli,Enrico (1934). 'Zar', *Encyclopædia of Islam* 1. Vol. IV, pp. 1215–24.
Constantinides, Pamela M. (1972). *Sickness and the Spirits: A Study of the Zaar Spirit-Possession Cult in the Northern Sudan*. Ph.D. thesis, University of London.
Darvishi, Muhammadriza (1991). *Muqaddamayi bar shinakht-i musiqi-yi navahi-yi Iran* (An Introduction to the Folk Music of Iran). Tahran, Huziy-i Hunari.
_____(1998). *Ayina va avaz* (Mirror and Singing). Tahran, Huziy-i Hunari.
_____(2001). *Dairatulma'arif-i Sazha-yi Iran* (The Encyclopædia of Iranian Musical Instruments). Tahran, Mahur, vol. 1.
De Goeje, Michael Jan (1890). 'Zâr'. *Zeitschrift der DeutschenMorgenlandischen Gesellschaft* , 44, 480.
Dimotheos, R. P. (1871). *Deux ans de séjour en Abyssinie*. Jérusalem, Typographie Arménienne du Couvent de Saint-Jacques.
De Jong, Frederik (1976–1977). 'Cairene Ziyâra-days: A contribution to the study of saint veneration in Islam'. *Die Welt des Islams*, 17:1–4, n. 24, 26–43.

Doumato, Eleanor Abdella (2000). *Getting God's Ear*. New York, Columbia University Press.
Duff Gordon, Luci Lady (1902). *Letters from Egypt*. Reedited by Janet Ross, London, R. B. Johnson.
Dykstra, Dirk (1918). 'Zeeraan'. *Neglected Arabia*, 107, 17–23.
Eickelman, Dale and Piscatori, James (eds) (1990). *Muslim Travelers: Pilgrimage, Migration and the Religious Imagination*. London, Routledge.
Fakhouri, Hani (1968). 'The zar cult in an Egyptian village'. *Anthropological Quarterly*, 41, 49–56.
Feilberg, C. Gunar (1952). *Les Papis, tribu persane de nomades montagnards du sud-ouest de l'Iran*. Kobenhavn, I kommission hos Gyldendal.
Ferrand, Gabriel (1922). *Voyage du Marchand Arabe Sulayman en Inde et en Chine*. Translation of *Silsilat al-tawarikh*, written in 851 with commentaries by Abu Zayd Hasan Sirafi (around 916). Paris, Bossard.
——(1924). 'L'Elément Persan dans les Textes Nautiques Arabes'. *Journal Asiatique*, 204, 193–257.
Fredriksen, Borge (1977). 'Slavery and Its Abolition in Nineteenth-Century Egypt'. Ph.D., University of Bergen, Bergen, Norway.
Frobenius, Leo (1913). *The Voice of Africa* 2, London, Hutchinson, pp. 569–72.
Gaffary, Farrokh (1986). 'Démons et extases en Iran'. In *De la fête à l'extase: transe, chamanisme, possession*. Actes des deuxième rencontres internationales sur la fête et la communication. Nice Acropolis, 24–28 Avril 1985, Nice, Editions Serre – Nice-Animation, pp. 93–7.
Gamst, Frederick. C. (1969). *The Qemant: A Pagan-Hebraic Peasantry of Ethiopia*. New York, Holt, Reinhart and Winston.
Gharasu, Maryam (2008). 'Musiqi, Khalsa va Darman: namuna-yi marasaim-i zar dar savahil-i janubi-yi Iran' (Music, ecstasy, and healing: Case study of *Zar* ritual in south coasts of Iran). *Mahur Music Journal*, 40, 115–38.
Goitein, Shelomo Dov. (1954). 'Two eyewitness reports on an expedition of the King of Kish (Qais) against Aden'. *Bulletin of the School of Oriental and African Studies*, 26:2, 247–48.
Harris, Grace (1957). 'Possession "hysteria" in a Kenyan tribe'. *American Anthropologist*, 59, 1046–66.
Harris, Joseph. E. (2003). 'African in Asian History'. In Joseph E. Harris (eds). *Global Dimensions of the African Diaspora*. Second edition, Washington, Howard University Press.
Hadi. (1928). *Persian Navigation*. London, Methuen and Co. Ltd.
Hentschel, Kornelius (1997). *Geister, Magier und Muslime: Dämonenwelt und Geisteraustreibung im Islam*. Berlin, Diederichs.
Holes, Clive (2000). *Dialect, Culture, and Society in Eastern Arabia*. Leiden, Brill, vol. 2.

Holy, Ladislov (1988). 'Gender and ritual in an Islamic society: the Berti of Darfur'. *Man* (N.S.) 23, 469–87.
_____(1991). *Religion and Custom in a Muslim Society: The Berti of Sudan.* Cambridge, Cambridge University Press.
Hourani, George and Carswell, John (1995). *Arab Seafaring: In the Indian Ocean in Ancient and Early Medieval Times.* Princeton, Princeton University Press.
Iqbal, Abbas (1949–50). *Mutala'ati dar bab-i Bahrain va jaza'yir va savahil-i Khalij-i Fars* (Studies on Bahrain and the Islands and Shores of the Persian Gulf). Tahran.
Iqtidari, Ahmad (1963). 'Zabanha-yi Mahalli va Fulklur-i Khalij-i Fars' (Local Dialects and Folklore of the Persian Gulf). In Rizazadih Shafaq; Mustawfi, Ahmad; and Muhammad Ali, Sayyid (eds). *Siminar-i Khalij-i Fars.* Tahran, vol. 2, pp. 119–32.
Issawi, Charles (ed.) (1971). *The Economic History of Iran, 1800–1914.* Chicago, University of Chicago Press.
Javaheri, Fatemeh (2006). 'Prayer healing: An experiential description of Iranian prayer healing'. *Journal of Religion and Health,* 45:2, 171–82.
Kahle, Paul (1912). 'Zar-Beschworungen in Egypten'. *Der Islam,* 3, 1–41.
Kapferer, Bruce (2003). 'Outside all reason: Magic, sorcery and epistemology in anthropology'. In B. Kapferer (ed.). *Beyond Rationalism: Rethinking Magic, Witchcraft and Sorcery.* New York, Berghahn Books, pp. 1–30.
Kapteijns, Lidwien and Spaulding, Jay (1996). 'Women of the Zar and Middle-Class Sensibilities in Colonial Aden, 1923–1932'. In R. J. Hayward and I. M. Lewis (eds). *Voice and Power: The Culture of Language in North-East Africa. Essays in Honour of B. W. Andrzejewski.* African Languages and Cultures. Supplement, No. 3, London, SOAS, pp. 171–89.
Kazemipur, Abdolmohammad and Rezaei, Ali (2003). 'Religious life under theocracy: The case of Iran'. *Journal for the Scientific Study of Religion,* 42:3, 347–61.
Kelly, John Barret (1925). *Britain and the Persian Gulf, 1795-1880.* Oxford, Clarendon.
Kenyon, Susan. M. (1991). *Five Women of Sennar: Culture and Change in Central Sudan.* Oxford, Oxford University Press.
_____(1995). 'Zar as modernization in contemporary Sudan'. *Anthropological Quarterly,* Possession and Social Change in Eastern Africa, 68:2, 107–20.
Khosronejad, Pedram (2011) (forthcoming). 'Seyids, Sheykhs and Sadats of Bakhtairi of Lali Plain'. In Catherine Mayeur-Jaouen and Alexandre Papas (eds). *Portrait of Family with Saints.* Leiden, Brill.
Klunzinger, C. B. (1877). *Upper Egypt: Its People and Its Product.* New York, AMS Press.
Kramer, Fritz (1993). *The Red Fez: Art and Spirit Possession in Africa.* New York, Verso Press.

Lambek, Michael (1980). 'Spirits and spouses: Possession as a system of communication among the Malagasy speakers of Mayotte'. *American Ethnologist*, 7:2, pp. 318–31.

_____(1993). *Knowledge and Practice in Mayotte: Local discourses of Islam, Sorcery and Spirit Possession*. Toronto, University of Toronto Press.

Leiris, Michel (1934). 'Le Culte des Zars à Gondar (Ethiopie septentrionale)'. *Aethiopica*, deuxième année, 4, 23–124.

Leslau, Wolf (1949). 'An Ethiopian argot of a people possessed by a spirit'. *Africa*, 19, 204–12.

Lewis, Bernard (1998), *Le langage politique de l'Islam*. Paris, Gallimard, Bibliothèque des Sciences humaines.

_____(1960). *The Arabs in History*. New York, Harper and Row.

_____(1979). *Race and Color in Islam*. New York, Octagon Books.

Lewis. I.M., Ahmed Al-Safi, and Sayyid Hurreiz (eds) (1991). *Women's Medicine: The Zar-bori Cult in Africa and Beyond*. Edinburgh, Edinburgh University Press for the International African Institute.

_____(1956). 'Sufism in Somaliland', *Bulletin of the School of Oriental and African Studies*, 18, 146–60.

Lindquist, Galina (2001). 'The culture of charisma: Wielding legitimacy in contemporary russian healing. *Anthropology Today*, 17, 3–8.

Littmann, Enno (1950). 'Arabische Geisterbeschwörungen aus Agypten'. *Sammlung orientalistischer Arbeiten*, VIII, Leipzig.

Macdonald, Duncan B. (1911). *Aspects of Islam*. New York, Macmillan Company.

MacPhee, M (2003). 'Medicine for the heart: The embodiment of faith in Morocco'. *Medical Anthropology*, 22, 53–83.

Makris, G. P. and Natvig, Richard (1991). 'The Zar, Tumbura and Bori Cults: A Selected Annotated'. In I. M. Lewis; al-Safi; and Sayyid Hurreiz (eds). *Women's Medicine: The Zar-Bori Cult in Africa and Beyond*. International African Seminars. Edinburgh, Edinburgh University Press, pp. 233–83.

Marsden, D. J. (1972). 'Spirit Possession on the Persian Gulf: a Precis and a Comment on the Book "Ahl-e Hava" by Golam Hosein Sa'edi.'. In C. F. Kücheman and G. A. Harrison (eds). *Historical Demography in Relation to Human Biology*. 1 (*DYN*), Department of Anthropology, Durham, Durham University, Vol. 2, pp. 23–42.

Martin, Vanessa (2005). *The Qajar Pact: Bargaining, Protest and the State in Nineteenth-Century Persia*. London, I.B. Tauris.

Marvazi, Šaraf-al-Din Ṭāher (1942). *Ketābṭabā'e 'al-ḥayawān: abwābfi'l-Ṣin wa'l-Tork wa'l-Hend*. Edited and translated by Vladimir Minorsky as *Sharaf al-Zamān Ṭāhir Marvazi on China, Turks and India*, London, Royal Asiatic Society.

Masquelier, Adeline (2001). *Prayer Has Spoiled Everything*. Durham, NC, Duke University Press.

Masudiyah, Muhammad T. (1977). *Musiqi-yi Bushihr* (Bushihr Music). Tahran, Surush.
_____(1985). *Musiqi-yi Baluchistan* (Baluchistan Music). Tahran Surush.
Mazumdar, Shampa and Mazumdar, Sanjoy (2002). 'In mosques and shrines: Women's agency in public sacred space'. *Journal of Ritual Studies*, 16:2, 165–79.
Mead, Margaret and Gregory Bateson (1942). *Balinese Character*. New York: Academy of Sciences.
Mernissi, Fatima (1975). 'Women, saints, and sanctuaries'. *Signs*, 3:1, 101–12.
Messing, Simon (1958). 'Group therapy and social status in the zar cult of Ethiopia'. *American Anthropologist*, New Series, 60:6, Part 1 (December 1958), 1120–6.
Meyerhof, Max (1917). 'Beitrage zum Volksheilglauben der heutigen Agypter'. *Der Islam*, 7, 305–44.
Mirzayi Asl, Behnaz A. (2002) 'African presence in Iran: Identity and its reconstruction in the 19th and 20th centuries'. *Revue Française d'Histoire d'Outre Mer*, 89, 229–46.
Miskawaihi, Ahmad Ibn Muhammed Ibn (2000). *Eclipse of the Abbasid Caliphate: Original Chronicles of the Fourth Islamic Century*. Edited and translated by H. F. Amedroz. Oxford, Aristide D Caratzas Pub.
Modarressi, Taghi (1968). 'The Zar Cult in South Iran'. In Raymond Prince (ed.). *Trance and Possession States*. Montreal, R. M. Bucke Memorial Society.
Moghaddam, Maria Sabaye (2009). 'Zar', *Encyclopædia Iranica online*. www.iranica.com/articles/zar.
Muhibi, Ilham (1995). *Barrasi-yi Zar: ravish-i sunati-yi darman-i bimari-yi ravani dar astana Hurmuzgan* (Study of Zar Ritual: Traditional Method for Healing Psychological Cases in the Province of Hormozgan). MA, Faculty of Medicine, University of Bandar Abbas, Iran.
Muhammad, Abbas Ahmad (1969). 'Al-zar aw al-rih al-ahmar 'ind al-Shayqiyya' (The Zar or the Red Wind Among the Shayqiyya). *Majallat al-Mujtama'*, pp. 16–33.
Muqtadir, Ghulam Husayn (1954). *Kilid-i Khalij-i Fars* (The Key to the Persian Gulf). Tahran, Amirkabir.
Nadvi, Syed Sulaiman (1966). *The Arab Navigation*. Translated from Urdu by Syed Sabahuddin Abdur Rahman, Lahore, Sh. Muhammad Ashraf.
Natvig, Richard (1987). 'Oromos, slaves, and the zar spirits: A contribution to the history of the zar cult'. *The International Journal of African Historical Studies*, 20:4, 669–689.
_____(1988). 'Liminal rites and female symbolism in the Egyptian zar possession cult'. *Numen*, 35:1, 57–68.
Nöldeke, Theodor (1890). 'Zâr'. *Zeitschrift der Deutschen Morgenländischen Gesellschaft*, 44, 701.

Nourse, Jennifer Williams (1996). 'The voice of the winds versus the masters of cure: Contested notions of spirit possession among the Lauje of Sulawesi'. *Journal of the Royal Anthropological Institute* (N.S) 2, 425–42.

Ong, Aihwa (1988). 'The production of possession: Spirits and the multinational corporation in Malaysia'. *American Ethnologist*, 15:1, 28–42.

Padwick, Constance Evelyn (1929). *Temple Gairdner of Cairo*. London, Society for Promoting Christian Knowledge.

Qaimmaqami, Jahangir (1962). *Bahrain va Masail-i Khalij-i Fars* (Bahrain and the Problems of the Persian Gulf). Tahran, Tahouri.

Rahim, S. I. (1991). 'Zar Among Middle-aged Female Psychiatric Patients in the Sudan'. In I. M. Lewis; Ahmed Al-Safi; and Sayyid Hurreiz (eds). *Women's Medicine: The Zar-bori Cult in Africa and Beyond*. Edinburgh: Edinburgh University Press, for the International African Institute, pp. 137–47.

Rasanayagam, Johan (2006). 'Healing with spirits and the formation of Muslim selfhood in post-Soviet Uzbekistan'. *Journal of the Royal Anthropological Institute* (N.S.), 12, 377–93.

Ricks, T. (1979). 'Persian Gulf, seafaring and East Africa: ninth through twelfth centuries'. *African Historical Studies*, 3, 339–57.

Ricks, Thomas M. (1988). 'Slaves and slave traders in the Persian Gulf, 18th and 19th centuries: An assessment'. *Slavery and Abolition*, 9:3, 60–70.

Riyahi, Ali (1977). *Zar, Bad, Baluch* (Zar, Bad and Baluch). Tahran, Tahuri.

Sa'idi, Ghulam Husayn (1967). *Ahl-i Hava* (The People of the Air). Tahran, Amirkabir.

Safa, Kaveh (1988). 'Reading Sa'edi's Ahl-e Hava: Pattern and significance in spirit possession beliefs on the Southern coasts of Iran'. *Medicine and Psychiatry*, 12, 85–111.

Salima, Niya (1902). *Harems et Musulmanes*. Paris, Lettres d'Egypte.

Savage-Smith, Emilie (eds) (2004). *Magic and Divination in Early Islam*. Surrey, Ashgate Publishing.

Seligman, Brende (1914). 'On the origin of the Egyptian Zar'. *Folklore*, 25, 300–23.

Sharifiyan, Muhsin (2002). *Ahl-i Zamin: musiqi va avham dar jazira-yi Khark* (People of Earth: Music and Hallucination in Khark Island). Tahran, Ghalm-i Ashina.

Shumovsky, T. A. (1964). *Araby i More* (The Arabs and Sea). Moscow.

Snouck Hurgronje, Christiaan (1970). *Mekka in the Latter Part of the 19th Century*. (1st edition 1889). Reedited, Leiden, Brill, 2 vols.

Strelcyn, Stefan (1972). 'Catalogue of Ethiopian manuscripts of the Welcome Institute of the History of Medicine in London'. *Bulletin of the School of Oriental and African Studies*, 35:1, 27–55.

Tafazulli, Muhammad (1969). 'Darya navardi-yi Iraniyan dar davranha-yi afsaniyi (Iranian Navigation in the Legendary Epoch)'. *Hunar va Mardum*, N.S. 18, 20–5.

Tapper, Nancy and Tapper, Richard (1987). 'The birth of the Prophet: Ritual and gender in Turkish Islam'. *Man* (N.S.), 22, 69–92.
Tett, Gillian (1995). 'Guardians of the Faith? Gender and Religion in an (ex) Soviet Tajik Village'. In C. F. El-Solh and J. Mabro (eds). *Muslim Women's Choices: Religious Belief and Social Reality*. Oxford, Berg. pp. 128–51.
Thompson, Anna. Y. and Franke, Elisabet (1913). 'The Zar in Egypt'. *The Moslem World*, 3, 275–89.
Torab, Azam (2006). *Performing Islam: Gender and Ritual in Iran*. Leiden, Brill.
Toussaint, Auguste (1966). *History of the Indian Ocean*. Translated by June Guicharnaud. London, Routledge and K. Paul.
Trimingham, J. Spencer (1965). *Islam in the Sudan*. London, Oxford University Press.
Van Beck, G. W. (1958). 'Frankincense and Myrrh in Ancient South Arabia'. *Journal of the American Oriental Society*, 77, 147–51.
Vollers, Karl (1981). 'Noch einmal der Zar'. *Zeitschrift der Deutschen Morgenlandischen Gesellschaft*, 45, 343–55.
Walker, John (1934). *Folk Medicine in Modern Egypt*. London, Luzac and Company Publishers.
Wiet, G. (1955). 'Les Marchands d'épices sous les sultans mamlouks'. *Cahiers d'Histoire Egyptienne*, 7:2, 81–147.
Winkler, Hans Alexander (1934). *Bauern Zwischen Wasser und Wuste*. Volkskundlisches aus dem Dorfe. Kimân in Oberägypten, Stuttgart, W. Kohlhammer.
Worrel, William. Hoyt (1909). 'Studien zum Abessinischen Zauberwesen'. *Zeitschrift für Assyriologie*, 23, 1–35.
Yinger, J. Milton (1957). *Religion, Society and the Individual: An Introduction to the Sociology of Religion*. London, Macmillan.
Young, Allan (1975). 'Why Amhara get 'kureynya:' Sickness and possession in an Ethiopian 'zar' cult'. *American Ethnologist*, 2:3, 567–84.
Zwemer, Samuel Marinus (1920). *The Influence of Animism on Islam: An Account of Popular Superstitions*. London, Central Board of Missions and Society for Promoting Christian Knowledge.

Filmography

Flaskerud, Ingvild (2003). *Standard-bearers of Hussein: Women Commemorating Karbala*/ 35'/ Norway.
Oskoui, Mehrdad (2004). *The Other Side of Burka (Az pas-i Burqa)* / 52' / Iran.
Rahmani, Mahmud (2007). *The Zero Degree Orbit (Madar-i Sifrdaraja)* / 26' / Iran.

Chapter Nine

SHAMANISM IN TURKEY: BARDS, MASTERS OF THE *JINNS*, AND HEALERS

Thierry Zarcone

Considering two regions of the Turkic world which are far away from each other, namely Turkey and Central Asia, the researcher on shamanism is surprised by the fact that an 'Islamised shamanism' still exists in Central Asia while it has almost totally disappeared in Turkey, although leaving its imprint on heterodox Sufism and popular Islam. In Central Asia, under the pressure of Islam, since the seventh and eighth centuries, shamanism has undergone many transformations in order for its pagan character to be veiled behind Muslim symbols and gestures. Depending on the places in the Turkic world where this process of Islamisation developed and the epoch involved, the results were 'far from being similar' and 'Islamised' shamanism presents various faces. In Central Asia, in general, where it was firmly established before the coming of Islam, shamanism didn't lose its main function, in spite of the pressure of the new religion, implicit being the negotiation/playing with the spirits and, additionally, healing through mediating with them. Nowadays, contemporary Central Asian shamans, called *bakhshi, emchi, parikhan*, etc., are essentially healers and seers. Conversely, in other regions of the Turkic world far from Central Asia, like Azerbaijan and Anatolia, the shaman, as a healer, has almost totally disappeared over the centuries or has undergone drastic changes and lost many of his characteristics.

The Sufi brotherhoods were instrumental in the Islamisation of shamanism and many Sufi symbols and ceremonial practices were adopted by Central Asian shamans (Vuillemenot 2000 and 2004; Garrone 2000: 242–54). This is the reason why I prefer to label Central Asian shamanism 'Sufised shamanism', as I have pointed out elsewhere (Zarcone 2000a), instead of

'Islamised shamanism', an expression coined by the late Vladimir Basilov. In 'Sufised shamanism', Sufism clearly serves the interest of shamanism. The situation is different in contemporary Anatolia where several elements exist – beliefs, practices, rituals – that show similarities to Central Asian Sufised shamanism that we would depict as 'shamanic'. These elements may be classified under two categories: 1) the first category is composed of a set of practices and beliefs with a genuine shamanic background, many integrated by antinomian Sufi trends[1] (Qalandar, Bektashi, Abdal, etc.) into their doctrine and ceremonies: this is the case of the animal dances and especially of the Alevi-Bektashi dance of the cranes (*turna semahı/oyunu*), the cult of the tree, the motifs of some peculiar animal families, deer family and wading birds etc.[2] I label this phenomenon 'shamanised Sufism' since shamanism serves here the purposes of Sufism.[3] Several books and articles published in Turkey about shamanism unfortunately focus mainly on this 'shamanised Sufism' which is not, although it is one aspect of shamanism, the major feature of healing which entails mediation with the spirits, as evidenced in Central Asia. 2) This category is constituted by a class of healers, called *ocaklı* (people of the fire-place/hearth), who heal through negotiating with the spirits and practise rituals that are close to those used in Central Asia. These *ocaklı* may be the Anatolian heirs of the Central Asian 'Sufised shamans'. Hereafter, I'll use the word 'shamanism' indiscriminately for 'Islamised' or 'Sufised' shamanism.

There are four sections in this chapter. The first section examines the case of the shamanic elements in the figure of the bard in the western part of the Turkic world (nowadays Turkmenistan, Azerbaijan and Turkey), from the sixteenth century up to the present day. The second section investigates the general case of the traditional healer in Turkey who is a therapist (also called a 'master of the *jinns*') who heals the sick through negotiating with spirits. And this leads us to the third section that highlights the particular role played by the class of healers called 'People of the fireplace' (the second category of shamanic elements observable in Anatolia). In the last section, some healing rituals performed by Anatolian healers are compared to Central Asian rituals.

The bard as an heir of the shaman?

In contemporary Turkey, the bards (*ozan, aşık*/lover) who are representatives of the popular culture are musicians, singers and poets, usually linked to the Alevi-Bektashi movement, a syncretistic religious trend deeply influenced by pre-Islamic beliefs, Ismaili-Batini ideas and Sufism. Although in Central

Asia the bard is still a shaman and a healer, there are very few cases now in Turkey when we see a bard healing a patient. The common characteristic of these two figures is that they are transmitters of the religious and cultural traditions of their own culture. Thus, the Central Asian bard is a living library of the Central Asian epics (Köroğlu/Köroglu, Alpamish, Manas) while the Turkish *aşık* ensures the transmission of a rich repertoire of mystical music and poetry. Nonetheless, history and literature show us that the situation was different centuries ago when the Turkish bard, the *ozan*, and the shaman were a single figure.

Korkut Ata, patron of the bards, singers and shamans in Central Asia

In the epics of Korkut Ata (ninth–eleventh century) and Köroğlu (sixteenth century), both linked to Anatolia and the Caucasian region, the heroes Korkut and Köroğlu are bards, soothsayers and healers. Korkut is regarded as the prototype of the bard (*ozan*) and of the Islamised shaman of Central Asia, also as the patron saint of musicians and singers and the inventor of the fiddle (*qobyz*), the favourite musical instrument (with the drum) of the shaman (Garrone 2000: 175–81; Karakoç 2006: 17–8). There is another patron of musicians and singers, Baba Qambar, who was credited with the invention of the *dutar* (a kind of lute). Most interesting, however, is the fact that Korkut and Baba Qambar have learned the art of making their instruments from the spirits (*shaytan*) (Garrone 2000: 179–80; Bayat 2003: 35–6; Karakoç 2006: 21–6). This is therefore the reason why musical instruments in general, and particularly those used by the shaman, were frequently considered 'demonic' (*shaytani*) artefacts and a creation of the demons (*shaytan ishi*). We know, for instance, of many poems written by the Anatolian bards to defend themselves against this accusation. Aşık Dertli in the eighteenth century wrote:

> Like Dertli, it [the *saz*/lute] doesn't wear a turban
> It doesn't have any sandals
> It has neither horns nor tail,
> Where is Satan here?[4]

In the western part of the Turkic world (today Turkmenistan, Azerbaijan, Turkey), the lute (*saz* and *dutar*) has gradually replaced the fiddle (*kobuz*) seen by Muslims as a pagan instrument. However, there were still bards playing the *kobuz* (*kobuzcu*) among the musicians of the Seljuk army and at the court of the Sultan Murad II (fifteenth century). In addition, the word *ozan* (bard) originally meant *kobuz* and the *ozancı* was a player of *kobuz*.

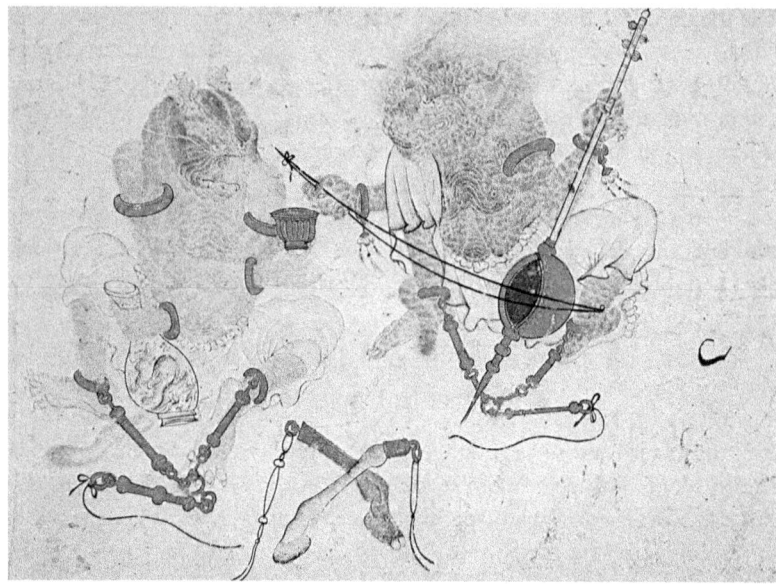

Figure 9.1. Drawing of demons playing the fiddle, end of fourteenth century ('Siyah Qalem', Manuscript 2153, Library of the Museum of Topkapı, Istanbul).

According to Abd al-Qadir Maraghi (d. 1435), there were different kinds of *kobuz* played by the Turks; one of them, called *kobuz-i ozan* or *ozan*, was a lute and not a fiddle, and was particularly the lute used by the bard (Başgöz 2001; Karakoç 2006: 73–8) (Figure 9.1). This means that though the instrument was forgotten its name was not, and is still respected. Actually, under pressure from Islam, the *kobuz* was replaced by the *çagur*, the *saz* and the *dutar*, all being the long-necked, plucked folk lute, and the *ozan* became an *aşık*. The *aşık* started to act more as a musician and a mystical poet than a magician and a healer.[5] This shift from the fiddle to the lute is supposed to have happened in the fifteenth and sixteenth centuries (Karakoç 2006: 77). From Muharrem Kasımlı, who wrote a study on the *ozan-aşık* art, we know that while some *ozan* became *aşık* under the influence of Sufism, others resisted and continued to work as shamans in areas far from the places where Islam was strong (Karakoç 2006: 58–60).

Köroğlu: the dervish and the shaman in Azerbaijan and Anatolia

The most interesting epic for our purpose is that of Köroğlu, which introduces, so I believe, the prototype of the *aşık*, that is the popular, wandering

Shamanism in Turkey: Bards, Masters of the Jinns, and Healers 173

Sufi poet of the Anatolian and Caucasian region who plays the lute (*saz*). Yet this epic was and still is very popular in the entire Turkic world with many variants, as it is among non-Muslims and non-Turkic people such as the Armenians (Reichl 1992: 318–33). This epic, we are told by Karl Reichl, most likely originated in Azerbaijan at the end of the sixteenth century, from where it spread north, east and west (Reichl 1992: 331). Furthermore, its Anatolian variant shows a deep mixture of shamanism and Sufism.

On the one hand, from the Azerbaijan variant, we learn that Köroğlu went wandering dressed as an *aşık* with his *saz* over one shoulder. Once, he was taught by a friend, an alchemist and seer (*kimyakar*),[6] how to heal a mad (*däli*) horse possessed by a *jinn* (*jin*). Köroğlu had to sit near the animal, playing the *saz* and 'reading' [poetry] (*saz chalına, söz okhuna*) for three days and three nights. He succeeded finally in expelling the *jinn*. What is striking, however, is the fact that at this time Köroğlu was ignorant of how to play the *saz* and he actually learned this art through the cure (Korogly 1975: 148). This story points to the capacity of music to expel evil spirits. More interesting, however, is that Köroğlu learned the art of playing the lute while playing the instrument and healing the horse, like the Central Asian shaman who learns the art of healing while being cured himself.

On the other hand, the Anatolian variant of the epic shows clearly how shamanism and Sufism mingle. Here, Köroğlu, still an *aşık*, is dressed like a dervish. He wears a long conical hat (*mervane küllah*) and holds a beggar's cup (*keşkül*), a stick (*asa*) and a rosary with 1,999 beads (*bin dokuz yüz doksan dokuz tesbih*). He also maintains that he belongs to the order of the Qalandars, a very popular antinomian Sufi brotherhood that had members wandering all over Asia, and to the other traditional 'twelve brotherhoods' (*on iki tarikat*), an expression which means that he is an 'achieved' dervish (Figure 9.2). Furthermore he presents himself as a 'dervish, a master of the *jinn*, a mulla, and a bard' (*hem devrişim, hem cindarım, hem mollayım, hem aşık*). As healer, he practised his art through mediating with the *jinns* (*cindarlık*) in mosques and making talismans (*muska*). The Muslims were convinced that he performed miracles (*keramet*) and the women, more attracted by the art of divination (*fal*) and healing than men, came to visit him. Köroğlu is also credited with the capacity to find objects and living beings (humans and animals) who are lost. Besides, it is thanks to his lute (*saz*) and his breath (*ben, bir afsun okur üfürürüm*), as recounted in the Azerbaijani variant of the epic, that Köroğlu heals the horse of a king (*Köroğlu Destanı* 1973: 200–205).[7] From this, we must understand that Köroğlu and the Anatolian bard (*aşık*) are the Anatolian prototypes of the shaman of Central Asia.[8]

Regarding the identification of Köroğlu with a Qalandar dervish, it is of interest to note from Clavijo, the Spanish ambassador to the court of

Figure 9.2. Drawing of a Qalandar dervishe (Ignatius Muradgea d'Ohsson, *Tableau général de l'Empire othoman, divisé en deux parties, dont l'une comprend la législation mahométane, l'autre, l'histoire de l'Empire othoman*. Paris, Imprimerie de Monsieur, 1791, vol 2, figure 137).

Tamerlane, that we know members of this brotherhood were healing the sick and playing music in Azerbaijan at the beginning of the fifteenth century.

> A place called Delilarkent a name which signifies 'the village of the madmen', for those who inhabit this place are all hermits of the Moslem creed [being dervishes] who here have the name of *kashish* [or priests]. The Moslem peasants from all the countries round come in pilgrimage hither to visit these holy men, and forsooth those who are sick regain their health...These dervishes shave their beards and their heads and go almost naked...As they walk alone night and day with their tambourines they chant hymns (Clavijo 1928: 139–40).

The capacity of dervishes to heal is confirmed by a poem attributed to Kaygusuz Abdal (fourteenth–fifteenth century), a Bektashi poet, who points to a particular group of wandering mystics named 'Abdal of Rum':

> The Abdal of Rum come calling upon the Friend,
> We wear the cloak, the felt and the rug,
> The sick come also to be healed,
> The sound one comes to my Master Abdal Musa.[9]

It is worth noting that the regretfully deceased Vladimir Basilov met in Uzbekistan in 1975 a female shaman chanting the epic of Köroğlu who depicted herself as a Qalandar, arguing that the epic was brought to her by spirits (*peri*) (Basilov 2000: 363).

As we shall see below, there are several themes in the epic of Köroğlu which have continued to influence Anatolia up to the present, although the bard has a looser connection to the art of healing. In contrast to the period when Köroğlu was also a dervish, a master of the *jinn*, a *mulla*, and a bard, these four figures are now independent, with the exception of the bard and the dervish who still embody a single figure in the Alevi-Bektashi tradition. The 'master of the *jinn*' (*cindar, cinci*) also exists in contemporary Turkey and the lute (*saz*) is sometimes required for some magical actions. Moreover, healing with the breath is widespread among the Turks, though the law has forbidden it as in 1925 the Kemalist government considered it a superstition.

We know that the contemporary Turkish *aşık* must experience a spiritual crisis, generally a love crisis, before being initiated as a musician. The beloved, i.e. God, is sometimes compared to a 'doctor' (*tabib*). The initiation of the bard occurs in part through dreams and he must sleep at a saint's mausoleum (*türbe/mazar*). In certain popular stories, while dreaming, the new bard listens for the strains of a *saz* and when awake he takes this instrument and improvises poems, and sings without any knowledge of this art (Başgöz 1967: 3–5; Günay 1999: 8–19; Yakıcı 2005; Serdarğlu-şişman 2006).[10] This dream motif complex was observed in the 1990s among the bards of Sivas (Central Anatolia); here, certain persons were made *aşık* after a dream or following a psychological crisis (*ruhi depresyon*) (Kaya 1995: 321). All this reminds us of the 'initiatory crisis' of shamans. Basilov collected similar stories during his fieldwork in Uzbekistan in 1983 and reported on spirits who used to bring a dreaming person to the world of music, inspiring him into playing a musical instrument (Basilov 1995) (Figures 9.3, 9.4).

Despite all these points, the Turkish *aşık* stopped acting as a healer along the model of Köroğlu and Central Asian shamans. In general, the great

Figure 9.3. Turkish bard playing the *saz*, 1865 (private collection, Istanbul).

majority of these bards belong to Alevi groups who play and sing during religious meetings (*cem*). Their position is highly respected as during ceremonies they always sit near the spiritual chief (*dede*) of the group and are greeted by all the participants and dancers. Yet, there is a practice mentioned in Köroğlu's epic that the *aşık* didn't give up. This practice, also observed among the contemporary Islamised shamans of Central Asia, especially the *közü achïk* of Kirghizistan (Duyshembiyeva 2005), is the searching and finding of lost objects or humans. This action is quite rare in present Turkey; however, we have an example from Sarıkamış (eastern Anatolia) in the village of Hamamlı Köy where a bard (*aşık*) named Durmuş Hoca played the *saz* while searching for lost objects (Kalafat 1990: 66–67).

Figure 9.4. The Turkish bard and poet Neyzen Tevfik (1879–1953) playing the saz, beginning of twentieth century (private collection, Istanbul).

The shamanic healer in Contemporary Turkey: 'master of the jinns'

The different figures under which Köroğlu presented himself are the dervish, the master of the *jinns*, the *mulla* and the bard, whose roles have become separated over time. In present Turkey, only the dervish and the bard are still associated and the *mulla* is exclusively considered a representative of orthodox Islam and, consequently, an opponent of popular Sufism and of the *aşık*. The fourth figure is that of the master of the *jinns* (*cindar*) who is a healer and seer. The term *cindar*, synonymous with *cinci* (or *cinci hoca*), and still in use in contemporary Turkey as it is in Azerbaijan, refers to a therapist who heals either by fighting and expelling the bad *jinns* or by summoning them to teach him how to cure the sick. As we'll see below, in present-day Turkey there are several ways to expel the spirits from a person who is possessed. Let us mention also that the masters of the *jinns* are known under various other names: the 'man who foresees', *bakıcılık* (*bakmak* = to see), the 'man who reads', *okuyucu* (*okumak* = read); the 'man who breathes', *üfürükçü* (*üfürmek* = to breathe), the man who 'reads and breathes' (*okuyup üflemek*), the 'magician', *büyücülük* (*büyü* = magic) and the 'amulet maker', *nushacılık/muskacılık* (*nusha/muska* = amulet).[11] According to tradition, many 'masters of the *jinns*' were black people originating in Sudan; Maghrebians and locals. Of interest is a ceremony called the 'day for collecting the plants' (*ot toplama gün*) directed by these black *cindar* and performed in Istanbul in the nineteenth and twentieth centuries on Fridays. The plants were cooked in a cauldron and the soup made from them offered to the spirits (*peri*) as a sign for the renewal of their relations with the humans. This ritual is reminiscent of the exchange of food and especially the giving of meat that is common in Siberian shamanism and in rare cases in Central Asia. The soup was also used to heal the sick (Abdülaziz Bey 1995: 370–71). There are other similar rituals in Turjey intended to please the spirits, such as the ritual of *şerbet dökmek*, 'to pour the sweet fruit drink': after reading prayers and breathing upon the juice or the juice of a fruit which the *cindar* poured secretly at a crossroad (Abdülaziz Bey 1995: 103). What is striking is the very detailed description of some 'masters of the *jinns*' in the memoirs of the Turkish ethnologist Mediha Esenel who carried out fieldwork in Anatolia in the 1940s.

> The *cinci hocas* [masters of the *jinns*] act as intermediaries between men and *jinns*. They save the people persecuted by the *jinns* and discover the concealed objects with the help of these spirits. The most renowned *cinci hocas* are black *hocas* (*zenci hoca*) about whom nobody knows from where they are coming. In the eyes of the locals, the aim of these *hocas* is different from that of the *hocas* based at the tombs of saints (*evliya türbeler*). These *cinci hocas* regarded as angels (*melek*), although they are humans, are creatures with satanic powers. They become enthusiastic [boil up] when having connection with the *jinns*, losing consciousness and foaming at the mouth.[12] To be successful in the cure, they need to be helped by good *jinns* and in order to deliver the sick persecuted by the evil *jinns* they have to gather all their powers and either burn the evil *jinns* or imprison them in a pot...(Esenel 1999: 141).[13]

This description is remarkable – being very rare, not to say unique, in Turkey – as it mentions a 'master of the *jinns*' who lost consciousness and foamed at the mouth when visited by the spirits. This collapse into rigid and inert trance is one feature of Siberian shamanism that is not very common nowadays in Muslim shamanism in Central Asia.

Then, Esenel learned from the Anatolian peasants the method used by the master of the *jinns* to assemble the spirits. Here, however, the *cinci hoca* assemble them in order that they may help him search for concealed objects instead of healing:

A great amount of tobacco was stolen in a village and the population called on a *cinci hoca*'s services to discover the thieves. The *cinci hoca* asked a nubile boy aged 12 years old to come to him. He spread on the palm of the boy's hand some purple ink and told the boy 'Look at your palm...You see many little people...' The boy looks at the palm and answered 'I don't see anything other than the purple ink.' 'Watch carefully, cried the *cinci hoca*, you will see'. The boy looks carefully and said 'Yes! the little people reaches my palm'. Then, the *cinci hoca* gives the boy several orders: 'tell them to sit on their chairs, to clean the place and to play'. The men who attend the ceremony were unable to see anything but the eyes of the boy have become bigger and he saw in his palm all the things the *cinci hoca* has told him. Therefore, the *cinci hoca* asked him 'Look at! Where did they put the tobacco stolen?' 'Near a chest' answered the boy who gave then a description of the place where this chest was situated. The *cinci hoca* became tired, he wiped away the sweat on his face. The boy then took fright and started to weep. The *cinci hoca* said 'Let's the *jinns* go away...Now you won't see anything'. And he dispersed the *jinns*. Then, I [Esenel] asked the people of the village if the stolen tobacco was discovered. They answered that it was not and that the explanation of the *cinci hoca* was the following: 'being foreign in this village, the boy didn't know the inside to the houses. On the contrary he would have discovered the thieves' (Esenel 1999: 141–2).

The names of the spirits invoked in Turkey are various and show that this country is at the crossroads of Africa, the Middle-East and Asia. The term *jinn* comes from the Arabic tradition,[14] but three others words, *peri*, *dev* (Persian in origin) and *alkarısı/albasti* (Turkish words) are inherited from Central Asia and almost totally unknown among Arabs. Another expression for the spirits is *iyi saatte olsunlar*, a Turkish expression used when having a bath at the hammam (bath) where *jinns* are supposed to dwell (Koz 1972: 6495–6; Abdülaziz Bey 1995: 371; Özbay 2007: 323).[15] To be possessed or smitten by the *jinns* is translated as *cin çarpmak, cin tutması* (*çarpmak* =

to beat, to trouble, to paralyse, to affect violently). Although the practices associated with magic, such as those performed by the *büyücüler* (sorcerer), *falcılar* (seer) and *üfürükçüler* (healer with the breath), were prohibited by the new Turkish government in 1925, these healers continue to practise their art today. It is striking that, as also evident in Russia and Central Asia in relation to shamanism, the practice of calling the spirit (*cindarlık*) mingles with 'spiritualism', implying a Western modern movement interested in calling the soul of dead persons and called '*alafranga cincilik*' (Frankish/western healer) by the Ottoman Ahmed Naim Bey since the beginning of the twentieth century (Çakan 2003: 35). Needless to say all these practices are fiercely opposed by orthodox Muslims and denounced as superstitions by the Turkish Ministry of Religious Affairs.[16]

Cinci and *üfürükcü* are frequently considered synonyms. According to Mediha Esenel, the second acts as an intermediary between men and *jinns*, as was the case in the epic of Köroğlu. Nevertheless there exists another category of *üfürükcü* who have no relations at all with the spirits (Esenel 1999: 139, 142–3). Healing with the breath, in the manner performed by the *üfürükcü*, is quite an old technique in Turkey; we know, for instance, in the fourteenth and sixteenth centuries of two Sufi saints of the heterodox Alevi-Bektashi trend, Hacı Mihman and Musa Beg, who were curing disciples with the breath (Ocak 2000: 147–8). Besides, the *üfürükcü* is usually associated with the act of 'reading' (*okumak*), actually the reading of the Qur'an, in the Turkish expression 'reading and breathing' (*okuyup üflemek*). Many Turkish healers argue nowadays that the breath brings great powers and we know that shamans of Central Asia also cure with the breath, though spitting is used more often than breathing. Actually both practices are linked (Garrone 2000: 212–6).[17] It may finally be observed that the master of the *jinns* and the *üfürükcü* belong to a wider category of healers called 'people of the fire-place/hearth of healing' (*ocaklı*) (see below) and that many *cindar* or *cinci* are called *ocaklı* and vice versa, as is also the case with the other healers.

Cinci and *üfürükcü* have drastically declined in Kemalist Turkey, as Esenel noticed in the 1940s, due to the growing modernisation of the country. The last among them were dwelling in remote areas, far from the towns (Esenel 1999: 139, 143–4). A contemporary researcher, Ünver Günay, who investigated the religious practices in Southeastern Turkey (Erzurum) in the 1990s, mentions many healers among whom are *cinci* and *cindar* (1998: 233, 236). Moreover, many healers were brought to the cities by rural people and there are now some urban *üfürükcü*, influenced by New Age ideas and Western esotericism, who are striving to revive this tradition and give it a 'modern' identity.

The 'people of the fire-place': a guild of healers?

The 'people of the fire-place' (*ocaklı*, also *urasa*) are either linked to a geographic place, or to a tribe or family, and sometimes to a mausoleum of a saint or to a sacred artefact (a magic stone usually). The natural decline of this trend was accelerated by the process of modernisation during the Republican era, after 1923, because healers, seers and magicians were declared superstitious and reactionary. Thus, as explained above, along with the 'masters of the *jinns*' (*cindar, cinci*) and the 'masters of the breath', the *ocaklı* healers became rare, except in the remote areas of Anatolia. Therefore, in the 1950s, shamanism benefited from the revival of Islam and of the implementation of a new policy that was more flexible in its attitude towards popular Islam and particularly tomb veneration. The 'people of the fire-place' (*ocaklı*) have thus undergone a re-birth and are now well represented in many areas in Turkey; for instance, they numbered only about 70 in the city of Zile, in Central Anatolia, in the 1970s, but increased considerably in number at Denizli and its surroundings in the 1990s (Öztelli 1974: 410; Öngel 1997: 26; Santur 1998). The *ocaklı* are specialised in the healing of specific diseases and follow various methods, i.e rituals, to heal: pouring of molten lead (*kurşun dökmek*), breathing (*üfürükcü molla*) or 'reading' Qur'anic prayers or invocations (*okuyan*).

Fatima: female patron of the shamans

The name *ocaklı* refers to the fire-place/hearth (*ocak*) according to legends collected by the Turkish anthropologist Gülnur Öngel at Denizli in Western Anatolia, in the 1990s. Muhammad, the Prophet of Islam, was making a fire when a voice reached him, which came from one side of the hearth. The voice told him that he could use the ashes of this fire, mixed with water, to heal the sick. So, the Prophet started to heal diseases but, after years, he became tired of doing this and decided to transmit this art to his daughter Fatima and 'authorised' (*izin*) her to carry it out. Hence Fatima 'took his hands' (*el almış*) and started healing. Becoming in turn tired of this, she transmitted the art of healing, in respect to the same ritual (*izin – el almış*), to her neighbour and close friend Lokman (Arabic, Luqman) – a famous figure in Islam – and his name was given to sura 31 of the Qur'an. Then Lokman spread this art to several places and people, setting up the tradition of the fire-place (Öngel 1997: 26).[18]

Thus, according to this legend, the Prophet Muhammad, his daughter Fatima and Lokman are the three first links in the chain of transmission of the healers' tradition. This chain is, as demonstrated below, clearly modelled upon the genealogies (*silsila*) of the Sufi lineages and of the guilds (craftsmen):

> Muhammad (the Prophet)
> ↓
> Fatima
> ↓
> Lokman
> ↓
> the *ocaklı*

However, Fatima and Lokman don't appear in any Sufi *silsila* and play no specific role in Sufism. In my view, this genealogy emphasises, on the one hand, the name of Fatima in order to show that the tradition of healing is under the patronage of that woman in particular and of women in general. On the other hand, it is not surprising to find Lokman as the third link in this genealogy as this legendary figure is the archetypal and emblematic doctor and wise man in Muslim tradition. He is still well known in Turkey under the name of 'Lokman Hekim', that is 'Lokman the doctor', and credited with knowledge of medicinal properties of plants (Özgen 2007: 13). Lokman is also frequently invoked by the contemporary Central Asian shamans (Basilov 1978: 161; Garrone 2000: 152–3) and, in Kharazm, he is considered the protector and transmitter of the art of healing (Snesarev 2003: 39). It is of importance to note finally that this genealogy associates the shamanic healing tradition represented by Fatima with the Muslim traditional medicine (called commonly Yunani/Greek) incarnated by Lokman.

The presence of the name of Fatima, as the first transmitter of the art of healing after the Prophet Muhammad, is confirmed by the fact that the great majority of the healers of the fire-place are female. This is also the reason why the name of Fatima (commonly Fadime Ana or Fatma Ana) is frequently evoked by the *ocaklı* during cures: thus, female healers when practising their art systematically pronounce the following formula: 'it is not my hand [that heals you] but that of our Fadime Ana' (Tanyu 1982: 483–4; Öngel 1997: 30–36). Besides, one of the conditions – among others – attached to becoming an *ocaklı* is to be chosen by Fatima Ana and to meet her through a dream and then to 'take her hand', a very ritualistic expression (see the next section in this chapter). This practice is still commonly used in the Yıldızeli (Sivas) district in Central Anatolia (Gökbel 2007: 662). The Turkish expression 'it is not my hand [that heals you] but that of our Fadime Ana' exists, with minor differences, in Central Asia, as reported by the Russian ethnographer Sukhareva in Tajikistan, in 1975. A female shaman, while healing and carrying out ritual gestures with her hand, said: '[this is] the hand of Fatima Zuhra, [this is] the hand of Khadicha [Khadija]' (*Fotima Zuhroni quli, Khadicha-Kibriyoni quli*) (Sukhareva 1975: 72; Garonne 2000: 216; Mustafina 1992: 91). In this case, Fatima is associated with another illustrious Muslim woman, Khadija, the first wife of the Prophet (an association that can also be observed in Turkey). The names of Fatima and Khadija under the form 'Bibi Fatimaju Zuhro Valilar' and 'Bibi Khatichaju Kubaro Valilar' (the saints Fatima and Khadija), are also present in the prayers/evocations of the Central Asian shamans (Murodov 1975: 103, 120).[19] A variant of this expression exists when Fatima is associated to God and his sons. A female shaman in the Uzbek enclave of Karamurt in Southern Kazakhstan said while healing: 'in the Name of God, the Merciful, the Compassionate, it is not my hand but, first, that of God, then those of Imâm Hasan, Imâm Husayn, Bîbî Fâtima and Bîbî Zuhra [still Fâtima]...'.[20] The 'hand of Fatima' is one of the most powerful talismans in Islam, and very popular in the whole Muslim world (Achrati, 2003).[21] However, among the Anatolian healers, the 'symbol' has been transformed into a 'ritual'.

On the other hand, it is striking that, according to the Russian ethnographer N. Pantusov in 1907, Fatima – under the name of Bibi Fatima as she is known in Central Asia – was regarded as the patron of Muslim shamans among the Turkic Taranchi tribe of the Ili Valley in Eastern Turkestan (China). From a manual of the guild of the *bakhshi* (*Bakhshilarning Risalasi*), presented by Pantusov and modelled on the manuals of other guilds of craftsmen, we know of the following legend concerning Bibi Fatima. The daughter of the Prophet was sitting in the shadow of a tree when a yellow bird descended from the heavens and stopped on one branch of this tree. The branch became dry immediately. Not long afterwards, the bird left the tree and the shadow of its wings covered the two legs of Bibi Fatima who became sick for seven days. Since no one was able to cure her, the Prophet Muhammad asked God for help. Then, 40 'perfect men' (*chihiltan*) were sent by God to heal her. Coming from the heavens, seven among these forty creatures reached the earth, alighting near a mausoleum (*gumbaz*). They put up a banner (*tugh*) in the house of Bibi Fatima who made some circumambulations around it and then recovered her health (Pantusov 1907: 61–2).

First, Fatima's sickness is clearly an initiatory ailment and the yellow bird that brings her the sickness is obviously a symbol of evil spirits. Secondly, the seven among the 'forty perfect men' (*chihiltan*) – that is the name of a famous set of Central Asian and Persian spirits (Andreev 1927; Basilov 1984; Garrone 2000: 163–5) – sent by God are none other than helping spirits who cure the daughter of the Prophet of Islam. Through her ceremonial circumambulations around the banner, a ritual usually executed by shamans (see below), Fatima clearly cured herself. The legend therefore reveals that she was 'chosen' or 'called' by the Invisible. Consequently, the art of healing passed from God and the *chihiltan* to Fatima and, therefore, from her to shamans.

Pantusov reports another legend about the origin of the art of healing that is more or less similar to the legend quoted above. In order to teach Muhammad how to cure his daughter, God sent the angel Gabriel to him. Travelling upon the wings of the angel, the Prophet was brought to the fourth heavens where 40 'invisible creatures' were absorbed in perpetual prayers. Seven among them travelled back to earth with Muhammad, all sitting upon the wings of the angel. Once in Fatima's house, the 7 'invisible creatures' put up a banner made of a rope and executed 72 'plays' (i.e. shamanic rituals), playing drums (*daf*), doing hubbub, running around Fatima and spitting on her. Finally, the daughter of the Prophet recovered her health (Pantusov 1907: 63–5).

A very symbolic and central element in the belief of the Turks is the banner (*tugh*) which is integrated here into the ritual of the shamans in Eastern Turkestan (as it is among the Turkmens,[22] but not in Western Turkestan). Turning around the *tugh* is the major shamanic ritual among the Uyghurs shamans, as pointed out by many Russian ethnologists and Tatar travellers, though rarely executed nowadays (Somfai Kara *et al.* 2007; Hujiexi 2009). The first Central Asian legend about Fatima as the patron of the shaman emphasises more profoundly than in Turkey the shamanic character of the daughter of the Prophet of Islam and the female domination of the art of healing. The second Central Asian legend, however, mingles deeply the shamanic and Islamic traditions. Particularly striking is the fact that the angel Gabriel brings Muhammad to the heavens where the spirits live, in the same way as, in the Qur'an, he helped the Prophet to perform the famous 'heavenly journey' – actually an 'ascension' (*mi'raj*) – that permitted him to be in close proximity to God. It is likely that Gabriel brings the 'invisible creatures' to Fatima.[23] The introduction of the *mi'raj* episode into the legend of the origin of shamanism is another way to integrate the shamanic more firmly into the Muslim tradition. Besides, in the second Central Asian legend, Fatima doesn't cure herself but the 'invisible creatures' do; therefore she cannot be considered a shaman in the manner indicated by the first legend.

Turning now to the Turkish legend of the origin of the fire-place, presented above, we note that Fatima never falls sick but learns from her father, Muhammad, the art of healing, thanks to the ashes of the fire. However, another origin (apart from any shamanic origin) for the use of ashes might be Islamic. The only data in any Muslim tradition recording the tradition of a healer of Fatima using ashes comes from Ismail Bukhari (eleventh century),

Shamanism in Turkey: Bards, Masters of the Jinns, and Healers 185

the famous author of a compilation of hadith. Bukhari writes that Fatima and her husband Ali nursed the wounds of the Prophet injured at the Battle of Uhud:

> [Fatima] used to wash the wounds, and Ali b. Abi Talib used to pour water from a shield. When Fatima saw that the water aggravated the bleeding, she took a piece of a mat, burnt it, and inserted its ashes into the wound so that the blood was congealed (and bleeding stopped) (Bukhari, 5, 277–8; 7, 126, quoted by Rahim 1989: 401–402).

Finally, it appears that in Central Asia and Turkey, the legend of Fatima is adapted to the particular way of healing as practised locally. Hence, Fatima appeared as a rival of Korkut Ata, the major patron of the shamans in a Muslim context. Lastly, the question arises: do the Turkish *ocaklı* healers work as a guild of craftsmen, as is the case in Eastern Turkestan? The fact that the Uyghur healers are organised into a guild with rules and possess a manual is attested not only by N. N. Pantusov, but also by S. E. Malov and Sergei Oldenburg (Ol'denburg 1918: 20; Malov 1918: 5, 15–6). The *ocaklı* have a genealogy that is only orally transmitted as they never collect and put down their teachings on paper in the form of a guild treatise (*risala*). And I have never heard of a guild of healers in Turkey.

To return to the 'healers of the fire-place' it is remarkable that the locals regard the 'fire-place' as the *locus* of the encounter between humans and spirits. According to an Anatolian tradition, when a fire is lit in the fire-place, the *jinns* flee far from there, frightened by the fire, but when the fire is over, they like to gather nearby (Tanyu 1976: 293). The fire-place is thus a place visited by the creatures of the Invisible and, consequently, a place where one can heal with their help. Let us note by way of a parenthesis that in neighbouring Caucasia the chimneystack is considered 'an entrance from one world to the other' (Arakelova 2006: 428). From a fieldwork trip carried on in Turkey in the 1970s, the folklorist Cahit Öztelli points out that the healer (*ocaklı*) strives to expel evil *jinns* from the body of the sick and reports the following example of a cure. Healing a child who suffers from his 'ears', the *ocaklı* reads the *besmele* ('In the name of God...') or any other prayers in Arabic to his ears, whereby he orders the *jinns* to leave his body. The healer finally informs the mother of the child that the *jinn* which has entered into his ears has now gone away (Öztelli 1974: 410). Öztelli gives details of other rituals executed at the fire-place to frighten and expel the *jinns*; one is to shoot hanging pans with arrows of a bow; the other is to simulate the stabbing of the stomach of the sick (Öztelli 1974: 410). To conclude this section, fire-places have a two-fold purpose in contemporary Turkey. In some rare cases, shamans heal through a negotiation or a fight with spirits but in the majority of the fire-places the shamans cure the sick without associating with spirits and using sacred artefacts. In this second category, the art of healing has obviously undergone a process of simplification that might imply, to the eyes of many who ignore its origin, that fire-places are one specific art of healing among many other Islamic magic practices without any link to shamanism.

The Sufi brotherhood (*tarikat*) pattern

As we can see from the above and from several descriptions of the rituals performed at fire-places, it emerges clearly that the framework of the *ocakh* is based on the Sufi initiation ritual. The art of healing is transmitted either within a healer's family (hereditary succession) or to a chosen person who does not belong to a fire-place. But in both cases the ritual is still the same: an authorisation (*izin*) is given, as in Sufism where this permission is generally called *icazet*. It is more relevant that the ritual during which a Sufi shaykh initiates a candidate is called 'giving the hands' (*el verme*), and, concomitantly, the initiated 'takes the hands' of the *shaykh* (*el almiş*). A similar ritual is carried out by the *ocakh* healers (Öngel 1997: 11; Şar 2005). Mahmut Makal writes in 1949: 'a healer who is about to die *gives his hand* to someone who then becomes a healer. So, the hearths continue – the customer too' (Makal 1991: 89–90).[24] Thus, the new *ocakh* is made an 'authorised' person (*izinli* – with permission), that means 'authorised' to heal and to transmit this art to somebody else.[25]

'Giving and taking the hands' is processed through various rituals among the *ocakh*: 1) by saying 'I authorise you'; 2) by drinking some water from the hands of the master where he has spat; 3) by the master spitting into the mouth of the disciple or by the latter licking ashes from the hands of the master. It also occurs, as seen above, during a dream (and it is usually Fatima Ana who transmits the art of healing through the 'giving and taking the hands' ritual). Moreover, only men can initiate men and women initiate women (Öngel 1997: 11, 77). The transmission ritual when the master spits into the mouth or in the hands of his new disciple is also attested in Central Asia and among the Yakuts (Basilov 1992: 142; Garonne 2000: 213). However, this ritual, as an aggregation/initiation and a healing ritual, is also attested in the Muslim tradition (Rubin 2005: 99). Thus, the Prophet Muhammad is credited with spitting in the mouth of Ibn Abbas, future father of the Qur'anic exegesis, in order to transmit to him the science of understanding and interpreting the holy book. Some Sufi lineages have also adopted this ritual for initiation (Gilliot 1985: 143; Moezzi 2006: 41–43). Obviously, it is not easy to know the precise origin of this initiation ritual as performed by the *ocakh* healers.

In some rare cases, the climax of the ritual of 'giving and taking the hands' corresponds to the Sufi ceremonial of shaking the hands (*musafaha*) that, according to the Sufis, symbolises the spiritual pact (*biat*) concluded between Muhammad and the first Arabs who converted to Islam. The expression 'giving and taking the hands' is not unknown among the Sufis of Central Asia (*kol berish* – giving the hand) and carries the same meaning as in Turkey.

From Calouste Constant, an Armenian living at Smyrna (Izmir) in the nineteenth century and certainly the first scholar to investigate traditional medicine and magic in this country, we know that such a ritualistic handshaking was practised by an Armenian female *ocaklı* at Smyrna/Izmir:

> The initiation doesn't consist in the lone transmission of prayers and passes; because the initiator must, at the end of the initiation, shake the hand of his disciple...(Constant 1863: 170).[26]

It is worth noting that the transmission of the art of healing is not limited to Muslims. The case of this Armenian healer is quite interesting for she was given the art of 'reading [prayers]' (*okutmak*, to read in Turkish and '*aghotèle*', to pray in Armenian) by her mother-in-law who also healed horses touched by the evil eye (*nazar*).[27] A member of the Asiatic Society of Paris and a representative of the French Society of Magnetism, Constant interpreted the art of healing as 'animal magnetism' (based on the idea of an all-pervasive fluid, a magnetism, which the magnetiser can sense, influence and direct) and published several drawings in the journal *Le Magnétiseur* (Genève) which show the Armenian healer curing a patient (Constant 1863: 162–71).[28] These drawings give details of the ritual followed by the healer which is of considerable ethnological interest (Figure 9.5). Besides, Constant points out that the healer yawned – common in shamanism – and, sometimes feels nausea or the desire to vomit (Constant 1863: 164). According to the folklorist Pertev Boratav, at the beginning of the twentieth century, a Greek priest who was given the permission to heal by a Muslim, conveyed it to his son and his grandson, the latter being interviewed by Boratav in 1950. The ritual of transmission was the same as explained above (Boratav 2003: 145).

Some *ocaklı* healers are linked to a saint's mausoleum (*türbe, mezar*) to which are attached certain prophylactic qualities. They usually pretend to be a descendant of the saint buried there. In this particular case, the capacity of healing is either transferred from the healer to the tomb or from the tomb to the *ocaklı*. There is another kind of transfer when the healer obtains a mysterious artefact, which has curative properties. The healer maintains that this artefact, generally a stone (stone of the Serpent; stone of Mecca,

Figure 9.5. A female Armenian healer healing a sick patient, mid-nineteenth century, Smyrna, Turkey (C. Constant, 'Le Magnétisme en Turquie. L'okoudmak, l'aghotéle', *Le Magnétiseur*, Genéve, 11, year 4, 15 February 1863).

etc.), was inherited by one of his/her ancestors who was a Sufi saint (*eren*), sometimes through the 'giving and taking the hands' ritual' (Constant 1862: 58–62; Roux 1970: 155–7; Öngel 1997: 13, 45–9; Boratav, 2003: 144). More important, however, is the fact that one can also become an *ocaklı* after going through an initiatory illness, as told by Mahmud Makal, a teacher in an Anatolian village in the 1950s, who collected many observations about the life of Turkish peasants. Makal noticed that a sick child aged six months, named İsmet, was brought to many *ocak* places by his parents, but all attempts to cure him failed. After a year and half, Makal persuaded İsmet's parents to bring the child to a doctor who healed him definitively with injections and drugs. But, during the cure, three or four worms (*solucan*) departed from a wound on his side. Makal writes:

> The people said that İsmet suffered from the *yılancık* (serpent). And that's how, since this moment, the child was recognized as a 'healer of *yılancık*' and therefore an universal healer (Makal 1963: 118–20; 1980: 45).[29]

Later, İsmet started working as a healer; he was just eight years old when Makal met him. The fire-places specialised in 'snake bite' (*yılancık ocaklı*) are nowadays widespread in all Anatolia (Öngel 1997: 45-9). In the opinion of the locals, the manifestation of the worms was a sign that İsmet was a healer. This is not surprising since the extraction of worms is a common practice in shamanism; let us also mention that in Central Asia the spirits frequently take the form of serpents that are very similar to worms.[30] Furthermore, the initiatory illness and the fact that Ismet survived this illness points to the shamanic characteristic of Ismet's story. Finally, there is no doubt that the Turkish *ocaklı* healers belong to a branch of shamanism similar to that existing in Central Asia, though the ritual and symbolism in use among the former is very simplified compared to that of the *bakhshi*, *emchi* and *parikhan* of Central Asia.

Remarks about some healing rituals

Healing by transfer

Having carried out much fieldwork on shamanism in Central Asia since 1995, I was very surprised on starting my research on the healers of Turkey, in 2007, that one of the rituals performed by these healers resembles closely a ritual performed in Central Asia. Actually this ritual is quite simple; it consists of waving a sacred object (musical instrument, cup of water, etc.) around the forehead and body of a sick person who is sitting with his head covered with a piece of cloth, a scarf for women, or blindfolded if male. Many shamanic 'seances' in Central Asia respect this ritual, particularly in Uzbekistan and Tajikistan. It is known that after playing the drums, the shaman waves this instrument above the head and around the body of the patient (Garrone 2000: 58 sq. and fieldwork in Tajikistan, Uratube, 1995). In Kirghizistan, a local anthropologist noticed that during a cure a female shaman filled a cup with some ashes and covered it with a piece of cloth. Then, she touched the body of the child from head to toe with the cup turned upside down (Duyshembiyeva 2005). Sometimes, as evidenced in the Tashkurghan district (former Afghan Turkestan), Northern Afghanistan, the patient is lying, but still covered with a wide cloth (Centlivres and Centlivres-Dumont 1988: 156–7).

Körkut Boratav attended a similar ritual at Ankara in 1945. It was executed by a 'master of the *jinns*' (*cindar*) while answering the questions asked by a patient. A child was covered with a wide piece of cloth and a bowl of water was placed nearby. The *cindar* called the *jinns* and asked the child to tell him the things he saw in the water of the bowl (Roux and Boratav 1968: 323). There is a variant of this ritual observed in Kars (Eastern Anatolia). According to local tradition, herpes (*uçuk*) have a satanic origin and appear on the lips of a person after being touched by Satan. A female healer linked to a fire-place (called *emçi kadın* or *ocaklı kadın* by the locals) used to cure herpes with a burning piece of cloth that she waved around the head of the patient before throwing it into a fire. Then, she applied a piece of bread to the herpes and later threw it to a dog (Kalafat 1990: 67).[31]

These rituals are obviously cures by transfer of which we know of very similar examples in Afghanistan and in Kharazm where they are named *alas* (a live coal in Persian) in both countries (Centlivres and Centlivres-Dumont 1988: 155–6), and even in Xinjiang (Du 1995: 50). This ritual, according to G. P. Snesarev, is 'the most popular of all "curative" ceremonies in Central Asia' and has several variants that are more or less complicated. It can, on the one hand, be performed in a very simple scenario by common people, and, on the other, in a more elaborate ceremony by shamans. A simple scenario implies the lighting of a small fire at the crossroads (*chorsuv*) which the patient walks around and steps across the flame thrice. Regarding the more elaborate ceremony, it is conducted by experts only, i.e. shamans (Snesarev 2003: 34–5).

Actually many of the rituals performed by Turkish *ocaklı* (with the exception of some analysed below) are essentially a cure by transfer rather than an 'archetype healing' ('guérison archétypale', an expression coined by Garrone 2000: 55); it is a more complicated ritual that is carried out by Central Asian shamans and is rare in Turkey, not to say non-existent, and consists of a long ceremonial process divided into several sections during which the healer, usually playing an instrument, heals through mediating with the spirits.[32] In the case of a cure by transfer, there is, in general, no elaborate ceremony for the spirits other than an offering ceremony. The situation in the Tashkurghan district will help me make the point clearer. There are three main healing rituals carried out in this area: 1) the *alas* ceremony which is cure by transfer; 2) the *qasida* ceremony, a reading of an evocation that is then written on a piece of paper and used as an amulet; 3) the *bakhshibazi* or 'playing of the *bakhshi*' which is the 'archetype healing' through mediation, i.e. playing, with the spirit.[33]

The best example in Turkey of cure by transfer is that of healing through pouring molten lead (*kurşun dökmek*), generally executed by a *kurşuncu hoca* (master of the lead) who belongs in most cases to an *ocaklı* lineage that specialises in this ritual (*kurşun dökme ocağı*, see Öngel 1997: 12; Demren 2008: 191–2). We have several descriptions of this ritual, one of which is a short video published on the Internet.[34] Here, however, the ritual is performed by a 'New Age' *kurşuncu hoca*, also an astrologist and a tarot reader, who is nevertheless very respectful of the traditional ritual, employing bread with water and lead. According to an observer of this cure in Istanbul at the beginning of the twentieth century, this ritual was executed in order to weaken the power of the *jinns* and the *peri* insofar as the amulets, charms and talismans were ineffective in healing the disease of the patient. The healer, in general an old female *ocaklı*, was 'authorised' (*izinli*) to perform it, i.e. initiated by a master. Molten lead was poured into a bowl with hot water and waved around several parts of the body of the patient including being placed on his head. Then, a piece of bread soaked into this water was given to a dog at the crossroads. The rest of the water was offered to the *jinns* and *peri* (Bayri 1972: 101–102). In a contemporary variant of this ritual, the slice of bread soaked in this water is then put into a cup of water which the patient must swallow from a couple of times. Finally, the cup with the slice of bread and the water are buried in a clean place in a garden (Özergin 1967: 4361–3).[35] From an explanation given by Muammer Kemal Özergin, the evil eye (*nazar*) and the disease are transferred to the lead, and the water is poured on the doorstep of the patient's house to avoid the disease moving to the healer (Özergin 1967: 4363).

The ritual of pouring lead is not only practised with lead but also with wax, as is the case in Azerbaijan and in Central Asia; here I observed during fieldwork (Jambul, Kazakhstan, 1996) a female *bakhshi* of Azerbaijani origin divining through a similar ritual with wax instead of lead. It has to be borne in mind, of course, that this ritual is also a way to tell the future as evidenced by the pictures suggested by the lead when thrown into the water.[36] This is also the case in Turkey where the ritual is sometimes performed in order to find out who has put a curse on a sick person. The visage of the malicious person appears when the lead is thrown in the water and the water is afterwards used as medicine (Makal 1963: 133–4).

Driving out and hunting the spirit *alkarısı*

There are some fire-places specifically used in fighting one particular spirit that is considered the most dreadful spirit; it is called *alkarısı* or *alcı* in Turkey. The *alkarısı* is famous all over Caucasia and Central Asia where he is known under similar names, *al, albastı, almaste,* etc. He is regarded as one of the most important spirits evoked by shamans and terrifies women with newborn babies since his main objective is to kill them. It would be too much of a departure for us to discuss here the complicated problem of this spirit, who is considered in Central Asia and in Turkey as either a spirit or a living non-human creature, sometimes half-spirit half-human.[37] Although several techniques exist for protection against the attacks of the *alkarısı,* we know of some 'healers of the fire-place' in Turkey, called *al ocaklısı* or *alcı,* who specialise in this task (Boratav 2003: 145–6; Özgen 2007: 107–108). It is likely that there are hunters of *alkarısı* in Central Asia (Sukhareva 1975: 13–17, 29–37; Basilov 1992: 246). At Sivas (central Anatolia), a hunter of *alkarısı (al ocaklısı)* inherited from his ancestors the art of protecting the villagers from this spirit. The healer used to catch and stab him with a needle *(iğne),* then force the *alkarısı* to repent *(tövbe).* Another scenario is to catch the *alkarısı* with pitch *(zift* – in French *poix).* Sometimes the healer gives a piece of cloth, which should be put near the bed of a newborn baby to remove the demon. The most important quality of the healer in this fight lies in his capacity to *see* the *creature* that, we must understand, is invisible to other persons, and to catch him. Another way to force the *alkarısı* to leave a room with a newborn baby in is to wave a sword in the four directions (Ülkütaşır 1939a; 1939b). As a shamanic practice, this ritual has spread throughout Turkey and the name of the *albasti* has become so popular in contemporary Turkey (where he still frightens the rural and uneducated population) that it has entered the 'fantastic' literature.

Conclusion

As demonstrated above, shamanic elements exist in Anatolia where arriving Turks have brought them from Azerbaijan and Transoxiana. The link with Central Asian shamanism is unquestionable. There are nevertheless some notable differences between the forms adopted in accordance with the ideas when they intermingle with Islam in these two regions of the Turkic world.

I would like to point first to the Anatolian bard *(aşık),* the major figure in the heterodox Alevi-Bektashi trend and, without any doubt, heir of the shaman. Many aspects of his doctrine (as seen generally in his poetry) and practices are reminiscent of the art of the healer, but the bard is one stage only, and the last in a process that started centuries before with the epic of Köroğlu. Originally the bard *(aşık),* dervish, shaman (master of the *jinns)* and *mulla* were interlinked; now in present-day Turkey the bard is a musician and a poet and no longer a healer or a shaman. There are some elements, however, that reveal his shamanic past; for instance, the dance of the cranes performed during the ceremony of the Bektashi-Alevi trend to which he belongs (Arnaud-Demir 2005), or the belief that he can transform himself into deer or stags, the shamanic animal *par excellence* (Zarcone 2000b). In addition, the bard still cultivates a special relation to his lute (*saz*) which he frequently considers a living creature. As Aşık Veysel (1894–1973), one of the renowned bards of Turkey, writes in a poem about his lute (*saz*):

I told you [the lute] my hidden pain,
I have striven to mingle my voice with yours...[38]

This example is reminiscent of the time when the instrument was a medium animated by the spirits (Figures 9.6, 40). Besides, it is highly likely that the initiation dream motif and the love crisis experienced by the contemporary bard at the beginning of his career have their roots in the shaman's initiatory sickness. However, some of these shamanic elements are slowly disappearing, as explained in 1991 by a contemporary bard, Aşik Ali Rıza (born 1949); he pointed out that bards (*aşık, ozan*) have lost many of their traditions that he called 'old beliefs, custom and habit' (*eski inanç, eski töre, esli adet kalmamış*). One example mentioned by Ali Rıza is that bards have no longer initiatory dreams, like in the past ('Günümüzde bir Aşık' 1991). Conversely, in Central Asia and in Xinjiang, many bards are still linked to shamanism and, in some areas, the term *bakhshi* (shaman) also means 'bard'. Korkut Ata, who is the prototype of the shaman and the healer, like Pir Aşık Aydın, is the patron of the bards and musicians; according to the legends, his fiddle/*kobuz* was buried with him (Reichl 2001: 53–4, 70; Garonne 2000: 180, 187–92). Consequently, the mausoleum of Pir Aşık Aydın at Kohna Urgench, Turkmenistan is nowadays, especially after the collapse of the USSR, a very popular pilgrimage place for Turkmen bards and shamans. A commemoration organised in 1991 at the grave of this bard, regarded also as the father of Turkmen poetry, attracted more than 50,000 visitors and pilgrims.[39]

Second, it must be kept in mind that the 'people of the fire-place' (*ocaklı*) along with some independent 'masters of the *jinns*' – if we except the 'modern' *cindars* who strive to revive traditional healing rituals in a New Age context – present many shamanic features. As seen above, the ritual carried out by *ocaklı* healers is less complex than in Central Asia, due, I believe, to the stronger pressure of Islam under the Ottomans and because of the remoteness of Central Asia, the original home of shamanism. On the one hand, the 'archetype healing' in Central Asian shamanism, to use Garrone's expression, is totally absent in Turkey where the only healing ritual is the cure

Figure 9.6. A miniature of Shehret ul-Nahr, the mother of the *jinns* with her 37 faces (from the 'Davetname', fifteenth century, manuscript of the Library of the University of Istanbul).

by transfer based on a very simple ceremony. On the other hand, the influence of Sufism, particularly that of the Sufi brotherhoods on the 'people of the fire-place', is limited to a few members, although there are notable rituals that differ from those existing in Central Asia (for example there are no rituals inspired by *dhikr*). The adoption by the fire-place healers of the Sufi ritual of reception ('giving and taking the hands') demonstrates that the *ocak* organisation is structured along the pattern of the Sufi brotherhood (*tarikat*). This aspect is consolidated by the existence of a genealogy, clearly inspired by Sufi and guild genealogies, which mixes the shamanic and Muslim healing traditions. This genealogy confers an Islamic legitimacy to the shamanic art of healing as the healers, like the Sufis and the craftsmen, are able to trace their art back to Muhammad the founder of Islam. The most notable characteristic of this genealogy, however, is the figure of Fatima the daughter of the Prophet of Islam who embodies in Anatolia and in Central Asian, with specific reference to Eastern Turkestan, the female prototype of the shaman. To conclude, Sufised shamanism is more Islamised in Turkey than in Central Asia, in the sense that it is supposed to be more acceptable in the eyes of the Muslim because of its link with the sacred family of Islam, and impregnated by the Sufi framework rather than Sufi ideas or practices.

Bibliography

Abdülaziz Bey (1995). *Osmanlı Âdet, Merasım ve Tabirleri* (Ottoman Customs, Rituals and Expressions). Istanbul, Tarih Vakfı.

Abdulla, Behlül (1993). 'Yesevîlik ve Azerbaydan'da şaman-derviş medeniyeti' (The Yeseviye and the civilisation of the shaman/dervish in Azerbaijan). In A. Yuvalı, M. Argunşah, and A. Aktan (eds). *Milletlerarası Hoca Ahmet Yesevi Semposyumu Bildirileri*. Kayseri, Erciyes Üniversitesi, pp. 1–8.

Achrati, Ahmed (2003). 'Hand and foot symbolisms: from rock art to the Qurân' *Arabica* 50: 4 , 464–500.

Acıpayamlı, Orhan (1969). 'Türkiye folklorunda halk hekimliği ve özellikleri' (Popular medicine and its characteristics in Turkish folklore). *DTCF Dergisi* 26: 1–2, 5.

And, Metin (2003). *Oyun ve Bügü. Türk Kültüründe Oyun Kavramı* (Dance and Sorcery. The Concept of Dance in the Turkish Culture). Reprinted in 1974, Istanbul, Yapı Kredi Y.

Andreev, M. S. (1927). 'Chil'tany v sredne-aziatskikh verovaniyakh' (The chiltan in the Central Asian beliefs). *Iz rabot Vostochnogo Fakul'teta Sredne-Aziatskogo Gos. Universiteta*. Tashkent, Izdanie Obshchestva dlya Izucheniya Tadzhikistana i Iranskikh Narodnostei za ego Predelami, pp. 334–48.

Arakelova, Victoria (2001). 'Healing practices among the Yezidi sheikhs of Armenia'. *Asian Folklore Studies*, 60: 2, 319–28.

_____(2006). 'Spirit possession. The Caucasus, Central Asia, Iran, and Afghanistan'. In Joseph Suad (ed.). *Encyclopaedia of Women and Islamic Cultures*. Leiden, Brill, pp. 426–29.

Araz, Rıfat (1995). *Harput'ta Eski Türk İnançları ve Halk Hekimliği* (Ancient Turkish Beliefs and Popular Medicine at Harput). Ankara, Atatürk Kültür Dil ve Tarih Yüksek Kurumu.

Arnaud-Demir, Françoise (2002). 'Quand passent les grues cendrées...Sur rune composante chamanique du cérémonial des Alévis-Bektachis'. *Turcica*, 34, 39–67.

———(2005). 'Entre chamanisme et soufisme: le *semâ'* des Alévis-Bektachis'. *Journal of the History of Sufism*, 4, 143–57.

Başgöz, İlhan (1967). 'Dream motif in Turkish folk stories and shamanistic initiation'. *Asian Folklore Studies*, 26: 1, 1–18.

———(2001). 'From gosan to ozan'. *Turcica*, 33, 229–36.

Basilov, Vladimir N. (1978). 'Nekotorye materialy po kazakhskomu shamanstvu' (Some materials about Kazakh shamanism). In *Polevye Issledovaniya Instituta Etnografii 1976*. Moscow: Nauka, pp. 158–66.

———(1984). 'The Chiltan spirit.' In Mihály Hoppál, (ed.). *Shamanism in Eurasia*. Göttingen: Herodot, pp. 253–61.

———(1992). *Shamanstvo u narodov Srednei Azii i Kasakhstana* (Shamanism among the peoples of Central Asia and Kazakhstan). Moscow, Nauka.

———(1995). 'Blessing in a dream. A story told by an Uzbek musician'. *Turcica*, 28, 237–46.

———(2000). 'Malika-Ata, peripheral forms of shamanism? An example from Middle Asia'. In Denise Aigle; Bénédicte Brac de la Perrière; Jean-Paul Chaumeil (eds). *La Politique des esprits. Chamanismes et Religions universalistes*. Nanterre [Paris], Société d'ethnologie, pp. 361–9.

Bayat, Fuzuli (2003). *Korkut Ata. Mitolojiden Gerçekliğe Dede Korkut* (Korkut Ata. From Mythology to Facts). Ankara, Kara M.

Bayri, Mehmet Halit (1972). *İstanbul Folkloru* (The Folklore of Istanbul). Istanbul, Baha Matbaası.

Boratav, Pertev Naili (2003). *Türk Folkloru* (Turkish Folklore). Istanbul, K Kitaplığı.

Çakan, İsmail Lütfi (2003). *Hurâfeler ve Bâtıl İnanışlar* (Superstitions and False Beliefs). Istanbul, Rağbet.

Çakır, Ahmed (1987). 'Türk halk oyunlarında hayvan motifleri üzerine bir Atlas denemesi' (A tentative cartography of the motifs of animals in the popular Turkish dances). In *III Milletlerarası Türk Folklor Kongresi Bildirileri*. Ankara, Başbakanlık Basimevi, vol. 3, pp. 75–85.

Clavijo (1928). *Clavijo Embassy to Tamerlane 1403–1406*. Translated by Guy Le Strange, London, Routledge.

Constant, C. (1862). 'L'Orient du *nazar* et ses prophylactiques'. In *Le Magnétiseur* (Genève) 4, year 4 (15 July), 58–62.

———(1863). 'Le Magnétisme en Turquie. L'okoudmak, l'aghotèle'. In *Le Magnétiseur* (Genève), 11, year 4 (15 February), 162–71.

Demren, Özlem (2008). 'Halk hekimliğinde ocakları ve şamanizm' (Hearths and shamanism in popular Medicine). *Folklor Edebiyat* 14: 56, 185–210.

Doutté, Edmond (1909). *Magie et Religion dans l'Afrique du nord.* Alger, Adolphe Jourdan Editeur.
Du, Shaoyuan (1995). 'Pratiques chamaniques des Ouïgours du Xinjiang'. *Etudes mongoles et sibériennes*, 26, 41–62.
Duyshembiyeva, Jipar (2005). 'Kyrgyz healing practices: some field notes'. In *The Silk Road* 3: 2, 38–48, www.silkroadfoundation.org/ toc/newsletter.html [accessed December 2009].
Elçin, Şükrü (1979–83). 'Türk halk edebiyatında turna motifi', (The motif of the crane in Turkish popular literature). *Türk Kültürü Araştırmaları* 17–21:1–2, 79–94.
Esenel, Mediha (1999). *Geç Kalmış Kitap* (A Late Book). Istanbul, Sistem Y.
Garrone, Patrick (2000). *Chamanisme et Islam en Asie centrale. La Baksylyk hier et aujourd'hui.* Paris, Jean Maisonneuve.
Gilliot, Claude (1985). 'Portrait mythique d'ibn 'Abbâs'. *Arabica*, 32:2 (July), 127–84.
Gökbel, Ahmet (2007). 'Yıldızeli yöresinde yaşayan Aleviler arasında ocak ve nazarla ilgili inanç ve uygulamalar' (Practices and beliefs regarding the hearth and the malignant look of an evil eye among the Alevis living in the district of Yıldızeli). In Filiz Kılıç and Tuncay Bülbül (eds). *2. Uluslararası Türk Kültür Evreninde Alevilik ve Bektaşilik Bilgi Şöleni Bildiri Kitabı.* Ankara, Gazi Üniversitesi, pp. 659–70.
Gölpınarlı, Abdülbaki (1977). *Tasavvuf'tan Deyimler ve Atasözleri* (Expression and Proverbs from Sufism). Istanbul, İnkılâp ve Aka.
Günay, Umay (1999). *Âşık Tarzı şiir Geleneği ve Rüya Motifi* (The Poetical Traditions of the Âşık Genre and the Motif of the Dream). Ankara, Akçağ.
Günay, Ünver (1998). *Erzurum ve Çevre Köylerinde Dinî Hayat* (Religious Life in Erzurum and its Surroundings). Erzurum, Erzurum Kitablığı.
'Günümüzde bir aşık' (1991) (An aşık today [Interview with Aşık Ali Rıza]). *Dergâh*, 11, 13.
Hamayon, Roberte (1999–2000). 'Des usages du jeu dans le vocabulaire rituel du monde altaïque'. *Etudes mongoles et sibériennes*, 30–31, 11–45.
Hell, Bertrand (1999). *Possession et Chamanisme. Les maîtres du désordre.* Paris, Flammarion.
Hujiexi, Gulibahaer [Ghojesh, Gulbahar] (2009). 'Keerkeze zu samande zhouyu he shenge' (Songs and incantations of the Kirghiz shamans). In Jinxiang Seyin (ed.). *Saman xinyang yu minzi wenhua* (Shamanic Beliefs and Nationalities Cultures), Beijing, Zhungguo shehui kexue chubanshe, pp. 383–413.
Işın, Ekrem (ed.) (2003). *ElemtereFiş, Anadolu'da Büyü ve İnanışlar – ElemtereFiş, Magic and Superstition in Anatolia.* Istanbul, Yapı Kredi Y.
Kalafat, Yaşar (1990). *Doğu Anadolu'da Eski Türk İnançlarının İzleri* (Remnants of the Beliefs of the Ancient Turks in Oriental Anatolia). Ankara, Türk Kültürü Araştırma Enstitüsü.
Karakoç, Dilek (2006). 'Muharrem Kasımlı'nın Ozan-Aşık Sanatı Adlı Kitabı Üzerine Bir Çalışma' (A Research About the Book of Muharrem Kasımlı

on the Art of the Ozan-Aşık). Yüksek Lisans Tezi, Kars [Turkey], Kafkas Üniversitesi.

Kaya, Dogan (1995). 'Sivas yöresi aşıkların çıraklık geleneği.' (Tradition about the apprentice bard/aşık in the Sivas district). In *İpek Yolu. Uluslararası Halk Edebiyatı Sempozyumu Bildirileri*. Ankara, Kültür Bakanlığı, pp. 321–30.

Kleinmichel, Sigrid (2001). *Halpa in Choresm und Atin Ayi im Ferghanatal. Zur Geschichte des Lesens in Usbekistan*. Berlin, Das Arabische Buch, ANOR 4, 2 vols.

Koç, Muhsin (1997). 'Doğu Anadolu aşık edebiyatında turna motifi' (The motif of the Crane in the bard literature of Eastern Anatolia). In *V. Türk Halk Kültürü Kongresi Halk Edebiyatı Seksyon Bildirileri*. Ankara, T.C. Kültür Bakanlığı, vol. 2, pp. 41–52.

Koca, Turgut (1990). *Bektaşi Nefesleri ve Şairleri* (Bektashi Poetry and Poets). Istanbul, Nacı Kasım İstanbul Maarif Kitaphanesi.

Koçu, Reşat Ekrem (1958–1971). 'Bakıcılar'; 'cinci'; 'cin çarpmak'. In *İstanbul Ansiklopedisi*. Istanbul, n.p.

Köroğlu Destanı (1973). Edited by Behçet Mahir, Ankara, Atatürk Üniversitesi.

Korogly (1975). Edited by M. H. Tahmasib, Baku, Känchlik.

Köprülü, Fuad (1986). 'Ozan' (The Turkish Bard). In *Edebiyat Araştırmaları* (Researches on Literature). Ankara, Türk Tarih Kurumu.

Koz, Sabri (1972). 'Kanbur Oğlan Masalı' (Story of the young hunchback). *Türk Folklor Araştırmaları*. 279, 6495-6.

Levchine, Alexis de (1840). *Description des hordes et des steppes des Kirghiz-Kazaks*. Paris, Imprimerie nationale.

Makal, Mahmout (1963). *Un Village anatolien*. Translated in French, Paris, Plon.

———(1954). *A Village in Anatolia*. Translated from the Turkish by Sir Wyndham Deedes, London, Valentine, Mitchell and Co.

———(1980). *Hayal ve Gerçek* (Dream and Reality). 5th edition, Istanbul, Derinlik Y.

———(1991). *Bizim Köy* (Our village). 1951, 3rd edition, Istanbul, Çağdaş Y.

Malov, S. E. (1918). 'Shamanstvo u Sartov' Vostochnago Turkestana' (Shamanism among the Sarts of Eastern Turkestan). *Sbornik Muzeya Antropologii i Etnografii*, 5, 1–16.

Moezzi, Mohammad Ali Amir (2006). *La Religion discrète. Croyances et pratiques spirituelles dans l'islam shi'ite*. Paris, Vrin.

Murodov, O. 'Shamanskii obryadovyi fol'klor y Tadzhikov srednei chasti doliny Zeravshana' (The shamanic and ceremonial folklore among the Tajiks in the central part of the Valley of Zerafshan). In G. P. Snesarev and V. N. Basilov (eds). *Domusul'manskie verovaniya i obryady ve Srednei Azii*. Moscow, Nauka, pp. 98–108.

Mustafina, R. M. (1992). *Predstavleniya kul'ty, obryady u Kazakhov* (An Introduction to the Cults and Rituals among the Kazakhs). Alma Ata, Kazak Universiteti.

Ocak, Ahmet Yaşar (2000). *Alevî ve Bektaşî İnançlarının İslâm Öncesi Temeleri* (The Pre-Islamic Origins of the Alevî and Bektashî Beliefs). Istanbul, İletişim.
Ol'denburg', Sergei (1918). 'Kratkiya zametki o peri-khon'akh' i dua-khon'akh' v' Kuchare' (A short note about *peri-khan* and *dua-khan* in Kucha). In *Sbornik' Muzeya antropologii i etnografii*. Petrograd', Akademii Nauk', pp. 17–20.
Orunzheva, A. A. (1983). *Azärbayjan Dilinin Izahly Lughäti* (Dictionary of the Azerbaijan Language). Baky, Elm Näshriyaty.
Öngel, Gülnur (1997). 'Denizli halk hekimliğinde ocaklar' (The *ocak* in popular healing at Denizli). Yüksek Lisan Tezi, [Turkey], Pamukkale University.
Özbay, Ekrem (2007). *Türkmenistan'dan Anadolu'ya (Örf-Adet ve Halk İnançları)* (Popular Beliefs, Usages and Customs from Turkmenistan to Anatolia). Istanbul, IQ Kültür Sanat Y.
Özergin, Muammer Kemal (1967). 'Kurşun dökme' (Pouring the lead). *Türk Folkloru Araştırmaları*, 212, 4861–3.
Özgen, Zübeyde Nur (2007). 'Adana (Merkez) halk hekimliği araştırması' (Research on popular medicine at Adana – centre). Yüksek Lisans Tezi, Adana, Çukurova Üniversity.
Öztelli, Cahit (1962). *Köroğlu ve Dadaloğlu*. Istanbul, Varlık.
_____(1974). 'Anadolu'da şamanlığın izleri' (Remnant of shamanism in Anatolia). In *1. Uluslararası Türk Folklor Semineri Bildirileri*. Ankara, Başbakanlık Y., pp. 410–413.
Pantusov, N. N. (1907). 'Taranchinskie bakshi. Peri uinatmak' (Sposoby igry i lecheniya bakshei' (The Taranchi bakhshi: procedure in playing and healing). *Izvestiia Turkeskogo otdela Imperatorskogo Russkogo geograficheskogo obshchestva*, 6, 38–88.
Rahim, Habibeh (1989). 'Perfection manifested: 'Alî b. Abî Tâlib's Image in Classical Persian and Modern Indian Muslim Poetry', Ph.D, Harvard University.
Reichl, Karl (1992). *Turkic Oral Epic Poetry. Traditions, Forms, Poetic Structures*. New York – London, Garland.
_____(2001). *L'Epopée orale turque d'Asie centrale*. Paris, Centre d'études mongoles et sibériennes.
Roux, Jean-Paul (1970). *Les Traditions des nomades de la Turquie méridionale*. Paris, Librairie Adrien Maisonneuve.
Roux, Jean-Paul, and Boratav, Pertev Naili (1968). 'La Divination chez les Turcs', in André Caquot and Marcel Leibovici (eds). *La Divination*. Paris, PUF, pp. 279–329.
Rubin, Uri (2005). 'Muhammad the exorcist: aspects of Islamic-Jewish polemics'. *Jerusalem Studies in Arabic and Islam*, 30, 94–111.
Santur, Alparslan (1994). 'Üfürükçülük-cincilik'. In *İstanbul Ansiklopedisi*. Istanbul, Tarih Vakfı, vol. 7, p. 335.
_____(1998). 'Eren (Evliya) mezarları etrafında oluşan şifa ve sağlık talebine yönelik inanışların etnologik değerlendirmesi' (An ethnologic analysis of the

beliefs regarding health and healing at the saint tombs). In *I. Uluslararası Türk Dünyası Eren ve Evliyaları Kongresi Bildirileri, 13-16 Agustos 1988*. Ankara, pp. 427–441.

Şar, Sevgi (2005). 'Anadolu'da halk hekimliği uygulamaları' (Practices in popular medicine in Anatolia). *Türkiye Klinikleri Tıp Etiği-Hukuku-Tarihi Dergisi* 13:2, http://tipetigi.turkiyeklinikleri.com [accessed October 2009].

Seleznev, A. G.; Selezneva, I. A.; Belich, I. V. (2009). *Kult' svyatykh v sibirskom islame: spetsifika universal'nogo* (The Cult of Saints in Siberian Islam). Moskva: Izdatel'skii Dom Mardzhani.

Serdarğlu-Şişman, Vildan (2006). 'Divan şiirinin iyileşmek bilmeyen hastaları âşıklar' (Bards 'who don't know how to cure their illnesses in classical poetry). In Nil Sarı et al. (ed.). *Proceedings of the 38th International Congress on the History of Medicine*, Ankara, TTK, vol. 3, pp. 671–82.

Shamlu, Ahmad and Russel, James R. (1985). 'Âl'. In *Encyclopaedia Iranica*, vol. 1, pp. 741–2.

Snesarev, G. P. (2003). *Remnants of Pre-Islamic Beliefs and Rituels Among the Khorezm Uzbeks*. First published in Russian in 1969, Berlin, Schletzer.

Somfai Kara, Dávid, Hoppál, M. and Sipos, J. (2007). 'The sacred valley of Jay Ata and a Kirghiz shaman from Xinjiang, China'. *Shaman*, 15: (1–2), 47–68.

Sukhareva, O. A. (1975). 'Perezhitki demonologii i shamanstva u ravninnykh tadzhikov' (The demonic and shamanic survivals among the Tajiks of the plain). In G. P. Snesarev and V. N. Basilov (eds). *Domusul'manskie verovaniya i obryady v Srednei Azii*. Moscow, Nauka, pp. 5–93.

Taizhanov, K. and Ismailov, Kh. (1986). 'Osobennosti doislamskikh verovanii u Uzbekov-Karamurtov' (Peculiarities of the pre-Islamic beliefs of the Uzbeks-Karamurts). In V. N. Basilov (ed.). *Drevnie obryady verovaniya i kul'ty narodov Srednei Azii*. Moscow, Nauka, pp. 110–138.

Talu, E. E. (1953). 'Eski üfürükçüler' (The old healers with breath). *Resimli Tarih Mecmuası*, 45, 2592–4.

Tanyu, Hikmet (1976). 'Tüklerde ateşle ilgili inançlar' (Beliefs regarding fire among the Turks). In *1. Uluslararası Türk Folklor Kongresi Bildirileri*. Ankara, Kültür Bakanlığı Y., vol. 4, pp. 289–304.

_____(1982). 'Fatma Anamız (Fadime Anamız) ve el ile ilgili inançlar üzerine kısa bir araştırma' (A brief study of Mother Fatma/Fadime and the beliefs about the hand). In *II. Uluslararası Türk Folklor Kongresi Bildirileri*. Ankara, G.Ü. Basın – Yayın Yüksekokulu – Basımevi, vol. 4, pp. 479–95.

Troickaja, A. L. (1925). 'Lechenie bol'nyh izgnaniem zlyh dukhov (*kuchuruk*) sredi osedlogo naseleniya Turkestana' (Healing the sick through the expulsion of the evil spirits (*kuchuruk*) among the sedentary population of Turkestan). *Byulleten' Sredne-Aziatskogo gosudarstvennogo universiteta*, 10, 145–56.

Ülkütaşır, Şakir (1939a). 'Albastı hastalığı, tekevvünü ve tedavisi' (The disease, the origin and the way to cure the albastı). *Halk Bilim Haberleri*, 8: 95, 241–2.

———(1939b). 'Alkarısına dair halk inanmaları' (Popular beliefs regarding the alkarısı). *Halk Bilim Haberleri*, 8: 95, 243–6.
Veysel, Aşık (2001). *Âşık Veysel. Hayatı ve Bütün şiirleri* (Âşık Veysel. His Life and his Poetry). Istanbul, İnkılâp.
Vuillemenot, Anne-Marie (2000). 'Danses rituelles kazakhes entre soufisme et chamanisme'. In Denise Aigle; Bénédicte Brac de la Perrière; Jean-Paul Chaumeil (eds). *La Politique des esprits. Chamanismes et Religions universalistes*. Nanterre [Paris], Société d'ethnologie, pp. 345–60.
———(2004). 'Quand un Bakhsi Kazakh évoque Allah'. *Journal of the History of Sufism*, 4, 131–41.
Yakıcı, Ali (2005). 'Gördüğü rüya sonucu aşık olmaya günümüzden bir örnek: sorgunlu Miskin Yusuf' (To be in loved after dreaming: a contemporary example: Sorgunlu Miskin Yusuf). *Millî Folklor*, 17: 68, 40–43.
Zarcone, Thierry (2000a). 'Interpénétration du soufisme et du chamanisme dans l'aire turque: chamanisme soufisé et soufisme chamanisé'. In Denise Aigle, Bénédicte Brac de la Perrière and Jean-Paul Chaumeil (eds). *La Politique des esprits. Chamanismes et Religions universalistes*. Nanterre [Paris], Société d'ethnologie, pp. 383–93.
———(2000b). 'Le Brâme du saint. De la prouesse du chamane au miracle du soufi'. In Denise Aigle (ed.). *Miracle et Karama. Hagiographies médiévales comparées*. Paris, Brépols, pp. 413–33.
el-Zein, Amira (1996). 'The Evolution of the Concept of the Jinn from Pre-Islam to Islam'. Ph.D, Georgetown University.

Chapter Ten

THE BEKTASHI-ALEVI 'DANCE OF THE CRANE' IN TURKEY: A SHAMANIC HERITAGE?

Thierry Zarcone

The Bektashi Sufi order and the Alevi movement are two syncretic Turkish religious traditions that have proximity to each other and originate from the same matrix, which emerged in Anatolia around the twelfth and thirteenth centuries. The notable characteristic of these two traditions is their combination of antinomian Sufism and extremist Shi'ism (Ghuluvv) with shamanic, Manichean, Zoroastrian and Christian elements.[1] Nowadays, a particular sacred dance that imitates the flight of the cranes, though quite different from any other Sufi dance, is performed by several Bektashi-Alevi groups. The origin of this atypical dance is undated and undocumented in hagiographical, historical and archival sources related to the Bektashi traditions. In these sources, only an 'ecstatic dance' is mentioned, but without any details about its precise choreography.[2] The 'Dance of the Crane' has, apparently, been kept very secret for centuries. Bektashi-Alevi poetry, however, provides some details about the dances, as sung poetry is an important element of the ritual that accompanies these exercises. Furthermore, this poetry has also been kept secret, and was sung in secret and closed assemblies exclusively. Thanks to Turkish ethnographers, folklorists and historians, this poetry has become better known since the nineteenth and, particularly, twentieth century. The only sources at our disposal to understand and analyse this dance are constituted by the oral traditions of the Bektashi-Alevi groups and the repertory of poetry.

As we will see below, the 'Dance of the Crane' could be a suggestive example of the integration of certain shamanic ideas by Turkish Sufism.

Two elements could confirm a probable shamanic origin of this dance or, more precisely, the shamanic origin of some of its elements: the first is the use of the word '*oyun*' ('play') – a term widespread in Central Asian shamanism where it refers to the shaman and/or the shamanic ceremony – to describe the Bektashi-Alevi dances, as well as the terms '*sema*' and '*raks*', the most commonly employed words for sacred and profane dance, respectively, in the Muslim world.[3] The second element is the imitation of the crane by the dancers, as with the dances of the Central Asian shamans, which imitates animals and birds.

This brief study will start with a description of one version among others of the 'Dance of the Crane', based on the reports of historians and ethnographers and my own observations. This description is augmented by the explanations provided by rare Bektashi-Alevi written sources and by Alevi informants. An analysis of the dance follows, with an emphasis on the two elements mentioned above.

The 'Dance of the Crane': choreographic aspects and poetry

The dances executed by the Bektashi-Alevis in contemporary Turkey are no more than one aspect of the ceremonial of this religious movement, which also includes complex initiation rituals. The so-called 'Dance of the Crane' (*turna semahi/turna oyunu*) is itself only one among many other dances, though the most prestigious. This dance is accompanied by the music of a lute (*saz* or *bağlama*) and sung mystical poetry. Men and women dance together, but they are required to maintain a certain distance from one another, as bodily contact is forbidden.[4] The dance described below was observed in Istanbul in 2008 at the Bektashi convent (*tekke*) of Merdivenköy. The dancers were young Bektashi-Alevis, all members of a 'dance and musician band' directed by Cafer Yildiz and linked to the Association of Young Alevis of this convent (Alevi Bektashi Gençlik Platformu).[5] Some elements of this group were also invited by the Centro Incontri Umani at Ascona to perform at the 'Shamanism and Healing Rituals in Contemporary Islam' on 22 November 2008. The number of the dancers varies, although it is usually odd, from three up to a maximum of twelve (Figure 10.1).

The choreography utilises line formations and an arrangement in which couples face one another, but the major figuration is circular. Forming a ring, the dancers go around slowly, raising their arms into the air and moving them from side to side. They are said to imitate cranes dancing and preparing to flight. After approximately 10 minutes, the whirling of the dancers goes

Figure 10.1. Alevis performing the dance of the crane at Merdivenköy, Istanbul, 2008 (Photograph: Th. Zarcone).

faster. This phase, regarded as a crucial period, is called *yeldirme* (take flight). The dancers jump and revolve on their own axes, at the same time as they circle about the hall with their arms still raised into the air and moving from side to side, as in the first stage. Some observers say that the fast movement is such that the dancers are said to whirl like spinning wheels (*charkh gibi dönerler*) (Markoff 1993: 1056; Dinçer 2000: 38; Onatça 2007: 73, 75; Bozkurt 2008: 39, 58).[6]

The lyrics which accompany the dances refer generally to mystical themes: divine love and separation from God, nature and universal reconciliation. There are also poems dedicated to the cranes: those which follow were song by an Alevi musician during the dance we observed at Ascona in 2008. They are well known among the Alevis:

> *İki turnam gelir de dost ellerinden*
> *Evrilir çevrilir döner göllerden*
> *Muhabbet getirir dost illerinden*
> *Korkmaz ki avcı var deyi yollarda.*

> My two cranes come from the country of the Friend [God]
> They are coming and going from the lakes

They bring love from the country of the Friend,
Don't fear the hunter who is on your route.

Yine dertli dertli iniliyorsun
Sarı turnam sinem yaralandı mı
Hiç el değmeden de iniliyorsun
Sarı turnam sinem yaralandı mı
Yoksa ciğerlerin parelendi mi?

Yoksa sana yad düzen mi düzdüler
Perdelerin tel tel edip süzdüler
Küskün müsün ne dediler üzdüler
Sarı turnam (alli turnam) sinen yaralandı mı
Yoksa ciğerlerin parelendi mi?

Again, you whimper so sadly
My yellow crane, is your heart wounded?
Although nobody has touched you, you whimper
My yellow crane, is your heart wounded?
Or were your entrails broken to pieces...

Or did they trap you?
Did they strain your feathers one by one?
Are you offended? What did they tell you? Did they apologise?
My yellow crane, my red crane, is your heart wounded?
Or your entrails were broken to pieces...[7]

From 'playing with the spirits' to 'dancing': how the shamanic ritual was 'Sufi-ised'

Centuries before, the term '*oyun*' was probably the generic term for sacred and Sufi dance in the Ottoman Empire, as demonstrated by a Turkish manuscript of the thirteenth century, later to be replaced by the word '*semâ*' (Levend 1955; Erseven 1996: 79–88; And 2003: 176–81). Nowadays, *oyun* refers to popular dances and, in some cases, to the dances practised by Alevis and Bektashis. Today, the reason why '*oyun*' characterises a dance is unknown to the great majority of the Turks and even to the dancers. The word is actually more widely used with the meaning of 'play' or 'game'. However, in Turkic Siberia, this term is intimately linked to shamanism proper and, in Central Asia, to Islamised shamanism. In Yakut language, *ojuun* means the 'shaman' and *ojuunnaa* means 'to shamanise'. Moreover, *ojuun* refers also to a jumper, a priest, a wizard and a spindle. However, as in Turkish, the word refers also to game and play (Lot-Falck 1977: 15; Hamayon 1999–2000: 22–3). The shaman actually plays with the spirits, 'dancing' with them in order to trick, to please, to appease them and, then, to obtain a beneficial support from these creatures: in brief, it is a 'ritual gesture'. In Islamised shamanism, the shamans describe their art as 'playing the spirits': for example, '*porkhan ojnayar*' in Turkmen and '*pîr oynata*' in Uyghur (Garrone 2000: 61–2, 190–91; Hamayon 1999–2000: 26–9). An Uyghur shaman (*baqchi*) in Xinjiang (China) said in 1915 that he 'plays the spirits (*pari* – fairies) to heal the females who are either possessed by *jinns* or those expecting a baby without success' (Yâûshef 1915: 334).[8] Besides, in the Uyghur language, although '*oyun*' is usually employed for the shamanic ceremonial and the term '*ussul*' for profane dance, as '*sema*' for sacred dance, we found expressions such as '*ussul oynimaq*' – 'to dance' and '*ussul oynighuchi*' – 'a dancer'. Thus, *oyun* and *oynash* also mean a 'game'.

The Uyghur term '*ussul*' (profane dance) is sometimes associated with the shamanic ritual in the expression '*perikhun ussuli*' ('dance executed to play the spirits'), a sign that the shamanic ritual resembles a profane 'dance' (Inayitillah 1998: 17). Many ethnographic sources report that the shamanic ceremony in the non-Muslim Turkic world is sometimes composed of uncoordinated gestures like whirling and circling. For instance, the Khakass shaman used to 'move in a circle, according to the path of the sun' (Alekseev 1997: 69). In this case, the shamanic ceremony has a very aesthetic and structured appearance:

> The seance of the Yakut shaman was not only a frenzied dance, placing him in an ecstatic condition. It was essentially a multiact, dramatic, at times comedic sequence, and containing many incantations of 'frightful' content, which were often delivered with eloquence. At times, these were poetic productions of high art (Alekseev 1997: 59).

In Islamised shamanism, we notice two kinds of circular movements executed by the shamans that are frequently depicted as 'dances': the first is circling of the assembly; the second is to circumambulate the sick (in Tajikistan and Xinjiang). In some cases, the assembly itself participates in the circling movement (in Kazakhstan: Vuillemenot 2000 and 2004; Garonne 2000: 124–5) or sit in the form of a circle (*charkh*) (in Xinjiang: Yâûshef 1915; Han 2003).[9] The aim of these uncoordinated or circular movements in both shamanism proper and Islamised shamanism is to 'play' the spirits and, if the ceremony is a cure, to force or to convince these invisible creatures to help the shaman in healing the sick.

Conversely, in the Bektashi-Alevis tradition, the term '*oyun*' refers to a mystical dance with a codified choreography. Over the course of time, under the influence of Islam, '*oyun*' became considered disgraceful and regarded as a despicable amusement, an inappropriate description of a sacred dance. It was consequently progressively replaced by the term '*sema*'. Probably facing criticism from orthodox religious opinion, Hacı Bektaş, the eponymous founder of Bektashism, is himself believed, according to a sixteenth-century source, to have condemned the use of 'play' for his sacred dance:

> *Haşa ki semâmız oyunçak değildir*
> *O bir aşk halidir, salıncak değildir.*
> In no ways, is our dance (*sema*) a play/game
> This is a mystical state, this is not an amusement
> (Erseven 1996: 130).

The tradition of calling the Bektashi-Alevis dances and other popular dances '*oyun*' has nevertheless never ceased in Turkey, especially in the rural areas and among nomadic and semi-nomadic tribes (Tahtacı, Yürük), who, though still linked to the Bektashi-Alevi tradition, are quite autonomous movements (Bektashim-Alevism is actually far from homogenous). Nowadays, the Bektashi-Alevi dances are usually qualified as '*sema*', like the other Turkish Sufi dances (for instance that of the whirling dervishes – Mevlevi). It is worth noting that the folklorist Vahit Lütfi Salcı (d. 1950), in his booklet *Gizli Türk Dinî Oyunları* ('The Turkish sacred and secret dances', 1941) which investigates Alevi dances, frequently used the expression 'to play the *sema*' ('*sema oynamak*'), a quite unusual compound which points to the fact, in our view, that these dances meld Sufi and shamanic elements. Although the words *sema* and *oyun* appear now to be interchangeable, a Tahtacı (Alevi) author writes that *oyun* refers to local and profane dances only and *sema* to sacred ones (Yetişen 1986: 126).

To conclude this section, I would like to point to the player of the lute (*saz*) who is obviously considered an eminent figure by the Bektashi-Alevi groups: the dancers, while circling, nod respectfully and never turn their backs to him (a gesture fully integrated in the choreography). The explanation is that his function is reminiscent of the ancient bard who was half-Sufi, half-shaman. His model is Köroglu, the hero of the sixteenth-century epic of the same name, depicted as a bard, a dervish and a master of the spirits (*cindar*) who healed the sick thanks to his lute and through mediation with the spirits.[10]

Wading birds and cranes

From the shamanic crane to the Sufi crane

Some animals and birds are imitated by non-Islamised shamans during the course of their rituals. In general, those imitated are of the cervid family (deer, stag, reindeer) (Zarcone 2000b), galliformes (hen, turkey etc.) or wading birds (crane, stork) (Hamayon 1990: 493). Among the wading birds, the migratory birds (crane, goose, swan) are the focus of great seasonal rituals: in Siberia, for example, swans are praised when arriving or leaving for their long migrations. Weakened after the end of winter, the shaman is given a new force by the swans, which are consequently regarded as 'bringing a vital principle'. These birds are also regarded as 'messengers' ensuring the circulation of souls between worlds, between life and death. Shamans imitate their cries when calling them (Hamayon 1990: 314–6). The cry of the crane, especially of the Asian Red Crown Crane, is especially striking because of its bourdon.

It is known that during their healing rituals, the Islamised shamans in Central Asia imitate, though not systematically, the movements and the cries of various animals and birds, such as horses. But the crane, although it plays a notable role in Siberian and Yakutian shamanism, is not a prominent symbol in Central Asian shamanism. There is one report only, by a Russian ethnologist in 1898, of a Kazakh shaman (*bakhshi*) 'Standing with the hands on the hips, hopping slowly up and down, sometimes rushing, as the cranes (*zhuravl'*) sometimes do, and crying something unintelligible' (quoted by Basilov 1990: 72). This shaman, however, never said that he imitated the crane; the link to this bird is the interpretation of the observer only. Cranes are indeed very popular in the whole of the Turkic world, from Anatolia and the Volga area to Xinjiang and even as far as inner China and Japan; this bird is also well represented in Central Asian epics and poetry. Unsurprisingly, in Anatolia also it is considered a sacred bird to be protected and not hunted, and it is frequently evoked in popular poetry and stories (Koç 1997: 50; Elçin 1979–83: 88–90). Worth mentioning is the transformation of men into cranes, as attested in the Central Asian Alpamish and Köroglu epics (Reichl 1992: 349–50; Koç 1997: 49–50) and in the early Bektashi-Alevi hagiographies. For instance, in the Bektashi epic *Velayetname*, several mystics (*eren*) from Central Asia flew from Khurasan to Turkestan in the form of cranes (*turna tonına girub*) (*Velâyetnâme* 2007: 102–103) (Figures 10.2, Plate 3).

In brief, the flight of these birds, together with their seasonal arrival and their particular movements, observed by all in Asia, has inspired various interpretations and influenced Turkic societies at different levels. The

Figure 10.2. Ottoman calligraphy of a crane in the form of the Arabic prayer 'Bismillah', by the artist Mustafa Rakım, dated 1808–08 (in Aksel Malik, *Türklerde Dini Resimler* (Religious iconography among the Turks), Istanbul, Elif Y., 1967, p. 77).

Anatolian people were not insensitive to the coming of migratory birds in spring either: there are many examples in Bektashi-Alevi poetry of a 'call' to them. This call is also present in the choreography of the 'Dance of the Crane', in the form of a hand gesture executed by the dancers (Arnaud-Demir 2005: 149–53). Another particularity of the cranes is the execution of amazing and graceful movements when in ponds. These are interpreted as a 'dance' – they bow, turn around, arch their necks and kick up their legs – and are no doubt one origin for the choreography of the 'Dance of the Crane' in Anatolia.

Surprisingly, the crane seems to have been more influential in Anatolia than in Central Asia, especially in the profane and sacred dances that explicitly refer to the bird. The majority of these dances of the crane are not mystical, but hint at the mating of the cranes (a phenomenon often observed in Siberian shamanism, see Hamayon 1990: 497–504). This is the case, for example, among the Anatolian Tahtacı and Yürük tribes, both of which are Alevis (Roux 1966: 245 and 1970: 249–50; Saygun 2007: 13). Here, nevertheless, the dance is neither called '*oyun*' nor '*sema*', but '*turna barı*', the latter term being another word for 'dance'. According to a survey of the Anatolian dances imitating animals and birds made by Ahmed Çakır in 1987, it appears that the 'Dance of the Crane' is the most represented in Anatolia, followed by dances of the horse, dromedary and eagle (Çakır 1987).

But the crane is not necessarily a shamanic element that the Bektashi-Alevi tradition inherited from Central Asia or Siberia, unlike the term '*oyun*', the crane may actually be no more than a symbol venerated all over Asia. If, however, we put forward the hypothesis that among the Alevis and Bektashis of Turkey this symbol has a shamanic background, as Françoise Arnaud-Demir does (2002; 2004), it must also be said that the Bektashi-Alevi tradition has reinterpreted this symbol with mystical/Sufi eyes, as will be demonstrated below. Conversely, if not a symbol inherited from shamanism, it must be regarded as no more than a Sufi metaphor integrated into a syncretistic ritual which might have a shamanic origin. Both hypotheses are perfectly tenable.

The symbolism of the crane in the dance

As mentioned above, the 'Dance of the Crane' is far from the only dance performed in the Bektashi-Alevi movement. One dance in particular, called the 'Dance of the Forty' (*Kırklar semahı*), has a prominent role in the foundation myth of this movement. As reported by a poem, the prophet Muhammad when performing his ascension (*miraj*) met the imam Ali and Salman Farisi, a well-known figure in Islam.[11] Muhammad and Salman were given a bunch of grapes by Ali that, after their return on earth, they bought to a Sufi convent named the 'Convent of the Forty' (i.e. of the 40 saint figures). The grapes were squeezed by an invisible hand, and all 40 living in the convent were intoxicated by the juice. Then, everybody, Muhammad included, started dancing (*sema*), singing the name of God (*Hüvellah Allah*) and *la ilaha illallah* – 'there is no god but God' (Yörükân 2002: 62–3).[12] The 'Dance of the Forty', integrated in the ceremonial of the Bektashi-Alevi assemblies, memorialises this event. It is nevertheless a purely Sufi dance, in the sense that the dancers experience the ascension of the Prophet when dancing and the climax of the dance hints at the intoxication from the beverage given by Ali, that is the wine of the pure knowledge.[13]

The 'Dance of the Crane' presents two elements in common with other Sufi dances: it is, as a whole, a ritual quest for the love of God or Ali, and for mystical intoxication. Only the symbol of the crane – whether or not this comes from a shamanic background – gives the dance its originality. However, this symbol is (re)interpreted through Sufism. First and foremost, the crane is identified with the spiritual leaders of the Bektashi-Alevi community: the prophet Muhammad; the imam Ali; the 12 imams; or the chief (*dede*, shaykh), musician or not, of a particular group (Elçin 1979–83: 91–3). The flight of the cranes in the sky is also a metaphor for the community of believers: all flying in a well-organised movement, one after the other (*katar katar*), like the cranes flying in formation and following the leading bird. The flight of birds is a widespread Sufi metaphor, as it hints at the flight of souls escaping the material world. So, the choreography refers both to the movement of the cranes on ponds and in the sky:

> *Yemen ellerinden beri gelirken*
> *Turnalar Ali'yi görmediniz mi*
> *Yer gök inileyip zarı kılırken*
> *Turnalar Ali'yi görmediniz mi*
>
> Coming from the countries of Yemen
> Cranes, didn't you see Ali
> Performing the *sema* in the sky
> Didn't you see our nice Shah?
> (quoted in Koç 1997: 51)

Because it is a migratory bird, the crane is regarded as a messenger; however, contrary to the messenger in shamanism, the crane here brings news and secrets from one heart to another (Elçin 1979–83: 87 and 91; Koç 1997: 45–7). Even if the symbol of the crane has a shamanic origin, it is clear that Sufi and pre-Islamic traditions are mingled and that the crane has definitively became a Sufi image.

More interesting is the identification of the dancers with the cranes, and consequently its identification with Muhammad, Ali or one of the 12 imams. In the twentieth century the Alevi poet Kırklarelli M. Fahri Baba writes:

> *Turna gibi göle kondum*
> *Göl içinde cevher buldum...*
>
> Like a crane, I settle on the lake
> Inside the lake, I found a jewel...
> (quoted by Salcı 1941: 51)

Being cranes, the dancers fly towards God, in search of a union with him. The *yeldirme* phase in the choreography hints at a mystical state of sacred ebullience, of enthusiasm (*coşluk*) (Yönetken 1944: 8). The cranes in flight are also compared to the moth (*pervane*) which flutters around a candle and, in the end, is consumed by the flames (Arnaud-Demir 2002: 55). The dance of these insects is also the motif of another Bektashi-Alevi dance. To conclude this brief enquiry, it must be kept in mind that the Bektashi-Alevi 'Dance of the Crane' embodies through its use of the term '*oyun*' a historical and anthropological link with Asian shamanism. Similarly, the musical instrument (*saz*) used by the musician and singer, whose commands the dancers obey, constitutes another strong link between the Bektashi-Alevi and the shamanic tradition. The musician is reminiscent of the Islamised shaman 'playing' the spirits and making his assistants (i.e. the dancers) circle, while not circling himself. The crane – although it has, like many other wading birds, a prominent place in Asian non-Muslim shamanism – is absent in Central Asian Islamised shamanism and seems to represent a mystical/Sufi metaphor in the Turkish Bektashi-Alevi groups, rather than a shamanic loan. To summarise, the Bektashi-Alevi 'Dance of the Crane' is, without any doubt, a Mystical/Sufi ceremony and no more, though based on some shamanic elements which have been reinterpreted over time.

Bibliography

Alekseev, Nikolai A. (1997). 'Shamans and their religious practices from shamanism among the Turkic peoples of Siberia'. In Marjorie Mandelstam Balzer, (ed.). *Shamanic World. Rituals and Lore of Siberia and Central Asia*. New York, North Castle.

Algar, Hamid (1990). 'Bektaš, Hâjî'. *Encyclopaedia Iranica*, vol. 4.

Ambrosio, Alberto, and Zarcone, Thierry (2004). 'Samâ' and Sufi dance: a selected bibliography'. *Journal of the History of Sufism*, 4, 199–208.

And, Metin (2003). *Oyun ve Bügü. Türk Kültüründe Oyun Kavramı* (Dance and Sorcery. The Concept of Dance in Turkish Culture). Reprinted in 1974, Istanbul, Yapı Kredi Y.

Arnaud-Demir, Françoise (2002). 'Quand passent les grues cendrées...Sur rune composante chamanique du cérémonial des Alévis-Bektachis'. *Turcica*, 34, 39–67.

———(2004). 'Entre chamanisme et soufisme: le *semâ'* des Alévis-Bektachis'. *Journal of the History of Sufism*, 4, 143–57.

Basilov, Vladimir Nikolaevich (1990). 'Dva varianta sredneaziatskogo shamanstva' (Two variants of Central Asian shamanism). *Sovetskaya Etnografiya*, 4, 64–76.

Berti, Daniela (1995). 'Observations on shamanic dance'. In Tae-gon Kim and Mihály Hoppál (eds). *Shamanism in Performing Arts*, Budapest, Akadémiai Kiadó, pp. 63–76.

Birge, John Kingsley (1965). *The Bektashi Order of Dervishes*. 1937, reprinted London, Luzac, 1965.

Bozkurt, Fuat (2008). *Semahlar. Alevilerin Dinsel Oyunları* (Dances. Religious Dances/Games of the Alevis). 2nd edition. Istanbul, Kapı.

Çakır, Ahmed (1987). 'Türk halk oyunlarında hayvan motifleri üzerine bir atlas denemesi' (A tentative cartography of the motifs of animals in the popular Turkish dances). In *III Milletlerarası Türk Folklor Kongresi Bildirileri*. Ankara, Başbakanlık Basimevi, vol. 3, pp. 75–85.

Dinçer, Fahriye (2000). 'Alevi semahs in historical perspective'. In *Dans Müzik Kültür*. Istanbul Boğaziçi Üniversitesi Folklor Club, pp. 32–42.

Duygulu, Melih (2004). 'Poésie et Danse chez les Bektachis des Balkans'. *Journal of the History of Sufism*, 4, 85–96.

Elçin, Şükrü (1979–83). 'Türk halk edebiyatında turna motifi' (The motif of the crane in Turkish popular literature). *Türk Kültürü Araştırmaları*, 17–21:1–2, 79–94.

Erseven, İlhan Cem (1996). *Aleviler'de Semah* (Dance among the Alevis). 4th edition. Ankara, Ürün Yayınları.

Garrone, Patrick (2000). *Chamanisme et Islam en Asie centrale. La Baksylyk hier et aujourd'hui*. Paris, Jean Maisonneuve.

Gölpınarlı, Abdülbaki (ed.) (1958) *Vilâyet-nâme, Manâkib-i Hünkâr Hacı Bektâş-ı Velî*. Istanbul, İnkilap ve Aka.

Hamayon, Roberte (1990). *La Chasse à l'âme. Esquisse d'une théorie du chamanisme sibérien*. Nanterre [Paris], Société d'Ethnologie.

———(1999–2000). 'Des usages du jeu dans le vocabulaire rituel du monde altaïque'. *Etudes mongoles et sibériennes*, 30–31, 11–45.

Han, Liang Bin. (2003) 'Huoyan shan zuihou de saman wushi' (The last shaman-sorcerer in the Flaming Mountains [Turfan Oasis, Xinjiang, China]). In Han, Liang Bin. *Huoyan shan. Gulao wenming de zuihou shouwang*, Beijing, Zito, pp. 194–99.

Inayitillah (1998). *Uyghur usul sän'iti* (The Art of Uyghur Dance). 1982, reedited, Kashgar, Shinjang Khälq Näshriyati.

Koç, Muhsin (1997). 'Doğu Anadolu aşık edebiyatında turna motifi' (The motif of the crane in the bard literature of Eastern Anatolia). In *V. Türk Halk Kültürü Kongresi Halk Edebiyatı Seksyon Bildirileri*. Ankara, T.C. Kültür Bakanlığı, vol. 2, pp. 41–52.

Levend, Agâh Sırrı (1955). 'Aşık Paşa'ya atfedilen iki risale' (Two treatises attributed to Aşık Paşa). *Türk Dili Araştırmaları Yıllığı*, 1955, 153–63.

Lot-Falk, Eveline (1977). 'À propos du terme chaman'. *Etudes mongoles et sibériennes*, 8, 7–18.

Markof, Irène (1990–91). 'The Ideology of musical practice and the professional Turkish folk musician: tempering the creative impulse'. *Asian Music*, 22: 1, 129–45

———(1993). 'Musics, saints and rituals: semâ and the Alevis of Turkey'. In Grace Martin Smith and Carl W. Ernst (eds). *Manifestations of Sainthood in Islam*. Istanbul, Isis, pp. 95–110.

Ocak, Ahmet Yaşar (1984). *Türk halk İnançlarında ve Edebiyatında Evliya Menkabeleri* (Popular Turkish Beliefs and Life of Saints in Literature). Ankara, Kültür ve Turizm B., 1984.

———(2000). *Alevî ve Bektaşî İnançlarının İslâm Öncesi Temeleri* (The Pre-Islamic Origins of the Alevî and Bektashî Beliefs). Istanbul, İletişim.

Onatça, Neş Ayışıt (2007). *Alevi-Bektaşi Kültüründe Kırklar Semahı. Muzikal Analiz Çalışması* (The Dance of the Forty in the Alevi-Bektashi Culture. Investigations on Music). Istanbul, Bağlam.

Rakhman, Abdurehim (2006). *Uyghurlarda Shamanism* (Shamanism among the Uyghurs). Beijing, Millätlär Näshriyati.

Reichl, Karl (1992). *Turkic Oral Epic Poetry. Traditions, Forms, Poetic Structures*. New York – London, Garland.

Roux, Jean-Paul (1966). *Faune et Flore sacrées dans les sociétés altaïques*, Paris, A. Maisonneuve.

———(1970). *Les Traditions des nomades de la Turquie méridionale*. Paris, Librairie Adrien Maisonneuve.

Salcı, Vahit Lütfi (1941). *Gizli Türk Dinî Oyunları* (The Turkish Sacred and Secret Dances). Istanbul, Nümune M.

Saygun, Ahmed Adnan (2007). 'Des Danses d'Anatolie et de leur caractère rituel'. *Journal of the International Folk Music Council*, 2, 10–14.

Seyit, Sabirjan (2003). *Uyghur Oyunliri* (Uyghur Dances/Games). Ürümchi, Shinjang Khälq Näshriyati.

Velâyetnâme. Hacı Bektâş-ı Veli (2007). Edited by Hamiye Duran, Ankara, Türkiye Diyanet Vakfı.

Vuillemenot, Anne-Marie (2000). 'Danses rituelles kazakhes entre soufisme et chamanisme'. In Denise Aigle; Bénédicte Brac de la Perrière; Jean-Paul Chaumeil (eds). *La Politique des esprits. Chamanismes et Religions universalistes*. Nanterre [Paris], Société d'ethnologie, pp. 345–60.

———(2004). 'Quand un Bakhsi Kazakh évoque Allah'. *Journal of the History of Sufism*, 4, 131–41.

Yâûshef, Nûrshîrvân (1915). 'Turkistan Chini'de sayahat (Kuchar'dan Kashghar'gha' (A travel to Chinese Turkestan – From Kuchar to Kashgar). *Shûrâ*, 11, 333–6.

Yetişen, Rıza (1986). *Tahtacı Aşiretleri. Adet, Gelenek ve Görenekleri* (Tahtacı Tribes. Customs, Traditions and Usages). Izmir, Memleket GazetecilikVe Matbuaacılık.

Yönetken, Halil Bedi (1944). 'Köylü samahları' (Villagers dances). *Ülkü. Milli Kültür Dergi*, 60, 7–8.

Yörükân, Yusuf Ziya (2002). *Anadolu'da Aleviler ve Tahtacılar* (Alevi and Tahtacı in Anatolia). 1928, reedited, Ankara, T.C. Kültür Bakanlığı.

Zarcone, Thierry (2000a). 'Interpénétration du soufisme et du chamanisme dans l'aire turque: chamanisme soufisé et soufisme chamanisé'. In Denise Aigle; Bénédicte Brac de la Perrière; Jean-Paul Chaumeil (eds). *La Politique des esprits. Chamanismes et Religions universalistes.* Nanterre [Paris], Société d'ethnologie, pp. 383–93.

———(2000b). 'Le Brâme du saint. De la prouesse du chamane au miracle du soufi'. In Denise Aigle (ed.). *Miracle et Karama. Hagiographies médiévales comparées.* Paris, Brépols, pp. 413–33.

———(forthcoming). 'Bektâshiyya'. *Encyclopaedia of Islam 3.* Leiden.

Chapter Eleven

DREAMING IN THE PRACTICE OF AFRICAN MARABOUTS IN PARIS

Liliane Kuczynski

Introduction[1]

The marabouts who constitute the subject of my research come from West Africa and are Muslims. It was in the 1960s that they began to emigrate to France. In West Africa they assume different roles: lawyers, teachers of the Qur'an, regulators of conflicts; they also celebrate births, marriages and deaths. They are also diviners, and provide people with predictions, advice or guidance, and amulets for all sorts of problems (work, love, residence permits etc.). In Paris, most of them assume only the role of diviner and healer (in a broad sense of the term) for many reasons which are particular to the Parisian context.[2] Attracting clients from all origins, they became a serious challenge to French diviners, reviewing and enriching the interpretations of illness and misfortune and the ways of healing; nonetheless they strove to maintain a subtle balance between exoticism and these practices, already well known in France before their arrival.

One of the practices marabouts use for healing is dreaming. Much has been written about the mainstream teachings of Islam regarding dreams and their interpretation (von Grünebaum 1967; Fahd 1987; Lory 2003, 2007). However, it is striking that none of this literature has dealt in any explicit way with Muslim social practices of dreaming. The purpose of this chapter is to provide some insights into this issue by describing several ways of dreaming used by marabouts in order to solve their clients' problems. It is divided in two parts: the first deals with current practices observed in Paris and in

Senegal; the second focuses on a case study, the examination of the special experience of a marabout whose biography I am currently writing.

Current practices of listikhar

As with shamanistic societies, the Islamic world places great value on dreams, and dreaming is an important component of Muslim people's everyday lives. Talking about one's dreams, guessing what they mean, and drawing knowledge, advice or warnings from them, are very common experiences. Just one example: during my fieldwork, Khadi, a young Malian student, told me that she saw in her dream a large white bird flying towards her, which she interpreted as a sign that something good would happen to her. But apart from such spontaneous experiences, dreams can also be induced through special prayers. Strictly speaking, what people are looking for is decision making via divine inspiration: this dawns upon the individual through dreams, especially in the last part of the night. Many websites explain how to perform this special prayer. It is well known that many religious young people now seek divine guidance through dreams before making any major decision, especially on questions of marriage. Two points should be borne in mind. First, that in Muslim societies, the power of dreams is widely acknowledged: they may predict the future, they may help to shape social behaviour, they may solve one's difficulties. Second, that, to some extent, everyone is able to draw lessons from their dreams.

However, if a person has a particular problem they cannot solve alone, they may seek the intervention of a specialist. They might also take this course if a dream remains unclear or predicts undesirable things. For example, a woman went to a marabout because she was frightened by her dream, which showed her sister in a very dangerous situation. It certainly meant something was threatening the sister, but the dreamer did not know whether it was an accident or an illness or some other unpleasant event. She asked the marabout to clarify this and to protect her sister. In such cases, it is up to the specialist to reveal the truth of the client's dream and to act, together with the client's cooperation, in order to avoid any gloomy predictions. For this, the marabout chooses between numerous techniques of divination. Although it may be replaced by more rapid techniques like geomancy or cowrie-shell divination, particularly in urban contexts,[3] one of the most frequently used methods, in West Africa as well as in Paris, is what marabouts call *listikhar* (Arabic *istikhara*). This corresponds roughly to the prayer that was outlined previously, which ordinary people can use to make a decision through divine inspiration, but which marabouts are presumed to hold in more elaborate and powerful versions. So, one can see that ordinary practices have similarities to those of specialists. The difference lies in the involvement with the esoteric sciences and the scale of the operations, rather than in the nature of the practice. A second observation is that claiming authority as a specialist can be a way of making a living as diviner and healer while using one's domestic religious knowledge. This occurs particularly in urban contexts.

When marabouts are aware of the problem or the request of their clients, they often need to 'look', which means engaging in this esoteric *listikhar* night consultation. They might also need this to verify if the client is sincere, or even to protect the marabout's own life. In West Africa, *listikhar* may also be used to solve more collective difficulties. For example, as Lamine O. Sanneh notes, the Jakhanke – a group of Islamic clerics of Senegambia – were known to perform *listikhar* for *jihad* war leaders in the nineteenth century; they helped them by predicting the outcome of a fight or advising them on precautions to take (Sanneh 1979: 193–4). This author also states that 'the Jakhanke have used prayer, including *al-istikharâh*, as part of the process of community renewal (*tajdîd*), particularly in the area of undertaking new ventures and founding new centres' (Sanneh 1979: 197).

Different techniques

I will now focus on four different techniques of *listikhar* that I was able to observe. The first combines writings and prayers and is made up of several related parts. After the initial interview with the client, the marabout waits alone till nightfall, when they write the first word (*bismillah*) of the first verse of the *Fatiha* (first sura of the Qur'an) on a sheet of white paper and shape the last letter into a five-pointed star. In every point of the star, they write the same number, which is determined by the addition of the name of the client to the name of their request (for example: work; in Arabic, *amal*); each letter of both names is converted into a number by following esoteric rules that depend on calculations called *abadjada*. Here begins the most important part of *listikhar*: the marabout recites the verse several times (often 313 times, which has a special meaning in esoteric Muslim practices[4]). Then they request Allah to help them solve their client's problem (he cites his name explicitly). Lying down on their right side, in imitation of the Prophet's position,[5] they slip the written paper under their head. While sleeping, the marabout is supposed to see 'somebody' in their dream that tells them what action to take. If this does not succeed, the marabout repeats their request, and possibly increases the number of prayers.

The second technique observed was that of a marabout of Fula descent. First of all, he cleans himself, wears a clean cloth, and lights candles and a brazier with auspicious scents, in order to urge the 'angels' to visit him. While many treatises on esoteric Islam correlate angels' names with particular scents (as well as with colours, stones ...), the marabouts' favoured scent is benzoin; but this man uses any kind of perfume. He does not write anything, but recites several suras that he has chosen. Before lying down in a comfortable position, he invokes the 'name of Allah' that is suitable to his request and 'calls' his client's name followed by their mother's name in order to identify them precisely. The number of prayers and callings increases with the difficulty of the problem to be solved. During his dream, angels (Arabic, *rawhan*) inform the marabout about the cause of the problem and instruct him as to what kinds of 'sacrifices' (Arabic, *sadaqa*)[6] and written amulets or talismans are required to solve it.

The third technique is quite different. On a new piece of fabric, the marabout writes an esoteric, undecipherable formula consisting of Arabic letters and numbers like those one can find abundantly in al-Buni's work (*ob.* 1225, one of the masters of the esoteric Islamic sciences, his work is known widely all over the Muslim world).[7] As in the first example of *listikhar*, he slips this paper under his head while lying down. Before sleeping, the marabout says aloud: 'Angels, take care of X (the client's name)!' and expresses their request. In the dreams, the diviner is supposed to 'see' what was asked for.

And finally, a rapid *listikhar* technique used by some Fula marabouts consists of putting a branch of a special tree, named *doki*,[8] under one's head before sleeping in order to raise a divinatory dream. It is to be noted that *doki* is believed by the Fula to have magic powers. It is especially used for building shelves that receive milk calabashes, which are particularly protected by all kinds of talismans; it is also used in healing.

Discussion

What can be inferred from these different ways of dreaming? Obviously they are all, except the last, totally immersed in Islamic teachings. In fact, the Arabic root of the term *listikhar* (*KH-Y-R*) refers to the placing of a choice in Allah's hands. And according to Pierre Lory's work concerning dreaming in Islamic doctrine, this can help in solving everyday problems as well as in spiritual exercises, in Sufi style. Evidence of the link between these ways of dreaming and Islam can be found in many elements: the prayers (oral or written), in the praises of the Prophet Muhammad; the reference to the angels (Arabic, *maleika* or *rawhan*); the gestures (which imitate the Prophet's position). It lies also in the special writing of Arabic numbers and letters. This knowledge (which is called in Arabic, *ilm al-asrar*, 'science of secrets') is part of the esoteric approach to Islam, which not all Muslims regard with the same respect that is granted to the *sunna*. It is based on the idea that the world was created with the letters of the Qur'an, and that these letters rule the world and stars. Each letter as well as each sura of the Qur'an is believed to be an 'angel' powerful enough to transform the world and to influence people. This is the reason marabouts use them to answer questions connected to the difficulties of everyday life. One may also note that only men are supposed to be skilled in this kind of science, for reasons of purity. Therefore, despite the numerous religious attacks against marabout practices since the fourteenth century (the major arguments being that there must not exist any mediation between Allah and his creation, that marabouts associate with Allah other mighty spirits – Arabic *shirk* – and that making a living out of predicting the future is prohibited),[9] it appears that *listikhar* is closely tied to Islam.

Actually, Islamic teachings reflect the importance of dreaming. In the Qur'an and in the hadith, one can read numerous stories of dreams that had a major influence on both Muslim history and doctrine.[10] Toufic Fahd states that all divinatory sciences (astrology, numerology...) have been severely attacked by Muslim theologians, philosophers and jurists, who all consider them as illicit (*haram*), except for physiognomy and dreaming. Many treatises on dream interpretation have been written since the seventh century. Besides Abd al-Ghani al-Nabulusi (1641–1731), the most famous author is Ibn Sirin (*ob*. 728), whose work remains one of the most valuable references on dreams in the Muslim tradition. One can buy different versions of his work in all Muslim bookshops (see Ibn Sirin 1992), including those in Senegal. Following Djibril Samb, Arabo-Islamic keys to dreams have in all likelihood accompanied the penetration of Islam into Senegambia from the very beginning (Samb 1998: 70). On some websites, one can enter a word corresponding to a vision in a dream and receive different possible meanings taken from an 'Islamic dictionary of dreams' directly inspired by Ibn Sirin's work. This is a quite mechanical version of a very popular activity in the Muslim world. In a recent issue of *al-Ahram* (2006), a widely read newspaper in Muslim countries, an article notes that '...dream interpretations have become a fixture of Arab satellite television. Some decipher dreams through the Freudian model, others eschew the father of psychoanalysis and focus on religious explanations'. The article goes on to describe the special programme on dreams available on an Egypt-based satellite channel: viewers can phone in to be enlightened by a popular dream interpreter, who interprets dreams by means of the Qur'an. Dreaming is indeed integrated into the *ilm* (Islamic teaching) and is traditionally considered as 1 of the 46 parts of the prophecy. But in its attempt to separate from other cultures with a rich tradition of dreaming and dreams interpretation, Islam developed a particular classification of dreams. There are many versions, but it commonly distinguishes between three types: first, the true dreams that come from Allah. These are the dreams of the Prophets and of the righteous people who follow them. They may also come to other people, but only to the true believers who are in accordance with the *sunna*. The second type is inspired by devils. In these dreams, which are rather nightmares, the individual is suffering or may hear angels telling them to do something forbidden. Such dreams are considered untrustworthy by nature. The third type, which is in fact the most common, comes from within the individual (*nafs*) and his desire. These are mostly remembrances of what happened in real life, or images of what the dreamer wishes would happen. They are considered to be virtually worthless and even meaningless. Unsurprisingly, as many authors note, Muslim thought is interested in the first category of dreams only, and considers the other types as irrelevant to Muslim life. So one can clearly conclude that Islam has attempted to regulate and to channel dreaming practices.

Returning now to marabout practices, I highlight some elements that show that 'sociological' Islam is much more complex than its theological construction.

1) I have noted that while dreaming some marabouts lie on their right side, in the Prophet's position, while other practitioners do not observe this recommendation. This diversity of gestures is a reminder that this religious custom is an Islamic reinterpretation of ancient traditions of dreaming, in particular the Greek incubation (see Meier 1967); moreover, the general influence of the Greek science of dreams on the Islamic teachings is well known. Thus, whether these gestures are considered today to go back to the Greek period or not, we can suggest that something of these ancient practices, not totally encompassed by Islam, remains; in the same way, Islam itself can be overlaid by other cultures. Just one example: one of the marabouts I worked with always used to make his dreaming experiences in the forest.

2) Another point to highlight is how varied the ways of making *listikhar* are. The first example that I gave deals explicitly with Allah's inspiration. In the third, the marabout orders the angels directly to grant his wishes. We have here two completely opposite attitudes towards the requested power: submission in the first case, domination in the second. The fourth technique of *listikhar* that I described is quite different: here Allah and the angels seem to be less powerful than nature (one recalls the branch of *doki*). The use of the forest (above) strongly suggests that nature may be an alternative or complementary powerful world for some marabouts. It should be recalled that in marabout thought nature is by no means a pleasant and smiling world, as in the representations of heaven's gardens.

It is conceived as ambiguous, hence potentially dangerous: the winds, the sun, the plants may be sometimes beneficial, sometimes harmful or nefarious; this contradictory, unpredictable power is the agent of all actions in the world. Therefore its appropriation and beneficial use can be experienced only by initiated and well-protected practitioners.

3) One important issue cannot be overlooked: besides Allah, marabouts invoke other beings' help before dreaming. Who exactly are these invisible beings, mighty enough to provide someone with help, advice and solutions to anxieties...? Marabouts generally use very allusive terms, like 'a person', or 'someone'; this euphemistic vocabulary is employed in order to avoid speaking about a highly dangerous invisible world. It designates a large group of beings that are supposed to exist between Allah and humans. Although some scholars have attempted to describe this invisible world as a hierarchical one (see for example Zempleni 1968), I believe that in a marabout mind, terms like 'angel', '*jinn*', 'spirit', '*rahwan*' and '*maleika*' are quite synonymous. As noted previously, the main feature of all these beings is that they are dangerous. For this reason, marabouts have to perform many rituals before invoking them, in order to persuade them to answer their requests. According to the Qur'an and the *sunna*, *jinns* are highly ambiguous: some of them are said to be Muslims, others not; all of them are able to take on any physical form they like (animals, whirlwinds, humans, noise...), and they are considered one of the origins of evil. The best way to seek refuge from the *jinns* is to pray to Allah. But marabouts are seen as able to collaborate with *jinns*. Having a nightmare is to marabouts the signal of a failure in this partnership and a serious warning to become stronger. Some of them mix invocations to Allah, to some of the well-known angels (like Jibril or Asrafil) and to the *jinns*. Some diviners are even closely related to particular *jinns*, which they appeal to in any circumstance and whom they consider their relatives – namely their wives. Marabouts are also believed to act on the partner *jinn* of the client; this *jinn*, which everyone has, is often viewed as the double of a person, and to be their most vulnerable aspect. The conclusion that arises is that the dreamer's inspiration depends upon a very composite world. It mixes Allah with an invisible group of powerful beings that are not clearly defined in Islamic teachings, and who give rise to all sorts of discussions, even from a religious perspective. In some marabout practices, it doesn't appear obvious whether *jinns* belong to a transcendent or an immanent world. Nature, as it appears in the forms that *jinns* may take, is not so distant or distinct a force. It may itself cause illness or misfortune. As we have seen, some marabouts pay special attention to the power of nature. My central contention is that it is not so easy to discriminate, let alone establish a hierarchical distinction,

between what would belong to 'the recognised, dominant religious tradition of the Muslim clergy who claim godly and angelic inspiration' (Dilley 1992: 77) and what would belong to the less institutionalised tradition of diviners inspired by a more composite spirit world.

4) The last element to be introduced concerns the flexibility of marabout practices. Many other versions of *listikhar* could have been described.[11] As with healing, each marabout holds his own recipes for dreaming. The salient notion here is that of secrecy (Arabic, *sirr*). Reputation and power are tied to the possession of secret knowledge, which assures this power, and, in some cases, is the very condition of it. For this reason, clients seek out practitioners willing to employ a secret on their behalf, in the same way that marabouts themselves seek out people presumed to have the most powerful secrets in order to reinforce and enrich their own knowledge and power. Elsewhere (Kuczynski 2000), I have analysed different modes of transfer of marabout knowledge, either following a hierarchical model or circulating among peers. What I want to emphasise here is that, to some extent, both ways are propitious for individual constructions or inventions. For reasons related to power, marabouts would hardly ever use a secret in the way it was revealed to them (sometimes sold, or exchanged for money or another secret). Furthermore, given that in most cases part of the revealed secret remains hidden by its transferring owner, on acquiring it the marabout must accommodate, reinterpret, complete and integrate it in the mould of their own knowledge. There are numerous processes involved in this personal appropriation of knowledge, not discussed here. But one should note that this is a very dynamic situation in which the personal expertise of each marabout is paramount.

A similar flexibility pertains to the interpretation of dreams. As mentioned, one can find a myriad of 'keys to dreams' in every Islamic bookshop. But marabouts really do not appreciate this kind of knowledge; they generally place more value on expertise that is orally transmitted. So the same situation as that just described applies, and opens the way to many personal variations and innovations.

Finally, the Islamic teachings themselves consider that the interpretation of dreams is never strictly codified or predetermined, and that it cannot entirely rely on the meaning of a symbol. Many other features have to be taken into account, such as the dreamer's general context, their feelings, the personal, social and psychological problems they face. During my fieldwork among marabouts, I was able to observe the many questions they asked their clients or themselves about their own dreams: were they frightened by their dream or not? Did they feel cold or warm? What did they smell, what did they hear? etc. All senses (not only vision) are involved in dreaming and in dream interpretation. Marabouts have many verbal and non-verbal exchanges with their clients, and their dream interpretation derives more from the interaction between the marabout and his client than from the mechanical implementation of a learned code. In his book on dreaming among Guajiro shamans, *Les Praticiens du rêve*, Michel Perrin argues that literate societies, where the keys to dreams are put down in books, are much more rigid in this respect than societies with oral traditions, where such keys play a less important role: 'Because literate societies have given a fixed form in writing to the keys to dreams, we attribute to them a rigidity which they do not possess in oral societies' (Perrin 1992: 62).[12] With the above discussion in mind, it is difficult to agree with Perrin's opinion. Quite the opposite. Marabout practices show us that the skills and the personality of the practitioner play a crucial role in dreaming and in interpreting dreams.

I will not attempt to compare shamanism and Islam with regard to dreaming, but I would like to mention some elements in which they echo each other: in the unobtrusive presence of nature that can appear in some versions of *listikhar*; in the intricate invisible world marabouts deal with, a world that seems to exceed a religious-sanctioned framework; and, finally, in the openness to personal creation and the importance of a practitioner's personal experience and expertise.

A case study

This section examines how a particular marabout, Dia, whose biography I am writing, experiences dreaming.

He was born some 75 years ago on the eastern bank of the Senegal River. He is of Fula descent and Fula culture is deeply ingrained in him. His male ancestors have been renowned *silatigi* for generations, in both paternal and maternal lineages. A *silatigi* is a diviner and a healer, and is particularly skilled in pastoral farming matters (Fula people are, in origin, shepherds). But a *silatigi* also knows how to deal with human misfortunes and wishes (such as those concerning relations between men and women, infertility, business, success in all fields, etc.). *Silatigi* are believed to hold secrets regarding the use of plants that originate in their close links with powerful *jinns*. These secrets may be communicated in a dream. Dia's family turned from 'traditional' religion to Islam three or four generations ago. They pray to Allah, and in addition Dia's father has affiliated to the Tijani Sufi order, as has Dia himself. He attaches great importance to the worship of Allah, and this seems to give guidelines to his practice as a *silatigi*. He defines himself as a Muslim and never works on Friday. But Dia never attended an Islamic school or learned Arabic. Only one of his brothers was taught by a marabout who used to live in Dia's family house for many years; Dia himself learned Muslim prayers with this man. None of the family was introduced to the Islamic science of secrets (*ilm al-asrar*). Thus, when Dia came to France, he ran into marabouts and tried to learn their trade by himself. He acquired secrets of *silatigi* practice from his father, and improved his knowledge with other elder Fula practitioners whom he met in Dakar. Unwilling to become a *silatigi* when he was young – he intended to involve himself in business – he finally began to practise in Dakar, then in Paris. He came to France in 1961, and has worked most of his life here.

I will now focus on Dia's experience of dreaming. He has a thorough knowledge of *listikhar*, thus he does not use the Islamic forms of it. But he is dream-prone and speaks very often about his experiences. From his experience of many months in the French Caribbean, he also likes to practise what is known in France as 'sleeping divination' (*'voyance dormante'*); for example, he used it in order to find a thief. But dreaming is by no means a harmless experience, because of the dangerous link with the invisible world. For this reason, he often feels tired or even ill, and he has to protect himself against the *jinns*' assault. For this purpose, he mostly washes with plant mixtures, but he also invokes Allah's names and those of *jinns* as well as other assistants in a Fula secret language. Although he is not really literate, he has written down a large part of his secret invocations in different languages, including Arabic, in a little notebook. Like most marabouts, he keeps this knowledge away from prying eyes. Once a week he also 'feeds' his assistants by spitting pieces of a white kola nut onto a horn serving as a sort of a portable altar.

His gift of dreaming originated in his childhood. He described how his parents were worried when they heard him screaming; some of his dreams were really threatening. In Fula culture, such a dreaming child is considered gifted for divination. But it is frequently a twofold gift, with a positive and a negative side. The positive is that the child is believed to become a *silatigi* (he is devoted to learning the practice). The negative side is that he may also be attacked by sorcerers called, in Fula language, *soucougnan*, or 'night-travellers', or 'blacks'. These wicked beings appear at night, taking the shape of threatening shadows or half-animal half-human creatures,[13] and are supposed to assault people and change them into sorcerers. These are mainly believed to be real creatures, and are widespread in West African cultures. The child has to be protected, but fighting against *soucougnans* demands special skills which are not within *silatigi*'s competence. Other specialists are thus requested. The protection against *soucougnans* has to be repeated regularly, as they can attack at any time. Dia describes numerous dreams of threatening *soucougnans* that he has had over the course of his life, leaving him exhausted, suffering and sometimes really ill. What appears in dreams becomes reality. He has had to cure himself and sometimes to request other specialists' help (including physicians). It is noticeable that he dislikes curing people he believes to be harmed by *soucougnans*. One might ask: What relation exists between this kind of dream and Islam? Sometimes it is direct: in one dream it was said to Dia that only Mohammadu Rasulilla could save him (meaning that he should pray to Allah). Fighting against *soucougnan* dreams (which means against *soucougnans*) can take several forms, and belief in this kind of sorcerer coexists with the worship of Allah.

Dia experiences other kinds of dreams. When he came to France in 1961, he did not make a living as a *silatigi*, using his skills only occasionally; he worked as a warehouseman in several factories. Nevertheless, dreaming was significant even in that kind of job. For example, he told me that he found the factory where he was to spend more than ten years thanks to a dream: he 'saw' the area, the street, details of the building, which he then 'recognised' while going round all the firms in a Parisian suburb. In the same way, he was able to 'see' how many clients would come in one day, at what time etc. These premonitory optimistic dreams can also turn into frightening warnings – they also have an obscure side. The most striking example is when Dia deals with talismans that have to be prepared in a cemetery. This kind of work takes place in Africa. He does not touch the body, but he sits at the head of the tomb invoking his *jinns* and other names while making the amulet. Dia explains that when leaving the cemetery he would always dream about somebody's death; and that this dream would quickly turn into reality (he would hear that someone really passed away). It is not actually clear to what extent Dia has to effectively deal with the deceased in the cemetery: Does he invoke them or not? This case deserves further enquiry. But what is suggested here is that dreams announce a dramatic exchange; and that these dreams not only give advice or knowledge for action, to some extent they become reality. It is almost the same situation as when Dia undertook dangerous practices that overstepped those that he was able to use in accordance with his age: then he had terrifying dreams that made him ill and warned him to stop his work. At that time (Dia was in his 20s) his father reinforced the warning of the dreams and advised his son to limit his work to easy questions.

Finally, I analyse a dream that Dia had in his late 30s, which had serious consequences for his whole life. At this time he was living in Paris and, as mentioned earlier, he was confined to petty work. Suddenly, he was assailed by terrible dreams that persisted for more than a month. In these dreams he heard and saw all sorts of animals: cows, birds, bees, camels, hyenas, snakes, locusts, ants, mosquitoes, worms, sheep etc; all of which cried out in his head. He explains that he even saw children, men, in brief, all creatures on earth, running to him. He adds: all creatures, but no angels. He was afraid of going mad and felt near to death. In order to help him to overcome this serious crisis and painful headaches, a marabout shaved his head. Dia also went to a physician who gave him some medicine: in both cases his condition worsened. A talisman against *soucougnans* seemed to calm his pain. But the most important thing, Dia explains, was what he describes as a real fight: he did not give up, he was not scared of this invading, swarming crowd; he remained firm. Gradually these fearsome dreams vanished. After overcoming this dangerous trial, which he calls an illness, and which left him forever bald, Dia felt stronger and more effective as a diviner. He stopped being a warehouseman – in the meantime, the company which employed him had closed down – and decided to work exclusively as a diviner and a healer. This opened the path towards social recognition and was the beginning of a fairly successful career in Paris.

Interpreting this dream is not easy. It seems to lead to a kind of 'initiation'. Dia was already given an 'initiation' by his father, who allowed him to work as a *silatigi* within the limits of his age. However, speaking of 'initiation' seems somewhat inappropriate in that case, for his father regularly transmitted knowledge and know-how to his gifted son. At the time of his trial, Dia's father had already passed away. So one can consider this dream as a second, more absolute legitimisation (rather than 'initiation') in a new context: Dia is alone, he is about 40 and he lives in Paris. The intervention of nature in this urban context is interesting – nature meaning animals (bush animals as well as domestic ones) and human beings.[14] Bearing in mind what has been explained about the skill of a *silatigi*, and the special links that this practitioner has with nature, it could be argued that overcoming nature in Paris leads to a full legitimisation of *silatigi* practices in this new context – which is not incompatible with all sorts of personal accommodations. It is noticeable, once again, that Dia's dream combines various features dealing with *silatigi* practices as well as with *soucougnans*. Islam does not seem to act in this dream (Dia explains that he did not see angels), unless we understand the shaving of Dia's head as an Islamic ritual purification – which actually failed to cure Dia! In my opinion, however, too much rationalisation here is dangerous and even meaningless. It appears that dreaming is not only a mediation establishing contact with the invisible world, it has in itself curative properties.

Conclusion

As a result of the present study, two observations need to be emphasised: first, as already highlighted, practices are always very mixed, and attempts to distinguish what belongs to Islam and what to shamanism seem irrelevant. In my opinion, the most salient points to be learned concern flexibility and personal accommodation.

The second observation is about the relevance of the separation of literate and oral societies in our analyses. As I have attempted to demonstrate, this distinction often makes little sense when regarding the world of diviners and healers, in which the personality and the individual experience of the practitioner is always paramount.

Thus, within a Muslim framework, marabouts are nowadays, in Paris as in Senegal, competing with practitioners who repeat the time-worn criticisms of marabouts as 'associationists' and 'innovators'. Aiming to return to a literal interpretation of Islam and pretending to be representatives of a more 'orthodox' Islam, these 'new' specialists promote a version of *listikhar* strictly based on the reciting of prescribed verses and totally excluding the invocation of spirits. Some of them also claim to draw from the medicine of the Prophet's time, and spread healing practices such as *ruqiya*, a way to cure misfortune and illness also exclusively based on prayers. But the different Muslim movements who claim to adhere to the original form of Islam (*tablighis, salafis...*) do not agree among themselves with the definition that may be given of ritual purism and heavily denigrate each other, much as they do marabout practices.

Bibliography

Dilley, Roy M. (1992). 'Dreams, inspiration and craftwork among Tukolor weavers'. In M. Charles Jedrej and Rosalind Shaw (eds). *Dreaming, Religion and Society in Africa*. Leiden, E.J. Brill, pp. 71–85.

Fahd, Toufic (1987). *La Divination arabe: études religieuses, sociologiques et folkloriques sur le milieu natif de l'Islam*. Paris, Sindbad.

Grünebaum, Gustav E. von (1967). 'La Fonction culturelle du rêve dans l'islam classique'. In R. Caillois et G. E. von Grünebaum (eds). *Le Rêve et les sociétés humaines*. Paris, Gallimard, NRF, pp. 7–23.

Hamès, Constant (2008). 'Magie-sorcellerie en Islam et perspectives africaines.' *Cahiers d'études africaines*, 189–190, 81–99.

Ibn Sîrîn (1992). *L'Interprétation des rêves dans la tradition islamique*. Lyon, Alif Editions.

Kuczynski, Liliane (2000). 'Fidélité et Liberté. Transmission du savoir chez les marabouts de Paris.' *Ethnologie française*, XXX: 3, 369–377.

———(2002). *Les Marabouts africains à Paris*. Paris, CNRS Editions.

Lory, Pierre (2003). *Le Rêve et ses interprétations en islam*. Paris, Albin Michel.

———(2007). 'L'Interprétation des rêves dans la culture musulmane.' In Constant Hamès (ed.). *Coran et Talismans. Textes et pratiques magiques en milieu musulman.* Paris, Karthala, pp. 75–94.

Meier, Carl Alfred (1967). 'Le Rêve et l'Incubation dans l'ancienne Grèce'. In R. Caillois and G. E. von Grünebaum (ed.). *Le Rêve et les sociétés humaines.* Paris, Gallimard, NRF, pp. 290–305.

Perrin, Michel (1992). *Les Praticiens du rêve: un exemple de chamanisme.* Paris, Presses universitaires de France.

Samb, Djibril (1998). *L'Interprétation des rêves dans la région sénégambienne, suivi de la clé des songes de la Sénégambie, de l'Egypte pharaonique et de la tradition islamique.* Dakar, Les nouvelles éditions africaines du Sénégal.

Sanneh, Lamine O. (1979). *The Jakhanke. The History of an Islamic Clerical People of Senegambia.* London, International African Institute.

Zempleni, Andras (1968). 'L'Interprétation et la thérapie traditionnelle du désordre mental chez les Wolof et les Lébou du Sénégal'. Thèse de doctorat en ethnologie, Faculté des Lettres et sciences humaines, Université de Paris.

Chapter Twelve

HEALING AMONG TRADITIONAL PRACTITIONERS OF THE ALGERIAN SAHARA

Faiza Seddiq Arkam

When facing the absence of a male ancestor, the Tuaregs claim that they are the sons of the *essuf*, of the emptiness, of solitude. As Dominique Casajus emphasises: 'in the myth the mothers of the first Tuaregs belonged to an already existing society when the *kel essuf* arrived, so that one can talk of an anteriority of maternal ancestry of the ancient Tuaregs for their paternal ancestry' (Casajus 1987: 286).[1] Tuareg myths not only give feminine ancestry to the group but also a 'shamanic', supernatural origin, claiming that the Tuaregs descend from a feminine ancestor and from her relationship with the *kel essuf*.

The Tuareg oral tradition is made of accounts based on real events (*taneqist*), mythical journeys, tales and legends telling the adventures of these spirits of the emptiness, the *kel essuf*, who get in touch with men in certain circumstances either to torment and possess them, or to help them make miracles as they are endowed with extraordinary powers. These myths are then updated in collective rituals and other rites of passage. For instance, a bride must be kept out of sight of other people and protected from the threat of the *essuf*, and the newborn child must be protected by burying the placenta, considered the substitute of the child; this applies also to the rite of hair-cutting during naming.

Mystical Islam has profoundly assimilated the local Tuareg culture, and it could not, or did not, try to curb the ancient customs completely. It sought to assimilate and incorporate them. It is tempting to speak of a religious 'bricolage', but this notion seems insufficient to me, insofar as in this case no clear disjuncture can be seen in the religious symbols. Most of the symbols are re-appropriated and absorbed by Islam, and one can observe their coherence. These ancient beliefs do not merely coexist, but always seek some legitimacy in relation to Islam, which is the dominant religion. When different 'ethnic' and cultural groups share a common territory, or when they have settled in close proximity, the different therapeutic measures that are specific to each become in time common property, which in turn is then reined into new individualised practices.

Social transformations

Tuareg society is undergoing massive changes. The upheavals experienced by these nomads have affected their physical as well as their psychological balance. One of the most important impacts of economic and social change has been the transgression of marriage restrictions in an urban environment, which have led to a weakening of the privilege granted to the feminine principle (Claudot-Hawad 1986), as the first persons to be made vulnerable by a certain form of social breakdown are women. In the past women used to own the tent, *ehen*, which represents shelter, as well as the *ebawel*, i.e. the inalienable belongings constituted by herds and other goods that come with it, all these being fundamental elements handed down from mother to daughter. It is women who break with the matrilineal tradition when they marry outside the group or when they divorce or become widows, destitute and vulnerable in a more and more difficult world. These deep changes, which affect all traditional societies, compel these populations to undergo some difficult and painful restructuring. In the semi-camps and villages in the bush, there are more women than men.

In the context of modernity, when several populations live next to each other, new alliances take shape, not least amongst different Tuareg categories, which undermine endogamy and consequently the upholding of the traditional hierarchies. The consequences of these destabilisations are profoundly different from one social milieu or group to another. These diverse ad hoc reactions show the disarray that emerges in a society in these unprecedented situations. Endogamy is transgressed. The loss of herds, non-existent or insufficient harvesting, the lack of profit from the work leading to a massive drain of resources, have brought about the extreme poverty of the nomadic population and have destroyed traditional channels of trade and exchange.

Once the hierarchical structures that used to uphold traditional power and the relationships of subordination were upset, some groups managed to break away from these structures, as in the cases of former slaves or *enaden* (blacksmiths). The blacksmiths lived a sedentary life that differed from that of the noble classes, the *ihaggaren*. The slaves could adapt by finding new means of subsistence that allowed them to find a new way of life a little more easily. Roger Bastide has mentioned that it is always people who are in contact, never cultures, which implies the need to consider the status and position of those communicating (Bastide 1971). According to their status (noblemen, slaves, clergymen) individuals react differently in situations of contact. In most ritual practices, the issue of 'syncretism' or of 'makeshift' is present. Knowledge becomes more and more fragmentary, and it is usual that when society evolves, it adjusts to a new culture or breaks up. Then, therapeutic activity acquiring some degree of autonomy (Hamayon 1990: 29) and the traditional practitioner essentially becomes seen as a healer.

One has to know that the fame of a traditional practitioner (seer or healer) does not only depend on an atypical individual journey, but also on the collective experience of his/her patients; it is specifically this factor that leads to collective recognition. At the end of a long therapeutic process the patients and their families confirm the reputation of a seer or a healer (traditional practitioner) according to the positive or negative outcome of the journey.

The individualisation of practices

In a context of the transgression of the sacred space linked to the world of the *essuf*, an adaptation of the ritual to urban space can be observed. It is striking that if one walks around the outlying districts of the city by night, one can hear a multitude of sounds coming from the numerous ritual celebrations and musical ceremonies organised by young Tuaregs at different parties, the smell of incense, the sound of drum, bodies 'in a trance', and the transgression of sexual taboos. Physical proximity favours the blending of feminine and masculine spaces, contrary to the traditional rituals that respect a certain code of behaviour. The transgression of the rule of the *ashak* (sense of modesty, honour) instigates a significant mutation in the Tuareg society.

It can be noted that the collective ritual practices that are linked to the management of disorder and affliction are becoming individualised, as with the traditional practitioner, as social actors become more and more important.

Former slaves, here without a particular brotherhood organisation, practise a possession ritual called *tazengharet* involving the spirits of the void, the *kel essuf*, which in many respects is reminiscent of those from Morocco as well as those observed in West Africa (Bori Haoussa, Jinnedon, etc.), although there is no sacrifice during the ritual. Sacrifice may, however, be mentioned in the songs. There is also no instrumental music. In the local Tuareg landscape there are also some female traditional practitioners, *tagahant* seers who can diagnose, or *tanesefert*, psychotherapists who heal numerous illnesses with plants. These women correspond with *ineslmen* (religious men), who are their specifically religious counterparts.

A form of resurgence of cosmogonic beliefs and an adaptation of rituals to new semi-urban spaces is also evident. This emerges in some of the new outlying districts of Tamanrasset, where communities that come from outside have settled and are stigmatised, being renowned as dangerous and as sources of disorder. The desert space next to the city, once reserved for the world of the *essuf*, with its symbolic barriers, was transgressed as new constructions were formed. The limits of the once sacred and feared space are constantly impinged upon.

Irrespective of the upheavals experienced by Tuareg society, music and musical ritual celebrations seem to bring these populations together and offer a space of 'release'. This is how the participants express both their happiness at being together and their anxiety. The sound of the *tazengharet* ritual and the noise of the *tindi* (mortar drum) act as a magnet: the celebrations, wherever they are taking place, irresistibly attract people. A musical ritual is the moment when a specific emotion or same state of communion is shared. This ritual moment brings together a suffering community. Above all, most of the people expect that the music will drive away the bad spirits and they will find harmony again in space and time. The ritual is like a barometer of the social climate, as can be seen in the work of François Borel in Niger (1986).

The complexity of the phenomena related to possession, entailing different forms of relations with the invisible, demand a global approach so as to comprehend the cosmology and the place of each category of traditional practitioner within this world. A specific role, status and position are accorded to each of them. It would be tempting to speak of a coherent system, but this would lead us to ignore the fundamental issues of the makeshift, the interpenetration of different cultures and symbols.

The symbolic representation of illness and spirits

The notion of illness among the Tuaregs is very complex as two conceptions are interwoven. The first, which comes from the Greeks and is present in the origins of Arab medicine, is based on the four humours and arrived in North Africa with the Muslim conquerors. It emphasises the natural causes of illnesses. The second is linked to a conception of the world and of human beings based on the translation of the conflict and effects of supernatural forces in the mundane world via an opposition between purity and impurity, and is largely influenced by Islam, but nonetheless obeys its own cultural logics and a duality between cold and hot.

Illness is experienced as a kind of breaking of the balance between man and the cosmos; an illness or misfortune never presents itself as an arbitrary curse. A cause is always found and named by the healer, who is also sometimes a seer. Tuareg women are very gifted in matters of traditional medicine and are the keepers of knowledge, of know-how in the field of prescription or of the preparation of traditional medicines, *isefren* or *imaglan*.[2] They also possess specialised mythological knowledge.

The medicine of humours, borrowed from the Arabs, proposes hot food to treat cold illnesses and vice versa, in order to re-establish the corporal balance. It coexists with prophetic medicine, called *doua ârab* (traditional Arab medicine), as well as one practised by witch-doctors in the form of incantatory formulae or of *tirawt* (sacred writing, Qur'anic amulets) and other ritual processes inspired by the *Sunna* (tradition) of the prophet. Spirits will probably be responsible for most of the cold diseases, some hot diseases and all mental illnesses (Hureiki 2000: 80). Thus, the *Kel essuf* are rife above all at night, especially at sunset. They strike with mental illnesses, haunting desert places and cemeteries; they possess their own territory.

Several illnesses are said to be caused by spirit possession. In these cases the sick persons are offered, according to their situation and social class, a musical ritual that takes the shape of a possession rite (*tindi* or *tazengharet*), or another religious ritual also closely linked to possession, which introduces sacrificial practices (Figures 12.1, 12.2). The latter is supposed to be therapeutic and is officiated by the *tolba*. But here also, it represents a 'cunning of therapeutisation' – 'ruse de la thérapisation' (de Sardan 1994: 7–27), and the possession rituals cannot be easily likened to practices that have exclusively therapeutic purposes. The translation of autochthonous terms can also lead to a 'religious or therapeutic' interpretation. The *essuf* designates solitude, melancholy. Having *essuf* implies that the ill person suffers from solitude and isolation.

Finding the meaning of an illness, by searching in family history for the origin of the 'evil', allows one to apprehend it better. All the more so since collective responsibility removes the dimension of guilt from the illness, making it more bearable. Illness crystallises the permanent link between life and death and disturbs the equilibrium of the society. The therapeutic system, which is essentially symbolic, is activated to combat this.

An ambiguity and an inaccuracy emerge in using the word *jinn* in connection to the spirits. According to a tradition derived from the prophet Mohammed, the *jinn*'s particular nature gives them the power to penetrate the human body. Were the remarks of the Prophet a parable or a genuine

Figure 12.1. Drawing of a healing ritual, performed during a pilgrimage at the mausoleum of Moulay Abdallah at Tarhananet (Ahaggar, Algeria). The healer is in trance with a sword in her hands, a women, playing the lute/*imzad* (the drawing was made by Didi Slimane, a male nurse and Tuareg, whose mother was a Kel Ferwen from the Air district and his father a Kel Ghezzi from the Ahaggar).

phenomenon? This is still debated by commentators. In this respect, possession can be considered an intense form of 'penetration'. Possession by spirits, appearing under different guises, often takes the shape of an initiatic illness. The repetition of illness within the same family indicates a story of legacy, of transmission through kinship, often genuine and uterine, but primarily symbolic. The relationship with spirits is flexible and varies according to their nature and how they contact men. The *jinn* is said to have the capacity of transformation (*yethaouel*), to metamorphose, and thus change its colour and aspect. Just as their contact with men varies, being struck by a spirit is not the same as being haunted. Each of these states evokes different symptoms. What sets the specialist, the ally of the invisible world, apart from the general run of people is that he/she manages to communicate with the spirits and maintains relationships with them, from negotiation to a declaration of war, depending on their disposition. Dirt and pollution contribute to the descent of the *kel essuf*, who are partial to dirty, impure places in which there is human excrement or the blood of killed animals. Isolation and solitude can also cause them to attack. The breath of any spirits, brought by the cold wind, causes paralysis and muscle weaknesses. The *kel essuf*, in the form of grains of sand, of moon beams, are responsible for almost all cold diseases (bone, articular, renal, respiratory, inflammatory, urinary, genital...). Some

Healing among Traditional Practitioners of the Algerian Sahara 237

Figure 12.2. Drawing of a ritual called *tindi* in the Air district. The sick woman (in the centre of the picture) is in trance. She holds a headband decorated with horns. The men circle her with swords in their hands (drawing by Didi Slimane).

illnesses are said to be hereditary, transmitted by maternal milk, while others occur during rites of passage, such as weddings or births. Susan Rasmussen (1995: 285) mentions the actions of spirits in the genesis of mental illnesses. The way the spirits enter (via the mouth, percutaneous) is of little consequence; their attack targets the head after lying in the stomach (*tedis*) and the liver (*tasa*). Men, if they do not take the precaution of covering their heads, of wearing sandals and of hanging a sword from the hoop of the tent, also risk being attacked. They may be unfortunate and walk on an *echel* (viper) or they may have to remove a scorpion found under their bed, both forms that spirits can take on. The *kel essuf* are responsible for many different bites and stings (rabid dogs, scorpions, vipers).

Most psychological and mental illnesses are caused by the spirits. Among them, we can mention the *agullel*, which designates a person who has lost any capacity to concentrate, as well as a loss of memory; this person is said to be *teraoul* (not present) and suffers from a 'loss of conscious awareness' (De Martino 1999). *Agullel* also refers to a person who has lost his or her bearing, who stands still unable to move forward. *Iggulelen* designates those who are taken over in a 'possession' dance, a term that designates, according to the

Western aetiology, nervous bouts, epilepsy, hysteria; ethnologists interpret these as signs of trance or possession.

Thus, an individual who has lost control of himself, meaning that he is possessed by spirits, must be replaced in a new situation (a new psychological state) that he will control, as a master or a king (*agellid*) over the spirits who torment him. In this view, a special ceremony is organised for that person which includes a dance of trance; at the end, this person 'is elected' (*esegelled*). The meaning of this election is that the person has become the master of some of these spirits and gained certain powers through them.

The handing down of disease and baraka *(blessing)*

I observed in different places in Algeria that many families who are in a state of affliction, when one member is ill or possessed, experience a kind of repetition. Indeed, the same phenomena may continue over several generations.[3] Psychoanalysts will be interested in such transgenerational transmission. In these families a permanent feature is evidenced: there is definitely something that is akin to transmission and which corresponds to particular conditions. But which conditions? It is as if a family destiny was continuing through individuals, through the members. I came across this same phenomenon with Tuareg initiates. Tales telling of the transmission of a sacred legacy (of a secret knowledge, of the *albaraka*, of illnesses and spirits) is a core issue that is constantly repeated in initiates' tales.

My first observations, from which came the first hypotheses of this work, led me to consider transmission through matrilineal descent. In the same family of initiates, a phenomenon is transmitted in the form of a spiritual gift. Tacheka, after going through an initiation voyage, received her gifts and the knowledge of sacred songs from her mother's *tazengharet*. Her story is that she conceived children in the other world and married a *kel essuf* spirit. The human lover is here the wife of the spirit; it is an alliance. Her account was followed by those of many other initiates, all showing the same permanent feature – the real and symbolic transmission of power born of an alliance with the supernatural. Most of these initiated women have entered into an alliance with an invisible being. Several examples taken in other contexts also attest to this hereditary phenomenon.

Transmitting through the matrix, the notion of ebawel

Some Tuareg illnesses linked to the spirits are said to be hereditary. They can even be transmitted through the mother's milk. A symbolic dimension is given to milk, and is found in the Tuareg expression *axh n ebawel*, which means the 'milk of *ebawel*'. *Ebawel* designates the inalienable goods (cattle, tents, palm trees) exclusively transmitted through the matrilineal line and symboliees the permanency of the lineage.

The spatial unity that best represents this image of the matrix for the Tuaregs is the tent, the *ehen*. For the nomad, the heart of the inhabited space is his tent first...each new tent must include at least a few elements of the maternal tent, the symbolic extension of the original shelter that allowed the family ancestors to 'exist' (Claudot-Hawad 1993: 46).

Indeed, for the Tuareg the tent is a feminine element; the man, as husband, is not its owner. It is around this concept of *ebawel*, or its opposite – the absence of *ebawel*: emptiness, solitude, the *essuf* – that Tuareg thinking circulates (Claudot-Hawad 1984). It is to these concepts that notions of balance and life are associated.

Ebawel refers to kinship, the *rahm*, which for the Arabs is the matrilineal matrix that gives one life. This kinship also corresponds to *tasa*, which in the Kabila language means the liver or the stomach, and matrilineal kinship, which symbolically designates the seat of maternal love. Among the Kabyles, who also are an *amazigh* (Berber) population from the north of Algeria, the phrases '*nghigh tasainou*' or '*etchigh tasainou*' literally mean 'I've killed my liver' or even 'I've eaten my liver' – a metaphor that means 'I've killed my offspring, therefore I've killed myself'. The liver represents the extension of life and is also 'the seat of the *baraka*' (Kuczynski 2003: 268). The *ebawel* is a notion which, in the Tuareg world, expresses the central place of feminine values. From an etymological point of view, this word means the 'hollow', the 'nest', the 'shelter', the matrix. All these terms point to the domesticated world of women.

It is primarily through dreams that a person gains access to ritual or religious knowledge that is recognised and legitimated by society. It is also through dreams that the Tuareg *albaraka* (Muslim *baraka* – blessing) is transmitted. But other modes of transmission come into play that differ from direct ties of filiation, in particular the elective modalities when some one is chosen to be sick. Not everyone is affected by the spirits. Yet spirits often touch humans, in particular family members. They roam around, especially after the death of one of their victims, looking for new prey inside the same family.

The choice of a new victim or of that election is often connected to a transgression, to lack of respect for the rules that govern the relationships with the spirits. But it is also connected to other aspects that are still obscure and linked to the affected person, to their path, to their personality – all aspects that are intrinsic to their personal biography. Why is such a person chosen to be the victim, and why does he or she later become the support for the spirit's words and not someone else? An answer to this is only provided when we look at the life narratives of the people concerned. Before briefly recounting the journey of some initiated women, we should look at how different actors appear in the Tuareg therapeutic and religious field to form a social and symbolic landscape. They lie in no hierarchy and neither do they constitute a homogeneous group. Though they were born in different social categories, each of them share the burden of the sacred and symbolic power associated with different therapeutic skills, each of which have a distinct role.

In the centre of the great village of Tamanrasset, where there is almost no anonymity, collective experience very quickly designates the individuals considered to be the most charismatic, the most efficient from a therapeutic perspective. The traditional practitioners are thus often considered to be outsiders whatever their social class, slave, intermediary class or with high status (*chorfa*, men of letters or religious dignitaries). They are actually twice outsiders; first, because there are mediators between the visible and invisible worlds. Each of them claims that they have at their service invisible spiritual entities, with different names according to their nature and functions. The entities with which they have formed an alliance allow them to act as a seer and to heal most of the time. Second, these traditional practitioners are outsiders due to their social position (blacksmiths, slaves).

On the one hand, there are among these traditional practitioners those that are despised and feared. They are black slaves and cultivators (*iklan* and *izzegaren*) who officiate during such musical rituals of possession as the *tazengharet*; herbalist healers and phytotherapists (*anesefer, tanesefert*); also blacksmiths (*enaden*), who are feared for their mystical power and known for their proximity to the supernatural. The latter's role is that of ritual mediator, sometimes also that of a seer. On the other hand, there are the religious men, or *ineslmen*, who include in various ways the *tolba* (religious student), *afaqih* (jurist) and *icheriffen* (noble), with admittedly better standing in the community, not only due to their status as clerics, but primarily because of their efficacy in healing rituals. They are feared because of the formidable and unpredictable strength of the *baraka* that they each possess in varying degrees.

Among the Tuareg breeders (*imuhagh*), designated as noble and free men, there are no experts, because they delegate this role to other social categories. Even if they know well the powers of the medicinal *isefren* and *ishkan* plants, being closely in contact to nature, they do not specialise in this field.

The initial hypothesis, which was confirmed by the data I gathered, was that this absence of experts among the Tuaregs is intimately connected with their relationship to pollution. In order to heal someone, one has to be in contact with such impure objects as blood, urine, saliva and other bodily fluids. Tuaregs even find it repellent to sacrifice their animals themselves during religious ceremonies. Being touched by blood provokes in them a feeling of profound disgust, called '*seghlef*'. The person on whom blood has splattered during a sacrificial ritual is said to be *emedhas* (polluted); the person must immediately take a complete ritual bath. We will see how this relationship with blood opposes two categories intrinsic, in symbolic terms, to the structure of this society. The consideration of these rituals has enabled me to record oppositions and make comparisons.

The initiates enter the different fields of religious and therapeutic knowledge and each of them is given a specific role according to their status and skills. I began my survey with Tacheka, a *taklit n ihaggaren*, a former slave considered by her family circle as an ally of the *kel essuf*. She is the leader who brings liberation to the young men possessed by the ritual song of the *tazengharet*. The *akli* (slave) is not concerned by the division of labour and the ritual/religious obligations. The *tiklatin* (former women slaves) are often accused of practising witchcraft. This was one of the reasons people described Tacheka to me as in the guise of an animal, or a part woman part animal figure. She herself spoke of her rivals in the cult, the *tizzegaren* women (black farmers), as *tinisemt* women, i.e. jealous women, endowed with magical powers. These women are *tibudalin* (from the Arabic *tabadala*: to transform oneself), i.e. women who can transform themselves into an animal with claws that are supposedly lethal.

Tacheka and the tazengharet

The *tazengharet*, which links ritual with possession, would have arrived in the Ahaggar at the same time as the first *iklan* (slaves) were plundered from the Sudanese regions. It is unknown in Ajjer country (near the Hoggar), which speaks in favour of its sub-Saharan origin. It would have the twofold role of leading festive events and of healing those mentally possessed. Such an event is also organised after a scorpion's bite, accompanied with anxiety crises (*teqlaq* in Arabic), in a way strangely reminiscent of the tarantula possession ritual in Southern Italy (Di Mitri 2006: 118), as well as in cases of melancholy and depression (*kwaswas*) in which the subject loses the power of speech or presents obvious signs of a breakdown (*egullel*). When the musical ritual is not brought to a successful conclusion – or in some cases concerning parturient women, when the ritual of the *mousse* (the knife), observed by a *tanesmagalt*, a traditional practitioner, does not appear to be efficient either –

then the last resort, and the most expensive, turns out to be the representative of the Islamic religion, the *taleb* (also called marabout), who is the only one able to bring about a recovery. Yet the illness connected to the spirits does not really come to an end with such a cure, as it is transmitted through the generations within a family. The spirits often attack women in a transition stage of the life cycle, when they are on the verge of getting married or giving birth to a child. Many women have experienced this, and it was the case of most of the initiated women whose stories I have undertaken to tell: they all lost a husband, as well as many children, when they were young.

In the musical ritual, derision, laughter and intense fervour are intermingled. The allies that lead the song are hence the symbolic mediators of speech that liberate the sick. Although the *tazengharet* is carried out by *tiklatin* women of servile origin, it is not exclusively a feminine cult.

Women lead men into 'trance' through a ritual song, and then the men dance on the floor and become possessed. The song serves as the frame. In one particular instance, a woman who can no longer control her body falls flat on the ground. She is immediately held up, and a group of women keep her in the background.

Tacheka, the wife of the spirits, 'works' with wild spirits, the *kel essuf*, and has the mission of giving drink, *saswequen*, to people painfully affected by the *kel essuf*. The slave woman, more than the man, is connected to the natural world, as in the case of Tacheka, who is identified as an animal and a witch. Witchcraft refers to the disorder as 'hidden in every society' (Balandier 1988) and the slave (the *akli*) is the medium of absolute otherness. Everything starts with this vague sense of belonging, this absence of fatherhood, of genealogy. Around this revolves the theme of excessiveness, of unrestrained sexuality; although old and barren the slave woman nonetheless remains fearsome, as occult powers are attributed to her.

Khadija, the tanesefert, *and Oum e sebian, the bird spirit*

The *tanesefert* belong to a different aspect of the management of illness. It is another feminine character represented by Khadija, a woman coming from the group of the *izzegaren*, black farmers who live in the district of Taberket in Tamanrasset. Khadija said that her grandparents were former slaves of the Sahelian Tuaregs: *ewellmeden* (Tuareg confederation in Niger) on her mother's side and *igdalen* (wandering religious in Niger) on her father's. Her own parents would have been emancipated by the masters who had acquired them from marabouts, *kel ansar*. Khadija is recognised by the local population of Tamanrasset for her healing powers with certain diseases affecting infants and illnesses linked to the sexuality and motherhood of women. For this, she is called a *tanesefert* (from *asefer* in the singular, *isefren* in the plural, which means 'plants that treat, or medicine'). A pregnant woman is prone to many complications and illnesses, for during her pregnancy she crosses a dangerous threshold. She must protect herself from the risk of losing her child or even of dying. Her body is half-open, and it can be easily penetrated by cold, by the *essuf*. Khadija undertakes to close her body.

A biographical survey and observation of her implementation of practices have shown that her knowledge goes beyond the framework of the so-called natural or biological illnesses, touching also upon the spiritual world (what would be designated the supernatural) and the invisible. This knowledge she prefers to remain silent about, even if she gets her recognition from it. For Khadija is, above all, a great expert on the wrongdoings of a feminine spirit called *taira* (the feminine word for bird), also known as Oum e sebian (the children's mother), recently introduced among the Tuareg, who have named it *tagadit*. She mentioned that Oum e'sebian in the *tamahaq* dialect is called *tagadit*, which also designates a bird. It appeared among the Tuareg not long ago, probably when they became sedentary and were affected by their new environment. This 'bird' has four udders and gives milk, reminding us of its human origin and the anteriority of its status as a mother, as described in the myth.

> If you want to experience it, to see her come, she told me, spread out something white in front of her, she will put some '*hayd*' on it, menstrual blood, she will stain this piece of cloth with her impure blood.

Oum e sebian is a mythical feminine spirit that has taken the shape of a bird (*taira*) in the Saharan imaginary world. This spirit is anthropomorphic, has udders, menses like a woman, drinks blood and fatally attacks infants. The types of illnesses related to motherhood that are treated by Khadija have even affected her own daughters, and she eventually confessed she was chased by the *taba'â* (the 'chaser'), a fearsome feminine spirit that keeps her in misery and makes her own daughters ill.

One day a child stricken with a fearful disease was brought to Khadija. It was the fever identified as black heat that provokes paralysis. After examining him minutely and touching his fontanelle, she prepared a medicine for him, taking roots of agar ground by her daughter. She burnt these roots as incense, and took leaves of *atil* or *agar*, a sacred tree known for being the home of spirits; she pulverised some onion and blended it with goat's urine (Figure 12.3).

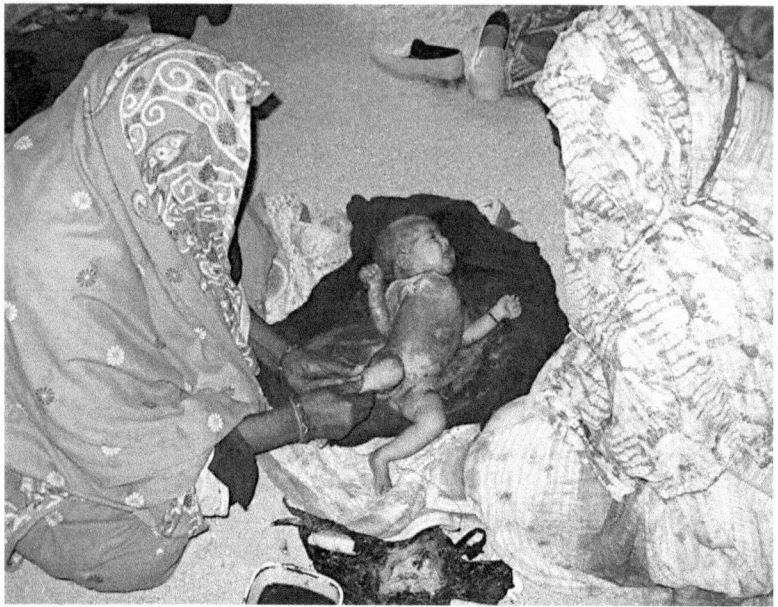

Figure 12.3. Healing ritual of a baby possessed by the female and bird spirit called Oum e Sebian. The baby is wrapped up in a black cloth and a black cream is put on his body. Black is the colour of this bird spirit (Taberket, Tamanrasset, Algeria, 2002).

For the black fever, a black remedy ('*skhana el kahla, edwa el khal*'). The whole body of the child was covered with this blackish product. Heat is associated with the colour black. Perfumes and aromatic substances, such as musk, amber and saffron (ritual perfumes), or very symbolic substances, like henna, the oil of cade, called *tar* or *qutran*, or human products 'from the inside or the outside', such as urine and blood, linked to stain and used in the *sihr* (magical processes), are all associated to the spirits, as is the colour black.

If one takes the term for the spirit, *oum e'sebian*, translated as 'the children's mother', it can be associated with children inasmuch as it could have become their foster mother after breastfeeding them during their sleep.

> The woman thus appears to be eminently ambiguous, both mother and woman, giving life, but also able to refuse to participate in her biological function of reproduction and feeding (Djeribi 1988: 45).

Could this be the same mythical and legendary character that assumes different feminine shapes, that of a 'devouring' mother, of a *ghoula* (ogress), of a *taba'â* (pursuer), of an ogress (*steriel*), of a seductive lover (*aicha*), of a saint, and finally a manifold image of the queen of an invisible kingdom (Saba)? In the myth told by the *tolba*, Oum e sebian would be none other than the mother of the spirits, the one who faced the Prophet and King Solomon.

Fatna, the tagahant *and divination on sand*

Women are also actors in an intermediary field that is part of the local religious and therapeutic landscape: divination, the ancestral practice to which nomad Tuareg women devote themselves in the evenings on the pre-Islamic tombs (*idebnen*). In the context studied here, divination comes into play with Fatna, a famous *tagahant*, a seer, who lives outside Tuareg society and practices geomancy, an ancient technique known by both the Tuareg and the Arab nomads.

I was sent to Fatna's house by Tuareg women who had recently moved to town and who were having a brutal experience of the social transformations of that city. Survival through social and family solidarity, through begging and sometimes even prostitution is the daily lot of the Tuareg women who have been deprived of any economic and cultural support. This is the dark picture of their forced urbanisation and the Tuareg's first experience of modernity. The massive exodus to the cities has had consequences on individual and collective destinies. It has led to deep social disruption, which has left indelible marks on the women, as well as on the men, who have been deprived of everything. Women suffer the attack of the spirits mostly during conjugal crises, after childbirth, or a change of environment, but the reactions are different according to their social position.

Fatna officiates in Tahaggart e choumera, a famous district of Tamanrasset containing a diverse population. She is a Saharan woman from Adrar who settled in Tamanrasset after the mysterious disappearance of her husband in the desert. Her invisible companion, about whom she talked to me immediately, is called Bel Ahmer, the red spirit. It provides some help to Fatna during all the ritual stages of divination, but she must follow very strict rules to make this cohabitation with her spirit beneficial, avoiding repercussions. This soothsayer is not Tuareg, she expressed herself exclusively in Arabic and claims descent from a prestigious Arab tribe, that of the conqueror Okba benou Nafee, as well as affiliation with a *zaouïa* (*zawiyya*, Sufi lodge) located between Adrar and Timimun. Sedentarised Tuareg women come to consult her, as do others in the local population.

The role of soothsayer concerns many initiates, but this woman appears to be an exemplar of her field of expertise, divination; she has succeeded in her profession and her career is quite remarkable. Her story shows her particular, painful and intimate relationship with the invisible in a sincere and unambiguous manner. Fatna admitted that she had allowed herself to be unfaithful, that she had worked with other *jinns*; for which Bel Ahmer has not forgiven her. Jealous and exclusive, the spirit could not bear her practising with other spirits, and she was punished for this. Fatna dreads her spirit, Bel Ahmer, just as she dreads this spirit's wife, which she dared to expel with *oum nass* incense. Because of this relationship, she said she lost five of her children from retaliation alone. Nevertheless, she talked about a real alliance, insofar as she takes her divinatory power from this spirit. Already as a child, this destiny was written in geomantic characters on a dune, a sign that she was able to decipher from knowledge received in a dream. In the case of this Arab woman the transmission is once again in the maternal line, though she comes from a patriarchal system.

One of the recurring features of the episodes relating the resistance of neophytes and the retaliation of the spirits, is signified by the loss of infant children or the death *in utero* of babies. Their children can also bear the marks of the spirits. Khadija's mother was impregnated by them, which would explain the strange appearance of one of her children. There is a profound relation between this form of shamanic disorder and feminine sexuality/fecundity, which in itself provides food for thought. The explanation of the initiate is that the spirits prey on children, they punish her for not meeting their demands, which were to fulfil the shamanic functions assigned to her. She knows she has been chosen to be the mediator between the invisible world of the *kel essuf* and the visible world of men.

The masculine world of the tolba

From the outset, two worlds seem to have been opposed: the feminine world presented to us through these initiated women, and a masculine world of men who treat the sick. Each intervenes to re-establish harmony in the group, and each represents a pole of the sacred.

These male healers, called *ineslmen* (Muslim notables), are skilled in scriptural and theological knowledge, and often affiliated to a mystical brotherhood. They are foreign to the zone of the Ahaggar, and most of them come either from Western Africa, where the centres are Timbuktu or Tademekkat in the kingdom of the Essuk, or from Maghreb, from Moroccan Tafilelt or the mythical Saguiet el Hamra (called Rio del Oro by the Spanish), which was a real breeding ground for saints.

In West Africa, which has long been dominated by animism, the 'religion of the ancestors', the brotherhoods, have fulfilled the roles of articulating and interpreting universalist Islamic messages and teachings. Monotheism, thus proclaimed, served as a historic link, among many others, between Black Africa, the Maghreb and the Arab world, through the Sahara: 'The desert is no high wall insulating from the rest of the world, it is an interior sea that invites to the passage from one side to the other'.[4] Timbuktu is the perfect example of a cosmopolitan Islamic city. Islam made itself accepted through Sufism,[5] which, considering its strong mystical connotations, offers Africans in general and Berbers in particular, who are avid for symbols, a religious framework of fulfilment adapted to the pre-existing religious environment and cosmogonic world.

These pious men, also called *chorfa*, are endowed with supernatural powers and are the objects of a deep worship. The *ziara* (*ziyara*) pilgrimage to saint's tombs helps to purify the country, to drive away the *essuf* (the void), to restore the balance between the exterior and the interior, to bring society together, to renew the ties of solidarity, and to undertake a new cycle after becoming impregnated with the *baraka* of the holy places. Possession rites are part of the religious landscape of a *ziara*. Celebrated in the proximity of the tomb of saints, they benefit from the sacrality of the place that surrounds his tomb. The offering meal, the *takute* or *sedqa*, has a resolutely religious nature: it brings the communion of the souls. The sharing of the donation of food is equivalent to that of the *baraka*. The *ziara* is a sacred feast in which excessiveness is desired, even looked for, in everything (food, habit, word and vigil), but with a control and sense of the limit, giving its sense to what Roger Caillois (1939) calls the 'resurgence of excess and chaos'.

Religious functions are spread throughout all classes of free men, but specialisation is the concern of these important religious groups. The *ineslmen* form, like the *enaden* blacksmiths, a social category that assumes the functions of mediation. But they are more prestigious than the *enaden*. They are mediators between the visible and the invisible world, between Islam and tradition, and thanks to their status as pacifists, between groups and individuals involved in relationships of honour. As such, they fulfil the function of arbiter and often play the roles of 'éminence grise' (Wallentowitz 2003: 44), of political advisers, of *imgharen* wise men, who are the holders of the *baraka*, embodying a spiritual counter-power that authorises them to sometimes take over from the war aristocracy in order to implement political decisions taken in the consultative assemblies. With sedentarisation, a religious community of the *ineslmen* has recently formed in Tamanrasset and constitutes an achieved entity, with a marked socio-economic power. The *chorfa* from the Saharan oases are often called by the honorary title of *mouley* (lord).

Some remarkable individuals are raised to the status of sainthood, of a *wali* (a friend of God), who tends towards the *ittihad* (the union with God) through asceticism and renunciation. The saint is described as an extraordinary man, who makes 'miracles' of *karamat* and who is endowed with healing powers. Coming from Sufism, this notion of sainthood has spread through Islam. Muslims consider that sainthood in the strict sense (expressed by the root *QDS*) only belongs to God. Only proximity with God (*walaya*) defines Muslim sainthood (Mayeur-Jaouen 2004: 14). The idea of *walaya* refers to relationships of proximity and intimacy, as well as those of protection and patronage related to the exercise of a power.

Among the Tuareg, there is a distinction between great *alfaqitan*, scholars, who are exegetes (*faqih*), and *inaktiban*, scholars, who are writers.[6] Both however write protective amulets and enter into direct relationships with the spirits. The anger of the saint who has *baraka* is feared by the whole society, for the strength that inhabits him is unpredictable, it spreads through space and time and can provoke commotion, misfortunes and even death for those who have transgressed. Eventually, for Raymond Jamous, the *baraka*:

> defines not only a belief, but values and a relation of religious subjection between its holders, the *chorfa*, and the secular believers...The *baraka* is not only set at the level of symbolic thinking, but also at the level of social practice (Jamous 1981: 204).

As for their invisible companions, *aljinnen* and other *kel essuf*, each *wali* has his servants, soldiers, caliphs, *rowahin* (souls, spirits) and *oukils* (delegates). They serve him in his healing of the sick and bringing of well-being to the community, but they can also strike the guilty, the profaners. Each *taleb* also has his invisible servants, maybe not of the same category, but some distinguish the *jinns* from the *afarit* (higher and powerful geniuses).

All these *ineslmen* told me that knowledge is held by the *mostahkem*, which designates the one who holds the *hikma* (from which *mostahkem* is derived, meaning the rule, the gift, wisdom) and who owns also the *sir*, the secret. The status of the *mostahkem* legitimates action against the knots of the sorcerers. In order to use the power that stems from the *hikma*, one must have received the *idn*, the divine permission. Everything that does not stem from the *roqia* (exorcism), according to some *foqaha* (jurists), resorts to other harmful invisible forces that wreak havoc inside the community if they are not controlled.

The *tolba* and amulet 'makers' have had privileges since the colonisation of the Ahaggar and the Sahara, and the independence of Algeria only strengthened their social position. Amulets are very expensive and the services of a *taleb* also attain high prices, so much so that an established, recognised and socially integrated *taleb* can survive easily, much better even than a farmer. However, they often also fulfil several functions simultaneously until their base is well established. Most of the time the title of *taleb* is inherited from father to son. The healing power is acquired through initiation. The direct descendent may not be able to carry out this mission, and therefore sometimes the *taleb* chooses his disciple, first among his relatives (his children, even his grandchildren, his nephews), and then among his followers. The legacy of knowledge is also patrilineal. On the other hand, the title of *taleb* spreads to other social categories in both urban and rural contexts. Most of the *tolba* are not *icherifen* (noble, descendants of the Prophet Muhammad), and some *icherifen* can serve as *tolba* when they officiate and settle as such, which is very rare (they occasionally do it when sick people solicit them to). They thus activate their *baraka* in order to bring health and comfort. A mere self-proclaimed *taleb* can be considered a powerful sorcerer and an amulet maker, manipulator of invisible forces, a true ally of the *afarit*. He gets in touch with the spirits through rituals involving pollution and stain, and some even manage to stain the sacred blood (with blood). Therefore, it can be noticed that the religious and therapeutic field has become, little by little, democratic and has opened its doors to other social groups. Other relationships of power are set up through new legitimacies.

The relationship with spirits is flexible and varies according to their nature and to the nature of the contact they have with men. The *jinn* is said to have the ability to transform itself into *yethaouel*, to be metamorphosed and therefore also to change its colour and aspect. Their kind of contact with men also varies, they can simply 'brush against', 'touch' and 'visit', just as they can 'strike' and 'inhabit' the bodies of men. The expertise of the specialist, the ally of the invisible world, is that he managed to communicate with them and that he is carried by particular dispositions to enter into a permanent relationship with them, unlike ordinary mortals.

The *taleb* apparently makes powerful talismans. In addition to his function as an 'unsorcerer', he is in charge of freeing the victims of possession. During this ceremony, in which the Qur'an and certain ritual gestures such as the laying on of hands and the absorption of sacralised water and incense intervene, the possessed person takes on a different voice and state, he/she starts to yell and gesticulate, and as they express themselves there is identification of the spirit concerned. The possessed person's body starts shaking, and one can easily talk of a state of trance with music. Exorcism has been too quickly evoked to designate this kind of ceremony officiated by religious men, though this is far from always the case, as the possessing spirits are negotiated with before any form of exorcism is contemplated.

Alliances with the invisible are not limited to the cults of possession of the descendents of slaves. Possession goes through different categories. Rituals regarding the management of the relationship with invisible forces involve the bodies of possessed people in entirely different contexts. A wide vocabulary shows the diversity of these states and practices. The spirits being chased (exorcised) are neither those with whom an alliance has been made, nor those with whom a negotiation is attempted through an offering, an exchange or a sacrifice.

Purity and impurity

What can be acknowledged is that Tuaregs delegate the management of the body and illness to specific social categories. This stems directly from their relationship with blood and with everything that falls into the register of impurity. But the opposition between purity and impurity as it is presented by some authors (Hureiki 2000, Rasmussen 1995), as being between different social categories (slaves/nobles, blacksmiths/religious men), seems to me more complex.

A whole combination of food taboos typical among the Tuareg inform the notions of purity and impurity. Excesses or violations of food taboos, as well as the bad management of sexuality, cause serious disorders and are often at the origin of the invisible's attack. Some types of food (onion, chicken, eggs, fish) are prohibited for nobles because they are signs of pollution. On the other hand, these types of food are eaten by the other social categories. These food taboos have nothing to do with any interdiction. They are indisputably pre-Islamic.

Islam is apprehended as the dominant religion giving rise to the notions of purity and order. It did not clash with pre-existing religions or beliefs by pushing them aside, but has absorbed them: first through compromise, then by integration. This is what is shown in the tales and practices of traditional practitioners. The heart of the problem essentially lies in the relationship to blood. The blood of sacrifice is managed by the *ineslmen* (religious men) and the blacksmiths. Apart from the big festivities, some women (*tiklatin*, female slave and *hartaniates*, free female cultivator) perform magical sacrifices at home. Instead of the goats, bulls or camels that are sacrificed by the *tolba*, they cut the throat of cats, dogs and lizards (varanus) following a rigorous procedure. Secretly, they take the step of transgression, because they have negotiated this status, and for their magic remedies they resort to sacrifices of illicit species, of wild species.[7] But they are not regarded as prestigious by the population, which fears them, and thinks that they are able to transcend categories, to take an animal shape. 'The woman who practices witchcraft often remains a believer' (Benkheira 1997: 94). Yet the social imagination has her closer to diabolical forces. In this they are designated by the word *tinisemt*, the envious ones. But this negative view of women concerns inferior social categories, it far from corresponds to the enhanced image of the noble Tuareg woman, who remains the linchpin of society. Here, the image of impurity related to these practices concerns certain social categories mixing men and women, and is not directly related to the opposition between masculine and feminine expressed in other forms.

The main categories of purity and impurity, related to cleanliness and stain, can be found in all ritual practices observed among Saharan traditional practitioners and indeed in the society as a whole. It can be found in the daily gestures of people, in their relationship to the world, space, objects, fluids, food...one can say that in this way a structural category spanning the entire symbolic system is set up. It is at this level that the transmission of knowledge, and through it the legitimation of the actors, takes place.

Saliva is an emblematic element, just like blood. It is stain, but also a medium for *baraka* and a conveyor of healing. Saliva heals, and power and knowledge are transmitted. The same can be said about milk. Another figure of impurity is the witch, with which most traditional practitioners have an ambiguous relationship. Witchcraft produces pollution and disorder, but it also allows the maintenance of a certain balance, or the reversal of an established order. Witchcraft, due to its subversive aspect, arouses fear, but it also has a pre-eminent social role. One cannot interpret correctly the rites using urine, menstrual blood, maternal milk, saliva etc. if one does not know that the body is a symbol of society, and that it reproduces on a small scale the powers and dangers attributed to the social structure.

Disorder is a source of danger and power, for it holds creative potentialities. Douglas (1971) has explained that the margins have their own power ('unarticulated'). In one way or another, the field of witchcraft affects all the actors linked to the invisible world. Most traditional practitioners, even if they claim they do not resort to it, have a close connection to witchcraft.

Tuareg society, as it is presented in origin myths, emphasises a permanent feature – a feminine ancestor and a supernatural parent – that underlines an origin that can be called shamanic. This is shared with other social groups within the same culture. Within the kinship system, the relation between brother and sister refers to the origin myths and the sacredness of those origins.

Women are indeed metaphorically related to this function of the matrix tent, *ehen ebawel*. *Ebawel* refers to the idea of hollowness, of the nest and to the idea of uterine kinship, in other words to the Arabic *rahim*, which is mentioned in the Qur'an. Women also transmit the 'milk' of the *ebawel* (*akh n ebawel*), which is the continuity of life, its extension, transmitting the *baraka* just like blood.

The world thus described is composite, and instead of blending different traditions, it integrates them together, reinterpreting them through a cultural prism that is progressively renewed. The nodal point remains the belief in the spirits, in the invisible world, and as for the *baraka*, it represents a real common value for all the Muslim populations from the Maghreb, as well as those from West Africa, as is shown in many research works.

What about *baraka* in women? Whether or not they come from saintly lineages, the women who are also invested by the divine blessing (*baraka*) must possess personal qualities (tenacity, generosity, courage, hard work...) to make this *baraka* effective. Then they will enable other women to enjoy this *baraka* in exchange for offerings, and will hand it down to their children by filiation, in the context of the transmission of knowledge, and through symbolic means, in particular through dreams, and milk. In Tuareg societies, the social rank of these women is important. Those who come from the prestigious religious *ineslmen* tribes (e.g. *ifoghas, kel Ansar*...) have nobility and *baraka* in their blood; they inherit it, just as they inherit a certain religious knowledge. They also have established complementary skills in the medicinal and divinatory fields, they know the secret of plants. Numerous are those who become *tanesmagalt*, respected traditional practitioners, women of honour, who also take part in the rites of passage.

Stories gathered among initiates – such as those describing running away in a forest in the middle of *ibakaten* trees (the spirits' trees) and staying in the well with the *kel essuf*, or in the spirits' mountain, *garet el djennoun* for instance, an initiatory high place – are best understood as allowing the initiate to become familiar, through dreams and faintness, with the natural places in which the spirits are supposed to dwell, to come near their world and know their secrets. The disease stops with the acceptance of the function, and the alliance and the intimacy with the spirits leads to the capacity to practise.

Possession defies the stranglehold of religious dogmas, and that is why it remains something that must be subjugated and controlled. It should be noticed that in folk wisdom the women who become saints are often given male characteristics. They often had a more or less chaotic sexuality and conjugal life from their earliest youth, and their image is intimately linked to that of the women spirits to whom a cult is devoted. So have the mystical feminine characters that have entered mythology, women spirits and legendary figures such as Aîcha Qondicha and Lalla Mimouna in the Maghreb or even war heroines to whom are attributed supernatural powers, such as the Kahina or Fatma Soummer in Algeria.

Religious practice by women is absorbed into their social activities and articulates with their life cycle. They do it naturally because they manage everyday life affairs, the lack of well-being inside their families and their communities, periods of pregnancy, births and illnesses or deaths of their children. It can be noticed that women have a much more intimate relationship with the body, that they are more in touch with it. They touch, massage and put anointments on the bodies of sick people. Emotion is also expressed more naturally during the musical ceremonies of possession. Most formal activities of the brotherhoods are reserved for men.

There is no formal opposition between feminine and masculine spaces. We have seen how during the *Tazengharet* women can participate in the initiation of men and how singing refers to Islam; and vice versa, when the saint spits in the hand of an initiated slave woman to whom he transmits the *baraka*. It is a matter of a symbolic exchange. It is true that for former slave women, this alliance frees them from constraints linked to their status as members of a dominated group, both from their subordinate position in the highly hierarchical society to which they belong and from their status as women who must submit to the desires of their master. In Tuareg society, free women have a privileged status. In their case, possession does not represent a counter-power but a possibility to express inner conflicts and to give free rein to a form of bodily expression. A free woman will not dance like a slave, no matter which spirit possesses her. On the other hand, she is finally able to express herself, and sometimes express her anger towards a careless husband or her in-laws. In this there does not seem to be a major difference between women and men, as both are as likely to be affected by the spirits. There are no more cases of possession among women than men and therefore it cannot be said to be a feminine phenomenon.

The relationship with the body also differs between the social classes. Noble women have learnt how to control their body in case they fall ill or get into a trance during a ceremony, or when they dance at a *tindi* organised by other women. Thereby they avoid endangering their status. Men can also refuse to give themselves up to the call of the possession music, and avoid the *tazengharet*, in which the bodies of the possessed are unleashed. The *tazengharet* mostly concerns the former *iklan* slaves. An unbounded sexuality is also attributed to *tiklatin* women, and then possession is experienced as an almost natural consequence, due to their status. On the other hand, sexual relationships between the spouses do not admit to excess among the Tuareg.

The discussion of emotions is intimately linked to the relationship with the body, and follows a long process of shaping the individuals' affectivity, of the self-control dictated by reason (Hell 2006). Trance is not only regarded with suspicion in Western society, but also in other cultures, for it represents a form of subversion. But instead of completely erasing and isolating it, many non-Western societies codify and ritualise it. Inside cultures in which possession is an almost daily reality, there are ritual spaces allowing the body to express it entirely freely. It then becomes a language, and quite often a message too (Hell 2006: 88).

Conclusion

To conclude, I would say that until this point analyses have shown how the system of beliefs in a tangible sacredness can provide a framework for feminine solidarity, a space of material as well as cognitive resources (De Gasquet 2003–2004). With regard to possession, these analyses put forward its liberating potential, the fact that it gives access to a network of feminine solidarity, that of the initiated possessed women, and even to a social status (therapeutic and religious responsibilities). The possession of women of a certain rank allows the justification of certain transgressions (adultery, betrayal, dissoluteness). Being lusted after and taken by a spirit can explain the 'surprising' or even 'immoral' behaviour of a woman who leaves her husband, and thus leaves a comfortable life to go back to a lover and live in a state of uncertainty and precariousness. It is a personal path that does not necessarily pave the way to a calling, but which allows movement through a delicate passage of life without suffering the negative judgement of society. This is thus how society retrieves transgressors back into the social order, thanks to these explanations. Thus, one can wonder where the opposition between the feminine and masculine practices lies, if not in the kind of relationship they have with the spirits? In all likelihood it has to do with power. Some contrast an institutional power with a traditional one. The status and role of each of these specialists of the invisible are far from set.

In Tuareg society free women have a privileged status, as possession does not represent a counter-power for them. It allows them to express their inner conflicts and to give free rein to a form of bodily expression. A free woman would not dance like a slave, irrespective of what spirit possesses her. On the other hand, a free woman will finally express herself, sometimes in anger against her careless husband or her in-laws. Moreover, there does not seem to be a major difference between women and men, as both are as likely to be affected by spirits. There are no more cases of possessions among women than men and it is not, therefore, a typically feminine phenomenon. This chapter has shown how the opposition between the masculine and the feminine is built from a symbolic point of view and how the categories of tradition and modernity, traditional sacredness and religious institutions, are being questioned by the complex journeys of individuals and by their practices that blur the gendered spaces, the sexual categories.

Bibliography

Balandier, Georges (1988). *Le Désordre, éloge du mouvement*. Paris, Fayard.
Bastide, Roger (1971). *Anthropologie appliquée*. Paris, Stock (reedited 1998).

Benkheira, Mohammed Hocine (1997). 'Alimentation, altérité et sociabilité'. *Archives européennes de sociologie*, 38, 237–87.
Borel, François (1986). 'La vièle, le tambour et les génies du mal'. In Hainard Jacques and Roland Kaehr (ed.). *Le mal et la douleur*. Neuchâtel, Musée d'ethnographie, pp. 199–205.
Caillois, Roger (1939). *L'Homme et le Sacré*. Paris, Gallimard.
Casajus, Dominique (1987). *La tente dans la solitude. La société et les morts chez les Touaregs Kel Ferwan*. Paris, MSH.
Claudot, Hélène and Hawad, Mahmoudan (1984). '*Ebawel/Essuf*, Les notions d'intérieur et d'extérieur dans la société touarègue'. *Revue de l'Occident musulman et de la Méditerranée*, 38, pp. 171–9.
Claudot-Hawad, Hélène (1986). 'La Conquête du vide ou la nécessité d'être nomade chez les Touaregs'. *Revue de l'Occident musulman et de la Méditerranée*, 41–42, 397–412.
_____(1993). *Les Touaregs. Portrait en fragment*. Aix-en-Provence, Edisud.
Cuoq, Joseph (1985). *Recueil des sources arabes concernant l'Afrique Occidentale*. Paris, CNRS.
De Martino (1999). *Le Monde magique*. Paris, Synthalobo, Les empêcheurs de tourner en rond, vol. 1.
De Gasquet, B. (2003–2004). 'Anthropologie féministe et cultes de possession: Reflet ou contestation des rapports de pouvoir entre les sexes'. Master in Sociology, EHESS, Paris.
De Sardan, Olivier (1994). 'Possession, affliction et folie: les ruses de la thérapisation'. *L'Homme*, 131, 7–27.
Di Mitri, Gino (2006). 'Les Lumières de la transe. Approche historique du tarentulisme'. In *Chamanisme et possession, Cahiers des musiques traditionnelles*. 19, 117–37.
Djeribi, Muriel (1988). 'Le Mauvais Oeil et le lait'. *L'Homme*. 'La fabrication mythique des enfants'. 28: 105, 35–47.
Douglas, Mary (1971). *De la souillure. Essai sur les notions de pollution et de tabou*, (1966). Translated in French. Paris, Maspero, 1971; (reprinted, La Découverte, 2001).
Gast, Marceau (1985). 'Croyances et Cultures populaires au Sahara'. *Mythes et Croyances du monde entier 2: le monothéisme*. Paris, Lidis-Brepols, pp. 370–82.
Hamayon, Roberte (1990). *La Chasse à l'âme. Esquisse d'une théorie du chamanisme sibérien*. Nanterre [Paris], Société d'ethnologie.
Hell, Bertrand (2006). 'L'Expérience du corps et des émotions dans les cultes de possession'. In *'Le Corps médiateur'. Revue Française de Yoga*, 33, pp. 87–107.
Hureiki, Jacques (2000). *Les Médecines touarègues traditionnelles, approche ethnologique*. Paris, Karthala.
Jamous, Raymond (1981). *Honneur et Baraka, les structures sociales dans le Rif*. Paris, Maison des Sciences de l'Homme.
Kuczynski, Liliane (2003). *Les Marabouts africains à Paris*. Paris, CNRS.

Mayeur-Jaouen, Catherine (2004). *Histoire d'un pèlerinage légendaire en islam. Le mouled de Tantâ du XIIIe siècle à nos jours*. Paris, Aubier.

Rasmussen, Susan J. (1995). *Spirit Possession and Personhood among the Kel Ewey Tuareg*, Cambridge, Cambridge University Press.

Wallentowitz, Saskia (2003). 'Enfant de Soi, enfant de l'Autre. La construction symbolique et sociale des identités à travers une étude anthropologique de la naissance chez les Touaregs (*Kel Eghlal* et *Ayttawari* de l'Azawagh, Niger)'. Ph.D, Paris, EHESS.

Part III

ISLAMISED SHAMANISM AND OTHER RELIGIONS

Chapter Thirteen

SHAMANISM AMONG THE GYPSIES OF SOUTHEASTERN EUROPE

François Ruegg

Southeastern Europe is known to be a place of acute and constant intercultural exchange. The borders of three Empires have shifted for many centuries and it has been the object of colonisations, deportations, exchange of populations as well as integration policies including forced religious conversions. Neither ethnic nor religious identities can be easily defined among the variety of populations settled in this region. Gypsies[1] (or assimilated groups) are a paragon example of this difficulty. Unanimously marginalised, they supposedly adopt the religion of the local majority, i.e. Islam or Christianity. However, within this apparently common religious affiliation, they rely on their usual survival strategies, integrating new confessions selectively. Their healing practices are but one illustration of this: under the formal adoption of Islam, they have maintained shamanic like healing rituals as do their Turkic neighbours. More recently, they adopted neo-Protestant charismatic ways in the context of Pentecostalism, which seems to suit both their longing for miracles and for partaking/joining a more successful community. Before addressing the question of Gypsies' healing practises, I would like to show how difficult it is to define their identity.

Multiple identities, national frontiers and census: impossible definitions

It is almost impossible to have a clear-cut picture of the various populations living in the Balkans. One cannot reduce multiple or complex identities by taking into account only one category i.e. 'nationality' (as the various 'ethnic groups' were called during the Communist regime), 'ethnicity' or 'minority', to say nothing about religious belonging and professional affiliations. As we well know, ascribed identities differ from self-ascribed ones. Receiving or adopting an identity does not mean sticking to it. Ethnic, national and religious identities are constantly mixed and confused. From a religious point of view, since we are speaking of healing rituals, formally adopting an official religion stopped no one from simultaneously practising others in what is known as syncretism.[2] In addition to these obstacles, the historical times in which observations and research are made refer to very different political and geographical frameworks, which add to the confusion of identities. Finally it is worth remembering that Gypsies and Turkic groups have often been nomadic, crossing borders easily. Therefore the limits of present Nation States (Romania *or* Bulgaria) are not pertinent to properly encompass these social groups.[3]

Today, Southeastern European nations still have a hard time trying to establish a precise census of their populations, globally divided in 'a national majority' and minorities, the latter sometimes being split in 'historical' and 'ethnic minorities' as in Romania. Gypsies are known to be particularly difficult to count for several reasons. Official governmental figures about the number of Roma/Gypsies are sometimes half of what Gypsy activists estimate, unless the government has political or economical reasons to show a larger Gypsy minority (Eminov 1997: 112). Following ethnic or religious affiliations criteria in the census makes also a big difference, not to mention the spoken language.[4] The ongoing discussions about the 'real identity' or 'origin' of Pomaks (*Muslim Bulgarians*) in Bulgaria and Gagauz (*Christian Turks*) in Romania, Moldova and Ukraine is a good illustration of the political dimension of identities and census. At a national level in Romania, the number of registered Muslims remains negligible. However, taking into account the regions of their major concentration, the Dobrudja province, they represent around 20 per cent of the population, regrouping Tatars, Turks and 'Turkish' Gypsies. In Bulgaria they represented 13.1 per cent of the population in 1992, mainly concentrated in the East of Bulgaria (Eminov 1997). How many Roma/Gypsies consider and declare themselves Turks because they are Muslims, or Bulgarians and Romanians because they are Christians, is difficult to estimate. This is nothing new and seems to have been a never-ending 'problem', as older studies and reports complain about (Arbore 1930). Under the Ottoman rule, Gypsies could certainly enjoy a better status if 'converted' to Islam than as serfs in the Romanian Provinces. However even as Muslims, they were considered the lowest social category (Cossuto 2001: 147–8).

More recently, the 'cultural trope' in European policies has encouraged minorities to regroup and create cultural associations and political parties which influence the choice of an ethnic/religious identity. Since the adoption of generous minority laws after 1989 in Romania, it can also be advantageous to belong to a religious/ethnic minority like the Turkish/Muslim or Tatar/Muslim one, who have a deputy in Parliament as well as the Roma/Gypsy community.

Finally, many 'minority' groups, not only among the Gypsies but also among 'Turks' or Pomaks and Tatars share a history of forced exile, colonisation and repatriation, conversion or 'atheisation' and, as regards Roma, even extermination. Sedentarisation affected Gypsies but also other nomadic minorities. The political history of Dobrudja over the last centuries did not contribute to the stability of the populations either. Under Russian rule from 1829 to 1856, it went back to the Ottoman Empire until 1878 when it was divided between Romania and Bulgaria. Romania received the 'Quadrilater' from 1913 to 1940 when it was given back to Bulgaria. Important migrations, deportations and colonisations took place, provoking confusion, not to speak of the imposition of new names during nationalist campaigns, in Bulgaria (Eminov 1997) as well as in Romania that managed to blur an already unstable situation.

Ethnicity and religion

In the context of the Ottoman Empire, the Black Sea littoral as well as the south Danube regions were colonised from the fifteenth century onwards with a variety of populations, mainly Turks and Tatars from various regions of the Empire, namely Yürüks from Anatolia (as early as in the sixteenth century), Tatars Nogay and Crimean Tatars, the latter fleeing the Russian occupation of Crimea (1856). This means that there is a clear 'Turko-Muslim' cultural heritage in this region, attested by a variety of religious monuments (Önal 1997: 335) which enables us later to localise some of the healing rituals.

For some scholars, historians or ethnographers, it is not only obvious that Muslim Gypsies came to the Dobrudja with Anatolian Turks, the above-mentioned Yürüks, but also that some of the latter were later assimilated to Gypsies (Strand and Marsh 2005; Cossuto 2001: 150–151) established in the region, because of their low social status and their belated sedentarisation. Önal (1997) who made extensive field researches in Dobrudja in the late 1990s affirms that among the Turkish Gypsies of today there are some former nomadic Anatolian Turks who mixed with the Gypsies. They are not as rejected[5] as they are everywhere else and are even seen as keeping Turkish traditions alive (Önal 1997: 33). Cossuto (2001) mentions that in Bulgaria, Gypsies are called Tatar and Yürük, for 'political reasons'. Eugène Pittard, who was primarily a physical anthropologist, measured and carefully noted the physical diversity in the Balkans (Pittard 1932). He distinguishes 'real Gypsies' from 'gypsified' groups. Other groups of Gypsies established in the Dobrudja, also studied by Pittard at the beginning of the twentieth century (Pittard 1903), called themselves *Turkish Gypsies, Tatar* or *Bulgarian Gypsies*. These groups have partially survived and are still Muslim. It is worth noting that today, some Gypsies have a commercial relation with the local Tatars: they play a Tatar musical repertoire for the Tatar neighbouring community (Dietrich 2001). This adds to the difficulty of using one common appellation for well diversified groups. On a more general note, Pittard observed how few nomads circulating in Europe were '*real*' Gypsies (1932: 3), according to his anthropometric approach.[6]

Religious affiliation and the sharing of a language (Turkish) seem to be more relevant than ethnicity for the identification of the group we are mainly interested in here. For Muslim Gypsies, the Romany language seems absent from their identity building and unless one specifically asks, they are 'naturally' included in the Turkish population. We have now seen that it is almost impossible to have a *clear picture* of the exact ethnic composition of the 'Turkish' or 'Turko-Muslim Tatar' minority. As I have already noted, one cannot reduce multiple or complex identities to just one category.

An important historical factor for understanding *healing practices* is the presence of diverse Alevis and Sufis orders in the entire region. Their notorious leaders travelled and eventually settled down in this part of Southeast Europe. The main Holy Muslim figure said to be buried in the Dobrudja and Deliorman region is the Bektashi saint, Sari Saltuk of Babadag (Kiel, 2002) attested already in the thirteenth century. In the sixteenth century, Demir Baba established himself as a hermit in Ruino (near Silistra), coming from the Persian border region. A Nakşibendi Shaykh, Sabri Husayn (Softa Baba) came from Bukhara at the end of the eighteenth century to Tutrakan where his tomb can be found. The tombs of these saints are still visited by pilgrims, some coming from Turkey. But the *türbe* (tombs, mausoleums) are also visited in the context of cultural tourism, promoted by the government and municipalities, proud of showing a 'true multicultural European state' (Figures 13.1, 13.2, 13.3). Otherwise Turks and Tatars in Romanian Dobrudja claim to belong to (Hanafite) Sunnism when asked (Dobrudja 2009) as the majority of Muslims in Bulgaria, even if they may be *in petto* (secretly) Alevis (Eminov 1997: 70–75). However Kizilbaş-Alevi, Halveti, Nakşibendi and Bektashi communities are attested and studied (Zarcone 1992; Clayer 1994; Cossuto 2001). They form an Islamic heterodox diaspora that, as we shall see, has touched the Muslim–Gypsy community. Because of their constant circulation and flexible identity, we can easily follow Strand and Marsh's (2005: 3) suggestion that 'the historical processes of Romani ethnogenesis

Figure 13.1. Mausoleum of Sabri Husayn (Softa Baba), nineteenth century, at Tutrakan, Bulgaria, 2011 (Photograph: F. Ruegg).

have produced a variety of related identities from a range of composite groups, amongst them Romani people who are Alevis'.

As is the case with Gypsy ethnicity, it is impossible to attribute one particular label of Islam to Muslim Gypsies and say that Gypsies are Sunnite or Alevis. Gypsies were and still are frequently said to have no religion or at least no religious feeling whatsoever. Muslim Gypsies are suspected of being either heterodox or not very 'religious'. According to Alexander Paspati, nomads and established Gypsies criticised each other not only for being not very serious about religion and religious practices, but also for being Christian and Muslim at the same time[7] (Paspati 1870: 13). They were always famous for practising different kinds of 'magical arts': divination, chiromancy, healing, practices that indeed add to their negative reputation.[8] It is in this

Figure 13.2. Entrance of the mausoleum of Sabri Husayn (Photograph: F. Ruegg).

syncretic context that we shall try to look for *healing rituals*. But before turning to some specific Gypsy rituals, it is important to first explore common religious practices among the various 'nations' in Southeast Europe.

Common sacred places, sanctuaries and healing rituals

On the periphery of three Empires (Austrian, Russian and Ottoman), it is unsurprising to face not only a multiplicity of cults but also various forms of syncretism issuing from centuries of cohabitation of different traditions, enriched by constant immigration. Romanian and Bulgarian folklorists have duly reported local 'archaic forms of religion' or 'traditional customs' among

Figure 13.3. A detail of the mausoleum with the tomb of the saint Sabri Husayn in the background (Photograph: F. Ruegg)

which witchcraft is always present. The practice and propagation of healing could well originate from as far back as the eleventh and twelfth centuries, a time when the Byzantine Empire was facing Turcoman incursions (Strand and Marsch 2005: 162).[9] Orientalists, travellers and observers in the nineteenth century noted the flexibility of religious practices and affiliations in Muslim Central Asia (Gobineau 1983: 243 ff). This certainly also applies to the flexibility of the religious practices among Gypsies, Christians or Muslims in borderland regions.

The role of stones, trees and forests in healing practices has been widely documented by historians of religions. (Healing) rituals performed on or through a stone[10] or a tree, in Dobrudja as well as in the whole region, are common. What is peculiar here, in contrast to similar phenomena observed across most of the world, is that a holy tree is planted right next to a sanctuary, Christian or Muslim, or that sanctuaries themselves are built next to an old, venerable and venerated tree (oak or lime tree), or even in a holy wood (forest) (Zarcone 2005). Paul-Henry Stahl (1965) has shown how what he calls *dendrolatric*[11] practices have been adopted in the Christian-Orthodox as well as in the Muslim contexts, in Southern Romania and Northern Bulgaria. With a functionalist or perhaps materialist trope, he explains the sacredness of trees and water by their scarcity in a desert land. Stahl mentions three particular places of the 'cult of the tree' near a tomb and near a well: A sanctuary in Nalbant around the ruins of a *tekke* (Sufi lodge) near Tulcea, the very well known Mosque of Babadag, and a *tekke* in the valley of Batova (Obrotchiste) that is equally famous. In a later article (Stahl 2006) he extends his reflections, explaining syncretism as the result of a common older 'popular religion'. He gives examples of churches established on former 'pagan' sacred places and eventually turned into mosques like the cathedral of Babadag (Stahl 2006: 300). The fact that Christian-Orthodox and heterodox Muslim call upon their saints for healing, visit their graves or relics and perform healing rituals is again well documented.[12] To be more specific, when speaking about the symbolism of the tree in religious practices, one could mention that in Orthodox theology and mystical poetry, as expressed in the *Triodon* for Lent for example, the tree, and especially the tree of life[13] from the garden of Eden from which the wood is said to have been used for Christ's cross, plays a central role in many liturgical occasions (Veneration of the Cross). It is said to have curative virtues.[14]

The use (and drinking) of holy water and wells is equally common in Orthodox Christian and Roman Catholic healing or prophylactic practises as it is in Muslim pilgrimage sanctuaries like the Demir Baba sanctuary. In the Dobrudjan village of Techirghiol I visited in 2009, a holy spring dedicated to Saint Panteleimon is venerated by pilgrims of all faiths. A monastery built on the site of this spring also contains a sanatorium. First restricted to clerics, the sanatorium was opened to the public by the Patriarchate of Romania: it thus offers both holy and healing waters. Similarly, in the Orthodox Monastery of Dervent in South Dobrudja, which has a long history of miraculous healings, pilgrims of all creeds use stones and wells for healing; some particular stones are even used for curing animals (Iliescu 2005).

To come back to the Bektashi *tekke* of Obrotchiste[15] as described by Felix Philipp Kanitz (1879: 211–215), it was still hosting 18 'permanent' dervishes and the shaykh at that time wore the title of 'Akiasli Dervish Sultan Tekkessi Kadiriden Istamboli Sheik Hafus Halil Baba'. Dervishes performed the 'chalka' (ritual dance, Turkish *halka*) in the presence of the author. The *tekke* is usually constructed around the tomb of the saint. Kanitz observed the pieces of cloth that pilgrims attached to a stick at the entrance of the *türbe*.

Another famous observer, the historian Nicolae Iorga, equally observed the presence of fragments of cloth attached to the branches of a nearby tree, evoking ancient popular custom (Stahl 1965: 299). Both Christians and Muslims were venerating the same tomb, the first affirming it contained the body of a holy man Nicholas, the latter the body of a Marabout (Stahl 1965: 300). Moreover, pilgrims of the two confessions lighted candles around the tomb and fixed small pieces of their clothes on the sacred tree next to the sanctuary (as *ex votos*). The same 'dendrolatric' practice is referred to by many others,[16] and also by Zarcone (1992: 8) who, also says that the sanctuary was vigorously disputed between the two communities in the nineteenth century. As far as the ritual of *attaching prayers* on a stick or a tree goes (or bringing a stone), it is common throughout the Muslim world (Kanitz 1879). Stahl (1965: 302) mentions that similar practices were performed in the cemeteries in southern Transylvania, as well as the practice of 'placing prayers' on a sacred tree planted next to a well in an Christian orthodox monastery (in Communist times). This shows an interesting permeability of what is considered the Western border.

Similar rituals have been documented in other places in Bulgaria as in Knjazevo, now a part of the suburbs of Sofia (Mikov and Kmetova: 1998, which I follow hereafter). The saint, Bali Efendi (who died in 1551 and was buried in Knjazevo), was 'a great teacher of the Yürük tribes'. This further shows the strong presence of Alevism (Bektachism)[17] in the midst of places inhabited by Christian and Muslim Gypsies. Moreover Bali Efendi had apparently founded a *zaviye* (Sufi lodge) 'and with his own hands planted a large forest, which is in existence to this day'. Similarly to the sanctuary of Obrotchiste, the Bali Efendi *türbe* is adorned with drawings of trees. 'There are three large trees on each side of the window, and just below it there are five small ones.' Furthermore, 27 old oaks of the primitive forest, said to have been planted by the saint, have survived and are kept alive with scrupulous care. As far as healing practices are concerned, the tomb (*türbe*) is said to have curative powers: 'They bring weak and sick people here, to touch with their face the holy grave and pray for good health' (Mikov and Kmetova 1998: 82). For the saint became a saint thanks to a miracle he performed, according to the legend, on a *vakf* (endowment, Arabic *waqf*) on which the sanctuary had been built. Until 1878 there was a mosque and a *tekke* next to the *türbe*, but the former were destroyed by Bulgarians and replaced by a church dedicated to Saint Elias. However the cults are performed in the courtyard on votive stones, by Bulgarian and by (Muslim) Gypsies, but not simultaneously.[18] As far as these cults are concerned, we only know that gifts were made to the saints and that pilgrims would, as mentioned earlier, touch the grave with their faces and pray. Gypsies as well as Bulgarians and Turks, Muslim and Christians would visit the *türbe*. Here again we find traces of the old traditional practices referred to earlier, but as far as the 'votive cloths are concerned' the pieces of cloth are attached to the window bars.[19] Sacrifices were carried out by the pilgrims, in the courtyard. An annual Gypsy festival on August 2 is still celebrated there too. Generally speaking, Gypsies are known for taking care of the graves of Muslim saints throughout the region.[20] As is common for Christian sanctuaries in Western Europe, Muslim sanctuaries in Southeastern Europe might have been used successively, first by priests of Bacchus[21] and later by Greek-Orthodox monks. The sanctuary of Demir Baba in Dulovo (Northeastern Bulgaria) is also known to have been once a 'pagan' sacred place.

The case of the island of Ada Kaleh and its thaumaturgist saints also refers to healing practices, performed on the grave of a *baba* (saint in Turkish). Precise references are made to the presence of trees (acacia and mulberry tree), which stand at the saint's grave. The marginal or even heretical practices of these (*Bektashis*) Muslims are attested to as well, including the use of alcohol. We find interesting information in a more detailed account on healing practices (Val Cordun 1971: 108–10): the use of medicinal plants for gastric illnesses and the distribution of amulets (*hamaili*) to pregnant women. But even more interesting for the anthropologist is the custom of symbolic adoption by the saint (*Miskin Baba*), a ritual by which ill (epileptic, for example) children would be cured. The fact that the same symbolic adoption ritual is also performed in a Christian context adds credence to the evidence of regional syncretism. It is also factually attested to by the succession of Christian and Muslim sanctuaries on the island of Ada Kaleh (Val Cordun 1971: 112–3).[22] The second ritual mentioned by Val Cordun relates to oracles that were consulted at the grave of the saint. Taking a handful of earth from the ground near the grave, one would sleep upon it and try to interpret the ensuing dreams (Val Cordun 1971: 110). The sad ending of this story is that the island of Ada Kaleh was covered with water from the Danube, when Ceaușescu decided to build the dam at the Iron Gates.

There are a multitude of older examples of such syncretism: Arthur de Gobineau, for example, offers remarkable observations dating from the middle of the nineteenth century, in his description of religions and philosophies in Central Asia (Gobineau 1983: 410):

> The Albanian Muslims consider it their duty to burn candles in honor of Saint Nicolas. The Mirdite Christians used to consult the dervishes with respect. The women from Khorsova, in Chaldea, make offerings to Notre-Dame to obtain a child. If successful they go to the church to thank Her. They also learn how the Christian rite is carried out and the prayers in association with it recited. Mostancha took me along to assist [at Baku] at a kind of celebration that was performed in one

of the temple cells which was accompanied by small Guebre cymbals. On the altar there were vases from the Parsi cult, Russian images of Saint Nicolas and the Virgin. Catholic crucifixes were set up near divinities from Shivaism. All these various relics were regarded with equal respect.[23]

These kinds of syncretic practises are still observable today, among a wide range of populations who have been Islamised but have either never given up their 'ancestral customs' nor adopted the traditional customs of their neighbours. This also applies to the twin sanctuaries[24] of Boliartsi in Bulgaria (Asenovgrad). It is a perfect example of shared rituals: two sanctuaries, a chapel and a *tekke* have been built near a holy fountain and are visited by pilgrims of both faiths, Alevi-Gypsies and Christian Bulgarians, who light candles on both places; a bridge allows the passage from one to the other. On the day of Saint George, two *kurban* (sacrifices) are offered: one by the Mayor for the Christian community and one by a Turkish (Alevi-Roma) family whose father was healed from cancer and who afterwards rebuilt the *tekke*. He claims that the Holy Virgin appeared to him in his dream and promised to heal him.

A different case is illustrated by a Turkish-Muslim middle aged woman who used to work in the USSR until 1980, and now lives in the city of Tutrakan on the Danube (Bulgaria). She built a small sanctuary for a *baba* she made contact with during her dreams after she had endured some pain. In her vision a spirit, who appeared to be white (like the late Pope John Paul II), was looking for a place to rest. This was interpreted as being the spirit of the nearby destroyed mosque and the spirit was named after this mosque (Kantar Djami Baba). She eventually built the small sanctuary under the stairs of her house, for the *baba* to rest there. The *baba* saved or cured several people and they still come to light candles to obtain favours from the 'saint'. This example of a cult to a saint and its accompanying healing rituals (as well as the construction of the 'sanctuary') show how these rituals can rise from private sources too.

Among these Islamised populations are the Gypsies, whose healing rituals we will now focus on. We have seen that they represent a marginal population whose religious identity remains adaptable but who also tend to retain older practices that are abandoned by their neighbours.

Shamanic-like healing practices among Gypsies

Shamans were perceived as diabolic magicians in the early accounts of travellers and missionaries who had in mind the 'civilisation' of the world. Ensuing ethnographic studies, because of their monographic/ethnic approach, too often identified shamanic healing practices with one particular tribe or social group. Gypsies, then, were associated with chiromancy, just as they were associated with playing music, travelling or showing bears. If we are to adopt the same ethnographic approach, it might sound inappropriate to speak of *shamanism* when referring to Gypsy healing practice. But we will see in the following two examples that these rituals are in fact very close to what has been described in classical shamanic ethnographical literature concerning the 'original' shamans of Northeast Asia.

The ethnographic literature provides very precise descriptions of the healing practices of Gypsies living in Southeastern Europe, particularly in the German scholarly tradition of the end of the nineteenth century. Heinrich von Wlislocki in his *Volksglaube und religiöser Brauch der Zigeuner*, describes the various healing rites and even specific healing medicines for specific illnesses that are performed and prescribed by Gypsy female magicians (*Zauberfrauen*) (Wlislocki 1891: 51).[25] They are able to cure physical as well psychic illnesses; the author adds that these magicians 'still play the same role as the priest used to play in indigenous societies (*Naturvölker*) before the separation between the spiritual and physical healer occurred' (Wlislocki 1891: 51 [my translation]).

A list of the requirements for a Gypsy woman to become a magician follows: among them the capability of chasing dead souls as well as controlling the weather (*Witterung zu regeln*).[26] Similarly, becoming a magician is strictly regulated, as it is for shamans by heritage or by supernatural election (Wlislocki 1891: 54), through an initially unconscious copulation with a *spirit* (Nivashi = water spirit), who also teaches the woman his art. Finally, illness is interpreted as the evil spirit's attempt to estrange the spirit from the body of the sick person (Wlislocki 1891: 60); therefore, the aim of the magician is to keep the soul in the body in order to avoid too big a gap between them that would cause death.

In serious cases, when spirits (*Dämonen*) appear to be very strong, the Gypsy (female) sorcerer will proceed with a divination rite consisting of the inspection of the bone of the left shoulder of an animal (lamb or pork) sacrificed and prepared by a member of the ill person's family. During the time of preparing the bone, the sorcerer executes an ecstatic round dance,[27] during which she calls the spirits in a '*monotonous*' song. She asks the spirits 'to whisper in her ear where the life of this sweet man was taken'. She then offers them some food (intestines) and promises to 'bury the bones for their sake'. She even promises animal hair and announces that if the bone breaks quickly, the soul of the man will come back into place 'nicely'. The last address to the spirits is an obscure threat: they should tremble with fear if they do not return the soul.

Shamanism among the Gypsies of Southeastern Europe 271

The actual divination scene follows this episode. The *Zauberfrau* sings until the clean bone is brought to her; she then adds a piece of wood to the fire and puts the bone in it until it turns black. She holds up the burned bone with a special pair of double pliers, spits several times on it, and guesses from the cracks and the form of the bone whether the person is going to survive or not.

The author further points out that this must be a very ancient practice among Gypsies and seeks to extend his description of the 'reading on the bone' practice, which I will summarise. The cavity of the articulation (of the bone) is important: a deep cavity means luck and success. The protruding bone of the shoulder-blade is called *life* and is used to predict the patient's recovery or death, or simply his or her life expectancy. Black spots on the smooth part of the bone, that are concentrated in the middle, are called luck (*baçt*) and bad luck (*bibaçt*) if they are to be found on the edge (Wlislocki 1891: 62). With regard to the cracks: if cracks on the under part of the bone cannot to be covered with the thumb of the left hand, it means that the patient or even a family member will die. The same applies if many cross-like cracks are found on the bone; on the other hand, the absence of cracks and the presence of 'elevations' of the flat part of the bone mean that there is hope of recovery; in this case the shoulder bone will be buried near the ill person in order to allow the vagrant soul to settle on it. This is why, in the case of an improvement, one says 'life (the soul) is sitting on the bone' and the Gypsy lady then brings the soul back to the body while at the same time trying to chase away the weakened bad spirit. She gives the patient a sudation agent (hot liquids) and, interestingly, draws a circle on the earth around the sick person and the place where the bone was buried. She then walks three times around the circle shedding snake powder and whispering again a magic formula (Wlislocki 1891: 62–3). The whole ceremony consists of a fight between the medicine lady and the bad spirits. Even if the *Zauberfrau* is able to bring the soul back to the body, the patient may still die in some circumstances. In this case the medicine lady explains to the family that the spirits had also attacked the body.

As a matter of fact, 'reading on the bone' is a very ancient practice also used as a divination ritual, practised, for example, by the Tartarian Khan Mangu himself in his palace, as Rubruquis witnessed during his stay during the years 1252–54.[28] It is still mentioned in the Balkans, notably among Aromanians (Vlachs) in Macedonia, in the first part of the twentieth century (Eckert 1944).

In a later account of Serbian Gypsies, I found a very interesting description of a different shamanic-like practice performed by Gypsy women, referred to as healing artist (*Heilkünstlerin*) as well as a soothsayer.

Gypsy women are able to cure any illness. They speak magic words, bathe the sick, extinguish charcoals (to unbewitch), withdraw worms from the nose, the eyes and the ears and in so doing pretend to alleviate the suffering of the sick, while always alleviating their purse!

The withdrawing of worms is an interesting juggling stunt. Although I was very attentive, I could not see how and from where they could extract a great quantity of worms from their patients. In order to extract the worms, Gypsies use a little tube which they place at the patient's ear or nostril or on their eye before sucking out a great number of worms from the concerned body part...the sick person feels better after such a treatment (Gjorgjevic 1903: 44–5, my translation).

There is little doubt that the practices referred to correspond to rituals commonly performed by shamans elsewhere including the supposedly original shamanic northern Siberia region. The whispering, the singing, the dancing and the extraction of worms are widely documented practices. The main element absent from the healing practices in these instances is however the drum.

In my recent fieldwork in the lower Danube region (2009), I met a Turkish-Muslim woman who acts as a *hoja* (sic) – Muslim cleric, prays over the sick and practises divination/healing with the use of lead. She lives among Gypsies in the Gypsy *mahala* (district) but presents herself as a Turk. Melting lead is poured into water above the head of the sick person which is covered with a cloth (compare Zarcone in this volume). The ritual of pouring lead serves the same purpose of extracting evil, as it allows her to identify the illness in the form taken on by the lead. Naming the evil is an important step in the cure. Pouring lead is said also to subdue post-traumatic fear. Similarly in Cobadin and Fântana Mare/Moş Pinar (Dobrudja), healing rituals using 'lead reading' were still performed some 50 years ago in the Turkish community (fieldwork 2009 interview of Ms. ZS).

Reading the Qur'an or the Bible over the sick is another common practice referred to by several informants and texts. This ritual has been performed by both Christians and Muslims since the Middle Ages, combined with other healing rituals.[29]

In religious matters, Gypsies are said to adopt the religion of their neighbours. I shall not bring up the question of whether Gypsies are 'good' or 'bad believers' in the different confessions they have adopted.[30] A long tradition of accounts from travellers has contributed to establishing an image of versatility and superficiality to their religious practices, particularly from those who have a fixed notion of what religious practice should be. Rather let us consider this from another view point, one that is more anthropological.

Gypsies are well known to be both very conservative and very flexible. Their capacity to adopt new customs and behaviour, as well as to find new 'niches', particularly in economic life, is comparable to their famous stubbornness in refusing to mix with *gadje* (non-Gypsies) or become regular citizens of their country. Tradition and flexibility can easily be combined in order to survive, as other classical examples have shown in other geographical contexts like Voodoo in Haiti or colonial and post-colonial Christianity in Latin America (Gruzinski 1999). The presence of both shamanic-like traditions and heterodox (or at least marginal) Muslim (Alevi) and Christian (Orthodox) practices in their heritage should not confine them to an obscure *pagan* past. On the contrary, it shows a capacity to adopt what appears to them as useful religious practices at different moments and different places. Taking care of the saints and their *türbe*, as it is the case in Southern Bulgaria, is also a job; so is palm reading and curing the sick. This is why I think it is necessary to examine more closely their conversion to charismatic forms of new Protestantism in the last decade, i.e. Pentecostalism, in the same complex context of tradition and innovation.

New forms of healing practices in the framework of Pentecostalism

Just as slaves in Brazil and Haiti mixed their old religious traditions with those of their new masters, Gypsies have always formally adopted the religion of their 'host' country, in the Balkans. This has not prevented them from continuing to practice their traditional healing arts, as shown by Wlislocki, at least until the twentieth century. As already discussed above, the direct link between shamanic-like practices and Muslim or Christian syncretism in Southeastern Europe can be reasonably and at least partially related to the long and documented presence of Turkmen and Tatar heterodox Muslim groups (Clayer 1994; Zarcone 1992), who were sometimes declared and assimilated to Gypsies. But Islamised Gypsies themselves could well have brought with them similar *mixed* healing practices and traditions from India, or from their subsequent stay in Central Asia and the Near-East (Marushiakova and Popov 1993: 12).

The wave of Gypsy conversions to Pentecostalism in Romania as well as in Bulgaria (Slavkova 2004; 2007) cannot simply be called a purely 'religious' movement. Syncretism can be seen as a long lasting adaptation strategy, irrespective of the purity of intentions of the converts (Fosztó 2009).

Converted Gypsies have not in this case migrated to new countries where they would have adopted the local faith. They stayed (with some exceptions during the exchange of populations between Turkey and Bulgaria) in Romania and Bulgaria. Here, their already converted fellow Gypsies or evangelical pastors who were active during the Communist period invited them to adopt a new religious affiliation (Benovska and Altanov 2009). They moreover entered into a new world after the fall of the Communist regimes, which provoked a vigorous 'return to religion' for the entire population. In adopting a new *religion*, Roma also convey non-religious messages, which have initially little to do with healing practices.

Conversions in general and conversions of Gypsies to new forms of charismatic evangelism in particular, have caught the attention of many social scientists[31] and become a common topic for research in the social sciences. We directed a three year research project on the wider topic of the mobility (social, economical and religious) of Gypsies in Romania and the Republic of Moldova. Massive conversions affect Bulgaria as well as Romania[32] (and the other Eastern European countries). It is noteworthy that some Pentecostal communities are mixed, as in Bulgarian urban areas. The general tendency seems to be to create mono-ethnic communities, i.e. Gypsy parishes,[33] in Romania as well as in Bulgaria, particularly in the countryside.

Social scientists are less interested in investigating traditional rituals than in investigating the invention of the new identity strategies by Gypsies/Roma that afford them social mobility and freedom from social and religious discrimination. As an example, many scholars mention the fact that Gypsies were never totally accepted in the traditional Orthodox communities, and that their cemeteries were often separated from their fellow-believers (Gog 2009). In this research, we associated conversions primarily with *identity and integration strategies* from a socio-anthropological perspective.[34]

On the other hand, it is also commonplace to observe that Gypsies perform their traditional customs[35] *within* existing local communities, sanctuaries and even during some feasts or holidays that pertain to their Orthodox or other Christian and Muslim fellow-citizen's calendar, as in the aforementioned case of Bali Efendis' graveyard or in Boliartsi.

Although we have access to some recent ethnographic research on the narratives of *converts* in Romania and Bulgaria, these are not very significant for our endeavour as they tend to repeat in a stereotypical manner the narratives of every new convert to charismatic churches in Western Europe or elsewhere; this includes a traumatic event interpreted as a meeting with God, followed by the conversion to a totally new life, particularly by following strict moral rules, namely the ban of alcohol and smoking.[36] As a matter of fact, born-again discourses and charismatic Christian healing practices are familiar and easy to view in the Western world. One can daily listen to them on Christian radio stations or TV channels. One of the first ethnographical studies on Gypsy conversion to Pentecostalism was devoted to the French Manouches who converted as early as 1950 (Williams 1991).

Pentecostalism is clearly about healing and therefore has an even more attractive potential to Roma, whose traditional religious practices and beliefs are linked, as we have seen, with healing processes and divination. Because of the *ecstatic-* and *possession-like* aspects of their healing liturgies, which in some aspects evoke the traditional (shamanic-like) healing rituals, being directed to the individuals, Pentecostalism has been very successful in all traditional shamanic communities, especially in Siberia. This is why we think conversions also deserve the attention of scholars working specifically on religious dimensions of conversions. In our case, we have to stress that these conversions occur also amongst *Muslim* Gypsies, at least in Bulgaria; some converted Bulgarian-Muslim/Turk-Gypsies have even been sent as Christian (Pentecostal) missionaries to Western Turkey (Benovksa 2009).

From shamanism to Pentecostalism: a process of continuity?

According to our research (but also according to that of Williams and others mentioned by him in studying the Manouches case in France) Gypsies' conversions to Pentecostalism are the religious expression of social adaptation to a new context: *urbanisation* in France and more globally, *modernisation* in the Balkans. This adaptation through a new Christian identity allows them to continue to belong to the Gypsy community and to a broader one, a purified and redeemed one (through baptism), which means escaping the negative stereotypes and also abandoning certain practices. The traditional cleavages between the Gypsy communities and families themselves and between them and the *gadje* are reformulated differently. Through their new religious affiliation they now are members of the global Pentecostal community which gives them an equal status, and they simultaneously form a new Roma/Gypsy community, regrouping all the Pentecostal Gypsies (a status they should have enjoyed in their former Christian communities, but were never able to depart from their low social status). Finally, in Romania at least, they proclaim that they are the *real Gypsies*. In affirming this, they also reject the other *traditional* Gypsies and their moral conduct.

From an almost exclusively sociological perspective and in a totally different geographical context, the Americas, Alvarsson (2003: 48–50) suggests five commonalities between shamanism and Pentecostal movements (equally successful). These would explain why, generally speaking, *shamanic cultures* easily adopt Pentecostalism:

1) The opportunity to protest against the majority (counter-culture).
2) The role of the spirit.
3) The egalitarian character of Pentecostalism.
4) The lack of doctrine or the ritual prevalence in communication.
5) The community of spiritual experience.

These points represent a good summary of our previous remarks, particularly as they refer to identity strategies. But I think that there are some specific points that have to be considered in the particular context of Southeast Europe.

Let us first recall that Gypsies have been mixed for centuries, identified with, and at the same time excluded from the two main official local religions: Islam and Orthodox Christianity. Let us also remind ourselves that Gypsies have been participating in peripheral, sometimes *heretical* expressions of these two religions, in which they have been able to perform their own rituals or traditional rituals. This flexibility and *syncretism* is equally expressed outside of a strictly religious context. In Serbia for example, Gypsies seem to have always gathered and conserved 'traditional Serbian' practices, which were disappearing among Serbs themselves[37] (Golemovic 2001). On the one hand they seem very conservative or at least attached to traditions, but simultaneously they quickly adapt to new situations.

It now seems possible to draw some more precise common features between shamanism and Pentecostalism that could partly explain, on a religious basis, the greater attraction that Pentecostalism exerts today on Gypsies, in contrast to that of Muslim and Christian Orthodox traditions.

1) Miraculous healing. In charismatic Pentecostal churches, conversion happens through or after a *miraculous healing* (or the acknowledgement of it), where the person claims that physical healing came with spiritual healing or even that it was the spiritual that brought the physical healing (which, by the way, is strictly in accordance with the Bible's narrative of healing miracles). The healing itself is accompanied by *possession*-like phenomena and followed by the mastering of some 'gifts': *glossolalia*, singing or prophesising under the influence of the Spirit (holy); possibly an ensuing *healing* gift.
2) Supernatural election. Pentecostal communities and the elected persons themselves equally claim a supernatural election. Such an election confers the authority to practice the gift of healing or other 'gifts' (tongues,

exorcism, divination, prophecy...). It also gives the elected person a status of Elder or Master.
3) Healing as a service to the community. Healing and directing the flock is not the only *profession* exerted by the pastor. Similarly to traditional healers, pastors/healers exercise other professional activities and do not make a living through healing.[38] This is verified among Gypsy Baptists and Pentecostal converts as well. In this sense, they do not constitute a clergy.
4) Techniques of healing. Except for the reading of the Bible,[39] the traditional techniques and healing rituals practiced for centuries by Gypsies, Muslims and Christians (as discussed above), cannot be found within the Pentecostal context.

Because Pentecostal movements are iconoclastic, as most Protestant churches are, we should not expect to find any of the old 'dendrolatric' or '*ex voto* on trees' practices, nor any 'cult' to the saint/healer or pilgrimage to his tomb in order to be cured. Similarly, other votive/healing customs like the lighting of candles to the saint, offerings etc., as are performed massively in Roman Catholic and Orthodox popular devotions, are absent. In the Pentecostal church, the individual is in a direct and *abstract* relation with God through prayers, invocations or even *possession* by the Holy Spirit.

Is it possible to affirm that the success of Pentecostalism among Gypsies is mostly related to the type of (ecstatic) healing rituals they perform and their efficacy, not only for physical and spiritual health but also for social healing?

I would at least argue that the *continuity* of healing practices seems to be more important than belonging to a particular religious confession.[40] An element in favour of this hypothesis is the fact that traditional (shamanic) forms of healing rituals have survived under Islam and Christian orthodoxy, openly or in a more hidden way. In some instances, this has even occurred with the blessing of the local church or *tekke*, as still seems to be the case for the grave of Bali Efendi. In other cases, the fact that a number of practices are explicitly forbidden[41] shows that these 'pagan' practices are surviving, as revealed, for example, by a poster fixed on a tree, in the sanctuary surrounding the tomb of Eyüb el-Ensari in Istanbul.

Finally, as shown in many studies with regard to the use of medicines, it is more important to people, Gypsy or not, to keep or choose the most efficient rites or medicines, as they are interlinking multiple identities (civic and religious), rather than to stick to a *simple* or unique identity. We also see therefore nomadic identities (social and religious) escaping the control of the State or the 'Church'. The above-mentioned fact that Gypsies carry on rites, which have disappeared among Serbs (Golemović 2001), seems a good illustration of my somewhat *functionalist* hypothesis (even if these rites have no direct healing purposes but are carried out to bring or stop rain). Similarly, although some Gypsies perform Muslim (unorthodox) rituals, revering the tomb of a saint, for example, it is not necessarily because of their Anatolian background, but rather because the inherited practices seem to function and to respond to their need for 'a sensible and ordered world'. It was a Christian family who asked the '*hoja*' to 'interpret the lead' for their injured son.

While the presumed origin or even the ethnic and religious 'identity' of healing practices is, of course, of little consequence to the healer and the patient – as long as they are effective – we as anthropologists like to ponder these questions. Should we then approach healing practices from a purely ethnic or religious point of view? Should we question whether or not they concern only Gypsies?[42] Syncretic practices, after all, constitute an interesting object of research in themselves.

Bibliography

Allard, Camille (1857). *Mission médicale dans la Tatarie-Dobroutcha*. Paris.
Alvarsson, Jan-Ake (2003). 'A few notes on conversion to Pentecostalism, especially among ethnic minority groups'. In Jan-Ake Alvarsson and Rita Laura Segato (eds). *Religions in Transition*. Uppsala, Uppsala Studies in Cultural Anthropology 37, pp. 33–64.
Arbore Alexandru P. (1930). 'Noi informaţiuni etnografice, istorice şi statistice asupra Dobrogei şi a regiunilor basarabene învecinate Dunarei' (New ethnografical, historical and statistical informations about Dobrudja and the Bessarabian Regions near the Danube). *Analele Dobrogei*, XI, 5–94.
Benovska, Milena and Velislav, Altanov 2009. 'Evangelical conversion among the Roma in Bulgaria'. *Transitions*, XLVIII: 2, 133–56.
Bergeron, Pierre (1735). *Voyages faits principalement en Asie dans les XIIe, XIIIe, XIVe, et XVe siècles*. Par Benjamin de Tudele, Jean du Plan-Carpin, N. Ascelin, Guillaume de Rubruquis, Marc Paul Vénitien, Haiton, Jean de Mandeville et Ambroise Contarini. Reprinted E. Müller, 1888 (wikisource/rubruquis).
Clayer, Nathalie (1994). *Mystiques, Etat et société. Les Halvetis dans l'aire balkanique de la fin du XVe siècle à nos jours*. Leiden, New York, Köln, E.J. Brill.
Charachidzé, Georges (1968). *Le Système religieux de la Géorgie païenne*. Paris, Maspéro.
Cossuto, Giuseppe (2001). *Breve Storia dei Turchi di Dobrugia*. Istanbul, Isis.
Dobrudja (2009) = fieldwork of the author.

Eckert, Georg (1944). *Das Schulterblattorakel bei den Aromunen*. Thessaloniki, Volkskundliche Miszellen aus Mazedonien, Heft 4.

Eliade, Mircea (1964). *Traité d'histoire des Religions*. Paris, Payot.

Eminov, Ali (1997). *Turkish and Other Muslim Minorities in Bulgaria*. London, Hurst and Company.

Fosztó, László (2009). 'Conversion narratives, sincere hearts and other tangible signs'. *Transitions*, XLVIII: 2, 109–132.

Gjorgjevič, Tihomir (1903). 'Die Zigeuner in Serbien. Ethnologische Forschung'. Diss. *Mitteilungen zur Zigeunerkunde*, Budapest.

Gobineau, Arthur de (1983). *Oeuvres II*. Paris, Gallimard.

Gog, Sorin (2009).'Post-Socialist religious pluralism: how do religious conversions of Roma fit into the wider landscape'. *Transitions* XLVIII: 2, 93–108.

Golemovič, Dimitrije (2001). 'Roma as an important factor in the development of Serbian ritual practice'. In Svanibor Pettan, Adelaida Reyes, Masa Komavec (eds). *Music and Minorities*, Proceedings of the 1st International Council for Traditional Music (ICTM), Study group: Music and Minorities, Ljubljana, Slovenia, June 25–30 2000, ICTM, Ljubljana 2001, pp. 199–205.

Gruzinski, Serge (1999). *La Pensée métisse*. Paris, Fayard.

Iliescu, Laura J. (2005). 'Des Saints et des miracles pour tous'. In L. Bârlogeanu (ed.). *Identité et Globalisation*, Bucarest, Editura Humanitas Educațional, 86–94.

Kanitz, Felix Philipp (1879). *Donau-Bulgarien und der Balkan. Historisch-Geographisch-Ethnographische Reisestudien aus den Jahren 1860-1878*. III. Band, Leipzig, H. Fries.

Kiel, Machiel (2002). 'Ottoman urban development and the cult of a heterodox Sufi saint: Sari Saltuk Dede and towns of Isakçe and Babadag in the Northern Dobrudja'. In Gilles Veinstein (ed.). *Syncrétismes et hérésies dans l'Orient seldjoukide et ottoman (XIVe–XVIIIe siècle)*. Leuven, Paris, Peeters, pp. 283–98.

Liebich, André (2007). 'Roma nation? Competing narratives of nationhood'. *Nationalism and Ethnic Politics* 13: 4, 539–54.

Marushiakova, Elena and Popov, Vesselin (2001). *Gypsies in the Ottoman Empire*. Hertfordshire, University of Hertfordshire Press.

Mikov, L. and Kmetova T. (1998). 'Bali Efendi of Sofia – a 16th century Moslem saint'. *Ethnologia Bulgarica* 1, 78–92.

Önal, Mehmet Naci (1997). *Din folclorul Turcilor Dobrogeni* (From the Folklore of the Dobrudjean Turks). București, Kriterion.

Paspati, Alexander (1870). *Etudes sur les Tchingianes ou Bohémiens de l'empire ottoman*. Constantinople, Coromela.

Pittard, Eugène (1903). 'Contribution à l'étude anthropologique des Tsiganes turkomans de Dobrodja'. *Bulletin de la Société des Sciences de Bucarest* XI: 4, 457–68.

_____(1932). *Les Tziganes ou Bohémiens, Recherches anthropologiques dans la Péninsule des Balkans*. Genève, Société générale d'imprimerie.

Slavkova, Magdalena (2007). 'Evangelical gypsies in Bulgaria: way of life: and performance of identity'. *Romani Studies* 17: 2, 205–47.

_____(2004). 'The "Turkish gypsies" in Bulgaria and their new religious identity'. Dr Todorovié (ed.). *Evangelization, Conversion, Proselytism* (Nis, JUNIR, XI), 87–100.

Stahl, Paul-Henry (1965). 'La Dendrolâtrie chez les Turcs et Tatars de la Dobroudja'. *Revue des études Sud-Est Européennes* III: 1–2, pp. 297–303.

_____(2006). 'Chrétiens et Musulmans balkaniques. Adversités et croyances communes: quelques notes'. *Revue des Etudes Sud-Est Européennes* XLIV: 1–4, pp. 291–320.

Strand, Elin and Marsh, Adrian (2005). 'Gypsies and Alevis; the impossibility of Abdallar identity'. In Hege Irene Markussen (ed.). *Alevis and Alevism. Transformed Identities*. Istanbul, Isis, pp. 155–74.

Val Cordun (1971). 'Les Saints thaumaturges d'Ada Kaleh'. *Turcica*, III, 107–16.

Williams, Patrick (1991). 'Le miracle et la nécessité: à propos du développement du pentecôtisme chez les Tsiganes'. *Anthropologie Urbaine Religieuse, Archives de Sciences Sociales des Religions* 73, 81–98.

Wlislocki, Heinrich von (1891). *Volksglaube und religiöser Brauch der Zigeuner*. Münster i.W., Aschendorff.

Wolf, Dietrich (2001). 'Rom music for the Tatar of the Crimea'. In: Svanibor Pettan, Adelaida Reyes and Masa Komavec (eds). *Music and Minorities*, Proceedings of the 1st International Council for Traditional Music (ICTM), Study group: Music and Minorities, Ljubljana, Slovenia, June 25–30 2000, ICTM, Ljubljana 2001, pp. 207–14.

Zarcone, Thierry (1992). 'Nouvelles Perspectives dans les recherches sur les Kizilbas-Alévis et les Bektachis de la Dobroudja, de Deli Orman et de la Thrace orientale'. *Anatolia Moderna: Derviches des Balkans. Disparitions et renaissances*, 4, 1–11.

_____(2005). 'Stone people, tree people and animal people in Turkic Asia and Eastern Europe'. *Diogenes*, 207, pp. 35–46.

Chapter Fourteen

SPIRIT HEALING IN A HINDU/MUSLIM AREA: SHADOW THEATRE IN JAVA AND BALI

Angela Hobart

> The deceased spirit ascends to heaven.
> He takes the rainbow as his path.
> His dwelling will be with the moon and stars.
> The Great Bear embraces him.
> The Pleiades clasps him close.
> We look to him to sow the rice.
> May you prosper; may I prosper.
> (Summarised from the Sa'dan Toraja chant
> for the deceased; van der Veen 1966: 5)

This chant was sung by the Sa'dan Toraja of Sulawesi in the Indonesian archipelago as part of their death rituals. The few lines cited give an inkling of the importance of ancestors in Indonesia and in Southeast Asia more generally, who are omnipresent in both past and present. If deceased spirits are not propitiated properly they can bring havoc to individuals, families or the community as a whole. This was poignantly illustrated after the genocide (Gestapo) of 1965 in Java and Bali, when thousands of people were massacred. During the rule of President Suharto (1967–98), government policies sought to obstruct funerary rites from being carried out for alleged Communists (PKI), which caused great anguish. Villagers point out that the deceased who have not had such rites became ghosts, demonic spirits (*buta cuwil*) that bring illness and suffering. On the other hand, if ritually purified, ancestral spirits protect, guide and heal family members.

Indonesia comprises about 1,000 inhabited islands. It has over 350 ethnic groups and about 220,000 million people. In this chapter, attention is focused on Java and Bali, where vigorous dramatic and ritual performances have been maintained. A large variety of theatrical forms exist, but the shadow theatre is the most venerated in both islands, and hence the subject of discussion here. Whilst a shamanic element is intrinsic to this theatre genre, Islam/Sufism has profoundly influenced shadow theatre in Java for reasons that will emerge. Balinese shadow play, on the other hand, emphasises the importance of social cooperation and reverence for the ancestors, and as such is related to spirit-healing seances.[1]

The Indonesian archipelago is the most populous Islamic, or nominally Islamic, country in the world. At the outset it is worth noting that the influence of the great Sufi master Ibn al-Arabi, an advocate of tolerance, clearly emerges in Indonesian Islam; this has a bearing on our subsequent discussion of theatre. Indigenous traditions of ancestor worship, shamanism, sorcery and animism, have blended with elements of the Great Religions: Hinduism, Buddhism and Tantricism. These derived predominantly from India and penetrated the archipelago around the middle of the first millennium A.D. Islam spread from the fourteenth century, initially within the coastal cities as a response to Arab trade, and brought the last major Hindu dynasty of Majapahit in east Java to a decline in the fifteenth century. Christianity arrived somewhat later, in the sixteenth century. Indonesia, together with the rest of the world, is now undergoing modernisation, technical progress and globalisation. The patterns, themes and motives inherent to the belief systems throughout the archipelago vary from island to island, in response to complex historical, political and social processes. Java and Bali are linked historically yet, as evidenced in theatre, they diverge culturally in significant ways.

Javanese shadow theatre

Java is the central island of the Republic of Indonesia, with a population of about 90 million people. At a natural crossroads for sea routes and international maritime trade between East and South Asia, Java has interwoven multiple cultures for thousands of years.

The legendary nine saints, or elect, among the Sufis, the *wali songo*, are considered the prime agents of the Islamisation of Java (Chambert-Loir

2002: 136). It is believed that the Sufi teachings were in part disseminated through the shadow theatre. Among the saints' descendants in contemporary times are Sufi teachers (*pir*) and ritual practitioners, who in certain instances have affinity with performers of the shadow theatre (*dalang*) or puppet masters, who may be attributed with supernatural and healing powers (*sakti*).

The shadow theatre, *wayang kulit* (*wayang* – shadow, puppet or dramatic performance; *kulit* – leather) 'is regarded by Javanese as the most important vehicle of Javanese religion' and refers to a complex of mystical beliefs (Peacock 1968: 4). Concomitantly, it also sets the aesthetic standard of Javanese theatre in general. Performances are given in grand ceremonies of rites of passage at the royal courts and to generate fertility and ward off illnesses in rural districts. The subject of the shadow theatre is extensive; hence the focus in this section is on its religious and political significance for the courtly elite, especially during the era of the sultanates from the seventeenth century to 1945, when Indonesia proclaimed its independence from Dutch colonial rule. After independence the state took over the patronage of many of the arts.

The origin of the shadow theatre in Indonesia is obscure. Hazeu suggested (see Holt 1967: 131) that it evolved from ancestor worship in prehistoric times. Deceased spirits were held to enter stone or wood images or leather puppets during rituals and speak through them to the living. However, Indian influences have left a distinct imprint on the shadow theatre. Most mythic stories dramatised on both islands are inspired by the great Hindu epics, the *Mahabharata* and *Ramayana*.[2] I will only concern myself with the *Mahabharata* here, as it is the more popular in Indonesia. The earliest version was written around the end of the tenth century in Old Javanese prose. The epic is concerned with the conflict between two families: the five semi-divine Pandawa brothers and their first cousins, the one hundred Korawa brothers, ogres incarnate. Their struggle culminates in the Great War, the Baratayuda, in which the Pandawa brothers emerge as victors over their wild, uncouth cousins. The heroes of most stories are the five Pandawa princes: Yudistira, Bima, Arjuna and the twins, Nakula and Sahadewa, whose genitors are gods.

Within the constraints of a short chapter, I want to draw special attention to the third Pandawa brother, Bima. He is a towering figure – tempestuous, bold and forceful, as befits the son of the Wind God. His long thumbnails signify that his five sense perceptions (*panca-indriya*) are united and focused. Bima in some ways epitomises the complex syncretic culture of which he is a part. The Dutch scholar Willem F. Stutterheim (1956: 107–43) persuasively argued that statues of Bima at sanctuaries on Javanese mountain-slopes of about the fourteenth century indicate that the hero pertained to a Tantric deliverance cult in which either Bima or Bhairava – both in these instances

Figure 14.1. Chatuhkaya with masks. Bali, Pejeng (W.F. Stutterheim, 1935. *Indian Influences in Old Balinese Art*).

being forms of the Hindu god Shiva – acted as redeemers. Evidence of this cult (Figure 14.1) is also present in Bali (Stutterheim 1935: 14, Plate XX).[3] The importance of Bima emerges again in shadow-play performances.

In its classical form shadow theatre evolved to its greatest efflorescence at the courts of the Sultans of Surakarta and Jogyakarta. It is during this period that the Sufi element permeates plays. The actors in the performances are flat puppets. A collection comprises about 150 puppets in 4 categories of character: deities, nobility, servant-clowns and ogres. It has been suggested that their extreme stylisation evolved during the era of the sultanates in order to remove them still further from any human semblance because of the Islamic proscription of image-making (Holt 1967: 135).

Spirit Healing in a Hindu/Muslim Area 285

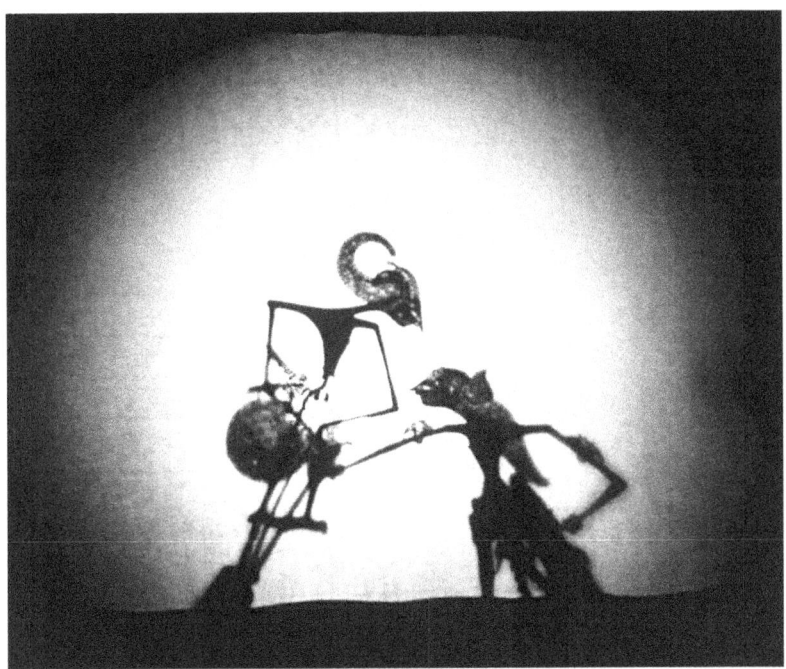

Figure 14.2. Shadows on screen: noble Prince and ogre (Photograph: Jeune Scott-Kemball).

The puppets in a play are manipulated by a *dalang* – a puppet master, teacher, storyteller and artist – who sits cross-legged on the stage, a lamp hanging over his head. In his role as performer he resembles a shaman (ibid.: 132) who entertains and officiates at efficacious communal rituals. The shadows of the puppets are projected onto a cotton screen where they 'dance' to the accompaniment of percussion music (Figure 14.2). Spectators these days watch shows either from the front or back of the screen. A show in Java and Bali always begins and ends with the appearance of the intricately carved leaf-shaped figure, the Cosmic Mountain or World Tree, Kayon (Figure 14.3). The figure also enters the play to mark the beginning and end of scenes. This figure is reminiscent of the shamanic axis mundi that intersects the three realms of existence: the underworld, middle world and celestial realm. As such it is symbolic of perpetual regeneration, or in Mircea Eliade's terms the primordial Centre from which all creation takes place (1974: 18). Birds and other creatures that accompany a shaman in his ecstatic ascent to the sky nestle in the branches of the tree.

In contrast to a shaman, however, a puppet master unfolds his visionary world through puppets, with which he evokes facets of the divine and

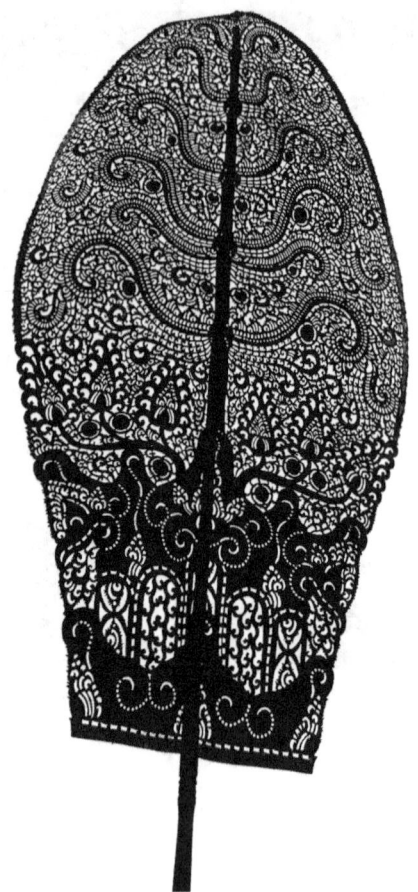

Figure 14.3. Kayon, Cosmic tree of life (Photograph: Angela Hobart).

the demonic. At the same time, the puppet figures constrain him to the mythological world they inhabit. A vast number of myths are perpetuated and disseminated by means of the shadow theatre, but most dramatisations revolve around the heroes of the Hindu epics. The central plot, however, is considerably improvised upon by the puppet master during the performance by interspersing the narration with poetic chants (*suluk*) that often have great aesthetic and spiritual merit. These *suluk* chants deserve our special attention. They are in verse, and predominantly refer to Sufi Islam and the pantheist doctrines of Hindu India (the Upanishads and Vedanta) that ultimately illustrate an ecstatic ascent to a transcendent and immanent Unity of God, whether called Brahman, Sang Suksma (He who is Immaterial) or Allah (Zoetmulder 1995: xvi–21). Essentially the chants mingle fragments from both Indian and Islamic ontological conceptions (ibid.: 110). Claire Holt writes 'that the *suluk* are the magic carpets on which the audience can float from scene to scene' (1967: 138).

The mystical teachings that direct the spectators' attention to a spiritual experience can be movingly discerned in the well-known play of *Bima Suci* (or *Ruci*), *Bima Purified*. The story tells of the prince's quest for the waters of life, i.e. initiation and illuminated insight. During the course of the narration Bima encounters ogres and monsters that he fights and defeats en route to the ocean. These obstacles are part of the hero's initiation process. On arriving at the seashore the prince plunges into the ocean's immense depth. At its bottom he sees a tiny replica of himself, Dewa Ruci, whom he enters.

The meaning of the play of *Bima Suci* has been eloquently discussed (1957) by the Sultan Mangkunagara of Surakarta VII (1895–1944). Quoting the puppet master, the Sultan describes Bima's existential state of concentration (referred to as *semadi*) which leads to divine revelation:

[The prince] turns to the purification of his heart and mind. He folds his arms, one over the other, and stretches his legs forward, closely joined. He suspends the functions of the nine openings of the body. Sounds do not penetrate him; forms are not distinguished by his eyes; his attention is fixed only upon the inhaling and exhaling of his breath while his gaze is kept upon the point of his nose. He concentrates his thoughts. The Lord of the Word hears his prayer (Mangkunagara 1957: 14).

Bima's mystic path to the 'Active Creator' is accompanied by rhythms played by the percussion orchestra in the background. The puppet master recites in a deep resonant voice while he knocks the puppet's chest rapidly with his mallet, like 'accelerated heart-beats of the *semadi*-practitioner' (ibid.: 19). These knocks punctuate the narration and enhance the audience's sensation of a divine reality where human suffering is transcended and the essential unity of God and man is experienced.[4] Mangkunagara (ibid.: 18) describes the spiritual depth of 'the ocean' (as) 'a world filled with light and no shadows'. Ibn al-Arabi already 'visualised the divine essence as a large green ocean out of which the fleeting forms emerge like waves, to fall again and disappear in the fathomless depths' (Schimmel 1975: 284). Such images are also found in Mawlana Jalal al-Din Rumi's poems when he speaks of the ocean of God (ibid.: 284). Throughout the play of *Bima Purified* the puppet master uses vague allusions, poetic images and metaphors. Magically the interplay of sound and meaning allude to a higher reality that is inaccessible to the commoner or uninitiated. This is a feature of all shadow-theatre performances. As the Sultan Mangkunagara wrote: the aim of the shadow play is 'to dare to lift a small tip of the veil to show how in *wayang* performance, lies hidden the secret knowledge concerning the deepest significance of life' (Mangkunagara 1957: 1). This orientation is more fully developed in the Javanese *suluk* literature, with specific reference to the poetic work *Centini*. There the following comparison is made:

> The screen is the visible world. The puppets which are set up to either side of the screen are God's creatures. The banana stem (into which the puppets are stuck) is earth. The *blencong* [lamp] hanging over the puppeteer is the lamp of life. The gamelan percussion music is the harmony of events. God's creations increase, [are] innumerable, but they are merely a hindrance to vision. One who receives no guidance does not see God, but remains attached to form and shape. His sight is obscured and confused and is lost in nothingness, because he sees the truth not...Thus the puppet Master is a 'true' image of the king, the king is the representative of the Prophet; the Prophet is the representative of the Most High (Zoetmulder, 1995: 245–7).

Such allegories are found cross-culturally – in Neoplatonism, in Islamic, Hindu, Sumatran and Javanese pantheist-monist teachings (Zoetmulder ibid.: 240). Schimmel (1975: 278) pointed out that Sufi Masters, such as Ibn al-Arabi, Ibn al-Farid and Rumi, all drew on imagery of the shadow play to hint at God's relationship to his loving servants. So, for instance, Ibn al-Arabi in his *Futuhat* writes: 'whoever wishes to gain understanding of God, let him consider the shadow-play (*khayal*) and the shadow-images (*suwar*) upon the screen' (Zoetmulder 1995: 241). This motif was taken up in later Persian and Turkish poems, and analogies to the shadow theatre were also made in eighteenth century India.

Traditionally, in rural areas the shadow theatre was bound up with exorcism and the invocation of ancestors and fertility. Yet such plays as that of *Bima Purified* given by a puppet master under the patronage of the sultans beg us to consider the ruler's relationship to this genre of theatre, and his role in the society – a subject which we can merely touch on here (forthcoming). In the early Hindu-Javanese kingdoms, from the eighth to thirteenth centuries, the king was at the apex of a highly stratified society. He was the highest spiritual authority, responsible for harmony and the well-being of his subjects. Even after the collapse of the Hindu kingdoms in the fourteenth century, these notions of kingship were reinstituted by the nominal Islamised sultanates. Classical art forms, with special reference to the shadow theatre, were deemed to help rulers and their dignitaries cultivate spiritual insight, poise, moral excellence and inner tranquillity – qualities vital to govern the country (Geertz 1960: 227–60; Anderson 1972: 1–69). This came to the fore vividly in Sultan Mangkunagara VII's interpretation of the story of *Bima Purified*. He envisaged such stories, when dramatised, as contributing to the subjective experience of God in his deepest essence. Inspired insight in turn empowered a ruler and his entourage truly to take care of the people, and to heal rifts in the social structure. In this context it is relevant to quote from Annemarie Schimmel's study: 'service to men has always been one of the first stages in the preparatory steps of the Path (*tariqa*), but it remains the true Sufi's duty throughout his life' (1975: 229).

Interestingly, even after the Dutch colonial era (mid-nineteenth century to 1945), presidents emphasised their right to rule by identifying with one of the Pandawa princes. In his youth President Sukarno gave himself the name Bima (Peacock 1968: 4); later presidents also identified themselves with mythic heroes who brought order and prosperity to their subjects. Some of my Balinese informants refer to Bambang Yudhayono as Bima. Although, in line with modernisation and globalisation, Yudhoyono's outlook is relatively secular, he has an imposing, forceful manner, like Bima in performances, and has brought in the eyes of some villagers a degree of 'democracy' and stability to the country.

Balinese shadow theatre

While the shadow theatre in Bali is as significant as in Java, a clear distinction has to be made between the genre in each island. In Bali it remained a rural art, its patterns of meaning being widely shared across the island (Hobart 1987). It never acquired the sophistication that it did in Java, where, as we have seen, it served a particular group, the courtly elite, as a route to divine revelation. Older religions than Sufism and Islam come to the fore in examining the Balinese shadow theatre. This also applies to the seances conducted by spirit mediums, discussed in this section because of the light they throw on important dimensions of Balinese ritual and aesthetic life.

Bali's population of over two million is concentrated in the fertile south of the island, which is also considered the heartland of culture, having been exposed to early Indo-Javanese influences from the eleventh century onwards; these were blended with ancient beliefs in shamanism and animism. The social structure is based loosely on the Indian caste system. Generally it is said that the high castes – Brahmins, Kshatriyas and Vaishyas – are descendants of aristocrats who came over to Bali from the great dynasty Majapahit when it disintegrated in the fifteenth century under the onslaught of the Islamicised sultanates. The commoners, the Sudras, comprise over 90 per cent of the population. Their predominance is reflected in theatre. Many Dutch and Javanese, as well as Balinese, have sought in recent decades to perpetuate the image of Bali as a 'paradise island' in order to attract tourists. This image was shattered after the bombings of 2001 and 2003. Tourism has picked up again in the last few years, but the clientele has changed.

In striking contrast to Java, the majority of Balinese practice a variant form of Hinduism, also called Holy Water Religion (Agama Tirta) as holy water is intrinsic to all rituals. Its importance also emerges in the Balinese version of the story *Bima Purified* (see below). Bali remained largely impervious to the spread of Islam. Only about 5 per cent of the people are Muslim, living mainly in the north and east of the island (Buleleng, Jembrana and Karangasem). Minimal Islamic influence is apparent in southern Bali (my research area) except in bigger towns. There is little evidence of a florescence of mysticism and heterodoxy among Balinese Muslims (Barth 1993: 179). They adhere to an orthodox form of Santri led by Muslim scholars (*kiyayi*), and frown on shadow theatre. For them it is above all the Qur'an which manifests aspects of Divinity, certainly not the Hindu epics.

Ancestor worship plays a crucial role in Hindu Balinese religion. Ancestors are intrinsic to the kinship structure, with descendency essentially being conceived as a spiritual relation of identity, and ascribed patrilineally. Each household has a temple containing shrines in which the family's deified ancestors are honoured with rituals in order to ensure that they guide and protect descendants.

Villagers emphasise that both the shadow theatre and medium seances draw on the spirit world for their power, and belong to the traditional healing system. Scholars have remarked on the meticulous poise and etiquette of the Balinese, which Clifford Geertz referred to as a 'kind of dance, a kind of worship' (1973: 400). Yet this view belies my own experiences when living in the village. Below the polite surface, tensions may be acute. Conflict in the family may be particularly acrimonious and bitter. As relationships in the household are so enmeshed, with boundaries between members diffuse, disagreements are rarely resolved satisfactorily. Villagers explain that ritual performances are crucial in counterbalancing community and family strife and disorder; essentially acting as 'medicine' (*tambe*) which 'cools' (Hobart 2003).

It is in this context that we can understand the place of the shadow theatre in Balinese society. Villagers associate the term 'shadow' (*bayang*) with *yang* or *hyang*, meaning deified ancestors (echoing Hazeu's view of the origin of the shadow play cited above). In tune with this interpretation, epic heroes in performances are often regarded as apical ancestors who came from Java, and ultimately India. This helps account for the magical and moral potency a well-presented performance may exert on spectators. A puppet master is primarily seen as an informal teacher, entertainer and healer, and by extension exorcist. Indeed, villagers say that the entertainment value of a play is crucial to making the moral teachings inherent in the epics accessible, especially to youngsters. Unlike his counterpart in Java, a Balinese puppeteer does not seek to initiate the beholders into a mystical religious experience, although he too has to be consecrated before performing. Generally puppeteers are peasants, commoners, like most of the spectators.

A standard puppet collection includes about one hundred puppets; fewer than in Java, although similar conventions underlie their iconography. Balinese puppets are simple and rustic in appearance. They have a lingering affinity with figures on reliefs of east Javanese Hindu temples erected before the penetration of Islam in the archipelago.

A play usually takes place in a temporarily raised booth, often set up in the village square. Most spectators watch the shadows of the puppets that are projected onto a screen, traditionally by a coconut-oil lamp. Curiously, Balinese villagers also draw attention to the symbolic nature of a shadow-theatre performance, which resonates with allegories made in Javanese poetic literature during the time of Sultan Mangkunagara VII of Surakarta in the twentieth century. In Hindu-Balinese philosophy the lamp is the sun. It animates the puppets that stand for all that exists. The screen is the sky, the banana stem the earth, the puppeteer the 'Creator God', invisible to the audience watching the shadows (Figures 14.4, 14.5).

The above analogies illustrate the force of the animistic-shamanic tradition in Bali. Before a show the puppet master, or 'world-maker', chants mantras to stimulate and evoke empathy in the spectators for the characters about to dance on the screen. As the play proceeds, the puppeteer unfolds a mythic story that explicitly seeks to benefit the village community. This differs considerably from the poetic sophistication which forms the basis of the Javanese shadow theatre, in which the individual seeks to dissolve his or her identity in the absolute Being of Allah through the dramatic experience. It came to the fore especially during the era of the sultanates, when Sufism and pantheistic-monist teachings intertwined with older religious beliefs surviving in much of the archipelago.

The main occasion for a shadow-theatre performance is in connection with the anniversary of a temple, once every 210 days. It is customary after such a celebration to have a dramatic performance for three nights running. The shadow play is often chosen, as it is the most revered genre of traditional theatre; moreover the stories are suitable, as they have moral content; it is also the cheapest genre.

A performance that I witnessed during my last research trip took place just outside the village death temple, dedicated to Durga, the goddess of death and transformation. The audience, as is usual, mainly comprised adult

Figure 14.4. Stage with puppeteer holding Prince Bima and musicians (Photograph: Per Horner).

men and youngsters, who sit cross-legged in front of the screen.[5] As in all performances, the shamanic Tree of Life, the Kayon, first appears on the screen. This figure evokes the cosmic frame of the narration. The puppeteer based his narration on *Bima Purified,* a story probably more popular these days in Bali than in Java because of its close association with the people's ritual life. The Balinese tale is similar to the one recounted in Java, although the shamanic element is more pronounced. Bima, like a shaman-voyager, ascends to the sky at the end of the play. There he meets the Supreme God Acintya (in Sanskrit, 'he who cannot be imagined'), from whom he obtains a gold casket with the Waters of Immortality, *tirta kamandalu* (generally identified with the elixir of immortality, *amerta*).

A few extracts from the story will illustrate the rustic, down-to-earth flavour of the play, befitting a theatre form that appeals primarily to villagers. The servant-clowns/fools in Balinese theatre deserve special mention. They do not appear in the epic literature, but stem from the folk tradition. They are probably still more critical in Bali than in Java. As is standard in all performances, what little the epic characters say is in Old Javanese. The servant Tualen[6] and his son Merdah translate and expand on their master's speech in colloquial Balinese, while improvising extensively on the main plot

Spirit Healing in a Hindu/Muslim Area 293

Figure 14.5. Shadows on screen: Prince Bima receiving Holy Water from the Supreme God (Photograph: Giacomo De Caterini).

and frolicking around, and in so doing they bring stories to life. In tales such as *Bima Purified* the servant-clowns also act as spirit guides to the heroes on their pilgrimage. The scene of the first extract is the woods in which Bima encounters an ogre, *raksasa*.

Ogre   Oh, a human is entering the forest. [Angrily to Bima] Who are you? Why have you come to the woods where I have authority?

Bima   Eh, ogre, you're talking with disrespect. I am the most important Pandawa brother [being the son of the God of Wind, Batara Bayu]. Hence I have strength, firmness and vital force. My brothers would be unable to unite without my life-spirit (*bayu*). I have come to fetch the Waters of Immortality (*tirta kemandalu*).

Tualen   Sang Bima is the child of the Wind God. His is sincere (*anak wiakti*), honest and focused in his intentions. Though not as learned as his brothers, they would not be able to form a united front without his vitality. You, ogre, do not heed *tata kerana*, the principles that give order to existence, but are carried away by your passions, devouring any creature that crosses your path.[7]

Merdah Sang Bima has come to fetch the Waters of Immortality, needed mainly in death rituals, *pitra yadnya*. They impart purity and life-spirit to the departing spirit in his or her journey to the beyond [to become a deified ancestor, *sang atma*, whom descendants worship]. Rituals are required throughout a person's life. As elucidated in the mantras recited by priests:

> Divine Kemandalu is the life-force of the Gods, the Holy Water of priests. It overcomes obstacles afflicting humans in the Middle Realm (between sky and underworld). It removes illnesses, memory lapses, weariness of the eyes. It undoes the detrimental effects of parents and grandparents (cf. Hooykaas, 1937: 277).

The conversation between Bima, his servants and the ogre continues in this vein for some time till the ogre tells them rudely to stop talking and confront him in battle. Fighting breaks out between Prince Bima and the ogre and his followers. Bima pierces the ogre's throat with his long thumb nail (*waspanak*) and he dies. His followers too are killed.

The play illustrates Prince Bima's sincerity, firmness and commitment; he does not shirk from taking risks to overcome obstacles before ascending to the heavens. His spiritual authority largely hinges on the fact that his genitor is the Wind God who grants life-force to all creation. The Waters of Immortality (*tirta kemandalu*) epitomise the human quest for spaciousness and liberation from illness, suffering and distress. Implicit are the misdeeds committed by ancestors; these may detrimentally affect development processes of descendants. Bima's qualities are particularly admired by headmen in the village or government officials who may seek explicitly to emulate them.

Unlike Javanese shadow-theatre plays – especially in the era of the sultanates – that tell of heroes' pursuit of mystic ecstasy or, in Ibn al-Arabi's conception, fusion of the personal entity with universal spirit (Zoetmulder 1995: 20), in Bali this theatre genre exalts above all the codes of etiquette and village principles. In the words of the locals, consciousness is 'purified' (*ngewatasin panca indriya*) through the plays that have instructive and concomitantly restorative importance, as they illustrate the moral values and norms that humans ought to uphold. These contribute to the integration and 'dynamic equilibrium' of the village community, in line with Victor Turner's (1957: 316) recognition that group unity transcends, but to some degree proceeds out of the mobility and conflicts of its component elements. Shadow-theatre performances, moreover, are frequently performed in the village community in conjunction with temple ceremonies, even these days, although pop music and soap opera are becoming increasingly popular. Hence, the continued reiteration and dissemination of the dramatised messages.

Spirit medium seances

Spirit mediums and shamans are found throughout rural Southeast Asia (Hobart 2003). Their practices reflect pre-historic traditions before Indian influences penetrated the area. In Bali I refer to such ritual practitioners as mediums, *balian tapakan* (from *tapak* to be entered), as they are vehicles for spirits in a seance who speak directly (*baos batara*) to clients. A medium has, I contend, a certain affinity with a puppet master, although he bases his narrations on the classical literature derived from the great world religions, in particular Hinduism, in Java also Islam/Sufism. Mediums and puppeteers have both to be consecrated before acting in the service of the people. Whilst the paraphernalia for a seance is much simpler, both puppet masters and mediums are in touch with the spirit realm when they perform. The ontological status accorded the spirits is however different. The actual presence of spirits dynamically engages clients in a seance; it draws them into the performative reality evoked by the medium, which is experienced as 'virtually real'. They are not spectators of a play articulated through puppets and silhouettes on the screen. It is noteworthy that a medium, like a shaman, has an initiatory crisis and a vision quest, which indicates to the community that she is called upon to become a village healer (*balian*) and an intermediary between the community and spirit world.

Mediums are generally low-caste women. During a seance they go into trance, or an altered state of consciousness, called *nadi* (from *dadi*, to exist); this may be very brief or continue for about 20 minutes. Mediums are still very much in demand. After the bomb blasts of 2002 and 2005, many villagers consulted mediums to enquire why a family member died or, if the corpse was missing, as to its possible whereabouts. In general clients consult mediums in relation to death rituals, psychophysical complaints, when sorcery may be implicated, or when all else has failed. The importance of ancestor worship comes to the fore in seances. It is primarily ancestral spirits who give advice, protection to clients or punish descendants when they follow wayward paths.

A case I recorded and discussed afterwards with the family members and medium is summarised here to give a flavour of the dynamics of a seance. The medium is referred to as Little Priest, Jero Mank Alit (Figure 14.6). She is small, friendly woman who is esteemed by villagers for the 'truth' value

Figure 14.6. Spirit medium (Photograph: Angela Hobart).

of her messages to troubled clients. Her household temple deserves special mention as it unusually elaborate. One of the shrines has magnificent statues portraying the five Pandawa princes with their two faithful servants, Tualen and his son, to either side. The shrine illustrates how Indian mythological motifs may resonate in a traditional healing ritual. The Pandawa protagonists, the ignoble Korawa, are not depicted. The medium explained that the shrine emphasises that clients have entered sacred space-time, where the mundane oppositions of life, intrinsic to the shadow theatre, have been transcended. It is intriguing that during a seance this particular medium points out that both deceased and mythic spirits may advise her when in trance on how to move patients from illness to health.

Case story

Five family members came to consult the medium. The uncle, who was eldest in the patriline, was the spokesman. The family requested the medium

Spirit Healing in a Hindu/Muslim Area   297

to contact the spirit realm to give advice on why their household was in a state of chaos (*buwut*). Quarrels were constantly breaking out. Children often became ill. Varied medical specialists had already been consulted, but with no avail. The 'Little Priest' is known for her capacity to unravel family problems by conveying clear messages from the unseen.

The seance lasted about fifteen minutes. The medium sat on her special elevated shrine, decked with bowls of offerings of fruit, rice cakes, new cloth and some ritual money (how much is not fixed) from the clients in reciprocity for her consultation. An entranced medium is empowered to make the inaudible become audible, the intangible take form. After chanting a short mantra, the Little Priest went into trance.

Medium	The ancestors seem dimly present. Have you [to the clients] placed offerings at your household temple, at the shrine [*kemulan*] dedicated to the deified ancestors?
Clients	Yes.
Medium	[Ancestors speaking] You 'red ants' [*semut barak*, an appellation used by deities to their subjects] have come because there are difficulties at home.
Client	[Not wishing to say much in order to test the medium's authenticity.] I am asking about my ancestors.
Medium	[Ancestors] The deceased grandparents followed by other spirits [four generations are mentioned] are descending to give advice so that you no longer grope in the dark. Mistakes were made in the past. You were given no clear direction how to cremate those who died. Hence they are 'stuck' in the hereafter and cannot transform into deified ancestors who are worshipped in the household temple. [In summary] you do not know your clan [*soroh*] temple. Hence you [descendants] are 'like humans who have no head' [*cara anak sing ngelah sirah*] and you wander hither and thither without any direction.
Clients	What is our clan of origin?
Medium	[Ancestors] It is not easy to answer this. The deceased spirits are still pondering. Not to bury a dead person without reference to his or clan identity is comparable to 'knowing what a banana is called, but not what it tastes like'.

The seance was compelling. As it progressed the clients become fully engrossed in the words of the ancestral realm – four generations of ancestors descended in this session. The clients' attention was focused on unravelling the words from the ancestors that were elusive and nebulous. In the discussion with the medium afterwards it emerged that the family had in fact not known their clan origin, which is rare in this community. Villagers say that it is grave indeed if a person does not know their clan roots and genealogical forbears. The proper rites cannot then be carried out, and suffering will undoubtedly follow. The family initially debated together, and also with other kin. Next, they set off to search for their temple of origin; eventually they were satisfied that it was located in another province on the island and elaborate rituals were carried out to the ancestral spirits to ensure their contentment and protection. The seance with the Little Priest soothed the family and helped them shift attitudes and transform deep structural family patterns. The session also gave them impetus to look unabatedly for the temple of origin. The offerings, incense, the holy water, the sound of the bell and the chant-like voice of the medium all reinforced the power and sanctity of the ritual.

Seances have an explicitly healing intent. Clients come always in groups of three or more family members. Hence sessions in some ways resemble family therapy. Western medicine strives to be objective, scientific and clear-cut, but spirit mediums link moral perspectives to illness and distress. This point has been made elsewhere. Arthur and Joan Kleinman (1997: 104–15), for instance, in their exploration of health and suffering in China, emphasise that health is inseparable from moral imagination. In discussing the shadow theatre in Bali, it also emerges that well-being in the eyes of the people hinges on generating in beholders a moral, spiritual and aesthetic commitment to principles that contribute to living a 'balanced', reasonably ordered life. But a shadow-theatre play in Bali is captivating above all because it entertains as well as instructs. Villagers say that the bawdy, humorous jokes and comic antics of the servant clowns in a skilled performance confound the intellect. In so doing, the buffoonery and inconsistencies contribute to human vitality and creativity.

Conclusion

In the context of this volume, it is important that we examine the healing performances of Indonesia, the most populous Islamic country in the world. There are an intriguingly wide range of healing practices found across the islands that these days coexist with biomedical systems introduced during the Dutch colonial period. While the constellation of characteristics intrinsic to the belief systems underlying healing performances vary considerably from place to place, and through time, they all resonate in varying degrees with an older religion – whether this is referred to as animism, shamanism or ancestor worship.

The focus in this chapter has been on the shadow play, the most revered theatre genre in Java and Bali, because of its socio-political, medical and spiritual connotations. As this form of theatre sets the aesthetic and structural standards for theatre in general it contributes to its significance on the islands. In the Balinese case, we examined spirit healing through seances conducted by mediums during which the dead speak directly to clients.

A shamanic element is clearly intrinsic to the shadow theatre. This is epitomised by the scenic figure of the Cosmic Tree that evokes perpetual regeneration. Appearing at the beginning and end of every performance, the great tree symbolises the centre of the mythic world revealed by the puppet master, directing vision skywards to the eternally sacred. Yet the orientation of the shadow theatre in Java differs from that in Bali. A poetic sophistication forms the basis of this genre in Java and came to the fore during the efflorescence of the sultanates from the eighteenth to twentieth centuries. Sufi and pantheistic-monistic teachings that point to Hindu India were conveyed to the courtly elite. As the Sultan Mangkunagara of Surakarta VII (1957) writes, performances encouraged introspection and mystic ecstasy. At the same time, it is interesting to note shadow play's' role in relation to the Indonesian state. For sultans and their entourage, and subsequently presidents and civil servants, the shadow theatre was deemed to encourage poise, equanimity and spiritual insight – qualities needed to bring, or perhaps more aptly to impose, order in the country, and to serve the people.

The shadow theatre in Bali, on the other hand, is not directed to a specific social group. It is deeply embedded in the village community, its meanings and patterns being widely shared across all sectors of the Hindu-Balinese society. The puppet master, if skilled, is not only a healer, but also entertainer and teacher – all three roles being intertwined in the eyes of villagers. It is interesting that the hero Bima in the Balinsese story of *Bima Purified* can also be envisaged as a shaman-voyager who flies up to the sky in order to fetch Holy Water that alleviates suffering and illnesses, and brings well-being to the community.

In conclusion, I want to bring up a remark made by the Sultan Mangkunagara about Prince Bima. In one instance the Sultan describes him as Lintang Bima Sakti, 'A Star of Powerful Bima'[8]: 'throughout moonless nights during the East-monsoon [the Sultan continues] this figure is clearly visible on the firmament' (1957: cover page). I suggest that irrespective of the Sufi and Hindu-Vedanta resonances of the shadow theatre in Java, especially during the period of the sultanates, ancestor worship is alluded to here. It is a feature of most Southeast Asia belief systems, as evocatively indicated by the chant for the deceased sung by the Sa'dan Toraja of Sulawesi, quoted at the beginning of the chapter:

> The deceased spirit ascends to heaven.
> He takes the rainbow as his path.
> His dwelling will be with the moon and stars...

Bibliography

Anderson, Benedict R. (1972). 'The idea of power in Javanese culture'. In Claire Holt (ed.). *Culture and Politics in Indonesia*. Ithaca, Cornell University Press, pp. 1–69.

Barth, Frederick (1993). *Balinese Worlds*. Chicago, Chicago University Press.

Chambert-Loir, Henri (2002). 'Saints and ancestors: the cult of Muslim saints in Java. In Henri Chambert-Loir and Anthony Reid (eds). *The Potent Dead: Ancestors, Saints and Heroes in Contemporary Indonesia*. Honolulu, University of Hawai'i Press, pp. 132-40.

Eliade, Mircea (1974). *The Myth of the Eternal Return*. Princeton, Princeton University Press. p. 18.

Geertz, Clifford (1960). *The Religion of Java*. Illinois, The Free Press of Glencoe.

———(1973). *The Interpretation of Cultures*. New York, Basic Books.

Hobart, Angela (1987). *Dancing Shadows of Bali: Theatre and Myth* (1987). London, Kegan Paul International.

———(2003). *Healing Performances of Bali: Between Darkness and Light*. Oxford, Berghahn Books.

Holt, Claire (1967). *Art in Indonesia: Continuities and Change*. Ithaca, Cornell University Press.

Hooykaas, Christian (1973). *Kama and Kala: Materials for the Study of the Shadow Theatre in Bali*. Amsterdam, Verhandelingen der Koninglijke Nederlandse Akademie van Vetenschapen, 79.

Kleinman, Arthur and Kleinman, Joan (1997). 'Moral transformations of health and suffering in Chinese society'. In Allan M. Brandt and Paul Rozin (eds). *Morality and Health*. London, Routledge, pp. 101–18.

Mangkunagara VII (1957). *On the Wayang Kulit, Purwa, and Its Symbolic and Magical Elements*. Trans. Claire Holt. Ithaca, Cornell University Press.

Peacock, James L. (1968). *Rites of Modernization: Symbolic and Social Aspects of Indonesian Proletarian Drama*. Chicago: The University of Chicago Press.

Schimmel, Annemarie (1975). *Mystical Dimensions of Islam*. Chapel Hill, University of North Carolina Press.

Stutterheim, Willem F. (1935). *Indian Influences in Old Javanese Art*. London, The India Society.

———(1956). *Studies in Indian Archaelology*. The Hague, Martinus Nijhoff.

Turner, Victor (1957). *Schism and Continuity in an African Society*. Manchester, The University of Manchester.
Veen van der, Hendrik (1966). *The Sa'dan Toraja Chant for the Deceased*. The Hague, Martinus Nijhoff.
Zoetmulder, Peter J. (1971). 'The *wayang* as a philosophical theme'. *Indonesia, Cornell Southeast Program*, 12: 85–96.
──────(1995). *Pantheism and Monism in Javanese Suluk Literature: Islamic and Indian Mysticism in an Indonesian Setting*. Trans. M. C. Ricklefs. Leiden, Koninklijk Instituut voor Taal- en Volkenkunde.

NOTES

Introduction

1 Dupaine's article was initially written in Dutch and entitled 'Een exorcist in Afghanistan. Sjamanisme of niet?'(Dupaigne 1996). It was subsequently updated.

Vladimir Nikolaevich Basilov (1937–1998) A Pioneer of the Study of 'Islamised Shamanism'

1 This volume was published as early as 1963 in Budapest, with the title *Glaubenwelt und Folklore der sibirischen Völker*. Its English translation, *Popular Beliefs and Folklore Tradition in Siberia*, came out as volume 57 of the *Uralic and Altaic Series* in 1967 (Budapest Bloomington The Hague).
2 At that time, shamanism was as a rule declared to be a relic of an early form of religion – hence primitive and wild – based on the specific neurotic character of some individuals, the shamans. Thus, Tokarev wrote: 'All observers unanimously report that the shaman is most notably a nervous, hysterical person, prone to seizures, occasionally an epileptic (. . .) The shamanic seance itself has much similarity to an hysterical attack' (Tokarev 1964: 292, quoted by Basilov 1984a: 140; Basilov 1990: 4). Tokarev himself only took up the current view in both Tsarist and Soviet Russia, previously expressed by Russian scholars as famous as V. G. Bogoraz (1910), D. K. Zelenin (1935) and many others, quoted by Basilov *ibid*. It was the official position set forth in the *Bol'shaya sovetskaya Entsiklopedia* 1978, XXIX, 278. For all of them, shamanism was only vestigial and doomed to disappear thanks to the progress of Russian colonisation or, later, of Soviet policy.

Chapter One

1 I am grateful to Angela Hobart and Thierry Zarcone for inviting me to take part in this stimulating conference and for their warm welcome in Ascona.

2 Initially, Siberian shamanism was apprehended as a religion, although a devilish one. Such was the evaluation made by the Russian archbishop Avvakum in his account of exile to Siberia (1672–75), which is known through two books, one in German (by Isbrant Ides, ambassador of Russia to China, translated into French 1699, into English 1706), the other in Dutch (by Nicolas Witsen 1692).
3 See for instance Kehoe 2000.
4 Thus, in Siberia, shamanising was often the main answer to changes and subsequent troubles. Henceforth, healing became prominent in shamanic practice and ordinary individuals increasingly resorted to 'shamanising' as a call for help to spirits. Among scholars, this resulted in a view of shamanic behaviour as psychopathological and of shamanic practice as therapeutic.
5 This point has been developed in African examples by Jean-Pierre Olivier de Sardan, 1994.
6 Objections of all kinds have been developed against this 'medicalising' view of shamanism over the last few decades. In particular, the assumption that the shaman's personality is pathological has been abandoned.
7 The author also recalls the difference between disease (which refers to biological or psychological malfunctioning) and illness (which refers to the patient's experiences and perceptions, including social responses to disease). This is why healing is often seen as secondary to curing: a patient can be healed (his integrity as a person can be restored) without being cured (Maskarinec 2004: 137–8).
8 Literally, this word means 'to imitate life by singing and dancing' (Vasilevich 1957: 151–63; Anisimov 1958: 26; Cincius 1975: 301b).
9 This paragraph is based on the data and analysis produced in Hamayon 1990: 373–424. It is conventionally written in the present tense, although it concerns the pre-Soviet or beginning of Soviet times. The view set out here is also valid for all those who practice hunting while belonging to herding societies and keeping domestic animals, a pattern found sporadically all over Siberia. A large part of its contents (namely the view of game animals as partners in an exchange relationship and the consequences of this) is still fresh in the minds of those who carried on living on hunting under the Soviet regime or returned to this way of life after its fall.
10 According to the view of the world of the Chukchee living on reindeer herding in Northeastern Siberia, human corpses should be eaten by wild bears, Bogoras explains extensively (1904–1910: 524–34).
11 Human beings are booty to spirits, just as reindeer are to human beings when they go hunting. This is also clearly stated by the Koryaks (Jochelson 1905–1908: 28), the Nganasans (Popov 1976: 34) and many others.
12 In the view of Samoyed peoples living in the Ienissei Basin, one should offer no help to a drowning person; that person has presumably been 'caught' by the water spirit that animates fish and therefore should not been taken back from the spirit (Khomich 1976: 21, Gracheva 1976: 58).
13 Smolev 1903: 6; Donner [1942]–46: 233; Zelenin [1936]–52: 174.
14 Young wild animals tamed and fed near to the hunter's home are mainly chipmunks (*Tamias striatus*) and fox cubs among the Buryats (Zelenin [1936]–52:

94, 121, and *passim*). They are mainly birds among the Tungus (Shirokogoroff 1935: 76), eaglets among the Selkups (Levin and Potapov 1956: 671).
15 Feeding the *ongon* is crucial also for the Khant-Mansi of Western Siberia (Gemuev and Sagalaev 1986: 150).
16 Sandschejew 1927–28; Manzhigeev 1960; Khangalov 1958–61; Hamayon 1990: chap. XII.
17 Shamans had a very important role in conflicts between clans before the integration of the Buryats into the Russian Empire in the seventeenth century, which put an end to such warlike conflicts.
18 Or such as the mere fact that one's soul has allegedly not returned into one's body after wandering out of the body during sleeping (Podgorbunskii 1891: 22).
19 'All troubles come from dead souls' is a commonplace in works by Buryat ethnographers (Baldaev 1975: 179; Manzhigeev 1960: 195; Khangalov 1958–1961, *passim*).
20 This is the title of a previous article (Hamayon 1978a) in which I have examined in detail this interrelation.
21 For examples of such negotiations about souls between the living and the dead, see Hamayon 1978b.
22 Thus, no fighting behaviour is observed during these rituals (at least nothing comparable to what Vladimir Basilov describes for Central Asian shamans). If Mongol and Buryat shamans do not use knifes, sabres and whips during healing rituals as in Central Asia (Basilov 1992), in some areas they may wear, hung on their coat, small metallic elements explicitly aimed 'to harm' (Badamkhatan 1962: 40 and 1965: 208); they are supposed to have their shaman ancestors use these iron miniature weapons on their clan's enemies. Significantly, during healing rituals, Buryat shamans still have a crown adorned with antlers as their headgear – a reference to the hunting lifestyle maintained in the semi-pastoral context – though not directly relevant to healing purposes.

Chapter Two

1 Although there are several terms in Central Asia to refer to the Islamised shaman, the latter is generally known under the denomination of *bakshi* or under other phonetically close names. In the present study, he will be referred to as 'Islamised shaman', a generic expression which gives an account of this figure of Central Asian ethnography and also underlines the historic bonds linking him with the Siberian shaman, of whom he is only a local and detailed variant (concerning the various terms used to name the Islamised shamans of Central Asia, see Garrone 2000: 9–21).
2 Shamanism will be considered as a religion in this study because it has often been treated as such by the ministers of rival religious ideologies.
3 In its most popular forms, however, Islam recognises this possibility for some of the faithful. We are referring here to the Sufis, though some commentators hold all forms of Sufism to be unorthodox. However, the mystical journey of

the Sufi is different from that of the shaman, as it is a 'journey into self', a kind of introspection (cf. the *safar dar vatan*, the 'voyage to the fatherland' of the Naqshbandiyya brotherhood). In addition, unlike the shaman, the benefit of the Sufi's acts are turned towards himself rather than others. Some Sufi do, however, possess recognised abilities to heal, but these are isolated cases or representatives of marginal forms connected with heterodox Sufism, such as the Qalandariyya or Ishanism.

4   The present study does not distinguish between the hunting and breeding types of Siberian shamanism even if, in the latter, healing occupies a prominent place. The expression 'original shamanism' is used to cover both variants, because only the possibility offered to the shaman of penetrating Supranature is referred to.

5   A Kazakh shaman thus asserted that he had travelled to Supranature, although he did not present this journey as a quest for the soul but as a means of seeking the cause of diseases or the entities responsible for disorders. I do not consider this an example of Central Asian shamanism in which the journey to Supranature survives, unaffected by the sudden emergence of Islam in the area; it rather seems an accommodation of local practices towards modernity and, particularly, the Western model in which a journey to Supranature is often considered the authentic sign of shamanism.

6   Laymen who do not possess shamanic powers only have an apprehension of this spiritual geography as believers. They only find a place in it as 'stakes' in a conflict between the powers that play an active role. These powers, that is the various classes of spirits and the shaman himself, interact and are the real protagonists of the drama.

7   The concept of 'definitive' fixation is quite relative. This fixation aims at being definitive, but in fact it is not. In fact, disease as such is basically incurable in the shamanic vision of the world since, consciously or not, it is part of the cycle of gift and counter-gift ensuring the permanence of life.

8   Although Anatolia is rather remote from Central Asia let us mention here the *kara kazan*, the large black cauldron of the Bektashiyya, another Sufi heterodox order in Hacibektash (Birge 1965: 175).

9   Let us note here that today a brotherhood similar to the Naqshbandiyya has not only succeeded in remaining stable in several places and re-emerging in some others but even seems to be flourishing.

10 For the sake of clarity we will systematically use the name Korkut even when the character introduces himself as Burkut or Burh in the examples mentioned in the text.

11 In our mind, the term 'assimilation' is *de facto* synonymous with 'disappearance' or 'eradication' in the sense that the previous form of what is 'assimilated', that is seized and integrated in a new perspective, simply vanishes.

Chapter Three

1   For more detailed descriptions of my fieldwork in Central and Inner Asia, see my articles published in the journal *Shaman* between 2004 and 2010.

2 The word *awliya* is the plural form of *wali* (from *wali u-llah*) 'Allah's friend', see Somfai 2004b: 580.
3 See Bayalieva 1972: 58 and Divaev 1899: 308–309.
4 The Arabic term means 'invisible'. It comes from the Muslim belief that some people do not die but disappear from the human world. Also see Bayalieva 1972: 114–16, Basilov 1992: 247.
5 Also called Müyüzdüü ene/baybiche 'Horned mother/lady', see Bayalieva 1972: 13–14 and Somfai 2008b: 189.
6 The meaning of the Arabic word *al-khidr* or *al-khadr* is 'green'. *Khidhr* is a mythological figure that is connected with life and vegetation.
7 The Persian term literally means '40 persons', see Basilov 1992: 246–64 and Bayalieva 1972: 115–16.
8 Kenin-Lopsan 1997: 115, Potapov 1991: 39–47.
9 See Johansen 2003: 29–49.
10 The word *bakshï* probably comes from Middle Chinese *bokshi*, which means 'master' or 'teacher'.
11 Russian *shamanstvo*, see Basilov 1992.
12 The Turkic word *tengri* means 'heaven' or 'sky'. It is a powerful spirit or deity who can grant special abilities to humans, see Somfai 2008b: 102.
13 See Bellér-Han 2004, Kehl-Bodrogi 2006.
14 Bayalieva 1972: 126 and Somfai 2007: 61.
15 See De Heusch 1971 and Hamayon 1993.
16 The Persian word *dewana* means 'crazy' or 'possessed by a demon', similar to the Arabic *jinni*. The Kirghiz term *kuugunchu* or *kuuchu* comes from the verb *kuu-* 'to chase away', see Bayalieva 1972: 96.
17 The Persian word *falgir* comes from the Arabic *fa'l*, 'divination', and the Persian *gir* (*giriftan*) 'to take/perform'. Its other forms are *falbin* and *falchi*, see Basilov 1992: 49.
18 See Basilov 1992: 48, Bayalieva 1972: 118–19 and Somfai 2004b: 579.
19 Aytpaeva 2007: 331.
20 See Somfai 2008a: 150.
21 The *dhikr* means 'mentioning [the name of Allah]'. The Arabic word *jahr* refers to the vocal performance of the *dhikr*. This contrasts with the more typical Naqshbandi practice of performing *dhikr* silently. In Kazakh and Kirghiz shamanic tradition both *zikr* and *jar* are vocalic invocations.
22 Zamanbek Kazakh *baksï* (Plate 4) sang in his *zikr* about the saints (*bab* or *baba*) who lived and were buried along the Sir-darya River; '*Otïrarda otïz bap, Türkistanda tümen bap, Sayramda sansïz bap, eng ülkeni Arstan-bap*' 'There are 30 saint in Otrar, many [10,000] saints in Türkistan, countless saints in Saryam, the greatest is Arslan-bab'. See Somfai 2005: 183.
23 Mélikoff 1987.
24 DeWeese 1994.
25 See Somfai 2003: 179–80.
26 Bayalieva 1972: 8.
27 See Aytpaeva 2007 and Somfai 2008c.
28 Sir-darya is sometimes mentioned as *suunun bashï Sulayman, suu ayagï Türkistan* 'The head of the river is Sulayman [Mountain] and the end of

it is Turkistan [former Yasi where Ahmad Yasawi is buried]', see Somfai 2007: 58.
29 See Somfai 2010b and Somfai 2007: 49–51.
30 See Bayalieva 1972: 113.
31 Aytpaeva 2007: 525 and Somfai 2004b: 579.
32 See Somfai 2007: 56.
33 Kirghiz Abdïkadïr's helping spirit appears in the form of a blue ram, see Somfai 2007: 54 and 59. Kazakh Batürkan's helping spirits are a camel and a magic snake, see Somfai 2006: 119.
34 The terms for demons have various origins: *jinn* is Arabic, *dew-pari* is Iranian, while *albastï* and *yel-moguz* have a Mongolic connection, see Somfai 2004b: 581.
35 See Bayalieva 1972: 113
36 See Somfai 2004: 162; 2005: 182 and 2007: 56. The term *oyun* is a Turkic word that means 'game or play'.
37 See Divaev 1899: 324; Basilov 1992: 238–42; Bayalieva 1972: 134.
38 See Basilov 1992: 67–72 and Somfai 2005.
39 The Arabic word means 'stick', but in Central Asia it is a magic stick only used by religious specialists, see Bayalieva 1972: 58; Basilov 1992: 76 and Somfai 2004a: 163.
40 See Somfai 2006: 118.
41 See Somfai 2007: 57.
42 See Basilov 1992: 87 and 188; Malov 1918: 4 and Somfai 2007: 59.
43 See Somfai 2008: 151.
44 See Bayalieva 1972: 45 and Potapov 1991: 68.
45 The expression *kutu/üröyü kachtï*, 'his/her soul ran away', nowadays means that someone got frightened, see Bayalieva 1972: 45–6.
46 See Somfai 2010a: 189–90.
47 Persian *pari-khwan* means 'spirit invoker'. The form *perikhan* is used by Uyghurs for a type of religious specialist (demon chaser), see Basilov 1992: 48.
48 See Somfai 2003: 188.
49 A young Polish author wrote a book on traditional Kazakh healing, where the traditional and post-Soviet healing traditions were not clearly distinguished, see Grzywacz 2010.

Chapter Four

1 This term is intended to cover the multiethnic population of the country of Kazakhstan, including people who are not Kazakhs.
2 On this topic see also Kosko 2002: 13–27.
3 The data presented here were gathered during the following field expeditions:

   1) From 1992 to 1997 in the course of doctoral research at the Free University of Brussels. Research was carried on in the regions of Almaty and Taldykorgan.

2) In 2003, research conducted under the aegis of CISMOC (Centre interdisciplinaire d'études de l'islam dans le monde contemporain), Catholic University of Louvain, in the southern part of Kazakhstan, in the region of Turkistan.

4 Part of our account of Kuat has already been published in French (Vuillemenot 2004: 131–41).
5 This term is used by Kuat when referring to other *bakhsis*, but also for doctors, psychologists and other foreign healers.
6 This word is used in Kazakhstan as a generic designation for Muslim spirit figures as well as pre-Islamic spirit figures.
7 The *kymalak* involves drawing from three times three piles of beans or small stones, containing from one to three pieces, for a total of 41 beans, and this drawing is useful for making predictions, as practised by *bakhsis* and other diviners in Central Asia, at marketplaces or in consultations at private residences. The soothsayer or diviner, male or female, mixes up the beans while uttering the name of the person for whom the consultation is being performed. Then he or she lines up three times three groups of beans on superimposed and parallel lines, forming a square. The arrangement of the beans is supposed to be made in an 'automatic' manner, without looking.
8 A Kazakh person is supposed to possess three different life-principles at birth: first there is the equivalent of what we call the soul, then there is the *kyt*, the potential for happiness or luck for a given individual, although this luck is collective in that it belongs to a line of direct descent. Finally there is the principle of breathing, which humans share with non-human entities, as for example when fog is considered the breath of the mountain (Vuillemenot 1998: 59–71).
9 With regard to questions about living spaces and yurts, see Hamayon 1979: 109–39; Sembin 1994: 63–8; Vuillemenot 2009: 115–9.
10 Nomadic habitations, circular huts made of felt.
11 Traditional iron cook pot, circular and concave, whose upper edge rests upon a circle above the central hearth.
12 Considering the time when these predictions were uttered (1995), and the course of later events, they seem quite prescient.
13 http://www.fsa.ulaval.ca/personnel/vernag/EH/F/cause/lectures/ chamanisme. html, accessed 7 July 2012.
14 Data on Khaiat was previously published in French; see Vuillemenot 2006.
15 As mentioned above, this is a divinatory practice using 41 beans or stones.
16 During 1994.
17 Cf. the very interesting work of Barba and Saverese (1985) about theatre and representation.

Chapter Five

1 'Sorcerers' can be *köz achïk*, who can be accused of harming others and are designated, by rival *köz achïk* as well as by the local community, by the word *kara köz achïk* ('black'). The most accused are those who advertise in

newspapers, boasting of their own merits, or those who earn a lot of money thanks to their activity. See Basilov 1992: 130; Garrone 2000: 98.

2   Some *moldo* practice healing rituals on patients and are supposed to take part in the 'Kirghiz way'.

3   This symbolic world is now at the forefront again (after having been kept clandestine in the Soviet era). Indeed, although in the countryside old people can be seen taking up such practices that were either abandoned for a long time or accomplished occasionally and clandestinely, an increasing number of young people, even in the cities, are also settling to practice as healer-diviners. This phenomenon was particularly strong just after the independence, because a lot of people lost their jobs and were consequently looking for a lucrative activity.

4   The majority of the Muslims in Central Asia are Sunni of *hanafi* rite, like in Afghanistan and throughout the Indian sub-continent. The *Hanafi*, as Stéphane Dudoignon explains, have distinguished themselves throughout the centuries by a great tolerance for practices that are foreign to Islamic jurisprudence, and have been confronted with hostility from other theological schools, notably the Hanbali school and its modern offshoots. The antagonism between *Hanafi* and the *Hanbali* in terms of the practices of Islam as well as ways of thinking has oriented the history of Islam in Central Asia throughout the modern and contemporary period; see Dudoignon 2001: 25.

5   *Jol* ('road') also designates in Central Asia the peculiar 'way' that a bard takes to sing an epic (the tone of the voice, repertoire, instrumental style), which corresponds to the ritual 'journey' of the shaman; see Zeranska-Kominek 1997; about the *zol* which comes from the same root than the Turkish *yol*, 'road', see Even 1988–9: 441. A similar idea can be found in the Tunguse peoples, who attribute 'roads' to the spirits as well as to the shamans, see the works of Laurence Delaby. A spatial dimension is thus bound to the relationships between clans as well as the relationships between the living and the dead.

6   Bad luck, for example, is perceived as an obstacle on an individual's road.

7   Some *köz achïk* say they can see, visualise through visions, the place where the object or the animal in question lies.

8   The function of *köz achïk* is, on principle, pragmatic and personalised. The failure of a prediction, or of a course of treatment, is not attributed to the symbolic world of which they partake, but to the specialist or the person behind the ritual. If the symbolic world is not questioned, those who implement it can be. The inventiveness and the atmosphere of rivalry and conflict among specialists hinder the institutionalisation of their power and the formation of corporatist groups.

9   Outlining these life stories not only considers the *köz achïk* as social actors through their mutations, but also takes into account the reverse perspective, that is the impact of the social context on their lives. I have tried to highlight the narrative patterns that emerge as well as the way in which the *köz achïk* stage themselves in accordance with a recurring thematic structure. Moreover, as there is an interaction between the storyteller and the addressee (the choice made by the *köz achïk* to emphasise certain elements rather than

others), the result is that these life stories are at the crossroads between real facts, interpretation and *a posteriori* reconstruction.
10 The linguist Kenneth Pike has established an opposition between the *etic* and *emic* points of views: the first is based on the standpoint of the researcher and his own culture whereas the second relies on concepts specific to the social actors under study; see Pike 1947.
11 See Dor 2004.
12 See Hamayon 1982: 25; Delaby 1976: 214.
13 The narrative pattern differs from one *köz achïk* to another, in particular the mode of sensitive contact with the spirits, the medium of a dream in Gülayïm's case, through visions and/or hallucinations for Joldoshbek during his wandering in the cemetery of his late father. Zarïlkan's visions still assail her and interrupt the flow of her everyday life.
14 As Gülayïm points out: 'All my family was for the *tabip* [doctor], they had a good comprehension of this people's medicine. When I fell sick, they told me to consult the *köz achïk*. They wanted me to get better. I consulted many *köz achïk* before going to see this gentleman. My grandparents respected the *kïrgïzchïlïk*. For years, despite the Soviet regime, we, the Kirghiz people, have understood the tradition of the *kïrgïzchïlïk*'.
15 In a society where each Kirghiz has to know the names of his seven direct patrilineal ancestors – one refers to ones ancestors by *jeti ata*, 'seven fathers', thanks to whom one has a precise genealogical position and thus a recognised social origin – and within which, moreover, privileges are inherited according to the paternal line, it seems however that the *kasiet* is handed down (and circulates) in the paternal line as well as in the maternal line. The filial connection between men and spirits allows retention of *kasiet* within the same lineage.
16 Bursulsun used a sheep's scapula during her divination sessions: 'I can see in it like in a mirror, there are sorts of sentences in Arabic or in Kirghiz that are appearing. My ancestors are showing me the road, the way.' Scapulamancy, or divination through the observation of a scapula, is a very common process in Central Asia.
17 Armed rebellion that took place in the region of Batken in the summer 1999, when several hundred armed combatants, under the command of the Uzbek Islamist Juma Khodjiev, called Namangani, held hostage four Japanese geologists, several hundred villagers and important Kirghiz figures for three months, before releasing them against a six million dollar ransom.
18 The *albarstï* is represented as a spirit that keeps attacking human beings in general. The *albarstï* was described to me either as looking like an old women with shaggy yellowish long hair, spoiled teeth (and red eyes) or as a being covered with hair. This spirit persecutes human beings, men and women, during their sleep and tries to smother them. See Garrone 2000: 168, and, in this volume, the chapter by Thierry Zarcone.
19 See, among others, Castagné 1930.
20 See Castagné 1951.
21 They condemn any form of cult of saints and visit to the saints' tombs (*mazar*). As they only recognise the Qur'an and the Prophet's Tradition

(*Sunna*) as sources of faith, they condemn Sufism and its practices such as the collective sessions of invocation of the divine Name (*dhikr*), the reading of the Qur'an on the tomb or at the deceased's address, the use of talismans (*tumar*) and of amulets, and so on.

22 We should nonetheless point out that what is at stake here is not to discuss the Islamic or non-Islamic nature of these practices and, consequently, to assess the part played by each of the components within this symbolic world, which represents a strictly impenetrable question, as the fusion of all the elements (the pre-Islamic elements as well as the Islamic ones, the elements specific to shamanism, to Islam, to Zoroastrianism, etc.) appears so intimate. See Basilov 1987, 1992; During and Khudoberdiev 2007; Rasanayagam 2006; Seleznev 2000; Vuillemenot 2000, 2004; Zarcone 2000, 2003.
23 They are criticised, paradoxically, for their lack of immediate results, of efficiency; 'most of the time', some mullahs explained to me, 'their predictions do not happen'.
24 This is rare, as the mullahs, in particular those who lived during the Soviet era, are blamed for their lack of theological knowledge.
25 A 76-year-old *köz achïk* from the village of Tamga told me that a young mullah had consulted her. She had asked for advice, for clarification regarding religion, from mullahs with whom she maintained, according to her, very good relationships.
26 Zarïlkan explained to me how she specialised in such an activity: 'Once a villager lost a horse. I am able to dream a week in advance of the place where the cattle is. This villager's horse had been stolen, its throat had been slit and then the horse had been sold. I was able to say in which street it had took place, in which house. We went there. The owners of the house protested and denied. Then I started to hear a voice reciting the Qur'an at the moment when I was standing in front of a young boy. My gaze focused on him and he admitted everything. At the beginning, I took care of people suffering from diseases, and then I specialised on the search for lost cattle. Sometimes some Kazakhs steal cattle using trucks and slit the throat of the animals in Kazakhstan. Until 2002, I received at home, about four or five patients a day. Now, one or two persons come here every week or I go to my patient's house.'

Chapter Six

1 This study is based upon fieldwork in the Turkmen Sahra region.
2 *Porkhani* is the term applied by Iranian Turkmens to those who cure patients of physical and psychiatric illness through a ceremonial rite in which music and dramatic gestures are used for this purpose. This rite has been common among various tribes of Turks in Central Asia, under different names, since the ancient times. It is called *ovzan* among the Turks of Azerbaijan; *qam* among the Turks of the Altay; *bakhshi* among the Turks of Kirghiz; *oyon* among the Turks of Yakut and *shaman* among the Turks of Tunguz.

3 Turkmen Sahra is a region located in the northeast of Iran, where the Turkmens reside. In all forms of the ceremony discussed – given different names by different tribes – there are significant similarities pointing to a unified underlying structure. Music, hymns performed by a choir on the basis of love poems, mystical poems, as well as poems praising nature, together with dramatic acts are the principal elements to be found in them; see Asghar 1976: 195.
4 *Ishan* is a term common among the Turkmens. It is on the one hand applied to *sayyids* (descendants of the Prophet of Islam). On the other, *ishan* refers to those who practise the healing of patients. Among the Turkmens, they can be either female or male. They are very religious and cure patients through reading certain prayers and acts of worship. They believe that any kind of disease or a problem is due to a *jinn*'s penetration into the bodies of individuals. *Ishan* therefore concentrate their efforts on reading prayers in order to drive the *jinn* out of the body of the sick person. Either through religious training, or through self-revelation and dreaming that happens all of a sudden, they gain the rank of *ishan*. However, this term has a history.
5 *Daamaar tutan/damar tutan* is a Turkmen word meaning a person who feels the pulse of the sick. It is in fact an indigenous healing method common among the Turkmens. The healer massages the body of the patient with a special mixture of animal oil and several medical herbs in order to find sensitive points. When these points are found, the healer uses certain techniques to remove the sickness from the patient.
6 *Qarakh Yaasin/qarakh Yasin* means to read the Sura Yasin of the Qur'an 40 times. It is one of the indigenous healing methods practised among the Turkmens. Forty people circle the patient and each of them reads the sura once, making a total of 40 times. This sura serves to remove the problems of the patient.
7 *Zikr-i khanjar* is changed into *raqs-i khanjar* (dagger dance) and only enjoys a dramatic aspect. It was one of the Turkmens' healing rituals in the past. In this ceremony, five men circle the patient while wearing special Turkmen costumes. They perform movements similar to dancing, and read spells in order to cure the patient, who is sitting inside the circle. In connection with the Turkmen tribe, the *zikr-i khanjar* is one of the dramas performed annually on certain occasions at the Vahdat Theater Hall in Tehran, as well as in other provinces. The younger generations of Turkmens see it as a drama characteristic of the Turkmen community. Non-Turkmens fond of art and music, who love to watch traditional ceremonies and rituals, attend this ritual and watch it with great enthusiasm.
8 Takiya Baba is a famous Turkmen shrine, located 60 kilometres from Gunbad Kavus.
9 Qadr Night is believed by Muslims to be the time when the Qur'an was sent down from God to humanity.
10 'Have you not regarded how [God created seven heavens one upon another]', Qur'an 71:15. This verse was revealed to the Prophet of Islam during a specific night.

Chapter Seven

1. A first version of this article was published in Dutch under the title 'Een exorcist in Afghanistan. Sjamanisme of niet?', in Alexandra Rosenbohm (ed.). *Wat Bezielt de Sjamaan? Genezing, Extase, Kunst*, Amsterdam, Koninklijk Instituut voor de Tropen, 1997, pp. 116–27. The present version is augmented.
2. Zorz and Dupaigne 1976.
3. Farhadi 1967; Sana 1975; Kieffer 1976–80; Barfield 1981; Dupaigne 1982.
4. Dupaigne 1976a.
5. Jarring 1939; Roux 1958.
6. Mir Haydar 1436.
7. Centlivres-Demont 1997.
8. Centlivres and *alii* 1971.
9. Jarring 1938; Çagatay and Sjoberg 1955; Schurmann 1962; Slobin 1976; Dupaigne 1976a; Sidky 1990.
10. Dupaigne 1976b.
11. Dupaigne 1976b.
12. During the same kind of rituals at Kashgar (Xinjiang), the healer plays also a *dâyra* instead of the old *kobuz* (communication from Sabine Trebinjac).
13. Jarring 1938: 89, n. 3.
14. Massé 1938; Nicolas 1972; Hamayon 1990; Lot-Falck 1953.
15. Lot-Falck 1953: 95.
16. Levchine 1840; Radlov 1870 and 1893; Castagné 1923 and 1930; Findeisen 1951; Krueger 1963; Menges 1968; Chadwick and Zhirmunsky 1969; Snesarev 1969; Basilov 1992.
17. Centlivres *et al.* 1971; Centlivres 1972; Slobin 1976.

Chapter Eight

1. I am grateful to many colleagues who shared their knowledge and also their materials with me. Special thanks go to R. Natvig, who was extremely generous to me in providing most of his works on *zar*, especially his fabulous bibliography. I would like also to thank: O. Fairless, S. Abtahi, N. Aghakhani, J. Boddy, M. Ebtehaj, R. Gleave, C. Holes, P. Luft, M. Rahmani, T. Ricks, D. Espirito Santo and Th. Zarcone for their kind help in providing most of the resources that I needed for writing this chapter.
2. Abu-Lughod 1993; Aghaie 2004, 2005; Doumato 2000; Flaskerud 2003; Holy 1988; Tapper and Tapper 1987; Tett 1995, Torab 2006.
3. See Azadarmak and Tezcur 2008: 211.
4. Flaskerud 2003, p. 35.
5. For example, see: Beck 1992: 46; Feilberg 1952: 144–53; Khosronejad 2011.
6. Palmistry.
7. Generally speaking, most Muslim communities commonly believe in magic (*sehr*) and explicitly forbid its practice. *Sehr* translates from Arabic as sorcery or 'black magic'. Like other Islamic countries, the Iranian state does not accept rituals, practices or any activities (sorcery, witchcraft, fortune-telling

and occults) under the title of sorcery (*jadugari*) or magic (*sehr*). The word *sehr* is a temptation for men for one too many things, especially for those who seek a miracle. In Islam, however, the practice of *sehr* (which means something that is hidden and its cause is unknown) is an act of *kofr* (disbelief). Therefore, magic and sorcery are forbidden and are considered *haram*.
8 The other ceremony is *Parikhani* or *Purkhani* which belongs only to Turkmen groups and nomads.
9 As far as I know, there are only three studies in this regard: Sa'idi 1967; Modarressi 1968; Riyahi 1977.
10 See: Aghakhani 1998, 2005; Aghakhani and Doubille 2002; Asadian 2004; Darvishi 1991, 1998, 2001; Fatimi 2005; Ghaffary 1986; Gharasu 2008; Masudiyah 1977, 1985; Moghaddam 2009; Muhibi 1995; Safa 1988; Sharifiyan 2002; Oskoui 2004; Rahmani 2007.
11 Possession belief may be found in a variety of contexts, altered states 'of consciousness' being only one such context. A belief in 'possession' may also be linked to the modification of a person's behaviour, capacities, or state of health, in the absence of an altered state of consciousness. We might speak of such non-trance possession as referring to an 'alteration of capacity' rather than of consciousness. Bourguignon 1973: 15.
12 Cerulli 1934; Constantinides 1991; Frobenius 1913; Natvig 1987; Seligman 1914.
13 The term 'spirit possession cult' refers to a cult in which ceremonial spirit possession is encouraged in individuals who become members of the cult by virtue at first of uncontrolled possession by a spirit, brought under control by the individual's incorporation in a cult group. For more information on 'Cult' in a religious context, see Yinger 1957.
14 Abyssinia may refer to the Ethiopian Empire that consisted of modern Ethiopia.
15 Amharic is a Semitic language spoken in North Central Ethiopia by the Amhara. It is the second most spoken Semitic language in the world, after Arabic, and the official working language of the Federal Democratic Republic of Ethiopia. http://en.wikipedia.org/wiki/Amharic
16 Kahle 1912.
17 Letter quoted in Thompson and Franke 1913: 281.
18 Meyerhof 1917: 321.
19 For more information on *jinn* and exorcism in Bahrain, see: Holes 2000: 27–31. Also on *zar* as a type of *jinn* in Dubai, see: al-Zakari 1998: 123–8.
20 Kapteijns and Spaulding 1996, p. 175.
21 Currently, the best bibliography of works made on *zar* is by Dr. R. Natvig and again I am grateful to him for sharing this document with me. In this regard, see: Makris and Natvig 1991: 233–283.
22 Lucie, Lady Duff-Gordon (1821–1869) was an English writer.
23 A plural form of *ziran* in the Omani dialect is noted by Cerulli (1934: 1217) in his article on *zar*. Also, Dykstra (1918) has mentioned *zeeraan* from Bahrein. In Egypt, the plural form *zarat* has been recorded by De Jong (1976–77: 32). Derivations of the word *zar* have also been noted, see: Vollers 1981: 344, Trimingham 1965: 175.

24 Belo 1960; Broch 1985; Harris 1957; Mead and Bateson 1942; Messing 1958, Nourse 1996.
25 Boddy 1989; Lambek 1980; Ong 1988.
26 '...Pour se livrer à leur fétiche (*zar*) qui consiste à chasser le démon du corps des possédés par des cris, de la musique, et des sacrifices de moutons.' Artin Pacha 1885: 185, n.
27 This manuscript was sent to me by the author (N. Aghakhani) and has no date. On *zar* rituals from the point of view of psychology, there are also three other articles by the same author to which I did not have access. For further information, see: Aghakhani 1998; 2005; Aghakhani and Doubille 2002.
28 For more information on maritime commerce during pre-Islamic periods of Iran, see: Iqbal 1949–50: 16–17; Muqtadir 1954: 7–8; Hasan 1928: 60–62; Qaimmaqami 1962: 37, 47; Belgrave 1952: 59.
29 Ferrand 1924: 193–257; Hasan 1928: 77–80; Hourani and Carswell 1995: 87–122; Tafazulli 1969: 20–25.
30 On the composition of the Persian Gulf's medieval societies, see: Iqtidari 1963: 119–32; Adamiyat nd: 144–51; Amam 1963: 46; Miskawaihi 2000; Amedroz and Margoliouth 1921: 155.
31 Amam 1963, pp. 47–8.
32 In 1851, the British Consul, Keith E. Abbott, reported that in the southwestern region of Sistan, 'the cultivators of the soil are, for the most part, slaves both black and white', quoted in Amanat 1983: 172.
33 Hennell to Wellesley, 8.5.1847, FO 248/129, quoted in Martin 2005: 166.
34 IO R/15/1/168, Jenkins to Jones, No.130, 5.11.1858, quoted in Martin 2005: 166.
35 This part of the article is based on Sa'idi's text.
36 Interview with Baba Salim, one of the *Baba Zar* of Salkh village situated in Qashm Island, quoted in Sa'idi, 1967: 46. For more information on *zar* and winds in other societies, see: al-Shahi 1984: 30; Nourse 1996: 425.
37 For more information on the role of blacks and slaves in *zar* rituals, see: Fredriksen 1977: 57; Macdonald 1911: 332; Meyerhof 1917: 310; Salima 1902: 255–98; Thompson and Franke 1913: 287; Winkler 1934: 15.
38 For more information on *zar* as red wind, see: al-Shahi 1984: 30, 35–36; Muhammad 1969; Kenyon 1995: 111.
39 For more information in this regard, see: Natvig 1987: 680.
40 For more information on the function of blood in *zar* rituals, see: al-Shahi 1984: 29, 34, 36; Boddy 1988: 4, 7–8, 10, 13, 16; Fakhouri 1968: 52–54; Kapteijns and Spaulding 1996: 187; Kenyon 1995: 115, 119; Littmann 1950: 7, 21; Natvig 1988: 59, 62–63, 65; Seligman 1914: 303, 305, 307, 316–317, 319–320.
41 Al-Shahi 1984: 28. For more information on Islam and the *zar* ritual, see: al-Shahi 1984: 28–29, 35–36, 38–40; Fakhouri 1968: 49–50; Kapteijns and Spaulding 1996: 171, 173, 178, 183–185; Seligman 1914: 300; Natvig 1987: 677; Young 1975: 571.
42 Relating *jinn* in *zar* rituals, Boddy (1988:10) writes: 'Most *jinns* are assimilated into three categories, coded by colour. White jinn are benign; possession

by one is not serious and in fact may go unnoticed. Black *jinn* or devils (*shawatin*) bring grave disease and intractable mental illness; possession by one is a dire matter, and curable, if at all, only by violent exorcism. Sickness caused by a black *jinn* might well result in death. Last, there are red *jinn* or *zairan*, whose color points to a characteristic association with blood and human fertility. These are pleasure-seeking, capricious, ambivalent beings that bring milder forms of illness which, though initially distressful, never result in death or severe mental dysfunction.' For more information on *jinn* and *zar* ritual, see: al-Shahi 1984: 30–31, 42; Boddy 1988: 10, 14; Padwick 1924; Seligman 1914: 305; Young 1975: 583.

43 For more information on the role of perfume in *zar* rituals, see: al-Shahi 1984: 29, 324; Young 1975: 572.
44 For more information on the role of alcoholic drinks in *zar* ritual, see: al-Shahi 1984: 29, 34, 36–7, 39; Kenyon 1995: 118.
45 For more information on purity and impurity in *zar* ritual, see: Boddy 1988: 6–7, 22–3; Seligman 1914: 320; Young 1975: 571.
46 For more information on the duration of *zar* ritual, see: al-Shahi 1984: 33–4, 42; Boddy 1988: 20; Fakhouri 1968: 50–51, 53–4; Kapteijns and Spaulding 1996: 178, 184; Kenyon 1995: 107, 114; Seligman 1914: 302, 314–5, 321–2; Natvig 1987: 676, 684.
47 For more information on washing the body during *zar* ritual, see: Natvig 1988: 59–60, 63, 65.
48 For more information regarding the same ritual in Bahrain, see: Holes 2000: 30.
49 For more information on singing songs during *zar* ritual, see: al-Shahi 1984: 33, 42; Kapteijns and Spaulding 1996: 172, 175; Fakhouri 1968: 51; Natvig 1987: 679, 683; Natvig 1988: 58–9, 68; Seligman 1914: 316, 318; Young 1975: 573.
50 For more information on votive meals during *zar* ritual, see: Boddy 1988: 6–8, 15, 20; Natvig 1987: 683, 687; Natvig 1988: 59, 65; Seligman 1914: 309; Young 1975: 572, 579–80.
51 See: Oskoui 2004; Rahmani 2007.
52 For more information on sacrifice during *zar* ritual, see: al-Shahi 1984: 34, 42; Fakhouri 1968: 49, 52–5; Kapteijns and Spaulding 1996: 172; Kenyon 1991: 198; Kenyon 1995: 115; Messing 1958: 1124–5; Natvig 1987: 672, 682–4, 687; Natvig 1988: 59–60, 63, 65; Seligman 1914: 303–304, 306–307, 310–312, 314, 319; Young 1975: 571–2, 576, 579–80, 583.
53 For more information on drinking blood or other liquids during *zar* ritual, see: al-Shahi 1984: 29, 31, 34, 36–7, 39, 42; Dimotheos 1871: 141; Fakhouri 1968: 52; Gamst 1969: 49–50; Kapteijns and Spaulding 1996: 174, 183, 187–9; Kenyon 1995: 115, 118–9; Leiris 1938: 23–124; Leslau 1949: 204–12; Natvig 1987: 681–3, 688; Natvig 1988: 59: 71; Seligman 1914: 305, 320; Trimingham 1965: 258–9; Worrel 1909: 30; Young 1975: 521.
54 For more information on the role of music during *zar* ritual, see: al-Shahi 1984: 33; Fakhouri 1968: 51, 53; Kapteijns and Spaulding 1996: 177; Natvig 1987: 673; Natvig 1988: 58–9, 65; Seligman 1914: 307, 317–20; Young 1975: 572.

55 For more information on the language of *zars* during *zar* ritual, see: Kapteijns and Spaulding 1996, pp. 173, 187; Messing 1958, pp. 1122, 1125; al-Shahi 1984, p. 31; Natvig 1987, pp. 677, 678, 679, 689.
56 For more information on *zar* requests during *zar* ritual, see: al-Shahi 1984: 28, 30–36, 39–40; Boddy 1988: 10–11, 13, 15, 19-20; Fakhouri 1968: 51-3; Kenyon 1995: 107, 110, 112, 114, 116–8; Leiris 1934: 120; Messing 1958: 1120, 1124–5; Natvig 1987: 681–3; Seligman 1914: 304, 307, 310; Young 1975: 571–2, 577, 579–82.

Chapter Nine

1 By 'antinomian' Sufism I mean, here, the Sufi lineages that do not respect fully the religious 'norm' imposed by the two dominant branches of Islam, Sunnism and Shi'ism; these norms are in general the five commandments, i.e. the five daily prayers, the pilgrimage to Mecca, etc.
2 More details in Elçin 1979–83; Çakır 1987; Koç 1997; Arnaud-Demir 2002 and 2005; Zarcone 2000a and 2000b; And 2003: 223–4.
3 I don't interpret, however, as relevant features to be classified in this section several other elements usually interpreted as shamanic by some writers, even if they are, in some cases, associated with shamanism; this is the case for the stone, mountain or nature cult (Köprülü 1929).
4 *Dertli gibi sarıksızdır,*
  Ayağı da carıksızdır.
  Boynuzu yok, kuyruksuzdur,
  Şeytan bunun neresinde?
  From Karakoç 2006: 26–7.
5 Köprülü 1986: 134–5, 142–44; Başgöz 1998: 2; Karakoç 2006: 17–32, 50–1. On the *kobuz*, see also Feldmann 1996: 117 9, 134 6.
6 Seer (*rämmal*), according to the Azerbaijani dictionary of Orunzheva 1983: vol. 3, 67.
7 The Persian word *afsun* (magic), generally associated with the Turkish verb *üfürümek*, means healing with the breath.
8 It exists in many poems by a Turkish bard named Köroglu living in sixteenth century but without any links with the author of the epic; the poetry of the former is, however, inspired by this epic and deals with Sufi themes; see Öztelli 1962.
9 *Urum Abdalları gelir dost deyu*
  Giydiğimiz hırka nemed post deyu
  Hastaler da gelmiş şifa isteyu
  Sağlar gelir Pirim Abdal Musa'ya.
  Koca 1990: 24.
10 Compare with Basilov 1992: 111; id. 1995: 241.
11 More details in Koçu 1958–71; Abdullah 1993: 7; Abdülaziz Bey 1995: 369–70; Santur: 1994; Ocak, 2000: 149, Boratav 2003: 101; Özbay 2007: 130, 319–26, 464; Günay 1998: 235–6; Öngel 1997: 19, 22, 24, 26, 38, 55.

A marvellous exhibition in Istanbul in 2003 was dedicated to the magic, talismans and amulets of Anatolia; see the catalogue of this event, Işın 2003.
12 The original in Turkish of this last sentence deserves to be quoted because of the Turkish terms used: *Onlar cinlerle temas ederken coşar, kendilerinden geçer, ağızlarından köpükler saçarlar*. The verb *coşmak*, to boil up, to overflow, to become enthusiastic, is also used by the Turkish Sufis to describe the mystical or 'ecstatic' experience. Karl Reich (2001: 77) points to the use by Uzbek shamans of a similar Turkish verb (*qaynamaq* – boil up) to describe the particular state they experience when reaching the climax during their song.
13 There is another example of a 'master of the *jinns*' (*cinci*) who searches out concealed objects, using a method quite similar to that adopted by the *cinci* described by Esenel (according to a story recorded in 1999 at Denizli, see story 2110 (1999 tape 2) at http://aton.ttu.edu, accessed July 2009).
14 On *jinn*, divination and seer, possession and exorcism among the Arabs, see el-Zein 1996: 126 sq., 305 sq.
15 The spirit *alkarısı* is famous in Turkey, as it is in the whole of the Turkic world and even in neighbouring Christian countries; see See Ülkütaşır 1939a; 1939b; Günay 1998: 237–8; Garrone 2000: 166–72; Boratav 2003: 102–4; Arakelova 2006; Shamlu and Russel 1985: 741–2.
16 Recently, in 2007, a popular newspaper mentioned that an *üfürükcü* was on trial in Istanbul.
17 On the *üfürükçü*, see Talu 1953; Makal 1954: 172–3; Makal 1963: 129–30; Santu 1994; Araz 1995: 166, 169; Boratav 1999: 147–8; Esenel 1999: 138–44 (fieldwork carried in the 1940s).
18 In the 1980s Hikmet Tanyu reported that the ashes coming from the hearth used by Fadime Ana for cooking were considered sacred and mixed with water to heal; Tanyu 1982: 484. This ritual is executed nowadays by *ocaklı* at Denizli (Öngel 1997: 30–31). Makal confirms that the ashes gained a prophylactic quality (Makal 1963: 135).
19 On Bibi Fatima in Central Asia see Kleinmichel 2000: vol. 2, 233–6. In Kharazm, the figure of Fatima is replaced by that of Ambar Ana, protectress of the women, wife of the Yasawi Sufi Sulayman Baghirgani who married therefore another famous Sufi of the same order, Zangi Ata. The popularity of the 'hand' of Ambar Ana in Kharazm is similar to that of Fatima in the rest of the Muslim world (Snesarev 2003: 184–5). This tradition has also spread among the Tatars of Siberia where it still exists; see Seleznev *et al.* 2009: 96–100.
20 Taizhanov and Ismailov 1986: 128.
21 In Northern Africa, the hand of Fatima refers to the 'white hand of Moses which operates many miracles', Doutté 1909: 327–7.
22 See Manijeh Maghsudi's chapter in this volume.
23 In general, the *chiltan* are presented as 'invisible people' or 'people coming from the Invisible, the hidden' (*rijal al-gayb* in Arabic), see Andreev 1927.
24 The Turkish text is: '*Ölenler kalanlara elini veriyor, böylece ocak tükenmiyor*'. The translation into English of this sentence by Sir Wyndham Deedes is not entirely correct since 'giving the hand', as we can read in Turkish, is very different from 'touching the hand' as Deedes – who ignored the cultural context – translated (Makal 1954: 86).

25 Acıpayamlı 1969: 5; Öngel 1997: 23. About the Sufi ritual of 'Giving and taking the hands', see Gölpınarlı 1977: 112.
26 The original in French is: 'L'initiation ne consiste pas seulement dans l'indication des prières et des passes, mais il est de rigueur que l'*initiateur* donne, à la fin de l'initiation, une *poignée de main* à son disciple...'.
27 'Reading' is usually associated with breathing (see above); about the expression 'to do reading' (*okutmak*), see Bayri 1972: 108–10. Victoria Arakelova (2001) shows some healing rituals among the Yazidis (an antinomian trend in Islam) of contemporary Russia that mingle Islam and Armenian Christianity.
28 There is another article by Constant on Turkish traditional medicine and on amulets published in the same journal: Constant 1862.
29 The original Turkish text is '*Çocuğun hastalığının Yılancık olduğunu söylediler. İşte o günden sonra İsmet, yılancık ocağı, derken her şey ocağı oldu*'.
30 On the extraction of worms see François Ruegg's chapter in this volume.
31 A very similar ceremony was observed in Tajikistan (Garonne 2000: 210, 214).
32 On the cures by transfer usually called *kuchuru* ('transplant' in Uzbek language) and *uchuk* ('herpes' in Turkish and Uzbek languages), see Garrone 2000: 200–201, 227–9, and Troickaja 1925. There is an interesting report about these two ceremonies in a travelogue by a Western traveller who visit the Kazakh steppe in 1840 (de Levchine 1840: 338).
33 On the cure as a play (*oyun* in Turkish) see Centlivres and Centlivres-Dumont 1988: 155–7; Hamayon 1999–2000; Garrone 2000: 20–21, 61–2. The term *'alas'*, as a cure by transfer, is used also in some other areas of Central Asia and even in Anatolian Turkey, see Tanyu 1976: 292. See also Bernard Dupaigne's chapter in this volume.
34 www.uzmantv.com/herkes-kursun-dokebilir-mi, accessed October 2008.
35 See several other descriptions of this ritual in Kılıç 1953: 691–2; Araz 1995: 177–8, and Sezik 1997: 52–5.
36 This ritual as a divination technique exists in Northern Africa, Hell 1999: 28.
37 More details are given in Ülkütaşır 1939a; id. 1939b; Günay 1998: 237–8; Garrone 2000: 166–72; Boratav 2003; 102–4; Arakelova 2006; Shamlu and Russel 1985: 741–2.
38 *Gizli dertlerimi sana anlattım*
   Çalıştım sesimi sesine kattım...
   (Veysel 2001: 235).
39 See the Turkish newspaper *Zaman* of 26 September 1992.

Chapter Ten

1 On the history and practices of these two traditions see: Birge 1965; Algar 1990; Ocak 2000; Zarcone 2000a and forthcoming.
2 This 'dance' (*semâ*) was spontaneous and the result of a state of 'boiling' (from the Turkish verb *coşmak*): *He 'boiled' up and entered the dance*; Gölpınarlı 1958: 36.

3   *Sema* (Arabic: *samâ'*) is literally a '[spiritual] audition'; see the bibliography on sacred dances in Islam in Ambrosio and Zarcone 2004.
4   See other descriptions of this dance with analysis in: And 2003: 181–6; Arnaud-Demir 2002 and 2004; Bozkurt 2008: 45–7; Dinçer 2000; Duygulu 2004; Erseven 1996: 134–6; Markof 1993; Onatça 2007: 74–5.
5   I would like to thank Cafer Yildiz for providing me with material about this dance, especially the texts of the poetry song by his group.
6   The *yeldirme* phase is also a characteristic of the profane dance in Anatolia; see And 2003: 144.
7   See the commentary about this poetry by Arnaud-Demir (2002: 55–6), who points to the identification of the feathers of the crane and the strings of the lute, as the Turkish word *tel* (string) refers to both.
8   '*Jinn sûqghân, bâlâ tâbmâghân khâtûnlargha pîr ûynimiz*'. On contemporary shamanism in Xinjiang see Rakhman 2006: 215–51.
9   Regarding dances executed by shamans in non-Turkic areas, see: Berti 1995.
10 See my chapter in this volume: 'Shamanism in Turkey: bards, "masters of the *jinns*" and healers'.
11 A Qur'anic event, the *miraj* is here reinterpreted by the Bektashi-Alevi tradition which shows the Prophet accompanied by Ali and Salman.
12 See also Birge 1965: 137–8.
13 This dance was also executed by the Association of Young Alevis of the Merdivenköy Tekke and presented at Ascona.

Chapter Eleven

1   I am by no means a shamanism specialist. In the course of extensive research on African marabouts in Paris, I am now writing the biography of one of them, whom I met many years ago during previous fieldwork. It was by collecting the words of this man that I realised how complex and varied his professional experience of dreaming was, compared to the position outlined in Islamic doctrine.
2   Owing to the need among Parisians for the services of diviners, it was finally decided in France to accept them with this status rather than consider them as religious figures.
3   *Listikhar* requires that the client visit the marabout twice: the first time to explain their problem and the second to hear the result of the divinatory dream. This twofold visit is believed to irritate impatient clients.
4   313 is considered a powerful number according to many different interpretations (there are 313 known prophets; there were 313 fighters at the famous Battle of Badr; it results from the addition of the numeral values of the letters of the prophet's name, etc.)
5   Imitation of the Prophet is the core of Muslim life; it is believed to be beneficial to spiritual life and a means of salvation.
6   The Arabic word *sadaqa* usually designates charity or alms-giving, which is a necessary part of Islam. West African Muslims use this same word (wolof, *sarakh*; fula, *sadaq*) for ritual offerings or sacrifices donated to Allah or the

jinns through a third party (who may be a poor person) in order to favour fortune. Islam merely tolerates this practice.
7   Concerning the progressive elaboration of Islamic esoteric sciences, see Constant Hamès 2008.
8   Botanical name: *Combretum glutinosum Perr.*
9   The Hanbali Ibn Taymiyya (1263–1328) was the first to violently denounce marabout practices.
10 Sura 8 describes two of Muhammad's dream experiences in the context of fighting against his opponents: Allah uses dreams to give Muhammad confidence in his final victory. According to the hadith (Bukhârî), the first revelation was given to the Prophet in dreams. I will not go into details here, as Toufic Fahd and Pierre Lory have so ably studied this issue.
11 For other descriptions, see Sanneh 1979: 192; Samb 1998: 196–7; Kuczynski 2002: 181–91.
12 Original version: 'les sociétés à écriture ayant figé leurs clés dans des livres, on leur prête une rigidité qu'elles n'ont pas dans les sociétés de tradition orale'.
13 Following Dia's description.
14 Dia's experience may be compared with that of an old Tukolor weaver described by Dilley: running into a female *jinn* in the bush, he could only utter *la* (beginning of *la ilaha illa'lah*) before he was struck dumb; but as he was not afraid, the female *jinn* appeared to him in a dream and gave him 'much weaving lore' that led to greater skill and ability. Dilley considers that the metaphor of the bush represents 'the origin of weaving and its source of inspiration coming from beyond the social world of men – that is from the *jinn* of the bush. It is the weaver who integrates and transforms these potentially threatening powers of creation into a socially useful activity such as weaving' (Dilley 1992: 78–80).

Chapter Twelve

1   'Les mères des premiers Touaregs appartiennent, dans le récit mythique, à une société déjà existante quand les *Kel essuf* viennent à elles, de sorte qu'on peut parler d'une antériorité de l'ascendance maternelle des anciens Touaregs par rapport à leur ascendance paternelle'. Most Tuareg groups refer to a feminine ancestor; for instance in Ahaggar, it is Tin Hinân, the ancestor of noble tribes. Among their neighbours in Niger, the *kel Ferwen*, they refer to Sabena, Casajus says. Most of the tributary groups of the Ahaggar claim that they also descend from a woman, Takema, the sister or the servant of Tin Hinân. *iklan* slaves too have invented a feminine ancestor for themselves.
2   At the moment this form of traditional medicine is the first resort in the encampments as well as in villages, and it raises the interest and hope of scientists with regard to certain recipes made from plants, which have turned out to be very efficient. There is a real enthusiasm for pharmacology that accompanies biomedicine.

3   I made this observation within my own family, as well as among many other families living in Algiers, amongst whom I carried out a free investigation/survey on this subject.
4   See Cuoq 1985: 25.
5   Al-Ghazali (1058–1111), one of the most powerful thinkers of Islam and the creator of 'pure love', states that the only way to reach moral and spiritual perfection of being was the practice of a contemplative and meditative life that would allow the reaching of a mystical reality with the heart. He made possible, thanks to his work, the definitive admission of Sufism into orthodoxy and influenced the outpouring of many brotherhoods that have a crucial importance in the life of Muslims by associating social and political actions with religious ones.
6   'The distinction between "writing" and reading sets up here a hierarchy between the *ineslmen*, for the study of sacred texts is considered as superior to a poor imitation of the work of good, paving the way to the diverting of religious knowledge to the benefit of magic' (Wallentovitz 2003: 10).
7   It happens at the end of the white winter, at the period of the great winds: 'Winds have a meaning in the mechanisms of the cosmos, of agricultural practices, the nutrition of men and their relation to the invisible forces' (Gast 1985: 373). A similar case was described by Edmond Bernus in 1985, and it was also observed by François Borel (who also told me about it with regard to the *kel eghlel* near Agadez).

Chapter Thirteen

1   Since we are considering a longer period of time, the recent appellation of *Roma* does not apply to most of the situations we are considering.
2   Gobineau observes this sort of syncretism in the middle of the nineteenth century in 'Central Asia' (Persia) and generously attributes the flexibility of religious identities to the 'Asian character' (Gobineau 1983: 601).
3   Not to mention biased religious, ethnic or political 'rehabilitative' perspectives.
4   'La langue prise ordinairement pour le signe distinctif des races, surtout pour les étrangers, n'est pas ici un léger obstacle. Il y a par exemple, en Macédoine, des Grecs qui ne parlent que le bulgare; presque tous les Grecs de l'Asie mineure ne parlent que le turc, et les musulmans de Candie ne parlent que le grec. Pour tous ces motifs, les statistiques commandées par des raisons politiques, non plus que celles puisées aux archives ottomanes par les voyageurs étrangers, ne méritent aucun crédit. Cependant, notre opinion à ce sujet, quoique assise sur des données certaines, pouvait être taxée de partialité, par suite de notre origine.' A. Bernardakis, 1878, quoted by Arbore (1930: 66).
5   'Ils ne sont pas un objet de répulsion en Turquie comme partout ailleurs; il n'est même pas rare de les voir s'allier avec les Turcs' (Allard 1857: 66).
6   Some biological researches are currently made as to determine specific Gypsy characteristics (DNA) see Liebich 2007.

7   The author adds that anyway Gypsies 'show no religious feeling since they have no feeling' a statement which is common in the literature devoted to Gypsies by travellers.
8   Poissonnier's hypothesis (1855, quoted in Allard 1857) of a possible link between the Gypsies and two African 'sects' the Derkaoua and the Aïssaoua (that are actually both Sufi brotherhoods) is the best example of the mixed feeling that the refusal of work (Derkaoua) and sorcery (Aïssaoua) have provoked in the 'Western' observer since Christopher Columbus.
9   'Sellers of relics and artefacts associated with both Muslim and Christian Saints and Prophets, and orthodox monks and Sufis seeking spiritual security in the chaos and disorder of early medieval Anatolia.'
10 One of the most famous healing stones is to be found in Moş Pinard/Fântana Mare. The ritual consists of possibly crawling through the stone or at least putting one's hand in the hole (see the Bocca di Verita in Rome).
11 For a critique of the concept of 'dendrolatry' and hence *animism*, see Charachidzé 1968: 659. The chapter describes a Georgian sanctuary in which a sacred oak is visited by an 'angel'. See also: Eliade 1975: 231: 'on ne peut donc parler d'un culte de l'arbre. Jamais un arbre n'a été adoré rien que pour lui-même, mais toujours pour ce qui, à travers lui, se "révélait"....'.
12 See Zarcone 1992 and the quoted bibliography.
13 Triodon, 3rd Sunday of Lent, Synaxaire, p. 255.
14 Friday of the 4th Week of Lent: 'Une étrange vision s'offre à nos yeux: la précieuse croix fait jaillir, comme une source, les dons spirituels, car elle écarte le péché, elle guérit les maladies, elle affermit les sentiments de ceux qui s'en approche en toute pureté'.
15 Or Akyazali/Akyazuku (BG) Akiazala (R) after the saint revered there. Kanitz mentions that the place was not on the map. For the history of the place and the Saint, see Zarcone 1992: 8.
16 The picture of the well of Demir Baba shows that although it is nowadays a historical monument, pieces of cloth are still fixed at the entrance of the cave.
17 But it is also said that he was fighting heresy (Mikov and Kmetova 1998: 79).
18 'Up until the end of the 1960s the votive cross and the round stone were recognised as ritual objects by Bulgarians and Gypsies alike. Now the Bulgarians make their offerings on the Feast Days of Saint George and Saint Elijah, the Gypsies making theirs on the Feast Day of Saint Elijah' (Mikov and Kmetova 1998: 86).
19 Ritual observances include: lighting a candle, offerings to the *türbe* – money, flowers, towel, *Martenitsas*, left on the window sill; tying a tread or a piece of cloth from one's clothing to the window bars; offering a prayer or a pledge, either orally in front of the *türbe's* window, or in writing on slips of papers left on the window sill (Mikov and Kmetova 1998: 88).
20 See Clayer 1994: 323: 'La formation de sous-réseaux dans les milieux gitans, est en effet un phénomène apparu au XXe siècle, qui n'affecte pas seulement la Halvetiyye. Depuis la fin de la domination ottomane, plusieurs *tekke* halvetis ont une clientèle composée exclusivement de Gitans ... En Macédoine orientale, d'après le şeyh Arid de Struga, les Gitans ont pris la place des Turcs qui sont partis.'
21 According to Kanitz, quoted by Stahl 1965.

22 The reproduction of the ceremony is worth mentioning: 'L'enfant était porté au tombeau de Miskin Baba et déposé à sa gauche ('du côté du cœur'). Puis la mère prononçait la formule d'adoption . . . la mère sortait du *türbe*, y laissant l'enfant seul quelque temps. Puis elle le ramenait à la maison. Dans certains cas, comme substitut de l'enfant, on déposait sur le tombeau sa chemise qui devait être propre, et on prononçait ensuite la même formule' (Val Cordun 1971: 109).
23 'Les musulmans albanais se font un devoir de brûler des cierges à Saint Nicolas. Les chrétiens mirdites consultent avec respect les derviches. Les femmes de Khorsova, en Chaldée, font des offrandes à Notre-Dame pour obtenir des enfants et si leur vœu a réussi, elles ne manquent pas de se présenter à l'église, afin de remercier, et elles prennent soin de s'informer des rites qu'il leur faut accomplir afin de faire leurs prières à la mode chrétienne . . . Mostancha me fit assister [à Bakou] à une sorte de service divin qui fut célébré dans une des cellules du temple avec accompagnement de petites cymbales guèbres; sur l'autel à côté des divinités sivaïques, se montraient des vases appartenant au culte parsi, des images russes de Saint Nicolas et de la Vierge et des crucifix catholiques; ces reliques si diverses étaient traitées avec un respect égal.'
24 This information was given to me by Prof. Irena Bokova from the New University of Bulgaria (Sofia) who has filmed these rituals.
25 In his foreword, Wlislocki mentions that he speaks mainly about the '*Donauländer* Gypsies', since they are more 'authentic' (*unverfälscht*) and testify about very ancient beliefs (XII). His other works are dedicated to South Hungarian and Transylvanian Gypsies.
26 Confirmed by Golemović (2001), in Serbia.
27 'tobt die Zauberfrau in dem nur durch düsteres Feuer erhelltem Zelte in wildem Stampfen und Sprüngen im Kreise umher, in dem sie die Dämonen in einem monotonen Gesange citiert' (Wlislocki 1891: 61).

I quote the text of the (rhymed) song in German as it has been translated by the author from the Romani. He offers both versions. Here is the German one:

> 'Ihr Dämonen kommt hervor!
> Flüstert leise mir ins Ohr
> Wohin habt ihr dann vertrieben,
> Dieses Mannes, dieses Lieben,
> Süsses, allersüsstes Leben?
> Will Gedärme nun euch geben
> Will die Knochen euch vergraben,
> Auch Tierhaare sollt ihr haben!
> Mannesseele her mir bringt;
> Wenn der Knochen schnell zerspringt
> In des Feuers Glut,
> Soll dem Manne, süss und gut,
> Kommen her das Leben,
> Vor mir sollt ihr beben,
> Wollt zurück ihr es nicht geben.'

28 '... et comme nous entrions, il sortit un serviteur portant des os d'épaule de mouton brûlés au feu et noirs comme du charbon, ce dont je fus étonné; leur ayant demandé depuis ce que cela voulait dire, ils m'apprirent que jamais en ce pays-là rien ne s'entreprenait sans avoir premièrement bien consulté ces os. Ils ne permettent à aucun d'entrer dans le palais avant d'avoir pris le sort ou l'augure de cette manière. Quand le Khan veut faire quelque chose, il se fait apporter trois de ces os, qui n'ont pas encore été mis au feu, et, les tenant entre les mains, il pense à l'affaire qu'il veut exécuter, si elle pourra se faire ou non; il donne après ces os pour les brûler. Il y a deux petits endroits près du palais du Khan où on les brûle soigneusement. Étant bien passés par le feu et noircis, on les rapporte devant lui, qui les regarde fort curieusement pour voir s'ils sont demeurés entiers et si l'ardeur du feu ne les a point rompus ou éclatés: en ce cas ils jugent que l'affaire ira bien; mais si ces os se trouvent rompus de travers et que de petits éclats en tombent, cela veut dire qu'il ne faut pas entreprendre la chose' (chap. 37 in Bergeron, 1735).

29 'Il avait une certaine racine qu'on appelait rhubarbe, qu'il coupa par morceaux, puis la mit en poudre dans de l'eau, avec une petite croix où il y avait un crucifix, nous disant que par ce moyen il connaissait si la malade se porterait bien ou si elle devait bientôt mourir; car mettant cette croix sur l'estomac de la malade, si elle y demeurait comme collée et attachée, c'était signe qu'elle réchapperait; mais si elle n'y tenait point du tout, cela montrait qu'elle en devait mourir. Pour moi, je croyais toujours que cette rhubarbe était quelque sainte relique qu'il eût apportée de Jérusalem. Il donnait hardiment à boire de cette eau à toutes sortes de malades. Il ne se pouvait faire qu'ils ne fussent beaucoup émus par une si amère potion, et le changement que cela faisait en eux était réputé pour miracle. Je lui dis qu'il devait plutôt faire de l'eau bénite, dont on use dans l'Église romaine, qui a une grande vertu pour chasser les malins esprits. Il le trouva bon, et à sa requête nous fîmes de cette eau bénite, qu'il mêla avec la sienne de rhubarbe où avait trempé son crucifix toute la nuit. Je lui dis de plus que, s'il était prêtre, l'ordre de prêtrise avait grand pouvoir contre les démons. Il me répondit que vraiment il l'était, mais il mentait: car il n'avait aucun ordre. Il ne savait rien, et n'était, comme j'appris depuis, qu'un pauvre tisserand en son pays, par où je passai en m'en retournant. Le lendemain, sur le matin, lui et moi avec deux prêtres nestoriens allâmes chez cette dame malade, qui était dans un petit logis derrière son grand; y étant entrés, elle se mit sur son séant dans son lit et adora la croix, qu'elle fit poser honorablement sur une pièce de soie auprès d'elle et but de cette eau bénite mêlée de rhubarbe et s'en lava aussi l'estomac. Alors le moine me pria de vouloir lire sur elle un évangile, ce que je fis. Je lui lus la passion selon saint Jean; si bien qu'enfin elle se trouva mieux, et se fit apporter quatre jascots, qu'elle mit premièrement aux pieds de la croix, puis en donna un au moine, et m'en voulait donner un autre, que je ne voulus pas prendre; mais le moine le prit fort bien pour lui; elle en donna à chaque prêtre autant, le tout se montant à quarante marcs. Outre cela, elle fit apporter du vin pour faire boire les prêtres, et je fus contraint de boire aussi de sa main en l'honneur de la très sainte Trinité... Le matin du jour suivant, nous retournâmes encore chez elle, et Mangu, ayant su que

nous y étions, nous fit venir devant lui. Il avait appris que la dame se portait mieux; nous le trouvâmes mangeant d'une certaine pâte liquide propre à réconforter le cerveau, accompagné de peu de domestiques, et ayant devant lui des os de mouton brûlés; il prit la croix en sa main, mais je ne vis pas qu'il la baisât ni adorât; la regardant seulement, il fit quelques demandes que je n'entendis pas. Le moine le supplia de lui permettre de porter cette croix sur une lance, comme je lui en avais dit quelque chose auparavant; à quoi Mangu répondit qu'il la portât comme il voudrait. Puis prenant congé de lui, nous retournâmes vers cette dame, que nous trouvâmes saine et gaillarde, buvant toujours de cette eau bénite du moine; nous lûmes encore la passion sur elle … Entre autres je vis là quatre épées à demi tirées de leurs fourreaux, l'une au chevet du lit de la dame, l'autre aux pieds, et les deux autres à chaque côté de la porte. J'y aperçus aussi un calice d'argent, qui peut-être avait été pris en quelqu'une de nos églises de Hongrie; il était pendu contre la muraille et était plein de cendres, sur lesquelles il y avait une grande pierre noire; de quoi jamais ces prêtres ne l'en avaient reprise, comme de chose mauvaise; au contraire, eux-mêmes en font autant et l'apprennent aux autres. Nous la visitâmes trois jours durant depuis sa guérison. Après cela le moine fit une bannière toute couverte de croix, et trouvant une canne longue comme une lance, la mit dessus et la portait ainsi. Pour moi, j'honorais cet homme comme un évêque, savant dans la langue du pays, encore que d'ailleurs il fît plusieurs choses qui ne me plaisaient pas. Il se fit faire une chaire qui se pliait, comme celle de nos prélats, avec des gants et un chapeau de plumes de paon, sur quoi il fit mettre une croix d'or, ce que je trouvais bon par rapport à la croix; mais il avait les pieds tout couverts de gales et d'ulcères, qu'il frottait avec des huiles et des onguents; il était aussi très fier et orgueilleux en paroles. Les nestoriens disaient certains versets du psautier (comme ils nous donnaient à entendre) sur deux verges jointes ensemble, que deux hommes tenaient, et le moine était présent à plusieurs autres semblables superstitions et folies qui me déplaisaient beaucoup; toutefois nous ne laissions pas de demeurer en sa compagnie pour l'honneur de la croix, laquelle nous portions partout chantant hautement le *Vexilla Regis prodeunt*, etc., de quoi les sarrasins étaient aussi étonnés que peu satisfaits' (Rubruquis, chap. 37, in Bergeron 1735).

30 A recurrent but not really useful discussion: see Marushiakova and Popov, Paspati etc.
31 Fosztó (2009) and Benovska (2009) present a good overview of the latest literature about conversions. As far as Manouches are concerned, see Williams (1991).
32 As our colleagues showed, it represents an important phenomenon in constant growth (for Romania see: Fosztó (2009), Gog (2009); for Bulgaria, Benovska (2009)).
33 The ethnic dimension of the conversion can be interpreted in both senses: an ethnification or de-ethnification process (Alvarsson and Segato: 2, 46).
34 According to the interviews we conducted recently in Romania and Moldova (2005–2008), conversions to Evangelism generally also correspond to the purpose of adopting a new *civic* identity, which allows the converts to

differentiate themselves from the rest or the *bad Gypsies*, those who are traditionally blamed for their laziness and other anti-social behaviours. At the same time the converts adopt a new ethical code, which tends to normalise them and make them good citizens who work successfully, do not drink nor smoke and bring their children to school. This aspect is relevant for the elite and Gypsies who wish to be integrated in the mainstream civil society.

35 As an example, an oath would be a major reason for Gypsies to go to church (Gog: 2009) or other non-liturgical celebrations like the sacrifice in the courtyard of Bali Efendi's sanctuary.
36 They may appear more exotic to researchers from Eastern and Central Europe who discovered them for the first time, as social relations among the faithful during 'assemblies' are of a totally different character to what they experienced in their traditional, national churches. See Fosztó (2009) for such narratives.
37 The author confesses however that the celebrations he is referring to, the Saint Lazarus dance and the rain-making rituals are 'pagan' and have been Christianised.
38 They are not even paid but can be given donations. Almost all historical accounts denounce the 'robbery' perpetrated by cynical Gypsy sorcerers and are doubtful about any religious belief among them.
39 The only Pentecostal practice that would perhaps be compatible with rites performed by Orthodox Christians and Muslims ones is the laying on of hands over the sick, again a gesture taken directly from the example of Jesus, which is also performed in healing rituals of other *denominations*. One could also mention the physical contact (holding hands etc.), accompanied by whispering prayers.
40 The continuity argument is also proposed by Alvarsson (2003: 48) and Williams (1991).
41 Information translated to me by Zarcone (2009).
42 This is clearly demonstrated in the Golemović folkloric-nationalistic approach of 'serbian' rituals which he claims were pagan before being Christianised.

Chapter Fourteen

1 In this article I want to acknowledge the assistance of the puppet master I Wija, and I Ketut Kacir's and his son I Wayan Suardana's help in recording and transcribing the Balinese story of Bima Suci and their explanations of it. Outside of Bali I want to express my gratitude to Vladimir Braginsky from the School of Oriental and African Studies for drawing my attention to relevant literature on Islam/Sufism and Javanese Hindu philosophy.
2 The *Mahabharata* is more complex than the *Ramayana*. Stories derived from it recount inheritance problems, family or community strife, romance and moral dilemmas – all situations that are familiar to the people. Locals often conceive of the *Mahabharata* as 'history', and as such it helps validate the

authority of the aristocrats or former god-kings. The *Ramayana* is more popular in mainland Southeast Asia.

3   The statue, called Catuhkaya, is from Pejeng in Bali (tenth to fourteenth century). It is composed of Bairawa-like figures, each with a mask portraying a symbol of Kala (a wrathful emanation of Shiva). Stutterheim (1935: Plate XX) suggested that these statues are connected to *kalacakra* deliverance sects in Java and Bali, known from India, particularly in Tantric Buddhism.
4   According to Ibn al-Arabi, *wahdat al-wujud* expresses the unity of God and man. It can be visualised as a raindrop that does not vanish in the sea, but becomes a precious pearl (Shimmel 1975: 284). Zoetmulder (1971: 92) in discussing the mystic-religious literature related to the shadow theatre refers to this exalted state as *wujudijah*.
5   Traditionally, women rarely watched shadow-theatre performances. They do not like the long drawn-out war scenes or the often inaccessible plots. In the past classical literature was the cultural sphere of men, but these days this strict distinction is breaking down.
6   The equivalent of Tualen in Java is Semar. The clown-servants are crucial characters in performances. In the folk tradition they are derived from the highest gods. Like the Fool in Shakespeare's King Lear they enjoy 'sanctioned disrespect' whereby they can question and criticise their masters. The servants also act as mediators between the celestial and human spheres.
7   The puppet master, I. Wija, is alluding here (through the servant Tualen) in veiled terms (referred to as *meseseret*) to the corruption in the country: ministers are like ogres who are carried away by their desires and passions. Although President Yudhayono has tried to eradicate corruption, this has proved impossible. Indonesia's judiciary is one of the most corrupt in the world. Learned puppeteers often sprinkle their narrations with critical allusions to situations or people. Generally, adult men in the audience immediately unravel such figurative idioms.
8   It is noteworthy that the Sufi poet Attar once compared the puppets to stars and the sky to the veil (Schimmel 1975: 278).

INDEX

Abadan, 134, 154–7
abadjada, 219
Abbot (K. E.), 316
Abd al-Ghani al-Nabulusi, 221
Abd al-Qadir Maraghi, 172
Abdal, 'of Rum' 170, 175, 318
Abu Zaid, 145
Abyssinia, 138, 140–1, 146, 315
acacia, see: trees, types of
Acintya, 292
Ada Kaleh, Island, 268
Aden, 139, 145
Adrar, 245
afaqih (jurist), see: *mulla*
afarit (spirit), see: spirits, names of
Afghan Turkestan, 190
Afghanistan, 33, 98, 115–26, 190, 310
Africa, XXI, XXIX, 134–5, 138–41, 144–7, 150, 179, 217–9, 226–7, 234
afsun (magic), see: magic
aggregation ritual, see: ritual; initiation
Aghotèle (praying), 187–8
agriculture, agriculturist, 20–1, 98, 115, 323
Ahaggar, 236, 241, 246, 248, 322
ahl-i ashq (people of love), 152
ahl-i hava (people of the Wind), 95, 148–9, 151–3, 158
al-Ahram (newspaper), 221
Aîcha Qondicha, 252
Aïssaoua / Isawiyya, see: Sufi orders

ajän (spirit-master), see: spirits, names of
Ajjer, 241
ajnaly (turning around), 66
Akayev (A.) (Kirghiz president), 85
akli (slave), 241–2
Aksu, 37
Akyazali / Akyazuku, 324
alas (cure or torchlight), see: ritual
alasta (smudging), 52
albasti, albarstï, see: spirits, names of
alchemist, 173
alcı, see: spirits, names of
alcohol, 14, 68, 70, 91, 151, 156, 268, 274, 317
Alevism, XXI, XXIX, 170, 175–6, 180, 192–3, 203–6, 208–13, 262–3, 267, 269, 273, 321; see also: Bektashism
Alevi Bektashi Gençlik Platformu, Istanbul, 294
Algeria, XXIX, 231–54
Ali ben Ali Talib, Imam, see: Islam, and
Ali, Mohammed, 141
aljinnen, see: *jinn*
alkarısı, albasti, albarstï (spirit), see: spirits, names of
Allah, 42, 51, 54–5, 68–9, 69, 72, 120, 219–23, 225–7, 286, 291, 307, 321–2; see also: God
Alliance with a spirit, see: spirit

almasti, see: *alkarısı, albasti, albarstï*
Almaty, 308
al ocaklısı, alcı, see: healer
Alpamish, 171, 209
altered state of consciousness, see: trance
Ambar Ana, see: Sufism
America, 275
Amerindian religion, XXI
Amhara, 315
Amir Kabir, 146
amulet, see: talisman
Anatolia, XXIV, XXVIII–XXIX, 40, 169–73, 175–6, 178–9, 181–3, 185, 188–90, 192, 195, 203, 209–11, 261, 278, 306, 319–21, 324
ancestor, 10–1, 19–20, 67, 81, 83–4, 89, 99, 192, 231, 239, 246, 251, 281–3, 288, 290, 294–5, 297–9, 305, 311, 322; see also: spirit
angel (*melek, maleika, rawhan*), XXX, 42, 81, 121, 123, 137, 178, 220–4, 228, 324
animal, XXIX, 6–10, 12, 34, 38, 48, 51–2, 65, 80, 87–8, 118, 120–1, 124, 126, 173, 204, 209, 211, 223, 226–7, 266, 270, 304, 310, 312–3; see also: spirit
  magnetism, 187
  transformation into an, 6, 8, 48, 51, 87, 120–1, 126, 193, 204–13, 223, 226, 241–2, 250
animals, type of:
  ant, 227
  bear, 304
  bees, 227
  bugra (male camel), 51
  camel, 51, 64, 102, 227, 308
  cat, 250
  chipmunk, 304
  cow, 118, 227
  deer, reindeer, stag, 8, 170, 193, 209, 304
  dog, 33, 152, 190–1, 237, 250
  dromedary, 211
  elk, 8
  faras (horse or possessed person) 147
  fox, 304
  goat, 88, 152–3, 243
  horse, 147, 173, 209, 211
  hyena, 227
  lamb, 118, 124, 270
  lizard, 250
  locust, 227
  mosquito, 227
  moth (*pervane*), 212
  ox, 124
  pig, 270
  ram (*kochkar*), 51, 308
  scorpion, 237, 241
  serpent, snake, viper (*yïlan*), 51, 86, 187, 189, 227, 237, 271, 308
  sheep, 33–4, 64, 67–8, 115, 142, 227, 311, 316, 327
  tarantula, 241
  worm, 189, 227, 272, 320
animism, XXIX, XXX, 99, 246, 282, 289, 298, 324
antinomianism, see: Sufism
Arabs, XXII, XXIX, 47, 115, 117–8, 121, 125, 138–9, 144–5, 179, 181, 187, 231–54; see also: Saudi Arabia
Aqasi, Mirza Haj, 146
Arakelova (V.), 320
arbak (ancestral spirits), see: spirits, names of
arga (mean), see: rite, ritual
Arjuna, 283
Armenians, 173, 187–8, 320
Arnaud-Demir (F.), 211
Aromanian (Vlachs), 271
Arslan-bab, see: Sufism

Index

art, 207, 210, 271, 283–5, 288–9, 313
Artin Pacha (Y.), 142
arvah (soul), see: spirits, names of
asa, see: stick
asa-Musa (stick of Moses), see: stick
asa-tayak, see: stick
asaid (spirit), see: spirits, names of
asceticism, 104–5, 247
ash, 181, 184–6, 189, 319
aşık (lover), see: bard
Aşık Dertli, 171
Aşık Veysel, 193
Asrafil, 223
astrology, astrologist, see: esotericism
Atagen (earth goddess), 99
Attar, see: Sufism
Austrian Empire, 264
Avvakum (Russian archbishop), 304
awliya, evliya (saint), 48, 51, 178, 307
axe, 51, 53
axis mundi, 34–8, 285
ayan (dream, vision), 49, 51–2
Ayinabini, 134
Azerbaijan, XXIV, XXVIII, 169–74, 177, 191–2, 312, 318

bab (Sufi master), see: Sufism
baba (Sufi master), see: Sufism
baba, see: healer
Baba Qambar, 171
Baba Tükles, 50
Babadag, 262, 266
babazar, see: healer
bad, bad-i dib or *div, bad-i jinn, bad-i pari, bad-i qul, bad-i zar* (spirit, wind), see: spirits, names of
Badr (battle of), see: Qur'an
Baghali, 118
Baghdad, 115, 145
Baghirghani, Sulayman, 319
bağlama (a kind of lute), see: musical instruments

Bahrain, 143, 315, 317
Baikal (Lake), 5, 10
bakhshi, see: healer
bakhshibazi, see: healer; ritual
bakıcılık ('the man who foresees'), 178
Bakiyev (K.) (Kirghiz president), 85
baksï, see: *bakhshi*
baksy, see: *bakhshi*
Baku (or Bakou), 268, 325
balger, see: healer
Bali Efendi, 267, 274, 277, 328
Bali Efendi sanctuary, 328
Bali Island, XXX, 281–300
balian, see: healer
balian tapakan, see: medium
Balkans, XXVII, 259–278
Balkh, 115
Baluchistan, Baluch, 95, 99, 144
Bambang Yudhayono, 289
Bandar Abbas, 95, 103, 146–7
Bandar Turkman, 99
banner, see: *tugh*
banning cure, 23
baptism, see: Christianity
baqsi, see: *bakhshi*
bâqum (healing ritual), see: ritual
baraka (blessing), 51, 238–9
Baratayuda war, 283
bard, XXIV, XXVIII, 52, 170–77, 192–3, 208, 310, 318
bargain, 12–3; see also: money
Bashagard, 131–2
Basilov (V.), XXII, XXXIII–VIII, 21, 33, 62, 69–70, 170, 175, 305
Bastani-Parisi (M.), 144
Bastide (R.), 233
bata (blessing), 70, 91
Batinism, see: Islam, and
Batken, 85, 311
Batova Valley, 266
bayu (life-spirit), see: spirits, names of
bean, 309

Bektashism, Bektashi Sufi order, see: Sufi orders
bell, see: musical instruments
belt, 118, 121
benzoin, 220
Berber, 239, 247
Bernus (E.), 323
Bhairava, 283
biat (initiatic pact), see: ritual; initiation
Bibi Fatima, see: Fatima
Bible, 272, 276–7
bid'a (innovation), 89
Bima, 283–4, 287–90, 292–4, 299, 328
Bima Sakti, 299
bio-energy, 87
birds, XXIX, 38, 183, 203–13, 218, 227, 242–3, 285, 305
  migratory, 209–10
  wading, XXI, XXIX, 170, 209–11, 213
birds, types of:
  chicken, 121, 250
  crane (*turna*), XXI, 170, 193, 203–13, 321; see also: dance
  eagle, 64, 211, 305
  goose, 209
  hen, 65, 117, 152, 209
  stork, 209
  swan, 209
  taira, 243
  turkey, 209
Bishkek, 85
Black Sea, 261
Blacksmith, 233, 240, 247, 250
blencong (lamp), 288
blood, 6, 41, 112, 118–9, 121, 148–50, 152–4, 158, 185, 236, 241, 243–4, 249–50, 251–2, 316–7
Boddy (J.), 135–6, 316
body, 6, 10–3, 22–3, 26–7, 32–3, 38, 52, 65, 69, 71, 85–7, 95–6, 101, 104–6, 108–9, 112, 125, 134, 142, 147, 150–5, 158, 185, 189, 191, 227, 235, 242–4, 249–50, 251, 253, 267, 270–2, 287, 305, 313, 317
Bogoraz (V. G.), 303
Boliartsi, 269, 274
bone, XXIX, 6, 33, 71, 236, 270–1, 327
boqimchi, see: healer
Boratav (P.), 187, 190
Borel (F.), 234, 323
Bori Haoussa, 233
bori ritual, see: ritual
Boushihr, 146
Braginsky (V.), 328
Brahman, Brahmanism, XXI, 286
Brahmin, 289
Brazil, 273
bread, 33, 190–1
breath, 48, 67, 69 114, 121, 173, 175, 178, 180–1, 236, 287, 309, 318, 320
bübü, see: healer
Buddhism, XXII, XXV, 25, 49, 61, 99, 282, 329
  Kalacakra, 329
  Lamaism, 25
  Tantricism, 282–3, 329
bugra (male camel), see: animals, types of
bugu-ene (spirit), see: spirits, names of
Bukhara, XXII–XXIII, 90, 262
Buleleng, 290
Bulgaria, Bulgarians, 260–4, 266–9, 273–5, 324
al-Buni, 220
Burh, see: Korkut Ata
Burkut, see: Korkut Ata
Buryat, Buryatia, 4–5, 10, 12–3, 304–5
Bushahr, 146

buta cuwil (demonic spirits), see: spirits, names of
butter, 119
büyücü (magician), see: magic
Byzantine Empire, 265

cafbini (psalmistry), 134
çagur (kind of lute), see: musical instruments
Caillois (R.), 247
Cairo, 142
Çakır (A.), 211
caliph, 100
camel, see: animals, types of
Candia / Candie, 323
candle, 51, 87, 116, 119, 219, 267–9, 277, 324
Caribbean, 226
Casajus (D.), 231, 322
cast system, 289
Castagné (Joseph), 28, 33
Caucasus, 145, 171, 173, 185, 191
cauldron, 41, 67, 178, 306
cem (Alevi meeting), 176
cemetery, 86, 227, 235, 267, 274, 311; see also: death; dead; tombs
Centlivres (M.), 125
Centlivres (P.), 119, 125
Central Asia, XXI, XXII–III
centre, 64, 68, 285, 299
Cerulli (E.), 138
Chabahar, 134
Chaek, 80, 84
changarak (smoke hole of the yurt), see: smoke hole
chant, see: song
charm, see: esotericism
chicken, see: birds, types of
chiltan, chihiltan (spirit), see: spirits, names of
Chimkent, 35
chimneystack, 185
China, XXII, XXVI, 47, 55
Chinese Turkestan, see: Xinjiang

chiromancy, see: esotericism
chorfa (men of letters, religious dignitaries), see: *mulla*
Christianity, XXI–II, 12, 135, 138, 203, 259–60, 263, 265–9, 272–8, 282, 319–20, 324, 328
  Armenian, 320
  Baptist, 275, 277
  and charismatic evangelism, 60, 273–4
  and churches, 136, 266–8, 274, 277, 328
  and cross, crucifix, 266, 269, 324–5, 327
  and the evangelical church, 274, 327
  and the Gospel, 121, 326
  and the Holy Spirit, 276–7
  and Isâ (Jesus), 121, 328
  and John Paul II (the Pope), 269
  and Nestorianism, XXII, 61, 327
  Orthodox, 10, 12, 266, 324, 328
  and Pentecostalism, XXIX, 259, 273–8, 328
  popular, 266–7, 277
  Protestant, neo-Protestant, 259, 273, 277
  and the Roman Catholic Church, 266, 273, 276, 326, 328
  and the Virgin Mary, 269, 325
Chukchee, 304
church, see: Christianity, and
cinci (master of the *jinns*), see: healer
cindar (master of the *jinns*), see: healer
circle, 64, 66–8, 74, 204–5, 207, 213, 237, 271, 309, 313; see also: dance
circumambulation, see: ritual
Clavijo, 173–4
cloth (ribbon), 10, 37, 40, 52, 64, 68, 108–9, 117, 119, 145, 153, 189, 190, 192, 243–4, 266–8, 272, 297, 324

coat, see: shaman
colonisation, colonialism, post-colonialism, 3, 79, 92, 133, 261, 273, 283, 289, 298, 303
colour, 71, 236, 244, 249, 316–7
Communism, 47, 82, 260, 267, 274, 281
concealed objects, see: stolen objects
Constant (C.), 187–8, 320
Constantinides (P.), 141
cosmic mountain, see: nature, and
cosmogony, cosmos, 137, 234–5, 247, 323
Cossuto (G.), 261
cow, see: animals, types of
cowrie-shell divination (*listikhar*), see: divination
craftsmen organisation, see: guild
crane (*turna*), see: birds, types of
Crimea, Crimean, 261
crisis (spiritual, initiatory, psychological or love crisis), see: Illness
cross, crucifix, see: Christianity
cross-road, 178, 190
curandero, see: healer
curse, 81, 191, 235
Cushites, 138
cymbal, see: musical instruments

Daamaar tutan, *damar tutan* (a person who feels the pulse of the sick), see: healer
daf (drum), see: musical instruments
Dah-i Zangiyan, 144
Dakar, 226
dalang (puppet master in Indonesia), see: puppet
dance, XXI, XXIV, XXIX, 51, 55, 64–6, 97, 106, 134, 142, 149, 152–3, 253, 290
  in Siberian shamanism, 8, 37–8
dance, types of:
  animal dance, 170, 203–13

'dance of the Forty' (Kırklar semahı), 211
'Devil dancing', 143
ecstatic round dance, XXIX, 270
halka (dance in circle), 266
oyun (dance, play), XXIX, 24, 170, 204, 206–8, 210–1, 213, 308
perikhun ussuli (dance executed to play the spirits'), 207
possession dance (Algeria), 237–8, 242, 253–4
Qalandar dance, XXIII–IV
raks, 204, 313
raqs-i khanjar (dagger dance), 313
Saint Lazarus dance, 328
sema, semah, sama ([spiritual] audition), 170, 204, 207–8, 210–2, 320–1
turna semahı (dance of the cranes), XXI, XXIX
ussul (in Xinjiang), 207
yeldirme (take flight), 205, 212, 321
Danube, River and region, 261, 268–9, 272
Dâoûd, see: David
David (the Prophet), 121
dâyra (drum), see: musical instruments
dead soul, see: death
death, 9, 11–4, 22, 42, 48, 62, 65–8, 71, 81–2, 84, 90, 122, 124, 151, 209, 227–8, 235, 239, 246, 248, 252, 270–1, 281, 291, 294–5, 305, 317; see also: cemetery
  and cult of the dead or ancestors 19–20
  ritual, see: ritual
  symbolic, 7, 62, 81
  voluntary, 7, 9
dede (Alevi cleric), 176, 212
Deeds (Wyndham), 319
deer, reindeer, see: animals, types of
degdzhush (bloody sacrifice), 41

De Goeje (M.), 140–1
Delaby (L.), 310
Deliorman, 262
Demir Baba, 262, 266, 268, 324
democracy, 289
demon, demonic, XXX, 3, 49, 51–2, 120, 123, 139–40, 142–3, 148–9, 171–2, 192, 222, 250, 281–2, 307–8, 326; see also: *div*
dem-saluu (to blow on a rosary), 87, 92
dendrolatry (cult of the tree), see: trees, types of
Denizli, 181, 319
Derkaoua / Darqawiyya, see: Sufi orders
dervish, see: Sufi brotherhood
Descola (Ph.), XXI
desert, steppe, see: nature, and
dev (spirit), see: *div*
devil, see: demon
devil dancing, see: dance
dewana, see: *dîwâna*
dhikr, *zikir* (Sufi recollection of God), see: Sufism
Dilley (R.), 322
disease, see: illness
div, *dev* (spirit), see: spirits, names of
Divaev (A.), 28, 35
divination, XXIX, 8, 11–4, 18, 60, 64, 72, 138, 179, 217, 219–20, 223–5, 228–9, 263, 270, 309–10, 321; see also: dream; diviner
  and arabic letters, 220
  on sand, 245–6
  with the bone of the shoulder, 270–1
  and healing, XXIV–V, XXIX, 8, 10, 84–5
  and *fal* XXV, 49, 134, 173, 307
  and *ilm al-asrar* ('science of secrets'), 220, 226
  and *kahana*, *kahina* (pre-Arabian soothsayer), XXV, 252
  and *kymalak* (divination with beans or small stones), 64, 72, 309
  with the lead, 181, 191, 272, 278
  and *listikhar / itikhara* (cowrie-shell divination), 218–20, 222–5, 229, 321
  and scapulamancy (divination with a scrapula), XXIX, 311
  and seer, soothsayer, XXV, XXVII–VIII, 3, 59–60, 169, 171, 173, 177, 180–1
  'sleeping', 226
  with stones, 82, 91–2
diviner, see: divination
dîwâna (Qalandar Sufi, demon-chaser), XXIV, 41, 49, 307
Djar (the Cushitic supreme god), 138
Dobrudja (Dobrogea), 260–2, 265–6, 272
doctor (*täwips*, *tabib*, *tabïp*), see: healer; medicine
dog, see: animals, types of
dombra (drum), see: musical instruments
dramatic art, 96, 102–3, 313; see also: shadow theatre
dream, vision, XXI, XXVI, XXX, 51–2, 81, 92, 97, 105, 107, 110–1, 117, 125, 175, 182, 186, 193, 217–29, 239, 246, 252, 268–9, 310–3, 321–2
dromedary, see: animals, types of
drum (*kymalak*, *dombra*, *daf*, *dâyra*), see: musical instruments
du'a (prayer), 51; see also: prayer
duana, see: *dîwâna*
Dubai, 143, 315
Dudoignon (S.), 310
Duff Gordon (L.), 140

dukhtaran-i hava (daughters of air), 152
Dulovo, 268
Durga, 290
During (J.), 69, 73–4
dutar (a kind of lute), see: musical instruments
Dutch, 283, 289, 290, 298, 304
Dykstra (D.), 143, 159
Dzhambul, 33, 191

eagle, see: birds, types of
earth, see: nature
East Africa, 21, 134, 144–6
Eastern Turkestan, see: Xinjiang
ebullience, enthusiasm (*coşluk*), see: trance
ecstasy, see: trance
Egypt, 138–41, 144–145, 221
ehen (tent), 232, 237, 239, 251; see also: yurt
ektraseans, see: New Age
election by the spirits, see: spirits
election-disease, see: illness, initiatory
elk, see: animals, types of
emchi, see: healer
emic / etic, 85, 89, 92, 311
enaden, see: blacksmith
'energy', see: New Age
environment, 13, 24, 26–7, 33, 38–9, 41, 44, 60, 90, 104, 232, 243, 245, 247
epic, XXIV, XXX, 50, 52, 74, 81, 171–3, 175–6, 180, 192, 208–9, 283, 286, 290–2, 310, 318; see also: Alpamish and Manas
epilepsy, see: illness, types of
eren (Sufi), 209
Erzurum, 180
esegelled (elected), 238
Esenel (M.), 178–80, 319
eshan, see: *ishan*

esotericism, esoteric sciences, 180, 219–20, 322
and astrology, astrologist, 191, 221
and chiromancy, palm reading, 263, 270
and geomancy, 218, 246, 273
and magnetism, animal magnetism, 187
and numerology, 221
and physiognomy, 221
and spiritualism, 4, 180, 187
and tarot, 191
essuf (emptiness), 231, 233–9, 241–3, 246–8, 252
Essuk Kingdom, 246
Ethiopia, 135, 138, 142, 150, 315
etic / emic, 85, 89, 92, 311
Evenk, XXII, 5, 9
evil, 12, 22–3, 27–9, 31–6, 50, 51, 59, 63, 71, 73–4, 80, 85–6, 223, 235, 270, 272; see also: spirit, evil
evil eye (*nazar, yaman köz*), 51, 85, 107, 120, 187, 191
evliya, see: *awliya* and saints
ewellmeden (Tuareg confederation in Niger), 242
exorcism, 87, 91, 116–7, 124, 142, 248–9, 277, 288, 315, 317, 319
ex voto, 116, 267, 277
Eyüb el-Ensari, 277

Fadime Ana (Mother Fatima), see: Fatima
Fahd (T.), 221
Fahri Baba (M.), 212
fal, falcı, see: divination
Falasha, 138
falbin, see: healer
falchi, see: healer
falgir, see: healer
faras (horse or possessed person), see: animals, types of possession

Index 339

Faryab, 115
fasting, 105–6, 108, 117
Fatiha (sura of the Qu'ran), see: Qur'an
Fatima (daughter of Muhammad), 181–6, 195, 319
Fatma Ana (Mother Fatma), see: Fatima
Fatma Soummer, 252
feast, see: sacred
fecundity, see: fertility
female, XXVI, 11, 50, 54, 69, 88–9, 91, 95–6, 106, 116, 118–9, 125, 140, 143, 150, 152, 159, 173, 175, 189, 192, 204, 225, 232, 234–6, 238–41, 245–6, 268, 270–2, 295, 311, 313, 329
   and Fatima, female patron of the shaman, 181–6, 195, 319
   slave, 135, 143, 241–2, 250, 253
   Sufism, saint, 134, 252
Ferghana, 79, 90
fertility, infertility, 8–9, 47, 52, 116, 151, 225, 246, 283, 288, 317
fiddle, see: musical instruments
figurine, see: puppet
fire, see: nature, and
fireplace, hearth of healing, 36, 66, 170, 180–1, 185–6, 195, 309, 319
Flaskerud (I.), 134
flesh, 67
folklore, folk tradition and beliefs, XXXV, 47, 49–50, 52, 95, 135, 138, 159, 172, 252, 292, 328–9
food, XXIX, 6–7, 10–3, 51, 67, 71, 178, 235, 246–7, 250–1, 270
foqaha (jurists), see: *afaqih*
forest, see: nature, and
fortune, see: misfortune
fountain, 269

France, 217–229
Franke (E.), 138
French Caribbean, 226
Freud, 221
Frobenius (L.), 138, 141
Fula, 219–20
fundamentalism, see: Islam, and
funeral rite, see: rites

Gabriel (the angel), 184
Gaffary (F.), 140
Gagauz (christian turkophones), 260
Garden of Eden, 266
Garrone (P.), XXII, XXXIV, 190, 193–4
gashtasuz (pot for incense), 149
Geertz (C.), 290
Geklen Turkoman (tribe), 37
genocide, 281
geomancy, see: esoterism
Georgia, Georgian, 324
ghaib (spirit), see: spirits, names of
al-Ghazali, 323
Ghaznavid (dynasty), 98
ghazza (holy war), XXIII
ghoula (ogress), 244–5
Ghuluvv (extremist Shi'ism), see: Islam, and
gift / counter-gift, 6, 8–9, 22, 62, 75, 83, 158, 226, 228, 235, 238, 248, 267, 276, 306
'giving and taking the hands' ritual, see: ritual
globalisation, 133, 282, 289
glossolalia, 276
Gnawiyya Sufi order, see: Sufi orders
goat, see: animals, types of
Gobineau (A. de), 268, 323
God, gods, 39, 48, 51–2, 72, 75, 83, 90, 92–3, 99, 104, 109, 111, 117, 119, 122, 124, 126, 138, 149,

God, gods (*cont.*)
  153, 175, 183–5, 205, 211–2,
  224, 247–8, 274, 277, 283–4,
  286–9, 291–4, 313, 329; see also:
  Allah, sky god and God-Heaven
God-Heaven, 138
Golden Horde, XXIII
Gondar, 142
goose, see: birds, types of
Gospel, the, see: Christianity
Greek religion, XXI, 222
guild (craftsmen organisation),
  XXIX, 181–3, 185, 195
Gumishan, 99
Gunbad Kavus, 99, 313
gumbaz, see: tomb
Günay (Ü.), 180
guvati (cure), 95–6
Gypsies, Manouches, XXIX,
  259–278, 327

Hacı Bektaş, 208
Hacıbektash, 306
hadith, see: Islam, and
hair, 106, 152
Haiti, 272
hajj (pilgrimage to Mecca), see:
  Islam, and
Hakim Ata, XXIII
halka (dancing in a circle), see: dance
Halvetiye Sufi order, see: Sufi order
hamaili (amulet), see: talisman, types of
Hamayon (R.), 83
hammam (bath), 179
Hanafiyya, see: Islam, and
Hanbalism, neo-Hanbalism, see:
  Islam, and
hand:
  'of Ambar Ana' (in Central Asia),
    319
  'of Fatima' 182–3, 319
  in rituals, see: rite, ritual
  as a talisman, see: talisman

handshaking ritual, see: ritual
Harris (J.), 144
Hartaniates (free female cultivator),
  250
Hausaland, 139, 141
Haydariyya Sufi order, see: Sufi order
headgear (of the shaman), see:
  shamanism
healer:
  al ocaklısı, alcı, 192
  baba, 148–55, 157–8
  babazar, 95
  bakhshi, XXV–VII, 17, 38, 48–9,
    54, 101, 116, 125, 169, 183, 189,
    190–1, 193, 305, 307, 312
  bakhshibazi, XXV, 190
  balger, 49–50
  balian, 295
  boqimchi, XXV
  bübü, 50, 54
  cindar, cinci (master of the *jinns*),
    173, 175, 177–81, 190, 193, 208,
    319
  curandero, 4
  Daamaar tutan, damar tutan (a
    person who feels the pulse of the
    sick), 313
  emchi, emchi-domchu, XXV, 49, 189
  falbin, XXV, 134
  falchi, 307
  falgir, 49, 307
  ishan, eshan, XXVIII, 50, 91, 97,
    104–7, 111, 113
  khalifa (also spiritual master), 96,
    118
  közü achïk, köz achïk (open eye),
    XXV, XXVIII, 51, 79–93, 311
  mama, mamazar, 95, 148–58
  ocaklı (man of the fire-place), 170,
    181–93, 319
  ovzan, 312
  oyon (chez les Yakuts), 312
  parikhan, pari-khwan, XXV, 189,
    308

pîr oynata, pirä oynitish, XXV, 50
purkhan, porkhan, XXV, XXVIII, 52, 95–126, 207, 312, 315
rämmal, raml, rammalji, XXV, 134, 318
sheikha, 143
silatigi (also diviner), 226, 228
tabib, tabïp, tabup, täwip (doctor), XXV, 49, 61, 88, 91, 175, 311
tanesmagalt, 241, 252
üfürükçü ('the man who breathes'), 178, 180–1, 318–9
health, 4, 8, 14, 20, 23, 51–2, 55, 63, 68, 80, 82, 84, 118, 174, 183–4, 249, 267, 277, 296, 298, 315
heart, 32, 82, 87, 111, 287, 323
hearth, see: fire place
heaven, see: world
Hell (B.), 61
Helmand, the River, 121
hen, see: birds, types of
herbalism, see: medicine
herding society, see: pastoralism
hereafter, see: nature
heresy, heretic, 268, 276, 324
herpes (*uchuk*), see: illness, types of
heterodoxy in Islam, see: Islam; Sufism
hikma (wisdom), 248
Hinduism, XXX, 282, 290, 295, 299
hoca, hoja (Muslim cleric), see: *khwaja* and *mulla*
Hoggar, 241
Holt (C.), 287
Holy Spirit, the, see: Christianity
Holy Water Religion (Agama Tirta), 290
horse, see: animals, types of
Hungary, 325
hunting, hunter, 6–8, 13–4, 18–9, 38, 139, 142, 191–2, 206, 209, 304–6; see also: spirit
Hurmuz, 145

Hurmuzgan, 131
Hut (tent), 9, 152; see also: yurt

Ibn Abbas, 186
Ibn al-Arabi, 282, 287–8, 294, 325
Ibn Farid, 288
Ibn Sirin, 221
Ibn Taymiyya, see: Islam, and
icazet (authorisation), 181, 186, 191, 248
icheriffen (noble, descendants of the Prophet Muhammad), 240
idn (permission), see: *icazet*
Ienissei Basin, 5, 304
igdalen (wandering religious in Niger), 242
iggulelen (possessed person), see: possession
ikenipke, 5
Ilkhanid dynasty, XXV
Ikhwani movement, see: Islam, and
Ili Valley (Xinjiang), 183
Illness, XXVII–VIII, 25–6, 33–4, 39, 52, 60, 63, 70, 73, 75, 79–82, 86–8, 100–1, 103–5, 112, 116–7, 120, 134–9, 148–51, 188, 217, 234–38, 294
crisis (spiritual, initiatory, psychological or love crisis), 81, 83, 170, 175, 193, 228, 295
initiatory, 3, 81, 183, 189, 236
psychiatric / mental, 312, 317
in Siberian shamanism, 3–5, 9–11, 13, 22–3
Illness, types of:
epilepsy, 49, 86, 238, 268, 303
herpes (*uchuk*), 190, 320
hysteria, 3, 238
puerperal fever, 124
talma (epilepsy), 49, 52, 55
ilm (Islamic teaching), see: Islam, and
Imam (the Twelve Imams), 211–2
Imam Ali, 211
Imam Hasan, 183

Imam Husayn, 183
Imuhagh (Tuareg breeders), 240
imzad (lute), see: musical instruments
incense, 153, 220, 233, 243–4, 249, 298, 317
incantation, magic formula, XXIV–V, 101, 120, 123, 139, 207, 235, 271–2, 313
incubation, 221
India, 123, 144–5, 147, 150, 152, 273, 282–3, 286–9, 290, 295, 299, 310, 329
Indian Ocean, 144–5
Indonesian archipelago, XXI, XXIX–XXX, 281–300
ineslmen (religious men), see: *mulla*
infidelity, infidel, disbelief (*kafar, kafir*), see: Islam, and
initiation, XXVIII, 51–2, 62, 64, 82, 117–9, 124–5, 187, 287, 320
  as aggregation ritual, 186
  as *biat* (initiatic pact), 187
  dream, 52
  and legitimisation, 228
  voyage, 238
  and illness, disease, 3, 81, 183, 189, 236
  by a spirit, 49, 51–2, 70–5
  Sufi ritual, 186–7, 195
initiatory crisis, see: illness, crisis
inspiration, 218
internet, website, 191, 218
invisible world, see: world
Iorga (N.), 267
Iran, XXV, XXVIII–IX, 95, 124; see also: Islamic Revolution of 1978–79
Iraq, XXV
iron, 124–6
Irtysh River, XXIII
Isâ (Jesus), see: Christianity; Jesus

ishan, eshan, see: healer
ishan, eshan, ishanism (Sufi leader), see: Sufi brotherhood
ishanism, see: Sufi brotherhood
Isïk-Köl, 92
Islam, 26, 28, 34–5, 44, 48–50, 54, 60–1, 69–72, 74, 88–90, 92, 103–7, 112, 119–120, 125, 132–4, 147, 195
  disease and healing in, 26, 103–4, 139
  conversion to, and Islamisation, re-Islamisation, XXII–III, 17, 19, 47–8, 50, 75, 79, 91, 99–100, 103, 125, 169, 187, 234, 282–3, 289–91
  heterodoxy in, XXIII, 40–3, 120, 125, 134, 149, 262–3, 266, 273, 290, 306
  orthodoxy in, XXIII, XXVI–VII, 23, 25, 42, 54, 79, 81, 89, 104, 106, 112, 132–3, 149, 177, 323
  popular, local, XXVII–VIII, 49, 59, 116, 120, 132, 134, 169–70, 181; see also: folklore
  prohibitions of, XXIII, XXVI–VII, 34–5, 36, 39, 41–2, 54, 70, 89, 91, 104–5, 125, 132, 134, 172, 221
Islam, and:
  Ali ben Ali Tàlib, Imam, 185, 211–2, 321
  Batinism, 170
  five commandments, 317
  fundamentalism, 53
  Ghuluvv (extremist Shi'ism), 203
  hadith, 322
  hajj (pilgrimage to Mecca), 90
  Hanafiyya, 79, 89, 91, 100, 262, 310
  Hanbalism, neo-Hanbalism, 79, 89, 310, 322

haram (illicit), 221, 315
Ibn Taymiyya, 322
Ikhwani movement, 89
ilm (Islamic teaching), 221
infidelity, infidel, disbelief (*kofr / kufr kafar / kafir*), 86, 147–8, 150, 315
Ismail Bukhari, 184–5, 322
Ismailism, 170
jihad (holy war), 219
jurisprudence, Islamic law, 23, 106, 310
Khadija (first wife of the Prophet Muhammad), 183
la ilaha illallah ('there is no god but God'), 211, 322
madrasa (Islamic school), 90, 107, 226
mosque, 90, 116, 159, 173, 266–7, 269
Muhammad (Prophet of Islam), XXIII, 71, 91, 121, 153, 181–3, 184–7, 195, 211–2, 219–20, 227, 235, 249, 288, 311, 313, 321–2
Musulmanchilik (Muslim tradition), 48
pre-Islamic beliefs, XXV, 23, 25, 42, 47–8, 50, 52–3, 59, 69, 75, 89, 123, 125, 134, 170, 245, 250, 309, 312, 316
proscription of image-making, 284
repent (*tövbe*), 192
revival of Islam, 181
Salafi movement, 89, 229
sayyid (descendant of the Prophet of Islam), 313
secrecy, secret (*sirr*), 224
'shamanised Islam', see: shamanism
sharia, XXIII
Shi'ism, 133–4, 143
shirk (associationism), 221, 229

Sunna, Sunnism, 100, 221–3, 235, 262–3, 310, 312, 318
Tablighi movement, 89, 229
taleb, pl. *tolba* (religious student, Algeria), 235, 240, 245–50
Taleban, XXVIII
Wahhabism, XXVI–VII
waqf, vakf (endowment), 267
Islamic law, see: Islam, and
Islamic Revolution of 1978–79 (in Iran), 106, 133–4; see also: Iran
'Islamised shamanism', see: shamanism
Ismail Bukhari, see: Islam, and
Ismailism, see: Islam, and
Istanbul, 178, 191, 204–5, 277, 319
Italy, 241
izin, see: *icazet*
Izmir (Smyrna), 187

jâdû (wizard, sorcerer), see: witchcraft
jahr (a kind of *dhikr*), see: Sufism
jakhanke (Islamic clerics), see: *mulla*
Jambul, see: Dzhambul
Jamous (R.), 248
jan (soul), 48
janda (a Sufi dress), see: Sufi brotherhood
Jaozjan, 115, 122–3
Japan, 209
jâr, see: *zar*
jar, see: *jahr*
Jarring (G.), 124
Java Island, XXX, 281–300, 329
Jayïl, 80
Jembrana, 290
Jerusalem, 325
Jesus (Isâ), 121, 266; see also: Christianity
Jeti ata ('seven fathers'), 311
Jews, XXVI, 145
Jibril, 223
Jidda, 145

jihad, see: Islam, and
jinn (spirit), see: spirits, names of
jin kapïr, jinn kafir (non-Muslim *jinn*), see: spirits, names of
Jinnedon, 233
jinngiri, 134
jin ooru (the diseases of the soul), 86
Job, Eyyüp sanctuary (Istanbul)
Jogyakarta, 284
John Paul II (the Pope), see: Christianity
Jonas (the prophet), 123
journey, voyage (shamanic journey); see also: shamanism; Sufism
Judaism, XXVI, 145
Juma Khodjiev Namangani, 311
Jumgal, 80, 83
jurist, see: *mulla*

Kabyle, 239
kahana (soothsayer), see: divination
Kahle (P.), 138–9
Kala, 329
Kalacakra, see: Buddhism
Kalalah, 98–9
kam (shaman), see: shamanism
kamarbandî (fasten the belt), 118, 121
kamchï, see: whip
kamlenie, kamalanye (cure), XXII, 24, 28–9
Kanam, 145
Kangirun, 146
Kanitz (F. P.), 266
Kapteijns (L.), 139
kara köz achïk (black sorcerer), see: witchcraft
Karakalpak, 52
karamat, keramet (miracle), see: miracle
Karamurt, 29, 32, 183

Karangasem, 290
Karbala, 134
Karnak, 59, 69
Kashgar, XXII, 314
kasiet (property [of healing]), 82–3, 90, 311
Kasımlı (M.), 172
Kaygusuz Abdal, 175
Kayon (tree of life), see: tree
Kazakhstan, Kazakh, XXII, XXVI–VII, 28, 33–4, 42, 47–56, 59–76, 99, 125, 183, 191, 207, 209, 306–9, 312, 320
Kazalinsk, 28
kazan (cookpot, cauldron), see: cauldron
Kazemipur (A.), 133
kel essuf (spirit), see: spirits, names of
kel ferwen, 322
Kemalism, 175, 180
kemulan (shrine), 297
kendek (umbilical cord), 68
Keramet, see: *karamat*
keşkül (Sufi paraphernalia), 173
Kettledrum (*mudendu*), see: musical instruments
Khadija, see: Islam, and
Khakass, 207
khalifa, see: healer
Khan Mangu, 271
Khant-Mansi, 305
Kharazm, Khwarezm, XXIII, 182, 319
khayal (shadow-play), see: Sufism
khayrât (benediction, thanksgiving), 118, 121
khereg (affair), see: sacrifice
Khidhr, Khadr, 48, 307
Khiva, XXII
Khurasan, 209
khuyag (shaman coat), see: shamanism

khwaja, khoja, hoca (saintly figures or Muslim cleric), 121; see also: *mulla*
Kipchaks, 52
Kïrgïzchïlïk (Kirghiz way), 79–80, 88, 92, 310
Kirghizistan, Kirghiz, XXII, XXVII–VIII, 47–56, 124–5, 189, 307, 311–2
Kirman, 144–5
Kish (island), 145, 147
kiyayi (Muslim scholar)
Kızılbaş, 262
Kïzïl-Oy, 80, 90
Kizilsu (Xinjiang), 38
Kleinman (A. and J.), 298
Klunzinger (C. B.), 140, 142
knife (sacred paraphernalia), 21, 29, 34, 51, 71, 86, 88, 91, 241, 305
Knjazevo, 267
kobiz, kobuz, qobyz (fiddle, viola-like instrument), see: musical instruments
köchür, 52
kofr, kufr (disbelief), see: Islam, and
Kohna Urgench, 193
Köktibie, 64
kol berish (giving the hand), see: ritual
koldoochu arbak, see: spirits, names of
Kondoz, Kunduz, 115
Korawa Brothers, 283
Korkut Ata, 40, 42–4, 171, 185, 193, 306
Köroglu, 171–8, 208–9, 318
Koryak, 304
Kosko (M. M.), 62
közü achïk, köz achïk, see: healer
Kramer (F.), 135
Kshatriya, 289
kuchuru (cure by transfer), see: ritual
külah (Sufi hat), 173
kurban (sacrifice), 269

Kurds, 124
kuugunchu, kuuchu (demon-chaser), 49, 307
kymalak, see: divination
kyt, kut (vital principle, soul), 51–2, 72

la ilaha illallah ('there is no god but God'), see: Islam, and
lake, see: nature, and
Lalla Mimouna, 252
Lamaism, see: Buddhism
lamb, see: animals, types of
Lambek (M.), 135
Langah, 146
Latin America, 272
lead (healing with), 181, 191, 272, 278; see also: divination
le Brun (E.), 142
Lévi-Strauss (C.), 73
Levshin (A.), 28
Lewis (I. M.), 135
Light, 125
listikhar / istikhara (cowrie-shell divination), see: divination
literate, illiterate, 105, 132, 225–6, 229
Littmann (E.), 138
liver, 237, 239
Lob Nor, 36
lohusa, see: *alkarısı*
Lokman, Luqman Hekim (Lokman the doctor), 181–2
Lot-Falck (E.), 124
luck, 3–14, 67, 271, 309–10
lung, 33–6
luqtcha (candle), 119; see also: candle
lute, see: musical instruments
Lutton (F.), 143

MacDonald (D.), 142
Macedonia, 323

madrasa, see: Islam, and
magic, magician, wizard, 112, 124,
    134, 138, 175, 178, 180–1,
    186–7, 220, 226, 241, 244, 250,
    263, 269–72, 287, 290, 308,
    314–5, 318–9, 323
    and *afsun*, 173, 318
    and magic carpet, 287
    and *sihr, sehr*, 244, 314–5
Maghreb, 178, 231–54
magnetism, see: animal magnetism;
    esotericism
Mahabharata, 283, 328
Mahmut Kashgari, XXV
Majapahit, Hindu dynasty, 282, 289
Makal (M.), 186, 189, 319
maleika (spirit), see: spirits, names of
Malov (S.E.), 37
mama, mamazar, see: healer
Manas, manaschï, 50, 52, 81, 171
Mangkunagara (Sultan), 287–9, 291,
    299
Manicheism, XXII
Manouches, see: Gypsies
mantra, 297
marabout, XXX, 217–29, 242, 267,
    321–2
markab (mount, possessed person),
    see: possession
marriage, alliance with a spirit, see:
    spirit
martyr (*shahid*), 48, 50
mashayikh (spirit), see: spirits, names
    of
al-Masudi, 145
mate (of animal), 210
mausoleum of a saint, see: tomb
mazar, see: tomb
Mazdak, 99
meal, 41, 116, 148, 152, 155, 247,
    317; see also: *sufra*
meat, 6–7, 9, 33, 121, 153, 178
Mecca, 22, 54, 71, 86, 90, 141,
    158

medicine, 63, 76, 79–80, 88, 148,
    182, 188, 191, 232, 270, 298,
    309
    alternative, XXVI, 59
    Arab, 234–5
    bio, 322
    Greek, XXI, 182, 234
    man, 4
    and pharmacology, 322
    and phytotherapy herbalism, 178,
        182, 223, 225–6, 234, 240, 243,
        252, 268, 313, 322
    prophetic, 235
    and psychoanalysis, 4, 221, 238
    and psychology, 309
    and psychotherapy, 234, 170, 177
    traditional, 182, 187, 235, 250,
        320, 322
medium, XXX, 23, 108, 112, 133,
    193, 242, 252, 289–90, 295–99,
    311
Merdivenköy, Bektashi convent of,
    see: Sufi brotherhood
Messing (S.), 142
Mevlevi, Mevlevism, see: Sufi
    brotherhood
Meyerhof (M.), 138
Middle East, XXI, 135, 141
milk, 220, 237–9, 243, 251–2
miracle, 61, 104, 173, 231, 248, 259,
    267–76, 315, 319, 325–6
mi'raj, mirac (ascension of the Prophet
    Muhammad); see: Qur'an
'Miraj-nâma' 116
Mir Arab Madrasa, 90
mirror, 311
misfortune, 3–14, 79–80, 82, 85–6,
    137, 217, 223
Miskin Baba, 268, 325
Modarressi (T.), 140–1
modernity, modernisation, 44, 60, 63,
    74, 92, 180–1, 232, 245, 254,
    275, 282, 289, 306
Moghaddam (S.), 142

moldo (Islamic religious), see: *mulla*
Moldova (Bessarabia), 260, 274, 327
monastery, 266–8
money, 8, 14, 108, 147, 224, 297, 310, 324; see also: ritual
Mongolia, Mongol, XXIII, XXV, 14, 40, 47, 112, 124–5, 308
monism, 288, 291, 299
monk, see: monastry
monotheism, 247
Morocco, 233, 246
Moses (the Prophet), 121, 319
mosque, see: Islam, and
Moulay Abdallah, 236
Mouley, 247
mountain, see: nature, and
Muhammad (Prophet of Islam), see: Islam, and
mulla, mollah, ulama (Islamic religious, jurist), 54, 59–60, 71, 79, 89–91, 104, 116, 132, 148–9, 173, 175, 177, 192, 221, 272, 278, 312
   afaqih, faqih, foqaha (jurist), 240, 248
   chorfa (in Algeria), 240, 247–8
   ineslmen (in Algeria), 234, 240, 246, 247–8, 250, 252, 323
   Jakhanke (in Africa), 219
   khwaja, khoja, hoca (in Turkey and Central Asia), 121
   kiyayi (in Indonesia), 290
   moldo (in Central Asia), 79, 90
Murad II (sultan), 171
Mûsa, see: Moses
musafaha (handshaking ritual), see: ritual
Muscat, 143, 146, 157
mushrikun (associators), see: Islam
music, XXII, XXVIII, 41, 69, 73–4, 95–6, 101, 103, 106, 109, 120, 142–3, 149, 152–3, 158, 170–5, 192–3, 204–5, 212–3, 233–5, 240–2, 249, 253, 262, 270, 285, 288, 292, 295, 312–3, 317
musical instruments:
   bağlama (a kind of lute), 294
   bell, 298
   çagur (a kind of flute), 172
   cymbal, 269
   dâyra (drum), 120–1, 123, 314
   drum (*kymalak, dombra, daf, dâyra*), XXI, 9, 29–31, 64, 72, 120, 123, 126, 134, 139, 143, 149, 153–4, 171, 184, 189, 233–4, 272
   dutar (a kind of lute), 101, 103, 109, 171–2
   imzad (a kind of lute), 236
   kobiz, kobuz, qobyz (fiddle), 29, 51, 60, 120, 126, 171–2, 193, 314, 318
   mudendu (kettledrum), 153–4
   percussion, 287; see also: drum
   saz (a kind of lute), XXI, XXVIII, 171–3, 175–7, 193, 204, 208, 213, 321
   tindi (mortar drum), 234–5, 237, 253
muska, see: talisman, types of
Muslims, see: Islam
Musulmanchïlïk (Muslim tradition), see: Islam, and
myth, mythology, XXX, 48, 68, 211, 231, 235, 243–6, 251–2, 283, 286, 289, 291, 296, 299, 307, 322

nadi (altered state of consciousness), see: trance
nail, 32, 283
Naim Bey, Ahmed, 180
Nakula, 283
Naqshbandiyya Sufi order, see: Sufi order
Nalbant, 266
Namangani, see: Juma Khodjiev

Narïn, 85, 91
nationalism, 60
nature, nature cults, 20, 22–8, 32–9, 100, 222–3, 225, 228, 240, 313, 318; see also: tree
supra-, 20, 22–28, 32–9, 43, 306
nature, and:
  cosmic mountain, 285
  desert, steppe, 32, 64, 147–8, 152, 234–5, 245, 247, 266
  earth, 11–12, 14, 33, 67, 99, 116, 123, 125, 147–8, 183–4, 186, 211, 228, 268, 271, 288, 291–2, 309
  fire, 28–9, 36, 66–8, 99, 124–5, 151, 170, 190, 271
  forest, 4–8, 18, 20, 222, 252, 265–67, 293
  lake, 50, 205, 212
  mountain, 32, 121–2, 147, 150, 252, 283, 285, 307, 309, 318
  natural world, 14, 26–8, 242
  rainbow, 300
  sand, 236, 245–6
  sky, XIII, 37, 99, 121, 123, 125, 212, 285, 291–2, 294, 299, 307, 329
  spring, 50, 115–6, 210, 266
  stone, rock, 32, 50, 91, 181, 187, 220, 265–7, 283, 309, 318, 324; see also: divination
  sun, 99, 116, 207, 223, 291
  water, 32, 33, 52, 88, 99, 181, 185–6, 189, 190–1, 249, 266, 268, 270, 272, 287, 290, 292–3, 293–4, 298–9, 304, 319
  weather, XXIX, 8, 270
  wood, 7, 30, 36, 102, 108–10, 116–7, 120, 152, 266, 271, 283
Natvig (R.), 136, 140–1, 315
nazar, see: evil eye
needle, 192
negotiation (with spirits), see: spirits

neo-*bakhsis*, neo-*bakhshi* XXVII, 59–61
neo-shamanism, see: shamanism
neo-Sufism, see: Sufism
neoplatonism, 288
Nestorianism, see: Christianity, and
New age, 44, 60, 180, 191, 193
  ekstrasens, 55
  ektraseans, 84
  'energy' 14, 73, 85, 87, 92, 109
Neyzen Tevfik, 177
Nganasan, 304
Niger, 234, 242, 322
nijasat (uncleanness), 151
Nile, the, 145
Niyazabad, 109
Nöldeke (Th.), 140–1
nomadism, semi-nomadism, XXII, XXIV, XXVII, 5, 10, 19, 21, 28, 30–7, 39, 43, 80, 98, 115, 232, 239, 245, 260–3, 277, 309, 315
North Africa, see: Africa
nuban (spirit), see: spirits, names of
Nubia, 141

Obrotchiste, 266–7
ocakli, see: healer
offering, see: gift
Oghuz, 98–100
ogre, 148, 283–5, 287, 293–4, 329
oil lamp, see: candle
Old Testament, 19, 22
Oman, 143, 146
Omdurman, 141
Öngel (G.), 181
ongon (young wild animal live or carved), 7, 305
open eye, 148; see also: *közü achïk*
oral tradition, see: tradition
Ordam, XXVI
orthodoxy, see: Islam
Orthodox Church, see: Christianity
Osh, 90

Ottoman Empire, XXIX, 145–6, 193, 206, 210, 260–1, 264, 324
Oskoui (M.), 143, 159
Otrar, 307
Oum e sebian (bird spirit), see: spirits, names of
ovzan, see: healer
ox, see: animals, types of
oyon (healer), see: healer
oyun (dance, play), see: dance
oyun, ojun (cure), see: ritual; dance
ozan, see: bard
Ozbek, see: Uzbekistan, Uzbek
Özbek Khan, XXIII
Özergin (K.), 191
Öztelli (C.), 185

paganism, pagans, XXIII, 138, 149, 159, 171, 266, 268, 273, 277, 328
Pakistan, 119
Pamirs, XXII
Pandawa, 283, 293, 296
Pantheism, 285, 288, 291
Pantusov (N.), 183–4
pari, see: spirits, names of
parikhan, pari-khwan, see: healer
Paris, 217–229
Parsi cult, 269
pastoralism, herding society, 5, 10–4, 21, 80, 225, 232, 304
Pavlodar, 63
payment, 5; see also: money
Pejeng, 329
Pentecostalism, see: Christianity
percussion, see: musical instruments
perfume, see: incense
peri, (spirit), see: spirits, names of
perikhun ussuli ('dance executed to play the spirits'), see: dance
Perrin (M.), 225
Persian Gulf, 131–2, 138, 143–7, 159
philosopher, 219

phytotherapists, see: medicine
Pike (K.), 311
pilgrimage, pilgrims, 50, 54, 61, 71, 91, 116, 146, 174, 193, 236, 247, 262, 266–9, 277, 293, 318
pir (Sufi master), 121
Pir Aşık Aydın, 193
pîr oynata, pirä oynitish, see: healer
Pittard (E.), 261–2
plant (use of), 178, 182, 223, 225–6, 234, 240, 243, 252, 268, 322
playing with the spirits, see: spirits
poetry, poet, XXI–II, 74, 148, 170–3, 175, 177, 192–3, 203–7, 209–10, 212, 266, 286–8, 291, 299, 318, 321, 329; see also: epic
pollution, see: purity, impurity
Pomaks, 260–1
pop music, 294–5
popular Islam, see: Islam
porkhan, see: healer
possession, XXIX, 49–50, 61, 69, 73, 85, 112, 150, 233–4, 275, 307, 315, 317; see also: spirit; ritual
cult, XXIX, 142, 159, 315
and *faras* (horse or possessed person), 147
and *iggulelen* (possessed person), 237
and *markab* (mount, possessed person), 147–50, 152, 158
in Siberian shamanism, 23, 26
and *tazengharet* (possession rite), 233–5, 238, 240–2, 253
prayer, 10–1, 36, 44, 51, 70, 74, 90–1, 97, 102, 104, 106, 116–7, 120, 184–5, 187, 210, 218–20, 226, 229, 267–8, 277, 287, 313, 318, 324, 328
pre-Islamic beliefs, traditions, see: Islam, and
Privatsky (B.C.), 61–62
Prophets (of Islam), 125

proscription of image-making, see: Islam, and
Protestant, neo-Protestant, see: Christianity
psychoanalysis, see: medicine
psychotherapist, see: medicine
psychotropic substances, 67
puerperal fever, see: illness, types of
pulse, 313
puppet, figurine, XXX, 7, 11–2, 283–8, 290–2, 295, 299, 328–9
purity, impurity, 125, 221, 235–6, 241, 249–53, 294, 317
purkhan, see: healer

Qadr Night ('night of destiny'), see: Qur'an
Qala Zangiyan, 144
Qalandar, Qalandariyya Sufi order, see: Sufi brotherhood
qalyan (shisha, waterpipe), 151
qam (shaman), see: shamanism
Qanbalu, 145
Qarakh Yaasin (*qarakh Yasin*) ritual, see: ritual
Qarakhanid dynasty, XXII
Qashm Island, 95, 143, 147, 316
qasida ceremony, see: ritual
qaytarma (cure), 24
qobyz (fiddle), see: musical instruments
Qoqand, XXII
Qôreysh, 115
Qur'an, 64, 69, 72, 87, 93, 106, 111, 126, 180–1, 184, 186, 217, 219, 221, 223, 249, 251, 272, 290, 311–3, 321
  and Badr (battle of), 321
  and *Fatiha* (sura of the Qu'ran), 87, 219
  and *mi'raj*, mirac (ascension of the Prophet Muhammad), 39, 116, 184, 211, 321
  and Qadr Night ('night of destiny'), 313
  and Uhud (battle of), 185
  and *Yasin* (sura of the Qu'ran), 313
Qusayr, 140

Rahim (S. I.), 135
Rahmani (M.), 143
rain-making ritual, see: ritual
Rakım (M.), 210
raks, see: dance, types of
ram (*kochkar*), see: animals, types of
Ramayana, 283, 328–9
Ramazân (month of), 116
rämmal, raml, rammalji, see: healer
raqs-i khanjar (dagger dance), see: dance, types of; and *zikr-i khanjar*
Rasanayagam (J.), 134
Rasmussen (S.), 237
rawhan (angel), 220
re-birth, see: ritual
Red Sea, 144–6
Reichl (K.), 173, 319
reincarnation, 68
reindeer, deer, rein, see: animals, types
relic, 266, 269, 324, 326
repentance (*tövbe*), see: Islam, and
Rezaei (A.), 133
rhubarb, 325
rijal al-gayb (the 'Invisible', the 'Hidden'), see: *chiltan*
ring, see: circle
Rio del Oro, 246
risala (manual of a guild of craftsmen), 183, 185
rites, 11, 18–20, 61, 63, 64, 66–9, 71, 74, 116, 136, 268, 270, 277–8

community, 44
funeral, 6, 86
pre-Islamic, 50, 125
of passage, 231, 237, 252, 283
ritual, XXI–II, XXX, 13–4, 24, 32, 34, 36–7, 39, 41–2, 44, 48–9, 51–2, 54–5, 61, 63–8, 71, 73–5, 79–81, 84, 86–9, 96, 100, 102–3, 106–10, 112, 124, 132, 135–8, 149, 153, 170, 183–4, 187, 193–5, 223, 234, 267, 276, 310, 313, 316
  adoption, 268
  African, XXX
  aggregation, 186
  alas, 118, 190, 320
  and *bakhshibazi* ('playing of the *bakhshi*'), 190
  bâqum healing, 124
  and *biat* (initiatic pact), 187
  bori, 138, 141
  and circumambulation, 116, 183–4, 207
  collective, XXXVI, 7–10, 12–3, 44, 54, 63, 231, 233
  death, 281, 294–5
  of 'giving and taking the hands' 186–8, 195, 319–20
  and hand, handshaking (in ritual), 35, 37, 64, 66–7, 87, 95–6, 102, 106, 109, 112, 117, 119, 120, 179, 181–3, 186–8, 190, 193–5, 209–11, 220, 253, 271, 328
  healing, XXIII, XXVI, 18–9, 31, 37, 42, 84, 104, 119–23, 135, 170, 181, 189–91, 236, 260, 264–9, 275, 277
  initiation, see: initiation
  and *kursç un dökme*, 181, 191, 272
  and laying on of hands over the sick, 328
  money, 297
  Muslim, XXIV, XXIX, 22, 89, 106, 108, 120, 134, 228–9, 235
  and *oyun*, *ojun* (play, game), XXIX, 24, 51, 55, 320
  possession, see: spirit
  and *qasida* ceremony, 190
  rain-making, 328
  and reading of the sura *Qarakh Yaasin* / *qarakh Yasin*, 313
  and re-birth, 68, 181
  of 'pouring molten lead'
  of 'pouring the sweet fruit drink' (*şerbet dökmek*), 178
  of 'shaking the hands' (*musafaha*), 187
  shared, XXI, XXIX, 50, 70, 240, 269, 289, 299
  of the shovel, 124–5
  Siberian shamanic (seance), XXV, XXVIII, XXXVII, 3–5, 7–14, 119, 178, 189, 207, 303
  Sufi, XXIV, XXVII, XXX, 50, 186–7, 195; see also: Sufism and Sufi brotherhood
  and tarantula (possession ritual), 241
  and transfer (cure, ritual by transfer), 23, 33–5, 52, 87–8, 108–9, 125, 147, 154, 187, 189–91, 193–4, 320
  and *zahal* (repair [ritual]), 11, 13
Roma, see: Gypsies
Romania, Romanian, XXIX, 260–4, 266, 271, 273–5, 327
rope (sacred paraphernalia), XXVIII, 37, 52, 102–3, 108–9
rosary (*tasbih*, *tespe*), 84, 87–8, 173
Rouget (G.), 69
ruh, *arvah*, *rowahin* (soul, spirit), see: spirits, names of
Ruino, 262
Rumi, Mawlana Jalal al-Din Rumi, 287–8
ruqiya, *roqia* (exorcism), 229, 248

Russian Empire, 261, 264, 269, 303–4, 305, 320

Sabena, 322
sabre, see: knife
sack (sacred paraphernalia), 101–2, 108
sacredness, 88, 116, 134, 195, 203–4, 206–8, 209–10, 212, 240, 243, 246, 249, 251, 254, 299
sacred:
 objects, XXVIII, 99, 181, 186, 189, 267, 324
 feast, 33, 41, 247, 274, 324
 place and space, 26, 51, 54, 89, 105, 139, 233–4, 247, 264–9, 296, 319; see also: tomb
 words and formulas, 64, 92, 235, 238, 323
sacrifice, XXI, 12, 34, 41, 86, 88, 118, 121, 124, 137, 142, 149, 152–3, 220, 234, 241, 250, 268–70, 316–7, 321, 328
sadaqa (sacrifice / charity, alms-giving), 220, 321
Sa'dan Toraja, 300
safi, see: *ahl-i ashq*
Saguiet el Hamra, 246
Sahadewa, 283
Sahara, XXIX, 145, 231–54
Sa'idi (G. H.), 131–2, 143, 146–8, 150
saints, sainthood, XXIV, XXX, 19, 48, 51–2, 89, 91, 104, 116, 120–3, 123, 171, 178, 180, 183, 188, 211, 245, 247–8, 252–3, 262, 266–9, 273, 277–8, 282–3, 307, 311, 324–6, 328
Saint Elijah, Elias, 267, 324
Saint George, 269, 324
Saint Lazarus dance, see: dance
Saint Nicholas, Nicolas, 267–9, 325
Saint Panteleimon, 266
sakti (healing powers), 283

Salafi movement, see: Islam, and
Salcı (V. L.), 208
saliva, 241, 251
Salkh, 316
Salman Farisi, 211, 321
Samangan, 115
Samanid dynasty, XXII, 98–9
Samarkand, XXII, 33
Samb (Dj.), 221
Samoyed, 304
sand, see: nature, and
Sang Suksma, 286
Sanneh (L. O.), 219
Sar-e Pol, 115
Sardan (J.-P. de), 304
Sarıkamış, 176
Sari Saltuk, 262
Sasanid (dynasty), 144
Satan, see: *Shaytan*
Saudi Arabia, XXVII, 90, 115, 143–4, 147, 150
Sayram, 307
sayyid (descendant of the Prophet of Islam), see: Islam, and
Sayyid Ata, XXIII
saz (a kind of lute), see: musical instruments
scapulamancy (divination with a scrapula), see: divination
scarf, veil, 106, 110, 119, 158, 189, 288, 329
scent, see: incense, perfume
Schimmel (A.-M), 289
seance, see: ritual
secrecy, secret (*sirr*), see: Islam, and
sedentary, 21, 27, 29, 31–3, 39, 115
seer, see: divination
Seligman (B.), 139, 141
Seljuk (Turkish dynasty), 98–100, 171
Selkup, 5
sema, semah, sama ([spiritual] audition/dance), see: dance

semadi (state of concentration), 287
Senegal, 218, 221, 229
Senegal River, 225
Senegambia, 219, 221
Serbia, Serb, 271, 276, 278, 325, 328
serpent, see: animals, types of
sexuality, XXVI, 11, 137, 233, 242–3, 246, 250, 252–4
shadow theatre (*wayang kulit*), 74, 281–300
al-Shahi (A.), 139
shahid (martyrs), 50
'shaking the hands', see: ritual
shaman, see: shamanism
shamanism,
    and coats (*khuyag, zebseg*), 11, 118–9, 305
    and headgear, 8, 305
    'Islamised' XXII–VI, XXXIV, 18, 20–2, 43–4, 169, 170–1, 305
    and journey, voyage (shamanic journey), XIII, 26, 37, 39, 42, 49, 65, 75, 125, 184, 231, 233, 238, 240, 294, 299, 305–6, 310
    neo-, 59–60
    and *qam / kam* (shaman), XXII, XXV, 312
    and shaman (the word), XXV, 312
    and 'shamanised Islam' XXVII, 43–4
    and weapon, 305
sharia, see: Islam, and
shaykh, sheik (Sufi leader), see: Sufi brotherhood
Shaykh Bidak (a *zawiyya* in Cairo), see: Sufi brotherhood
shaytan, sheytân, sheyâtûn (spirit), see: spirits, names of
Sheberghan, 121
sheep, see: animals, types of
sheikha (female healer), see: healer
shifa (healing power), 51

Shi'ism, see: Islam, and
Shiraz, 134, 145
shirk (polytheism), see: Islam, and
Shiva, Shivaism, 269, 284, 329
shoulder, 270
Siberia, XXI, XXII–III, 3–14, 18–27, 32, 34, 36, 38–9, 44, 48–9, 52, 61, 124–5, 178–9, 206, 209–11, 272, 275, 304–6, 319
sickness, see: illness
sihr, sehr, see: magic
silatigi, see: healer
Silistre, 262
silsila (Sufi genealogy), see: Sufism
sir, sirr (secret), 248; see also: Islam, and
Sir-darya River, 21, 28, 44, 50, 307
Siraf, 145
Sistan, 95, 316
Sivas, 175, 182, 192
skull, 33, 120
sky, see: nature, and
slave, slavery, 132, 143–6, 159, 233, 241–2, 249–50, 253–4, 273, 316, 322
smoke-hole, 9, 34–5, 37–8
Smyrna, see: Izmir
snake, viper, see: animals, types of
Snesarev (G. P.), 190
Snouck Hurgronje (C.), 139, 141, 143, 153
soap opera, 295
Sofia, 267
Softa Baba, 262–3
Sogdiana, 59
Solomon (King), 245
Somalia, 150
song, XXII, XXIV, 12, 28, 32, 35, 41, 50–1, 66–7, 101, 109, 120, 134, 139, 143, 148, 152, 154, 158, 170–2, 174–6, 205, 211, 213, 234, 238, 241–2, 253, 270, 272, 276, 281–2, 286, 291, 297–8,

song (cont.)
304, 313, 317, 319, 300, 321, 327
sorcery, see: witchcraft
soucougnan (night-travellers, sorcerer), see: witchcraft
soul (of the dead), 125
South America, XXI, 4
Soviet Union, XXXIV–VI, 4–5, 12, 17, 54–6, 60–3, 80, 88, 90, 303–4, 310–2
spatula (sacred paraphernalia), 102–3, 109
Spaulding (J.), 139
spell, see: incantation
spirit, XXV–VI, 28, 48–51, 62, 66, 79, 82–7, 99–100, 117, 119, 134, 137, 140, 150–1, 155–7
  alliance, marriage with a, XXVI, 8, 84, 238, 246, 249–50, 252–3, 270
  of the ancestor, XXVI, XXX, 81, 83, 89, 99, 141, 192, 281–3, 288, 290, 294–5, 297–9, 305, 311, 322
  animal, 5–10, 48, 51, 87, 121, 193
  cult, XXIX
  evil, demonic, 22–3, 27–9, 32, 34–6, 39, 51, 71, 87, 91, 95–6, 108–9, 121, 125, 142, 147, 173, 170, 173, 183, 270–1, 281–2
  helper, helping, protective, XXIV, XXVI, 23, 27, 32, 35, 37–8, 41, 50–2, 69–70, 72–5, 117, 121, 123–6, 183, 308
  hunting, chasing a, 139, 142, 191–2, 270
  initiatory, 71
  possession, XXV, 131, 133–7, 139, 142, 150, 159, 178–9
  tutelary, 82–3, 88
  world, see: world
spirits:
  call from the, 81, 117, 126
  election by the, XXVI, XXXVI, XXXVIII, 25, 35, 55, 81–4, 86, 137, 184, 238, 276
  expulsion of, 28–31, 39, 125, 173, 177–8, 185, 246
  fight with the, XXV, XXVIII, 18, 70–1, 87, 120, 125, 177, 185, 191–2, 219, 226–8, 271, 305
  mediation with the, XXVIII, 84, 170, 190, 208, 221, 228, 247, 295, 329
  negotiation with the, XXV, XXVIII, 12, 86, 90, 169–70, 185, 236, 250, 305
  offering to the, XXIX, 6, 8–9, 178, 190
  playing with the, 125, 169, 184, 190, 206–9, 213
spirits, names of:
  afarit, 248–9
  ajän (spirit-master), 123
  alkarısı, albasti, albarstï (Central Asia, Turkey), 51, 86, 123–4, 179, 191–2, 308, 311, 319
  arbak (ancestral spirits), 82–7
  asaid, 139
  bad, bad-i dib or *div, bad-i jinn, bad-i pari, bad-i qul, bad-i zar* (wind) (Iran), 148
  bayu (life-spirit), 293
  bugu-ene, 48
  buta cuwil, 282
  chiltan, chihiltan (Central Asia, Iran), 48, 183–4, 319
  div, dev, XXX, 51, 179, 147–8, 179, 308
  ghaib, 48
  ibakaten trees ('spirit trees'), 252
  jin kapïr, jinn kafir (non-Muslim jinn), 86
  jinn, XXVIII, XXX, 23, 26, 35, 51, 65–6, 69–71, 86, 90–1, 101, 103, 105–9, 111–2, 117–9, 121–5,

134, 140, 148, 151–2, 170, 173, 175, 177–81, 185, 190–94, 207–23, 225–6, 227, 235, 236, 246, 248–9, 307–8, 313, 315–7, 319, 321–2
kel essuf (Algeria), 231, 233, 235–8, 241–2, 246, 248, 252, 322
koldoochu arbak (Kirghizistan), 82–3
maleika, 220, 223
mashayikh (Iran, Persian Gulf), 146, 148
nuban, 146, 148–9
Oum e sebian (bird spirit), 242–5
peri, pari, XXX, 51, 121, 147–8, 175, 178–9, 191
ruh, arvah, rowahin, 48, 52, 248
shaytan, sheytân, sheyâtûn, 86–87, 120, 124, 171, 190
Umay-ene (spirit of fertility), 47, 52
wind (*bad*, Iran), 81, 95–6, 99, 146–53, 158, 223, 293
yel-mawïz, yel-moguz, 51, 308
zar, XXIX, 131, 135–43, 149–59, 314, 316
spiritualism, 4, 92, 180; see also: medium
spit, 28, 52, 66, 68, 88, 180, 184, 186, 226, 253, 271; see also: saliva
spring, see: nature, and
stag, see: animals, types of
Stahl (P.-H), 266–7
steriel (ogress), 245
sterility, see: fertility
stick (sacred paraphernalia), 51, 152, 157, 173, 267, 308, 327
stolen objects, concealed objects, 80, 118, 178–9, 312, 319
stolen soul, 12, 42, 125
stomach, 185, 237, 239
stone, rock, see: nature, and
stork, see: birds, types of
storyteller, 30, 52–3, 285, 310

Strelcyn (S.), 138
Struga, 324
Stutterheim (W. F.), 283
subterranean world, see: world
Sudan, 139, 141, 145, 178, 241
Sudra, 290
Sufi brotherhoods, 40–3, 79, 81, 91, 100, 169, 173, 233, 246, 262, 323–4
and dervishes, XXVIII, 40, 67, 172–5, 177, 192, 208, 266, 268
and *ishan, eshan, ishanism* (Sufi leader), 91, 306, 313
and Merdivenköy, Bektashi convent of, 204, 321
and *shaykh, sheik* (Sufi leader), 23, 89, 186, 212, 262, 266
and Shaykh Bidak (a *zawiyya* in Cairo), 142
and *tariqa, tarikat, turuq* (initiatic path), XXIX, 186–9, 195, 289
and *tekke*, see: *zawiyya*
and *zawiyya / zaviye* (Sufi lodges), 142, 204–5, 245
Sufi orders:
Aïssaoua / Isawiyya, 324
Bektashism, XXI, XXIX, 170, 175, 180, 192–3, 203–4, 206, 208–9, 210–13, 261, 266–8, 306, 321
Derkaoua / Darqawiyya, 324
Gnawiyya, XXIX
Halvetiye, 262, 324
Haydariyya, 40
Mevlevism, 208
Naqshbandiyya, 91, 100, 262, 306–7
Qalandariyya, XXIII–IV, 40–2, 170, 173–5, 306
Tijaniyya, 225
Yasawiyya, XXIII, 40–41
'Sufised shamanism', see: Sufism
Sufism, XXI, XXIII–IV, XXVIII–XXX, 40–3, 50–1, 59–61, 63–5, 67, 69, 73–5, 89,

Sufism (*cont.*)
91, 100, 134, 170, 172–3, 220, 282–4, 289, 291, 295, 312, 323, 328; see also: Baghirghani; Hacı Bektaş; Hakim Ata; Ibn al-Arabi; Ibn Farid, initiation; Rumi; Sayyid Atta; Zangi Ata; Yasawi
and Ambar Ana, 319
and antinomianism, XXIII, XXIX, 170, 173, 203, 318, 320
and Arslan-bab, 50, 307
and Attar, 329
and *bab* (master, leader), 307
and *babas* (Sufi masters), 269, 307
and *dhikr, zikir* (Sufi recollection of God), XXIV, 50, 51, 63–7, 69, 73–5, 105–6, 140, 193, 195, 307, 312
heterodox, 305–6, 318
and *ittihad* (union with God), 247
and *jahr* (a kind of *dhikr*), 50–1, 307
and *janda* (a Sufi dress), 40, 42
and journey (of the Sufi), 305–6; see also: *mi'raj*
and *khayal* (shadow-play), 288
neo-, 59–60
and *'safar dar vatan'* (journey into the self), 306
and Sufi lineage, Sufi genealogy (*silsila*), 182
and 'Sufised shamanism', 43, 169–70, 195
and *suwar* (shadow-image), 288
and *wahdat al-wujud* (unicity of being), 329
sufra (votive meal), 148, 152, 155, 158
sugar, 70–71
Suharto, President, 281
Sukhareva (O.A.), 33, 183
Sulawesi, 281, 300

Sulayman (mountain), 307
Sultan Mahmud, 98
sun, see: nature, and
Sunna, Sunnism, see: Islam, and
superstition, 95, 116, 175, 180, 327
supranature, see: nature
sür, sünesün (vital principle)
Surakarta, 284, 287, 291, 299
suwar (shadow-image), see: Sufism
swan, see: birds, types of
sword, dagger (sacred paraphernalia), 21, 28, 102, 108–110, 192, 236–7, 327
symbolic world, XXVIII, 79–81, 83, 85, 88–9, 92, 310, 312
symbolism, symbols, XXI, XXVI, XXVIII–IX, 18, 20, 29, 33–4, 36–7, 38, 41, 51, 62, 66, 68, 71–3, 79–81, 83, 85–6, 88–9, 92, 95–6, 101, 108–9, 117–9, 169, 183–4, 187, 189, 211–2, 224, 232, 234, 239, 247, 310
syncretism, XXIII, XXVI, 17–44, 170, 203, 211, 233, 260, 264, 266, 268–9, 273, 276, 278, 283, 323
Syria, 144

taba'â (pursuer), 245
Taberket, 242, 244
tabib, tabïp, tabup, täwip, see: healer
Tablighi movement, see: Islam, and
taboos, 22, 233, 250
tademekkat, 246
tafilelt, 246
tagahant (seer), 234, 245–6
Tahtacı (Turkish nomads), 208, 210
taira, see: birds, types of
tajdid, 219
Tajikistan, Tajiks, XXIV, XXVII, 21, 30, 31–3, 50, 125, 183, 189, 207, 320

Takema, 322
Takhar, 115
Takiya Baba (shrine), 108, 111, 313
Taldykorgan, 59, 63 308
taleb, pl. *tolba* (religious student), see: Islam, and
Taleban, see: Islam, and
talisman, 44, 124, 137, 191, 217, 220, 227–8, 249, 318, 320
talisman, types of:
   hamaili (amulet), 268
   'hand of Ambar Ana' (in Central Asia), 319
   'hand of Fatima', 183
   muska (in Turkey), 173, 178, 319
   tawiz, 116
   tirawt (in Algeria), 235
   tumar (in Central Asia), 312
   'white hand of Moses' (in Algeria), 319
talma (epilepsy), see: trance; illness, types of
Tamanrasset, 234, 240, 242–5, 247
Tamerlane, 115, 174
tanesmagalt, see: healer
Tängeri (sky god), 99
Tantricism, see: Buddhism
Tanyu (H.), 319
Taranchi, 183
tarantula (possession ritual), see: ritual; animals, types of
tariqa, tarikat, turuq (initiatic path), see: Sufi brotherhood
Tashkent, XXVII, 41
Tash-Qorghan, 125–6, 189–90
Tatars, 184, 260–2, 273, 319
täwip (doctor), see: healer
tawiz, see: talisman, types of
tazengharet (possession rite), see: rites
tekke (Sufi lodge), see: Sufi brotherhood
Tengrism, 48

tespe, see: rosary
theatre, see: shadow theatre and dramatic art
theology, theologian, XXIV, 89, 104, 221–2, 246, 266, 310, 312
therapy, see: medicine
Tian-Shan, XXII
Tijani, Tijaniyya Sufi order, see: Sufi order
tiklatin (female slave), 241–2, 250, 253
Timbuktu, 246
Timimun, 245
tindi (mortar drum) see: musical instruments
Tin Hinân, 322
tirawt (instruments sacred writing), see: talisman, types of
tobacco, smoking, 70, 274
tolba, see: *taleb*
tomb, mausoleum of a saint (*türbe, mazar, ziyara*), XXVI, XXX, 42, 50, 89, 105, 108, 111, 116, 122, 159, 175, 178, 181, 187, 193, 227, 236, 245, 247, 262–5, 266–7, 277–8, 311–2, 325
torchlight, see: *alas*
totemism, 99–100
tourism, 262, 290
tradition, XXIV, XXIX–XXX, XXXV, 3, 5, 17, 26, 47–51, 53–6, 59, 60–3, 72–5, 80, 88–9, 92–3, 109, 115, 118, 123, 125, 134, 136, 138, 141, 149, 152, 170–1, 173, 175, 179–80, 181–2, 184–7, 190–1, 193, 195, 203, 208, 211–3, 221–2, 224–5, 231–54, 261, 264, 267, 269, 273–7, 282, 290–2, 295–6, 307–8, 311, 313, 319–22, 329; see also: folklore
   matrilineal, 232, 238–9
   oral, XXII, 141, 185, 203, 224–5, 229, 231, 322

traditional medicine, see: medicine
trance, XXI, 49–53, 69, 73, 120, 126, 136, 142, 149, 158, 233, 236–8, 242, 249, 253, 275, 277, 295–7, 315
  and altered state of consciousness, 73, 135, 295, 315
  and ebullience, enthusiasm (coşluk), 212, 319
  and ecstasy, XXIII, 20, 50, 96, 101–2, 111, 136, 140
  and ecstatic round dance, XXIX, 203–8, 213, 238
transfer (cure, ritual by transfer), see: ritual
transformation into an animal, see: animal
transgression, 10–11, 232–3, 239, 248, 250, 254
Transylvania, 267, 325
tree, 50, 116, 183, 265–8, 277
  cult of the, 170
  and dendrolatry (cult of the tree), 266–7, 277, 324
  and forests, 4, 5–8, 18, 20, 221–2, 252, 265–7, 293
  of life, XXX, 266, 286, 292
  world, 285
trees, types of:
  acacia, 268
  atil, agar (tree, home of the spirits), 243
  cosmic tree of life, XXI, XXVIII, 286, 292, 299
  doki, 220, 222
  ibakaten ('spirit trees'), 252
  lime, 266
  mulberry, 268
  oak, 266–7, 324
  palm, 238
Tsarist Russia, see: Russian Empire
Tuareg, 231–54, 322

tugh, tug, tuu (banner, flag, rope), 36–8, 52, 55, 183–4
Tulcea, 266
tumar, see: talisman, types of
tunduk (piece of felt in the 'smoke hole' of a yurt), 35–6
Tungus, Tunguz, XXII, 3, 305, 310, 312
türbe, see: tomb
Turkestan (the region), XXIV, XXV, XXVI, 52, 59, 69
Turkey, XXI, XXVIII, 169–95, 203–13, 262, 274–5, 319–20
turkey, see: birds, types of
Turkistan / Türkistan (the city), 307, 309
Turkman, Turkmen, XXVIII, 28, 37, 52, 95–113, 125, 184, 193, 207, 265, 273, 312–3
Turkman Sahra, XXVIII, 95–126, 312–3, 315
Turkmenistan, XXIV, 17, 98, 170–1, 193
turna semahı (dance of the cranes), see: dance and crane
Turner (V.), 294
Tutrakan, 262, 269
tuu, see: *tugh*
Tyumen, XXIII

uchukta- (spitting water), 52
üfürükçü ('the man who breathes'), see: healer
Uhud (battle of), see: Qur'an
Ukraine, 260
ulama, see: *mulla*
Umay-ene (spirit of fertility), see: spirits, names of
underworld, see: world
unguent (*ma'jun*), 152
Upanishads, 286
Ura Tepe / Uratyube, 31–2
urasa, see: healer

urey, üröy (soul), 52
urf u 'ada (customs), 89
urine, 241, 243–4, 251
ussul, see: dance
ustat, ûstâd (master), 118
usturlab, 134
Uyghur, XXVI, 50, 52, 125, 184–5, 207, 308; see also: Xinjiang
Uzbekistan, Uzbek, XXVII, 21, 29, 32–3, 50, 52, 79, 89, 115, 123, 119, 123, 125–6, 175, 189

Vaishya, 289
Vedanta, XXX, 286
veil, see: scarf
Velayetname (Turkish epic), 209
Virgin Mary, the, see: Christianity
vision, see: dream
vital force, vital principles, 5–6, 8, 13, 20, 67, 72, 209, 293
Volga, XXII, 209
Voodoo, 273
voyage (of the shaman), see: journey

wading birds, see: birds, types of
wahdat al-wujud (unicity of being), see: Sufism
Wahhabism, see: Islam, and
wali, see: saints
Wali songo (nine saints), 282
Walker (J.), 140
water, see: nature, and
wax, 191
wayang kulit, see: shadow theatre
weapon, see: shamanism
weather, see: nature, and
well, 266–7
West Africa, see: Africa
Western Turkestan, see: Turkestan
whip (sacred paraphernalia), 28, 51, 70–1, 86, 88, 91, 108, 120–1, 305
wick (sacred paraphernalia), 121

Williams (P.), 275
wind (spirit), see: spirits, names of
witchcraft, 3, 50, 51, 79, 85, 180, 226–7, 241–2, 248–51, 265, 270, 282, 309, 314–5, 328
and *jâdû, jadugari*, 124, 314–5
and *kara köz achïk* (black sorcerer), 309
and soucougnan (night-travellers, sorcerer), 226, 228
Wlislocki (H. von), 270, 273, 325
women, see: female
world (in shamanism), XX, XXVIII, 3–4, 14, 20, 22, 34–9, 65–6, 68, 71, 74–5, 112, 117, 185, 209, 212, 223–4, 226, 228–9, 233–4, 238, 240, 313, 242–3, 246–7, 251–2, 278, 285–6, 287–8, 290–1, 294–5, 299, 304, 306–7, 310, 312; see also: nature symbol
cosmogonic, 247
and heaven, 20, 25, 183–4, 222, 281, 294, 300, 307, 313
human, 67, 71, 307
immanent, transcendent, 223, 286
invisible, XXVI, 79–93, 184–5, 192, 207, 223, 225–6, 228, 234, 236, 238, 240, 243, 245–52, 254, 291, 307, 319, 323
material, 26, 212
middle, 285
mythic, mythological, 30, 286, 299
spirit, spiritual, 48, 51–2, 137, 224, 243, 290, 295
supernatural, 20, 24, 26, 32, 37, 79, 83, 86, 111, 117, 134, 234–5, 238, 240, 243
subterranean, under-, 148, 285, 294
visible, 246, 288
World Bank, 80
worm, see: animals, types of

Xinjiang, XXIV–VI, XXIX, 37–8, 43, 55, 125, 183, 185, 190, 193, 207, 209, 314

Yakut, Yakutians, 186, 206–7, 209, 312
yaman köz, see: evil eye
Yasawi, Ahmad, 50, 308
Yasawiyya Sufi order, see: Sufi orders
Yasi, 308
Yasin (sura of the Qur'an), see: Qur'an
yawn, 84, 187
Yazidi, 320
yeldirme (take flight), see: dance, types of
yel-mawïz, yel-moguz (spirit), see: spirits, names of
Yemen, 212
yethaouel (transformation), 236, 249
yilan (snake), see: animals, types of
Yıldız (C.), 204, 321
Yıldızeli district, 182
Yudhayono (President), 329
Yudistira, 283
yunani, Greek medicine, see: medicine
Yurt, 34–5, 37–8, 68, 116, 309
Yürük (Turkish nomads), 208, 210, 261, 267; see also: Alevi

Zabuli, 103
zahal (repair [ritual]), see: ritual
Zaman (newspaper), 320
Zangi Ata, 319
Zangiabad, 144
Zanzibar, Zanzibar coast, 145–6, 150
zaouïa, see: *zawiyya*
zauberfrauen (Gypsy female magician), 270
zaviye, see: Sufi brotherhoods
zar (spirit), see: spirits, names of
zâra (to visit), 139–40
Zara, 140
Zarcone (Th.), 267
zârt, zârit, see: *zar*
zawiyya / zaviye (Sufi lodge), see: Sufi brotherhoods
zebseg (shaman coat), see: shamanism
zenghi, see: Gypsies
zikir (healing ritual), XXIV, 61, 63–7, 69, 73–5
zikr, see: *dhikr*
zikr-i khanjar (also *raqs-i khanjar*), 97
Zile, 181
ziyara, ziyarat, ziara, zîârat (pilgrimage), see: tomb; pilgrimage
Zoroastrian, Zoroastre, XXII, XXVI, 59–61, 99, 203, 312
Zwemer (S.), 140

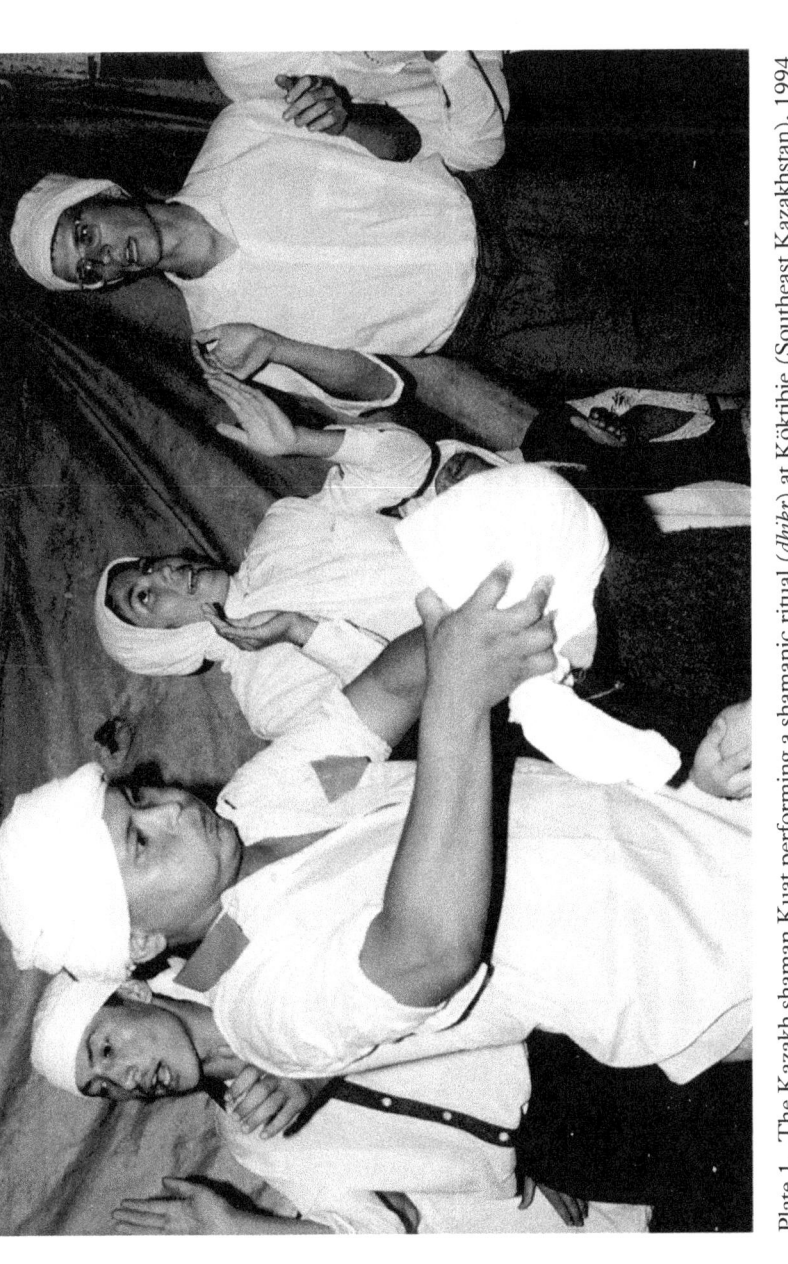

Plate 1. The Kazakh shaman Kuat performing a shamanic ritual (*dhikr*) at Köktibie (Southeast Kazakhstan), 1994 (Photograph: A.-M. Vuillemenot).

Plate 2 Spirits with bull heads praying, from 'Ajaib al-Makhluqat', fifteenth century (Archives Mazja And Istanbul)

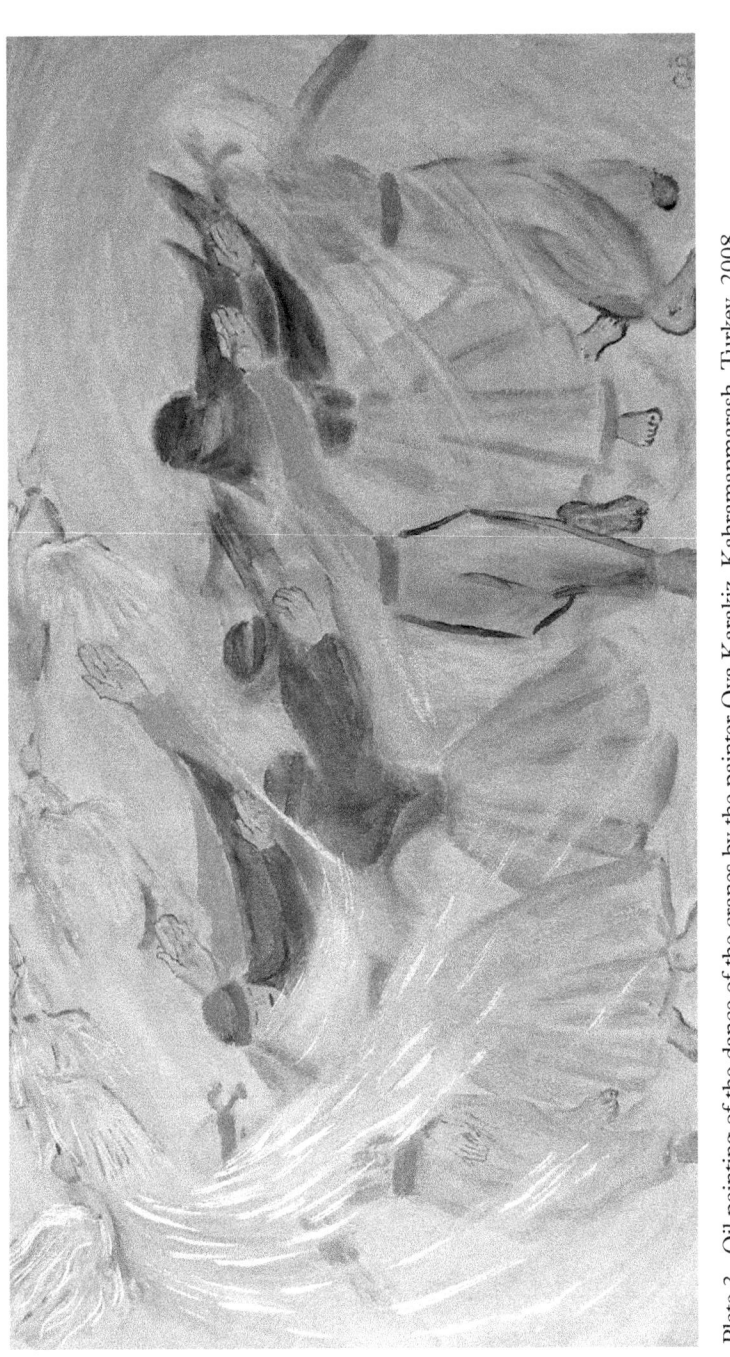

Plate 3. Oil painting of the dance of the cranes by the painter Oya Karakiz, Kahramanmarash, Turkey, 2008.

Plate 4. Zamanbek, a Kazakh shaman playing the fiddle (kobïz), Sayram, Kazakhstan, 1994 (Photograph: Jozsef Torma during fieldwork undertaken with D. Somfai Kara).

www.ingramcontent.com/pod-product-compliance
Lightning Source LLC
Chambersburg PA
CBHW070008010526
44117CB00011B/1465